Palgrave Studies in the History of the Media

Series Editors: **Professor Bill Bell** (Cardiff University), **Dr Chandrika Kaul** (Department of Modern History, University of St Andrews), **Professor Kenneth Osgood** (McBride Honors Program, Colorado School of Mines), **Dr Alexander S. Wilkinson** (Centre for the History of the Media, University College Dublin)

Palgrave Studies in the History of the Media publishes original, high-quality research into the cultures of communication from the middle ages to the present day. The series explores the variety of subjects and disciplinary approaches that characterize this vibrant field of enquiry. The series will help shape current interpretations not only of the media, in all its forms, but also of the powerful relationship between the media and politics, society, and the economy.

Advisory Board: Professor Carlos Barrera (University of Navarra, Spain), Professor Peter Burke (Emmanuel College, Cambridge), Professor Denis Cryle (Central Queensland University, Australia), Professor David Culbert (Louisiana State University, Baton Rouge), Professor Nicholas Cull (Center on Public Diplomacy, University of Southern California), Professor Tom O'Malley (Centre for Media History, University of Wales, Aberystwyth), Professor Chester Pach (Ohio University)

Titles include:

Laurel Brake, Chandrika Kaul and Mark W. Turner (*editors*)
THE *NEWS OF THE WORLD* AND THE BRITISH PRESS, 1843–2011
Journalism for the Rich, Journalism for the Poor

Jane L. Chapman
GENDER, CITIZENSHIP AND NEWSPAPERS
Historical and Transnational Perspectives

Jane Chapman, Anna Hoyles, Andrew Kerr and Adam Sherif
COMICS AND THE WORLD WARS
A Cultural Record

Andrew Griffiths
THE NEW JOURNALISM, THE NEW IMPERIALISM AND THE FICTION OF EMPIRE, 1870–1900

Chandrika Kaul
MEDIA AND THE BRITISH EMPIRE

Michael Krysko
AMERICAN RADIO IN CHINA
International Encounters with Technology and Communications, 1919–41

Christoph Hendrik Müller
WEST GERMANS AGAINST THE WEST
Anti-Americanism in Media and Public Opinion in the Federal Republic of Germany 1949–68

James Mussell
THE NINETEENTH-CENTURY PRESS IN THE DIGITAL AGE

Neal M. Rosendorf
FRANCO SELLS SPAIN TO AMERICA
Hollywood, Tourism and Public Relations as Postwar Spanish Soft Power

Joel Wiener
THE AMERICANIZATION OF THE BRITISH PRESS, 1830s–1914

Palgrave Studies in the History of the Media
Series Standing Order ISBN 978–0–230–23153–5 (hardback)
                    978–0–230–23154–2 (paperback)
(*outside North America only*)

You can receive future titles in this series as they are published by placing a standing order. Please contact your bookseller or, in case of difficulty, write to us at the address below with your name and address, the title of the series and one of the ISBNs quoted above.

Customer Services Department, Macmillan Distribution Ltd, Houndmills, Basingstoke, Hampshire RG21 6XS, England

The *News of the World* and the British Press, 1843–2011

Journalism for the Rich, Journalism for the Poor

Edited by

Laurel Brake
Birkbeck, University of London, UK

Chandrika Kaul
University of St Andrews, UK

and

Mark W. Turner
King's College London, UK

palgrave
macmillan

First published 2016 by
PALGRAVE MACMILLAN

Palgrave Macmillan in the UK is an imprint of Macmillan Publishers Limited, registered in England, company number 785998, of Houndmills, Basingstoke, Hampshire RG21 6XS.

Palgrave Macmillan in the US is a division of St Martin's Press LLC, 175 Fifth Avenue, New York, NY 10010.

Palgrave Macmillan is the global academic imprint of the above companies and has companies and representatives throughout the world.

Palgrave® and Macmillan® are registered trademarks in the United States, the United Kingdom, Europe and other countries.

ISBN: 978–1–137–39203–9

This book is printed on paper suitable for recycling and made from fully managed and sustained forest sources. Logging, pulping and manufacturing processes are expected to conform to the environmental regulations of the country of origin.

A catalogue record for this book is available from the British Library.

Library of Congress Cataloging-in-Publication Data

The News of the World and the British press, 1843–2011 : journalism for the rich, journalism for the poor / Laurel Brake, Birkbeck College, University of London, UK, Chandrika Kaul, University of St Andrews, UK, Mark W. Turner, King's College London, UK.
        pages cm.—(Palgrave studies in the history of the media)
    Includes bibliographical references and index.
    ISBN 978–1–137–39203–9
    1. News of the world I. Brake, Laurel, 1941– editor, author. II. Kaul, Chandrika (Lecturer) editor, author. III. Turner, Mark W., editor, author.

PN5130.N48N49 2015
072'.1—dc23   2015023517

Contents

List of Illustrations

List of Tables

Acknowledgements

The editors are very grateful indeed to three institutions, whose support has made the research and the project itself possible. The British Library produced an enabling microfilm surrogate of the *NOTW* early in the work, and made it available during the lacuna between the closure of Colindale and the opening of the newsroom; it also granted us permission to use a range of images in this book. We would like to thank The British Library Board specifically for permission to use the images in Chapters 2 and 3. The English Department at King's College London hosted the original study day, along with *Media History,* and helped to fund publication, including the bibliography, the index and the use of the masthead. Lastly, Nick Mays from the archives at TNL Archives, London, a late discovery on our part, was patient and generous with advice and information. We are grateful to him for supplying the circulation figures from the *News of the World* archive and permission to publish them in Appendix 1. His enabling Note on the contents of the archive may be found at the end of the Bibliography. This book has been much improved by his unstinting replies to our queries.

Library staff from the Guildhall Library, London, and the new British Library newsroom also helped us to ferret out material. Matthew Engel went well beyond the call of duty, into the attic, in locating the source of the elusive 1890s hoarding; Dr Andrew Hobbs, Professor Andrew King, Professor Louis James and Professor Tom O'Malley repeatedly provided expert advice, and have helped us muster evidence. Thanks also to Andy Eccles at the School of History in St Andrews who helped reproduce the images from *Punch* included in Chapter 6. Dr Melissa Score produced the bibliography.

Notes on Contributors

Neil Berry is the author of *Articles of Faith: The Story of British Intellectual Journalism* (2002; rev. ed. 2008). He has written reviews and articles for many publications, including the *Guardian*, *Times Literary Supplement* and *New Statesman*. Since 2002, he has been a columnist for the English-language Arab daily newspaper, *Arab News*.

Adrian Bingham is Reader in Modern History at the University of Sheffield. He has written widely on the history of popular journalism, including *Gender, Modernity and the Popular Press in Inter-War Britain* (2004), *Family Newspapers? Sex, Private Life, and the British Popular Press 1918–1978* (2009) and (with Martin Conboy) *Tabloid Century: The Popular Press in Britain, 1896 to the Present* (2015).

Laurel Brake is Professor Emerita at Birkbeck College, University of London. Her recent work includes *NCSE* (the *Nineteenth-Century Serials Edition*; www. levesoninquiry.org.uk), a digital edition of seven nineteenth-century periodicals; *DNCJ* (*Dictionary of Nineteenth-Century Journalism*) and *W.T. Stead, Newspaper Revolutionary*, both co-edited. She is the author of numerous other books, chapters and articles on nineteenth-century serials and print culture.

Martin Conboy is Professor of Journalism History and the co-director of the Centre for the Study of Journalism and History at the University of Sheffield. He is the author of ten books on the language and history of journalism and is on the editorial boards of *Journalism Studies: Media History, Journalism: Theory, Practice and Criticism* and *Memory Studies*. He is also co-editor of the book series *Journalism Studies: Key Texts*.

Alexis Easley is Professor of English at the University of St. Thomas in St. Paul, Minnesota. Her first book, *First-Person Anonymous: Women Writers and Victorian Print Media*, was published in 2004. Her second monograph, *Literary Celebrity, Gender, and Victorian Authorship*, was published in 2011. Her most recent works appeared in three 2012 essay collections, *Women Writers and the Artifacts of Celebrity*, *Women in Journalism at the Fin de Siècle*, and *Centenary Essays on W.T. Stead*. She is currently co-editing the *Ashgate Companion to Nineteenth-Century Periodicals and Newspapers* (with John Morton and Andrew King). She also serves as editor of *Victorian Periodicals Review*.

Chandrika Kaul is Lecturer in Modern History at the University of St. Andrews in Scotland. She is the founding co-editor of the book series,

Palgrave Studies in the History of the Media (Palgrave Macmillan). She sits on the editorial board of the international journals *Media History* and *Twentieth Century British History*. She serves as editor of *Exemplar*, Journal of the South Asian Studies Association, USA. Her monograph entitled, *Reporting the Raj, the British Press and India* (2003), is the first detailed study on the subject. She has also edited *Media and the British Empire* (Palgrave Macmillan 2006, 2013), *Explorations in Modern Indian History and the Media* (2009) and is co-editor of *International Circuits of News* (2011). Her most recent monograph is titled *Communications, Media and the Imperial Experience: Britain and India in the Twentieth Century* (Palgrave Macmillan, 2014).

James Mussell is Associate Professor of Victorian Literature at the University of Leeds. He is the author of *Science, Time and Space in the Late Nineteenth-Century Periodical Press* (2007) and *The Nineteenth-Century Press in the Digital Age* (2012). He is one of the editors of the *Nineteenth-Century Serials Edition* (*NCSE*, 2008) and *W.T. Stead: Newspaper Revolutionary* (2012). He is currently editor of the Digital Forum in the *Journal of Victorian Culture*.

Alison Oram is Professor of Social and Cultural History in the School of Cultural Studies and Humanities, Leeds Beckett University. She has written widely on the history of sexuality in twentieth-century Britain, including *Her Husband Was a Woman! Women's Gender-Crossing in Modern British Popular Culture* (2007) and *The Lesbian History Sourcebook: Love and Sex between Women in Britain from 1780 to 1970* (2001, with Annmarie Turnbull). Her recent research examines how the themes of queer sexuality, gender and the family appear in public history, especially in historic houses open to the public.

Julian Petley is Professor of Screen Media in the Department of Social Sciences, Media and Communication at Brunel University. He is the editor of *Media and Public Shaming* (2013), a member of both the editorial board of the *British Journalism Review* and the national council of the Campaign for Press and Broadcasting Freedom, and gave both oral and written evidence to the Leveson Inquiry.

Kevin Rafter is an associate professor at Dublin City University. He has written widely on media and politics in Ireland and is the author/editor of ten books including *The State in Transition* (2015), *The Irish Presidency* (2014), *Independent Newspapers: A History* (2013) and *Irish Journalism Before Independence*: *More a Disease Than a Profession* (2011). His research has also been appeared in *Media History*, *Press/Politics* and the *European Journal of Communications*. Prior to 2008 he worked as a political journalist and held several senior editorial positions including with the *Irish Times*, the *Sunday Times*, the *Sunday Tribune*, *Magill* and RTÉ, the Irish national broadcaster.

James Rodgers is Senior Lecturer in Journalism at City University London, where he teaches the History of Journalism, the reporting of armed conflict and Television Journalism. He is the author of *Reporting Conflict* (Palgrave Macmillan, 2012), *No Road Home: Fighting for Land and Faith in Gaza* (2013) and *Headlines from the Holy Land: Reporting the Israeli-Palestinian Conflict* (Palgrave Macmillan, 2015). He is a former foreign correspondent, editor and producer for BBC News and Reuters Television.

Melissa Score After a career in journalism at Dow Jones Newswires, Melissa completed her doctoral thesis entitled 'The Development and Impact of Campaigning Journalism in Britain, 1840–1875' at Birkbeck College, London. She has been an editorial assistant for Birkbeck's online journal *19: Interdisciplinary Studies in the Long Nineteenth Century* and taught on the BA Honours English degree programme. Her articles on compositors, gender and technology have appeared in *Victorian Periodicals Review*.

John Stokes is Emeritus Professor of Modern British Literature at King's College London and Honorary Professor of English and Drama at the University of Nottingham. Together with Mark W. Turner, he has edited two volumes of Oscar Wilde's journalism for Oxford English Texts (2013).

Mark W. Turner is Professor of English at King's College London, where he teaches literature and culture from the nineteenth century to the present. His works include *Trollope and the Magazines* (2000), *Backward Glances* (2003) and two volumes of Oscar Wilde's journalism, co-edited with John Stokes, for the Oxford English Texts collected works series (2013). He is one of the editors of the journal *Media History*.

Chris Williams is Professor of History at Cardiff University and Head of the School of History, Archaeology and Religion. He is principal investigator on the Heritage Lottery Funded project 'Cartooning the First World War in Wales' (cartoonww1.org), and a Royal Commissioner with the Royal Commission on the Ancient and Historical Monuments of Wales.

Kevin Williams is Professor in the History and Classics Department at Swansea University. His most recent works include *International Journalism* (2011) and *Read All about It! A History of British Newspapers* (2009).

List of Abbreviations

DNB	*Dictionary of National Biography*
Express	*Daily Express*
ILN	*Illustrated London News*
Lloyd's	*Lloyd's Weekly Newspaper*
Mirror	*Daily Mirror*
NOTW	*News of the World*
ODNB	*Oxford Dictionary of National Biography*
Reynolds's	*Reynolds's Weekly Newspaper*

Introduction

The lamentable closure of the *NOTW* in 2011 and the public attention it attracted provoked this book. Its germ was a small-scale study day, set up to investigate this title – suddenly history – in its existence across three centuries, from 1843 to 2011. In the summer of 2011, News International (part of Rupert Murdoch's News Corp) made the decision to close the paper, in the midst of a deepening scandal that purported to implicate the paper in 'phone hacking', that is, accessing messages on private mobile phones in order to gather information about celebrities, royalty and the general public. Such allegations had been made since 2006, but they came to a head in 2011, with suggestions that the phone of Milly Dowler, a murdered British schoolgirl, had been hacked after her death, a gross personal violation that led to a serious backlash from the public and from advertisers. The phone hacking scandal led to the Establishment of the Leveson Inquiry – a public inquiry set up to investigate the practices and ethics of the British press, including the *NOTW* but extending well it beyond.[1] This was not an august end for a paper that had been, as this volume demonstrates, central to the cultural life of Britain at various points, and among the world's highest selling newspapers.

The chapters here address the span of the run, with seven contributions on the nineteenth-century broadsheet, seven on the twentieth century and two on its truncated twenty-first century life. Our collective research has enabled us not only to scrutinise the title in a book-length study, the first undertaken by scholars,[2] but also to unearth obscure facts from diverse sources, to examine themes and periods in detail and to assemble a working bibliography of previous work that future scholars can consult. In its aim, it might be compared with recent collective work on the journalism of *Blackwood's Magazine*, Charles Dickens, G.W.M. Reynolds, and W.T. Stead, having taken up their subject afresh for the twenty-first century.[3]

Scrutiny of the origins of the paper is informative. To many contemporary readers' surprise in 2011, the *NOTW* was one of the oldest surviving Sundays, along with the *Observer* (1791 ff) and the *Sunday Times* (1822 ff). It was also notably respectable and news rich from the beginning. During the greater part of the nineteenth century, it was a demanding read, like almost all of its immediate competitors. A densely set, unillustrated, six-column broadsheet, it adhered to its aim of providing an entertaining and informative weekly for readers across the classes – 'journalism for the rich, ... journalism for the poor' – at an affordable price. Its interest in reform, domestic and international politics, entertainment and news of various kinds was instantly signalled to readers by the contents of its front page. Its breadth of coverage is indicated by its inclusion of weekly market prices (it was the official reporter for the *Grocers' Gazette*, for example), a literary page with serious reviews and court reports. For nearly 50 years, from 1843 until 1891, the *News of the World* was owned and probably edited by family members of its founder and first editor, John Browne Bell. This dynasty was succeeded by another newspaper family, that of Henry Lascelles Carr, who purchased it in 1891. His nephew Emsley Carr edited it for another 50 years, and succeeded his uncle as proprietor in 1902. It was from Emsley's son, William Carr, that Rupert Murdoch purchased the paper in 1969.

The first seven chapters locate the paper in the genre of the nineteenth-century Sundays, with the dual role of entertainment and information gathering. Melissa Score's Chapter 4 on the role of campaigning in such a genre examines the resulting tensions in the early years – between a broad-based appeal across class and politics, the drive for change between the Reform Acts and the allocation of space for news and entertainment. In Chapter 5, Alexis Easley explores the *NOTW* in relation to what she calls the 'feminisation' of the emerging mass market press, not only friendly to but also cultivating female readers. In these different ways – investigative reporting and gendered interests – the nineteenth-century paper resembled its descendants, more familiar to us. However, contrary to expectation, as Chandrika Kaul argues in Chapter 6, on political questions of Empire the *NOTW* proved enlightened and moderate, balanced and informed rather than intemperate and jingoistic. Through the first in-depth case studies of the *NOTW*'s coverage of the Great Indian Rebellion (1857–58) and the first royal tour of the sub-continent by a Prince of Wales in 1875–76, she concludes that the paper displayed a remarkable prescience and engagement with imperial issues.

Chapters 1–3 by James Mussell, Laurel Brake and Mark W. Turner map the history of the paper over the nineteenth century, assessing the initial intentions announced in its manifesto, its multiple editions and problems of distribution and its actual range of contents. They gauge how it responded to the roller coaster of changes accompanying the removal of taxes on news-papers between 1855 and 1861. What were the implications of its decision to remain a cheap title after 1861 at 2*d*., but not the cheapest at 1*d*., like most of its competitors? Rather than defining the paper as one merely of declining sales between 1855 and 1891, we show that it was responsive to the new environment of sensationalism and the New Journalism, dropping its price to a penny in 1880 and adding fiction to its contents in 1881, long before its competitors. Once its new owners – the Carrs – took charge, enlargement of the format of the paper, introduction of illustrations, cartoons and enhanced sports coverage gradually followed, so that by the end of the century it hardly resembled its earlier 'self'. Chris Williams's Chapter 8 on J.M. Staniforth's weekly cartoons on page 1, from 1893 to 1921, offers a pithy account of the refashioned paper – its politics, its format and artists, who were a recent addition to the categories of its staff.

A persistent aspect of the paper throughout its history is the symbiosis among its crime reports, sensation and entertainment and, appropriately, this crops up in all of the essays here. Our collective findings suggest that these elements of the *NOTW* vary – in definition, format and prominence – at different periods in the paper's long run. While crime reporting was part of all weekend papers in the nineteenth century, in the *NOTW* it remained throughout the period as it was initially, part of the news reporting of the various courts, comparable to Parliamentary reporting in the daily press, which was similarly often spiced with verbatim quotation and interesting detail. In a genre that did not generally include fiction, these court narratives had elements of developing 'stories'.[4] As the arrival of the cheap press and sensation fiction coincided in the 1860s, so the crime reports in the *NOTW* and the other Sunday press began to spill outside of the court reports and to acquire at times of a major trial, for example, the prominence of war or civic news, along with the sensational style of such reports. The 'entertainment' element of the Sessions, Magistrates', Old Bailey and divorce court reports was intensified in a hybrid type of contents, with 'news' and 'entertainment' elements finely balanced.

By the late 1880s–90s, just as the new iteration of the *NOTW* was being crafted, the tales of Conan Doyle's Sherlock Holmes, 'sensational crime stories', begin to appear in the monthly *Strand Magazine*. Doyle describes a character who 'reads nothing but the criminal news and the personal adverts' and 'knows every detail of sensational literature and the history of crime'. He is a 'Walking Calendar of Crime'. The *NOTW*'s appropriation of its crime and court material to headline-grabbing, sensational and entertaining stories is reflected in Conan Doyle's simultaneous alertness to the importance of crime in popular culture, and its translation into fiction. Realised in the character of Sherlock Holmes, popular and entertaining crime is distributed by Doyle in the New Journalism form of linked short fiction tales, a genre tailored for the new monthly, the *Strand Magazine*, in which they appeared.[5]

In the twentieth century, the *NOTW* was probably remembered most for two things – its apparent sensationalism and its extraordinary circulation figures, it being at one point the highest selling Sunday paper in the world, with a huge readership. As Alison Oram, Adrian Bingham and other contributors suggest here, 'sensationalism' is not a stable term across historical moments and the uses of 'sensational' or scandalous narratives are multiple and sometimes surprising. Scoops of various kinds, crime reporting and celebrity coverage – all play their part in the formation of what gets loosely termed 'sensational' material, but the paper's contents were always more varied. Martin Conboy, for example, assesses the paper's 'residual radicalism' in his overview of the popular Sunday press, and the extent to which the *NOTW* continued to exploit its appeal to readers' taste for scandal and sensation until its closure.

The twenty-first century *NOTW* is defined by its place as a tabloid, a transformation that occurred in 1984, in the hands of Rupert Murdoch, who took over the paper in 1969. A sensational broadsheet and a sensational tabloid are different cultural products, and while the *NOTW* may now be recalled more in its tabloid than broadsheet form, it is important to understand the long history of this transformation from one kind of newspaper to another. Chapters here by Kevin Williams, James Rodgers and Julian Petley all focus our attention on the *NOTW* in relation to shifts in popular journalism in the twentieth century, with regard to regulation, emerging technologies, news gathering methods and the impact of a media mogul.

The astonishing longevity of the *NOTW*'s popularity remains one of the most compelling features of its history. George Orwell, tongue in cheek, reminded readers of its role in 'The Decline of the English Murder' in 1946.[6] John Stokes takes the measure of this popularity at a high point in the 1950s, when the title pervaded all aspects of British cultural life at that time, straddling class in fascinating ways. Kevin Rafter tracks the paper's strength by tracing its history in Ireland in the twentieth century, arguing that the paper moved from a place as an 'outsider' publication to one with a nearly semi-official status. Both Stokes and Rafter demonstrate the depth and breadth of the paper's reach across class, nation and culture. While the contents of our book chart the changing nature of the *NOTW* from 1843 to 2011, they also make clear that such material is embedded in an economic and technological context and a newspaper text of considerable variety – news rich, investigative, business and reader oriented and outward looking. The impact of new printing machines – the Hoe Press – in the 1890s, for example, enabled the paper to print thousands of copies per hour, preparing the way for mass circulation over the next decade or two. The recent 'phone hacking' scandals remind us that news and newsgathering technologies can operate in a delicate ecology. Both examples, however, suggest ways in which newspapers are always developing and changing in relation to the new technologies available to them, a theme at the centre of James Rodgers's Chapter 15. The final contribution here, the 'Afterword' from Neil Berry, differs from other chapters on these topics, in that it provides a more reflective space in which to think about the Leveson Inquiry and recent events in the wake of phone hacking over the past decade. Perhaps too soon yet to be considered 'history', Leveson offers us an important moment in which to consider a whole range of issues connected to press regulation and freedom and, more broadly, the role of the press – of the popular press like the *NOTW* – in the contemporary world. Berry's piece opens out, we hope, into wider discussions in a narrative that continues to be written.

Part of the aim of this study is to establish more precise dates and accurate names from what can be gleaned so far about the *NOTW*'s business history and key events in the early stages of its purchase by Rupert Murdoch. Much remains unknown, but in aid of future research we have begun to identify important lacunae, as well as resources. Among the latter is the newspaper's archive from 1891 at News UK.[7] Among the former is uncertainty about the identity of the editors between 1877 and 1891. This is directly attributable to a lack of information about the proprietors in these years, Walter and Adolphus Bell, who appear in the most skeletal fashion in Eamon Dyas's *Scoop!* and not at all in the *Oxford Dictionary of National Biography*.[8] What has been striking for many of us undertaking new research for the volume is the way in which important figures from the history of the press can be largely absent from major resources like the *Dictionary of National Biography (DNB)*, as well as from obituaries and other sources where researchers might hope to glean important information. This is partly a reflection of the culture of the period, not simply the attitudes of the gatekeepers. For nineteenth-century sources and twentieth-century ones before the war, such as the *DNB* and newspaper obituaries, journalists and wealthy newspaper proprietors were of relatively low social status. Mitchell's *Newspaper Press Directory* of 1854 noted 'that the conductors and members of the press have no recognised standing',[9] and this is endorsed retrospectively by E.T. Raymond who avers that in the 1880s and 1890s journalists were barely professional, proprietors were commercial 'tradesman' and it was 'part of the character' of editors 'to be anonymous'.[10]

Circulation is another area of uncertainty, especially between 1855 and the early twentieth century. Even when figures are offered by various commentators or ex journalists, they differ considerably. This may be explained by A.P. Wadsworth, who dubs the 1850s through the 1930s 'the period of secrecy', when 'all but a few papers jealously guarded the volume of their sales'.[11] A tantalising glimpse of the circulation of the *NOTW* in these years is provided in the visual testimony of a wall hoarding probably mounted on the occasion of the achievement of sales of 1 million by *Lloyd's Weekly Newspaper* on 23 February 1896. In highlighting this event, remembered and described by an employee of the *NOTW*, some 25 years afterward, and *not* accompanied by an image of the poster, which has proved untraceable,

R. Power Berrey's point is that at this time, the *NOTW* was not even in sight of circulation of a million, despite its claims to the contrary:

> *Lloyd's Weekly News* had a huge poster on prominent hoardings. This depicted a yacht race, with a buoy labelled 'The Million Mark.' A splendid craft with the word Lloyd's on the mainsail was rounding the buoy while a string of boats representing other Sunday newspapers straggled far behind. The *News of the World* was not even in the picture. It was beyond the horizon: listing heavily, presumed more or less sunk.[12]

This is borne out by figures for these years compiled by UK News from secondary sources in the *NOTW* Archive, which suggest that for 1896 the *NOTW*'s circulation was 99, 539 copies per issue.

The various newspapers' descriptions of themselves in advertisements for the press directories tend to obscure the facts rather than clarify them, and the press directories' own brief assessments of the titles tend not to reveal hard numbers.[13] The *NOTW*, for example, describes itself in the early 1890s as having 'one of the largest circulations in the world' and as being 'one of the first in point of circulation of all the journals exclusively devoted to public intelligence and the general business of a newspaper'.[14] The *People* similarly 'claims to be the biggest Sunday penny paper' with 'Millions of Readers every week! The Sale of "The People" now considerably exceeds that of its older rivals with, possibly, a solitary exception'.[15] *Reynolds's Weekly Newspaper* advertises its 'enormous circulation', with 'more than two million readers',[16] and *Lloyd's* is said by Mitchell's to appeal 'to the million on the two great principles of quantity and cheapness'.[17] Readership, as opposed to circulation and value for money in relation to pages offered per penny were used to puff a title that sought to position itself as a market leader. In other words, unsurprisingly, hyperbole prevailed in the press directories, whose chief purposes were to sell advertising space and to ensure a robust industry, making it difficult to pinpoint exact figures with any real precision at this time.

As the editors of the first scholarly volume of its kind to undertake close examination of the *NOTW*, we are conscious that the research contained here comes from individuals working in a range of disciplines – English, History, Journalism Studies and Media Studies – with specialisms that reach across visual and print media. All of us, however, are engaged in the practice of what we collectively understand as 'Media History', a rich and diverse field that seeks to understand the history of the media from a variety of angles. The kind of methodological difference that one can detect across the chapters that follow in part indicates that the field of Media History has multiple nodes. All of us, however, believe that understanding the media requires an understanding of the historical circumstances that shape the media – its content, financial structures, policies and relations to other institutions. The varied practice of media history – in part spearheaded by the journal *Media History*, which organised and sponsored the research day out of which this volume arises – is manifest here. Some articles focus on content analysis, others on historical mapping of the title's changes across time, and still others on the socio-cultural impact of the title, that is, the relationship of the *NOTW* to society at large. What it means to 'do' Media History, what it looks like in practice, is not singular; rather it borrows from a range of methods across disciplines – textual and discourse analysis, archival approaches and visual studies.

Among the constraints common to all researchers of Media History, however, is limited access to the material being studied. That is, not all researchers have access to material equally. Rescarching the *NOTW* has been a sobering reminder of this point for many of us, and the research realities came as something of a surprise. The simple point to make is that full runs of the paper are scarce, even in the UK where the paper was based. There are *only two full runs* of the *NOTW* in the UK: one in the public domain at the British Library (where you can easily consult it on open access microfilm, if you can get to central London) and one in private hands at News UK (now the UK trading name of Rupert Murdoch's News Corp). There are partial runs on paper – mostly since the late 1960s, in a few universities and at the National Library of Scotland, online access from 1996 or 1998 on Factiva and Lexis Nexus in a cluster of other universities and odd volumes or a few issues at even a smaller handful of university libraries in the UK. Because the title has hardly been collected by libraries and was not digitised before 1996, the entirety of the nineteenth- and most of the twentieth-century runs are only available in the UK in London, at the British Library, News UK and in the British Library Reading Room at Boston Spa. This situation, i.e. that the first 150 years of the run is not in one of the databases of digitised print material (such as British Newspapers Online) that have emerged in recent years, has been a serious impediment to research.

This reminder of the uneven access to the run may account for something that has struck many of us in undertaking our research, that is, the relative paucity of scholarly material focused on the *NOTW*, in most periods of its history. For most of the twentieth century, the *NOTW* was the UK's highest selling Sunday paper, and its founding in 1843 made it among the oldest of papers until it closed in 2011. The majority of recent criticism focuses on the paper post-1969, in the Murdoch era; however, considering its prominence in British culture and its longevity in media history, we might expect to see more scholarship addressing its longer history. Lack of access to the paper itself might account for much of this striking absence, but there are other things at work here. The history of newspaper scholarship – in the UK's and elsewhere – has tended *not* to focus on the Sunday or weekend press, and to privilege the daily press above all else. Virginia Berridge's seminal synoptic essay on the Sunday press of the mid-nineteenth century, published in 1978, remains an important touchstone for scholars. However, the questions that she raised more than 37 years ago, and the frameworks through which she read and conceptualised the Sunday press, have been too little challenged since then.[18] It might be that re-reading the Sunday press (if you had access to it) would lead to a rethinking of some of the categories that have become settled in our understanding of it, in relation to popular culture, politics, readership and class. Furthermore, the broadsheets usually, though not always, take precedence over the tabloids when it comes to serious academic study, so the *NOTW*'s shift to tabloid form after Murdoch became proprietor perhaps helped to ensure that it remained adrift from academic study. New histories of the British press, by Kevin Williams and others, have helped to remind us of the importance of the Sunday and weekend papers, along with other areas of media history that remain under-researched.[19]

Contributors to this volume have found a number of books that document the history of the *NOTW* and provide enormous amounts of useful material and information, deriving from archival work, interviews and other sources. Cyril Bainbridge and Roy Stockdill's *The News of the World Story: 150 Years of the World's Bestselling Newspaper* published in 1993, Matthew Engel's *Tickle the Public* and Peter Burden's *News of the World? Fake Sheikhs & Royal Trappings* have done valuable work. However, these books are written as 'popular history', addressed to the general reader, and they often lack detail of their sources. We have found and followed many leads offered in these and other places and, where possible, contributors have verified facts and figures or demystified information, with rigour. We are especially indebted to the News UK Archive in this respect. It is because of this kind of work that we feel confident that ours will be a significant volume on which future scholars can build and develop further thinking. With future projects in mind, we include a bibliography of sources upon which we have collectively drawn.

Notes

1. For the Leveson Inquiry, see www.levesoninquiry.org.uk. Leveson's first report, the full text of which can be accessed on the Leveson website, was published in 2012. A second report may follow once all of the criminal cases are completed. In other words, the fallout from the phone hacking scandal, which led to the closing of the *NOTW*, is ongoing.
2. Extant work has been written by journalists – memoirs by staff of the *NOTW* (such as Berrey, Emsley Carr and Somerfield), or journalists on other papers (Bainbridge and Stockdill, Matthew Engel, and E.T. Raymond). Media historians who have treated the title or Sundays more generally include most notably Virginia Berridge and James Curran. See Bibliography.
3. D. Finkelstein (ed.), *Print Culture and the Blackwood Tradition, 1805–1930*, Toronto, 2006, H. Mackenzie and B. Winyard (eds), *Charles Dickens and the Mid-Victorian*

Press 1850–1870, Buckingham, 2013, A. Humpherys and L. James (eds), *G.W.M Reynolds, Nineteeth-Century Fiction, Politics, and the Press*, Aldershot and Burlington, VT, 2008 and L. Brake, E. King, R. Luckhurst, and J. Mussell (eds), *W.T. Stead, Newspaper Revolutionary*, London, 2012.

4. See J. Knelman, 'Subtly Sensational: A Study of Early Victorian Crime Reporting', *Journal of Newspaper and Periodical History*, 8.1 (1992) pp. 34–41, which discusses affinities between the narratives of fiction and those of crime reporting in the daily press in the nineteenth century.

5. The *Strand Magazine* (1891), which took up and circulated Doyle's tales was a new title founded by the publisher of the wildly popular *Tit-Bits*, George Newnes, who had founded it in 1881. Quotations are from Doyle's notebooks and curatorial Labels at the Sherlock Holmes Exhibition, the Museum of London, 2015. For Holmes and his use of newspapers, see C. Pettitt, 'Throwaway Holmes' in A. Werner (ed.), *Sherlock Holmes. The Man Who Never Lived and Will Never Die*, London, 2015, pp. 185–95.

6. See G. Orwell, 'Decline of the English Murder', in *Tribune*, 15 February, 1946, and *Shooting an Elephant and other Essays*, London, 1952, in which Orwell writes, tongue in cheek, 'It is Sunday afternoon, preferably before the war. The wife is already asleep in the armchair and the children have been sent out for a nice long walk. You put your feet up on the sofa, settle your spectacles on your nose, and open the *News of the World*.'

7. See the Bibliography for a note by Nick Mays on the holdings of the News UK Archive.

8. *Scoop!* is a biographical dictionary of journalists and newspaper history, accessible by subscription and also available in some libraries.

9. 'The Power and the Character of the Press', Mitchell's *Newspaper Press Directory*, [1854?], p. 4.

10. E.T. Raymond, 'Old and New Journalists', *Portraits of the Nineties*. London, 1921. pp. 291 and 293.

11. A.P. Wadsworth, 'Newspaper Circulations, 1800–1954', *Transactions of the Manchester Statistical Society 1954–5*, Manchester, 1955, p. 1.

12. R. Power Berrey. *The Romance of a Great Newspaper*. London, n.d. [1922?], 46; quoted by M. Engel, *Tickle the Public. One Hundred Years of the Popular Press*. London, 1996, p. 208. The editors wish to thank Matthew Engel for his considerable effort and help in attributing this account to R. Power Berrey. Berrey attributes the hoarding to 'c. 1891', but *Lloyd's* only attained a circulation of a million in February 1896. In this period of secrecy about circulation, the implication of the poster that the *NOTW*'s circulation remained below a million in 1896 is also implied by Bainbridge and Stockdill, in *The News of the World Story: 150 Years of the World's Bestselling Newspaper*, New York, 1993, p. 61, who note that in 1898, only 56,500 copies were sent to direct agents outside London. Circulation figures from the *NOTW* News UK archive suggest that it reached a million (1,173,309) only in 1906.

13. This is not for want of trying. See Deacon's note on 'Newspaper Circulations' in *Newspaper Handbook and Advertiser's Guide*, London, 1881, pp. 26–28, for example, which described its pursuit of proprietors for circulation figures, most of whom did not supply them. From that date, the first available in the British Library in London, Deacon's included the note annually. In 1883, the subtitle of the *Handbook* records its frustrations, reading 'And their circulations, where attainable.' By 1894, Deacon's is plainly exasperated with the proprietors, and

adds pointed text (pp. 58–60) to the annual note on circulations: 'In any case of doubt,' they write, 'we refuse to print the figures, leaving the matter open for advertisers to form their own opinions or to obtain ours by direct communication with us' (p. 59). An entire paragraph is added, giving examples of 'the reckless manner in which some publishers will exaggerate the circulation of their newspapers' (p. 60). The final sentence is equally admonitory: 'We would not have thought that such gross exaggeration as these are general amongst newspaper publishers, but we believe that the figures of circulation given in this book may be generally relied upon as being as nearly as possible correct' (p. 60). As early as 1854, Mitchell's *Newspaper Press Directory*, adjacent to an article on 'The Power and the Character of the Press', p. 4, published the stamp returns figures as the basis for circulation for the previous three years, but once the compulsory stamp was abolished in 1855, newspapers could boast circulation figures for which there was no sure way of testing, as Deacon's later noted.

14. Mitchell's *Newspaper Press Directory*, London, 1890, p. 225.
15. *Willing's British & Irish Press Guide*. London, James Willing, 1891, p. 130.
16. Ibid., p. 362.
17. Mitchell's *Newspaper Press Directory*, London, 1894, p. 66.
18. See K. Williams, *Read All About It! A History of the British Newspaper*, London, 2009, and comments here in Chapter 2.
19. See K. Williams, 2009 and *Get Me a Murder a Day: A History of Media and Communication in Britain*, 2nd edn. London, 2010.

1
The Foundation and Early Years of the *News of the World*: 'Capacious Double Sheets'

James Mussell

Introduction

The *News of the World* (*NOTW*) was established in 1843 and quickly found a readership. By 1846, when Charles Mitchell first published his *Newspaper Press Directory*, the *NOTW* was claiming a weekly circulation of over 35,000. In this chapter, I consider how the *NOTW* carved out such a remarkable place for itself in the mid-nineteenth-century market, becoming one of the largest-selling newspapers of all time. The Sunday newspaper was fairly well established, the first – *E. Johnson's British Gazette and Sunday Monitor* – had appeared in 1779, but it was the papers that emerged in the 1840s that demonstrated the large potential audience for cheap weekly newspapers. These papers, led by Edward Lloyd's *Lloyd's Illustrated Newspaper* (later *Lloyd's Weekly London Newspaper*, then *Lloyd's Weekly Newspaper* 1842–1931), took advantage of the reduction of the newspaper stamp duty in 1836 to keep their prices as low as possible while orienting their contents towards the interests of this emerging market. Their success in identifying and cultivating a readership amongst the working- and lower-middle classes meant that they reached more readers than newspapers ever had before. It is in this context, as a pioneering publication in the vanguard of a new and successful newspaper genre, that we should consider the *NOTW*.

The success of the cheap Sunday newspaper is generally attributed to its generous coverage of violent crime and close attention to the more scandalous proceedings in the courts. However, while the *Newspaper Press Directory* recognised that the *NOTW* was emblematic of a particular genre, it did not mention this type of content at all. According to the *Press Directory*, the *NOTW* was 'one of the many papers which compresses into a capacious double sheet the news of the week.'[1] All weeklies contained the week's news: what was remarkable about the *NOTW* and its rivals was the amount of news they contained given their price. For the *Newspaper Press Directory*, what made these papers distinct was the way they were oriented towards 'a class of readers who, though respectable, may be supposed – through incessant occupation in the week – not to have had much opportunity before the Saturday evening for newspaper reading.'[2] It was these busy readers, unwilling to pay for a daily paper and without the time to read it, who constituted the market for the cheap Sunday press. These readers might have wanted to read, in a mixture of prurience and shock, of the latest murder, but these were not the motives recorded by the *Newspaper Press Directory*.

The *Newspaper Press Directory* was aimed at advertisers and newsagents and, while it did not shy away from noting a paper's politics or orientation to the police courts, tended to present papers positively. As the *NOTW* was a cheap weekly, it might not have been necessary for the *Press Directory* to make explicit the type of content printed in its pages. Nonetheless, its delineation of this new genre is important, as it situated it on grounds other than those for which it has become known. As Raymond Williams, amongst others, has argued, the cheap Sundays laid the foundations for the commercial mass press.[3] One of the key arguments for the reduction of the newspaper stamp duty in 1836 was that it would enable the more respectable publications to compete with the radical unstamped papers that crowded the bottom end of the market. The success of the cheap Sundays, when they appeared 16 years later, appeared to have achieved this end, displacing the unstamped press with newspapers whose politics and contents, although not ideal, were tolerable to the Establishment. To understand the appeal of this new genre is to understand the broader political shift, as early nineteenth-century radicalism gave way to an increasingly hegemonic Victorian liberalism. The *NOTW*, both less sensational and less radical than its two closest rivals, was the most representative of the genre. To recognise its appeal, we must do more than look to its more lurid contents.

What follows is in two parts. The first describes the foundation of the *NOTW* and its place in the market for Sunday newspapers. The paper's founder, John Browne Bell (1779–1855), was well placed to launch a new, cheap Sunday newspaper as he already had substantial experience in the print trade. The success of *Lloyd's Weekly Newspaper* made apparent the market for cheap, unillustrated Sunday papers: Bell, who already owned one Sunday paper, launched the *NOTW* in an attempt to develop this new market. The second part explores the way the *NOTW* positioned itself as a new cheap Sunday newspaper. While it followed *Lloyd's Weekly* in an attempt to win a share of its working-class readers, the *NOTW* presented itself as an up-market alternative available for the same price. Its rapid success suggests that Bell judged the market correctly, and the *NOTW* remained remarkably consistent in both form and content for the next 30 years. However, the newspaper market changed radically over this period, particularly after the repeal of the final tax on knowledge: the removal of paper duty in

Gladstone's 1861 budget. The *NOTW*'s refusal to follow its competitors and reduce its price to a penny has been cited as the reason for its declining fortunes. It had conceived of itself as a respectable newspaper, aligned to the interests of working- and lower-middle-class readers and at a price they could afford. While the *NOTW* succeeded in adapting the upmarket newspaper for lower-class readers, after 1860 it was no longer a cheap weekly and so had to sell itself on other grounds.

John Browne Bell and the Sunday newspaper in the early nineteenth century

The market for Sunday newspapers was inaugurated by *E. Johnson's British Gazette* in 1779 and, by 1795, there were five Sundays published in London.[4] Despite concerns about the sanctity of the Sabbath, these new Sunday papers closely resembled those published during the working week. *E. Johnson's British Gazette's* only concession to the Sabbath, for instance, was the inclusion of the 'Sunday Monitor' column on its front page, where the theatre advertisements would otherwise be placed.[5] In 1796, John Browne Bell's father, John Bell, entered the market with *Bell's Weekly Messenger* (1796–1896). John Bell was a well-regarded (and well-connected) figure in the London print trade. He was a member of the syndicate behind The *Morning Post* (1772–1937) and his periodicals, the *World, or Fashionable Advertiser* (1787–94) and *La Belle Assemblée* (1806–47), were important pioneering publications in their respective genres. His *Weekly Messenger* was a successful innovation of the Sunday newspaper genre, developing its review-like aspects to increase its appeal over the course of the week. Bell ensured its respectability, moderating its content and refusing to take advertisements, to make it suitable for families. At 7 ½*d* it was fairly expensive but the paper was considered good value (it expanded in 1802, 1810 and 1828) and found a market, particularly amongst country readers. Its circulation was modest – around 6,000 a week in 1803, climbing to 14,000 at the time of Nelson's funeral in 1806 – but this was sufficient to establish the paper, and it prospered, surviving until 1896, when it became the *Country Sport and Messenger of Agriculture*.[6]

The market became more competitive in the early years of the nineteenth century and, by 1812, there were at least 12 papers published on a Sunday.[7] *The Observer* (1791–) and the *Weekly Dispatch* (1795–1961) were already well established, but they were joined by the *Sunday Times* (1821–, originally as *The New Observer*) and *Bell's Life in London* (1822), amongst others. The name 'Bell' clearly operated as a signifier for a type of Sunday newspaper. The *Weekly Dispatch*, which was edited by an Irish barrister called Robert Bell, had appeared as *Bell's Weekly Dispatch* for the first six years of its run; when *Bell's Life in London* appeared in 1822, Robert Bell made clear that it was nothing to do with him (it was founded by another Robert Bell[8]) and noted, too, that the *Weekly Dispatch* was unconnected with John Bell of the *Weekly Messenger.*[9] The market was clearly attractive but, because of the rise of the newspaper stamp duty in 1804 to 3 ½d, there was little room to compete through price. Instead, the papers differentiated themselves through their content. The *Weekly Dispatch* (8 ½d) and *Bell's Life in London* (7d), for instance, were both more radical and more seedy than the *Weekly Messenger*, targeting a knowing, London-based, male readership.

John Browne Bell made a number of attempts to establish himself in this market before the launch of the *NOTW* in 1843. He was motivated by a combination of commercial astuteness and personal grievance, often pitching his publications directly against those of his father. Bell's origins are a little murky. The *Dictionary of National Biography* (*DNB*) claims that John Bell 'appears never to have married and left his estate to his niece', but this appears to have been a deliberate attempt to disinherit his son.[10] John Browne Bell's record as a publisher certainly suggests he was aggrieved. In 1806 he launched *Le Beau Monde*, a three-shilling monthly that directly imitated his father's *La Belle Assemblée*, which had appeared just a few months previously, even going so far as to take its title from one of *La Belle Assemblée*'s sections. In January 1808, he entered the Sunday market with his *National Register* (subtitled 'The King, Constitution, and Laws'), an 8d. weekly that combined foreign and domestic news, commercial intelligence and police reports with a review of national political institutions. The paper was not a success, and in January 1809 Bell merged it with *Le Beau Monde*. The resulting paper, *Le Beau Monde and Monthly Register* lasted a few more months before being sold in April 1809, and Bell and his publishing partner, John de Camp, were declared bankrupt the following year.[11] In 1824 Bell returned to the monthly periodical market, publishing the *World of Fashion and Continental Feuilletons* (1824–51), another attempt to compete with his father's *La Belle Assemblée* with a title that also evoked the latter's *World, and Fashionable Advertiser* (1787). The *World of Fashion* was a success, partly no doubt due to its close association with Mary Ann Bell, who had previously managed the fashion section of *La Belle Assemblée* before it was sold by John Bell in 1821.[12] However, it was after the death of his father, in 1831, that Bell attempted a new Sunday paper and this new venture represented his most audacious attack on his father's reputation to date. The new publication was called *Bell's New Weekly Messenger* (1831–55), evoking his late father's *Weekly Messenger* while suggesting that it was both a continuation and successor.

While his father's *Weekly Messenger* circulated widely in the country (it would absorb the *Farmer's Journal* in 1834), *Bell's New Weekly Messenger* was intended for metropolitan readers and was modelled on established publications such as the *Weekly Dispatch* and *Bell's Life in London*. This made commercial sense, as, according to James Grant, these were the two papers with the highest circulation of any paper, 'daily or weekly, in the United

Kingdom'.[13] Bell disavowed any connection with his father's paper, which he referred to as 'that old journal, commonly called in the country "My Grandmother's Newspaper".'[14] Instead of its country interests and moderate Toryism, Bell espoused a form of liberalism that Grant thought verged 'on extreme radicalism'.[15] In this, the *New Weekly Messenger* positioned itself between *Bell's Life* and the *Weekly Dispatch*, which Grant thought were 'moderately Liberal' and 'Radicalism in its purest form' respectively.[16] In a move that he would repeat again with the *NOTW*, Bell entered a market that had already been opened up by his competitors and then attempted to compete on content. *Bell's New Weekly Messenger* had 16 pages and contained 64 columns, larger than all of its rivals for more or less the same price.

Bell's New Weekly Messenger was initially 8*d*. (the *Weekly Dispatch* was 8 1/2*d*. and *Bell's Life* 7*d*.), but, like most weeklies, it reduced its price to 6*d*. after the reduction of the newspaper stamp duty in 1836. Despite their politics, these long-running weeklies made little attempt to compete with the cheaper, usually unstamped publications at the lower end of the market. It was in this area, however, that the *NOTW* would take shape. In the 1840s, there were a number of unstamped weeklies, usually with connections to radical politics and the chapbook and broadside traditions, that attempted to mimic the more respectable Sunday press. For instance, Edward Lloyd launched his *Penny Sunday Times and People's Police Gazette* (1840), its title alluding to both *The Sunday Times* and *Cleave's Weekly Police Gazette* while conflating them both under the master-sign of the penny. In the same year a *Penny Weekly Dispatch* appeared. In 1841, this titular dexterity reached its climax with *Bell's Penny Dispatch, Sporting and Police Gazette, and Newspaper of Romance, and Penny Sunday Chronicle* (1841).[17] Nothing to do with John Bell, Robert Bell or John Browne Bell, this paper included 'Bell' as one of many markers of genre in its title intended to demonstrate its capaciousness while masking its generic resemblance to its other penny rivals.

Edward Lloyd proved a particularly astute reader of the market. Observing the success of the *Illustrated London News* (*ILN*), a sixpenny illustrated weekly published on a Saturday, Lloyd launched *Lloyd's Illustrated London Newspaper* on 27 November 1842. Appearing on Sunday not Saturday, it explicitly mimicked the front page of *ILN*, with a similar masthead, a large topical engraving and the same number of columns. At tuppence, *Lloyd's Illustrated London Newspaper* significantly undercut the *ILN*, but, as Lloyd's paper was stamped, it also signalled his interest in developing the cheap end of the legitimate market. After accounting for the stamp duty, Lloyd's income was still a penny per issue but, selling at tuppence, his newspaper was in a different market. Despite the paper's success (in December 1842 he claimed that circulation was 100,000, 65,000 of which were in London[18]), Lloyd clearly believed that a different kind of publication was needed in this new market. From its eighth issue, dated 15 January 1843, Lloyd expanded the paper's size, redesigned the masthead so that it no longer resembled that of the *ILN*, removed the engraving and hired Douglas Jerrold as editor. He also increased the cover price to 2 ½d, suggesting that he believed that readers would be willing to pay more for a larger paper.[19] In this new guise, the paper, now called *Lloyd's Weekly London Newspaper*, with its five columns rather than three and on larger paper, more closely resembled the established form of the newspaper rather than the cheap illustrated weekly from which it was derived. In September 1843, he increased the price by another halfpenny, making it 3d, while adding another sheet to make it twelve pages rather than eight. Each increase in price raised Lloyd's revenue substantially and, although sales must have been affected each time, any losses were soon absorbed by the growing readership at the new price.

This was the newspaper that demonstrated the viability of the market for a cheap, stamped newspaper. Just as he had with *Bell's New Weekly Messenger*, John Browne Bell watched one of his rivals establish a niche and then launched his own competing publication. On the 1 October 1843, the *NOTW* appeared, printed and published by James John Rogers at 30 Holywell Street, London, an address well known in the trade as the former shop of the late printer and publisher Thomas Dolby. A threepenny Sunday newspaper, it was a marked departure for Bell and it placed him in direct competition with *Lloyd's Weekly London Newspaper*. However, he was not simply an imitator, following where others led. The *NOTW* might have been aimed at a similar set of readers, but this new paper would appeal on its own terms.

The *News of the World*

The entry for the *NOTW* in the *Newspaper Press Directory* of 1846 gives a sense of the new paper's place in the market. After noting that it is 'one of the many papers which compresses into a capacious double sheet the news of the week', the entry goes on to describe the *NOTW*'s content:

> It has no very distinctive feature in its composition, which simply aims at giving as much news as possible; and of a general as well as political character. There is some attention given to literature; and a small selection of sporting news. Its commercial intelligence is good, and its 'Grocer's Gazette' seems to mark it out as favoured by that class of traders. It is well suited for the respectable tradesman and intelligent persons in that sphere; and its being cheaper than any newspaper (except one), tends of course to enlarge the circle of its readers.[20]

The emphasis is on economy and the amount of material the paper contains for its price, rather than anything exceptional about its contents. For the *Newspaper Press Directory*, the *NOTW* was a cheap, respectable weekly aimed at the upper working and lower middle classes.

If anything was distinctive about the *NOTW*, it was that it provided what looked like an upmarket newspaper for just three pence. The *NOTW* was a double sheet, with eight pages of six columns, and claimed that it contained the maximum amount of type permitted under the Stamp Act.[21] Although *Lloyd's Weekly* had twelve pages, it was printed on smaller paper and only ran to five columns. On larger paper, the *NOTW* could not only compete in terms of size, it also looked more upmarket. In advertisements prior to the appearance of the first issue on 1 October 1843, Bell boasted that the size of the *NOTW* 'will be equal to that of the *Times*, the largest newspaper in the Kingdom'.[22] This was a claim that the new newspaper was capacious, but it also situated it amongst expensive dailies rather than the cheap weeklies with which it was in direct competition.

Its title, too, differentiated the *NOTW* from its predecessors. Plenty of papers used astronomical terms in their titles – the two evening papers, *The Globe* (1803–1921) and *The Sun* (1792–1900), for instance – and Bell himself published *The Planet* (1837–44) and the *World of Fashion*. Yet, for the *NOTW*, 'the World' encompassed both the newspaper's coverage and its proposed readership. What was unusual for a Sunday paper was that the title lacked the name of a specific person. The market was dominated by publications whose titles featured somebody's name and so the 'News of the World' would have sounded strikingly new (as well as a little presumptuous). By not including his name in the title, Bell disassociated the newspaper from any of his other publications, particularly *Bell's New Weekly Messenger*, but he also distanced the new paper from the genre of the Sunday paper. The name 'Bell', whether or not it referred to an actual individual, had become so closely associated with the Sunday newspapers of the past 40 years that by rejecting it, Bell signalled a clear break between the *NOTW* and its predecessors.

The sense of inclusiveness suggested by 'the World' also informed the way Bell imagined the *NOTW*'s contents. In a column called 'The Politician' on the front page of the first issue, Bell suggested that the paper could transcend class interests by aligning itself with 'truth':

> Journalism for the rich man, and journalism for the poor, has up to this time, been as broadly and distinctly marked, as the manners, the dress, and the habitations of the rich, are from the customs, the squalor and the dens of the poor. The paper for the wealthy classes is high priced, it is paid for by them, and it helps to lull them in the security of their prejudices. The paper for the poorer classes is on the other hand, low priced, and it is paid for by them; it feels bound to pander to their passions. TRUTH, when it offends a prejudice, and shews the evil of passion, is frequently excluded from both.[23]

'Truth' was what was missing from each of these class-bound forms of journalism but, it was implied, this absence is also what defined them. By aligning itself with 'truth', the *NOTW* created a space distinct from what it presented as class interest: a useful common ground to unite this otherwise divided readership.

'Truth' might have provided a conveniently apolitical perspective from which to pitch a new newspaper, but the *NOTW*'s own class position was much more complicated. Rather than take the best aspects of each type of journalism, the *NOTW* used aspects of journalism for the rich to remedy those inherited from the poor. Whereas journalism for the rich was 'remarkable for its talent, for its early intelligence', journalism for the poor was notable 'for the absence of talent, and the staleness of its news'. The supposed superiority of the former dictated both the shape of the *NOTW* and its place in the market. For instance, although Bell insisted that the 'general utility of all classes' was the founding motivation of the *NOTW*, its appeal was to be different for different classes. Whereas the paper was designed to suit the limited means of the 'poorer classes', it was its (at this stage predicted) 'immense circulation' that would command the attention of 'the middle, as well as the rich'. When Bell hoped that by combining the 'attractions of the rich newspaper' with 'the smallness of its price' he could 'secure a circulation amongst the poor and the rich', he actually intended a paper for the poor that, because of its circulation, would be noticed and approved of by the rich.[24] The *NOTW* was presented as a cheap newspaper, not a radical one: this was to be rich man's journalism at a price suited to the poor.

While it has been common for historians to assume the *NOTW*'s radicalism, its politics were carefully judged in order to cultivate as wide a readership as possible.[25] As Virginia Berridge has noted, radicalism was 'axiomatic in popular papers of this type', but it was a radicalism commodified 'to provide an easy appeal'.[26] For Raymond Williams, the *NOTW*, and other cheap Sundays that appeared in the 1850s, espoused a 'a more generalised social radicalism, of a kind corresponding to the alliance between middle-class and working-class political forces before 1832, in which rich and idle could be isolated as villains, but with innocence and magic (respectability and Providence) as the only effective alternative forces.'[27] For Williams, this radicalism took on the form of melodrama, emptying out politics to tell tales of vice and victimhood. As Williams argues, the cheap newspaper was both attuned to and a representative of a 'new urban popular culture' that was made visible in commercialised and commodified forms.[28] The *NOTW*, with its distinctive title and masthead, was particularly implicated in this new culture. For Stanley Morison, it was a 'poor but flamboyant design', but as it incorporated 'a common sign-writer's lettering' it 'would have been familiar to the patrons of the old London music halls'.[29]

The *NOTW* shared the generic radicalism of its rivals, expressing sympathy for a range of radical causes, but tempered this with moderation. For instance, in the first 'The Politician', the *NOTW* offered the unpopularity of the Poor Law as 'a neutral ground – It is that of humanity, and of charity – on which the rich and the poor – the Whig, the Tory, and the Radical can meet together – can make their voices heard by the Government'.[30] Surveying what it saw as widespread apathy amongst the governing classes, the column notes the Rebecca Riots, Chartism, calls for repeal in Ireland and the Anti-Corn Law League as promising signs of activity, but rather than advocate any one of these movements it opted for the paternalistic course of ameliorating the widely despised consequences of the Poor Law. Looking back in a leading article at the end of 1844, this sympathetic but noncommittal politics was restated. The *NOTW*, it claimed, was 'devoted to the eternal cause of TRUTH', every political question was 'dispassionately considered' and 'no one class [...] upheld at the expense of others'. The newspaper was 'dedicated to THE GENERAL WELFARE OF THE COMMUNITY' and supported reform so as to 'relieve INDUSTRY of its heavy burthens, and TRADE of its unjust restrictions, without endangering the property or the institutions of the Country'. This was conventional liberalism, but it tempered its support for free trade with a radical afterthought. While the paper admitted 'the sacred Rights of Property', it nonetheless maintained that 'Property has its duties also; – that Labour has its Rights; and that the poor man's privilege should be sacred as the rich man's prerogative'.[31]

Its contemporaries tended to view the *NOTW* in these terms. In 1846 the *Newspaper Press Directory*, for instance, described its politics as 'liberal', making no further reference to its political opinions in the entry.[32] By 1851, it had modified this to 'Ultra Liberal', differentiating it from the solidly middle-class liberalism of the *ILN* ('Liberal in its general tone; in Politics, neutral') and the politics of its rivals amongst the cheap Sundays, *Lloyd's Weekly* ('Democratic and Anti-Poor-Law') and *Reynolds's Weekly* ('Chartist').[33] Twenty years later, James Grant registered the politics of the *NOTW* in the same way, offering it as an apolitical representative of a genre against which other publications might be judged. In his *History of the Newspaper Press* he described the politics of *Lloyd's Weekly* as 'thoroughly Liberal', but noted that it was 'not so extreme in that direction as those of some others of its weekly contemporaries'. Foremost amongst these was *Reynolds's Weekly*, which Grant described as the 'organ of extreme Republicanism throughout the country'. For the *NOTW*, however, he noted its principles were 'Liberal' and that 'original political discussion' was not one of its features.[34] Given that 'The Politician' had been a fixture of the *NOTW*'s front page from the outset, this judgement reflects the way that its specific politics were subsumed within the expected orientation of papers of this type.

As the *Press Directory* entry makes clear, what made the *NOTW* noteworthy was the amount of news it furnished for its low price, not its political stance. It took its boast to contain the news 'of the World' seriously, with a regular department, 'Foreign News', occupying most of page two. *Lloyd's Weekly* also published the news of the world as 'Foreign Intelligence', usually running to two or three columns and printed prominently on the front page. Although tucked away inside the paper (the front page was dedicated to advertisements, 'The Politician' and a column of 'Jokes' from *Punch*), the *NOTW*'s coverage was both more extensive and better organised, ranging from East Asia, the Indian sub-continent and North America to Europe. News from Ireland, then Scotland, often followed 'Foreign News', operating as a transition before 'Country News', usually starting on page three. As was common in weekly newspapers, the leading articles were published at the centre of the paper, on page four, and were followed by 'Last News', which included late items from London, the rest of the country and abroad. It was not unusual for news items to move from this section of the paper to nearer the front over the course of the paper's three editions. For instance, the third edition of the *NOTW* for 8 October 1843 has two reports of a murder on the front page. In the second edition, they had been printed on page four in column six, following the leading articles. In the third edition, these reports displace two royal proclamations, one asking for information regarding the Rebecca Riots, the other recalling some gold coins. Royal proclamations were news, but they were not exclusive to the *NOTW* and they were less attractive to its readers.

As a weekly, the *NOTW* could draw upon the rest of the week's press for news. However, the necessity of Friday publication for country readers meant that it did not simply reprint or rewrite content from elsewhere. Bell knew that country readers were important if the *NOTW* was to sell enough to turn a profit, so different editions were published from the outset. The first edition went to press on Friday evening 'so as to be forwarded to all parts of Europe that night, by the General Post' and did not contain any news received after seven o'clock that evening, including the day's gazettes.[35] Bell overstated the newspaper's circulation here as the Friday edition was more likely intended for more distant parts of Britain than for readers abroad.[36] The Saturday edition was published at six o'clock on Saturday morning and then continued to appear over the course of the day. This edition, according to the paper, contained 'all the news that reaches London, together with every occurrence that transpires in the metropolis, so that residents in the country are furnished with the news up to the latest moment'. Published on a Saturday, rather than a Sunday, this edition avoided any reservations by distributors and newsagents about sales on the Sabbath. The third and final edition went to press at six o'clock on Sunday morning and continued to appear throughout the day. This edition, for a London readership, contained 'all the information that can be collected being inserted as it arrives at our office'.[37]

This pattern of publication, which was established from the newspaper's first issue, ensured that readers across the country would receive the newspaper – if not exactly the same newspaper – at the same time. The *Newspaper Press Directory* of 1846 thought that this was particularly noteworthy, speculating that the paper, due to its editions, was 'designed in a great degree for country circulation'.[38] A few years later, the *Press Directory* discriminated further between the *NOTW*'s readers and those of its rivals. In 1851, it described *Lloyd's Weekly* as 'peculiarly the poor man's paper' giving 'prominence to police reports, and similar matters of *popular* interest', but suggested that the *NOTW* was most likely read by busy tradesmen (on account of its 'Grocer's Gazette') who, due to 'incessant occupation in the week', had little 'opportunity before the Saturday evening for newspaper reading'.[39] However, although the *NOTW* thought of itself as 'a Miscellaneous Newspaper fit for family perusal, and enjoyment by the fireside', it was well aware of the commercial appeal of sensation reports of scandal, crime and violent accident.[40] These could often be found at the front of the paper (murder was still news, after all), but they tended to be printed on page five, to fill the space after the leading articles, before the regular 'Literature' column on page six, and on page seven, where columns such as 'Central Criminal Court', 'Police', 'Robberies, &c' regularly featured.

That such content passed unremarked by the *Press Directory* demonstrates its generic nature. Sensational material was an important component of the newspaper in general, but the extent to which it was employed and the way that it was written played an important part in distinguishing between papers and situating them within the marketplace. The *NOTW* fully recognised the commercial appeal of such content, but took steps to ameliorate the generic associations that went along with its low price. As mentioned above, on large paper and unillustrated, the *NOTW* did not look like a cheap publication, and it took pride in this appearance.[41] Looking forward in December 1843 to the New Year, for instance, the *NOTW* boasted about the quality of its paper (by Venables, Wilson and Tyler) and its type (by Vincent Figgins).[42] In 1852, the paper announced its move into new offices on Exeter Street and the installation of 'new steam machinery with all the latest improvements for the effective production of our newspaper'.[43] The paper's 'Literature' column also established a level of respectability. There was no original literature, only reviews, and these tended to be for non-literary works ranging from travel to popular science. When literary works were reviewed, they were judged both according to their literary merit and their likely appeal to the *NOTW*'s readers: when Tennyson's *Maud and other poems* was reviewed in 1855, it was judged flawed because it was 'inaccessible to ordinary intellects'.[44]

The *NOTW* asserted its respectability in order to market itself to advertisers. In May 1844 it claimed that its character guaranteed its 'circulation among the most respectable families in the kingdom' making it 'a most eligible medium for advertisements'. It went on to challenge the idea that the paper, because it was three pence, 'circulates amongst persons not interested in the perusal of Advertisements' instead arguing that its 'Readers are the most respectable and influential classes of society, and many thousand copies are sold weekly'.[45] While the *NOTW* wanted to sell as many papers as possible, it tried to do so with a paper that could appeal to a particular type of reader. In 1844, the *NOTW* claimed it had sold a total of 175,000 copies, based on the stamp returns from September, October and December 1843, a total higher than all other papers but *The Times* at 258,333 (it did not give totals for either the *Northern Star* or *Lloyd's Weekly*, probably the *NOTW*'s chief competitors).[46] The figures were deliberately flattering, aggregating stamp returns with no regard to the periodicity of the publications, but the *NOTW* also began to volunteer weekly sales. On 1 September 1844 these were 13,876; by the end of the year they had reached 17,500. At these levels, income from sales dwarfed that from advertisements. To give an example, on 22 September 1844 circulation was 15,153 and the paper contained about 173 lines of advertisements.[47] On the basis of their advertised rates, this meant that the paper received £187 10s. from sales and £2 8d. from advertisements (and this sum for advertisements assumes that the *NOTW* derived an income from advertising Bell's other publications, The *World of Fashion*, the *Gentleman's Magazine of Fashion* and *Bell's Historical Scrapbook*). However, with a business model based upon only a small return per issue (the *NOTW* claimed only a farthing was left to cover costs), advertising income, because it was free of overheads, was vital. In 1851, with a weekly circulation of 60,000, the paper was still declaring that 'its readers are the most intelligent and respectable classes or society' while teasing advertisers that 'only a limited space' was allotted for them.[48]

Fox Bourne, in his *English Newspapers* (1887), claims that the *NOTW* promised 'to emulate all the virtues and avoid all the vices of the other papers' but 'hardly kept its word':

> Its radicalism was more violent than that of *Lloyd's*, and it was more freely supplied with offensive news; but it pleased many readers, and in the course of twelve years it attained a circulation of nearly 110,000, being some two or three thousand ahead of *Lloyd's*.[49]

While it was true that the *NOTW* rapidly found a market and was able to increase its circulation week by week, reaching 110,000 a week by 1855,[50] it was neither more radical nor more bloody than its rivals. It was certainly aware of the commercial appeal of both radical politics and sensational news and it employed both astutely, but the *NOTW* presented itself as a respectable newspaper at a cheap price. Fox Bourne's judgement, some 43 years after the paper first appeared, shows both the ability of the genre – the cheap Sunday paper – to overwhelm the characteristics of that genre's representatives and the effect that this had on the *NOTW*'s reputation, which had become fixed.

Yet the significance of the *NOTW* depends upon recognising its distinct place within the market. For Virginia Berridge, the origin of the cheap Sundays 'lay not in a natural outgrowth of working-class consciousness, but in a shrewd assessment of the possibilities of an expanding working-class market.'[51] Each paper found its own niche within this market and its own way of addressing and appealing to its readers: for the *NOTW*, this was by marketing itself as a paper that was affordable by everyone and contained as much news as possible. If, as for Berridge, the cheap Sundays' 'commercial synthesis of radicalism and sensationalism resulted in manipulation of the old traditions of radical journalism so that the real roots of social and economic distress were effectively ignored', the *NOTW* was particularly important as it represented the fullest example of this synthesis.[52] More moderate than its closest rivals, the *NOTW* was an explicit attempt to create what would become the popular press. Capitalised and commercialised, the *NOTW* presented itself as an apolitical yet democratic product, available to all, that contained everything, apparently, that its readers needed to know.[53]

Conclusion: 1855, 1861 and the refusal to charge a penny

The achievement of the *NOTW* was striking. The paper was launched in 1843 into a new market but, rather than imitate its predecessors, it struck out distinctly on its own. This initial innovation paid off for the paper and it attracted a readership that grew for nearly two decades. This was a publication that was confident of its market. After the repeal of the newspaper stamp in 1855 the *NOTW*, like its rivals, reduced its price by a penny. The paper claimed that tuppence 'was always our price, the additional penny being paid to Government for the stamp' and then restated its universalist aims:

"THE NEWS OF THE WORLD" will always contain NEWS FOR ALL READERS. The Fullest Intelligence from the Seat of War, including Original Correspondence and Official Despatches – News from all the Foreign Courts – News from all the Colonies – News from the Gold Fields – News from all parts of England, Scotland, Ireland, and Wales – News for the Politician – News for the Diplomatist – News for Citizens and for Country Gentlemen – News for the Ladies – News for the Family Circle – News of Everything for Everybody.[54]

Even accounting for the expected self-aggrandising hyperbole common in such pronouncements, that the *NOTW* chose this moment to restate its aims so fully shows how it perceived itself – and wanted its readers to perceive it – in the market. Its cheapness was at the service of its accessibility, and the paper took care to exorcise the various less-savoury connotations that were associated with it.

From the first of July 1855, it was available on unstamped paper at two pence, although a stamped impression at three pence was also produced for despatch in the post. Although it attempted to present itself as a political conduit for (relatively) unmediated news, the *NOTW* was nonetheless committed to a certain relationship with its readers. The paper knew that sensational news reports and some sort of sympathy, at least, with radical politics were not only expected in a cheap Sunday newspaper, but were essential for its survival. Nonetheless, when its rivals began to reduce their price by another penny in 1861, the *NOTW* did not follow them. John Browne Bell had died in 1855 and the paper was held in trust by his son, John William Bell, for his younger siblings, Walter John and Adolphus. A further reduction in the price of the paper would have halved its income from sales: even with the increase in the number of advertisements in the paper in the 1850s and 1860s, sales were still the paper's major source of revenue and so such a reduction would have substantially reduced the estate. The *NOTW*'s rivals, especially *Lloyd's Weekly*, were in a similar commercial position but, for them, the reduction in price paid off in continuing increased sales. As it would be decades before the *NOTW* would follow suit, it suggests that the paper thought that it would retain its position in the market at tuppence. Whereas previously the paper had competed directly with the other Sundays, maintaining its price at tuppence meant that it now occupied a position of its own. The gamble was whether its readers would recognise – and so pay for – its distinctiveness, or would simply see the paper as a more expensive version of the cheap Sunday paper represented by its rivals.

Notes

1. 'The News of the World', *Newspaper Press Directory*, London, 1846, p. 79.
2. 'The News of the World', p. 79.
3. Raymond Williams, 'The Press and Popular Culture: An Historical Perspective', in George Boyce, James Curran and Pauline Wingate (eds), *Newspaper History: from the 17th Century to the Present Day*, London, 1978, pp. 41–50.
4. Stanley Morison, *The English Newspaper: Some Account of the Physical Development of Journals Printed in London between 1622 and the Present Day*, Cambridge, 1932, p. 229.
5. Morison, *English Newspaper*, p. 229.
6. Alison Adburgham, *Women in Print: Writing Women and Women's Magazines From the Restoration to the Accession of Victoria*, London, 1972, pp. 185–86; Stephen Koss, *The Rise and Fall of the Political Press in Britain*, 1981; London, 1990, p. 51; Cheryl Law, 'Bell's Weekly Messenger: The Country Gentleman and Landowner's Journal (1796–1896)', in Laurel Brake and Marysa Demoor (eds), *DNCJ: Dictionary of Nineteenth-Century Journalism*, Gent and London, 2009, p. 47.
7. G.A. Cranfield, *The Press and Society: From Caxton to Northcliffe*, London and New York, 1978, p. 86.
8. Harold Herd, *The March of Modern Journalism: The Story of the British Press from 1622 to the Present Day*, London, 1952, p. 83.
9. Morison, *English Newspaper*, p. 243.

10. See Morison, *English Newspaper*, p. 241; Adburgham, *Women in Print*, p. 227; Francis Williams, *Dangerous Estate: The Anatomy of Newspapers*, London, 1957, p. 55; Dennis Griffiths, *Fleet Street*, London, 2006, p. 109. Morison denied a family connection between John Bell and John Browne Bell in his *John Bell, 1745–1831: A Memoir*, 1930; Cambridge, 2009 (see p. 52) but subsequently changed his mind in *English Newspaper*. For a contemporary assertion, see [James Grant], *The Great Metropolis*, 2 vols, 2, London, 1837, p. 141.

11. See, for instance, 'Bankrupts', *Manchester Mercury*, 26 March 1811, p. 3. Bell and de Camp are described as 'booksellers, printers, publishers, dealers and chapmen'.

12. There is some discussion as to Mary Ann Bell's identity. Adburgham suggests she must be either John Bell's wife or daughter-in-law (*Women in Print*, p. 227). Either way, the *World* was published from Mary's shop in 1832, and John Browne Bell was also listed at this address (see Morison, *John Bell*, p. 75). Mary Ann does not appear in the 1840s and perhaps this is connected to the death of Browne Bell's youngest son in 1844. See the *Morning Post*, 4 March 1844, p.8.

13. [Grant], *The Great Metropolis*, p. 134.

14. Morison, *English Newspaper*, p. 250; Herd, p. 84.

15. [Grant], *The Great Metropolis*, p. 142.

16. Ibid., p. 135 and p. 137.

17. Morison, *English Newspaper*, p. 257.

18. 'To Advertisers', *Lloyd's Illustrated London Newspaper*, 11 December 1842, p. 20.

19. James Grant, *History of the Newspaper Press*, 3 vols, 3, London: George Routledge, 1871, p. 92. See also Ian Haywood, *The Revolution in Popular Literature: Print, Politics and the People, 1790–1860*, Cambridge, 2004, pp. 163–64.

20. 'The News of the World', pp. 79–80.

21. See 'The News of the World', *NOTW*, 8 October 1843, p. 4.

22. The advertisement ran in a number of provincial papers in the weeks preceding publication, including the *Taunton Courier*, *Leeds Times*, *Worcestershire Journal*, and *Sherborne Mercury*. See for instance 'The Novelty of Nations and Wonder of the World', *Leicestershire Mercury*, 16 September 1843, p. 1.

23. 'The Politician', *NOTW*, 1 October 1843, p. 1.

24. 'The Politician', p. 1.

25. For the *NOTW* as ultra-radical, see S. Maccoby, *English Radicalism, 1832–1852*, London, 1935, p. 420; John Hartley, 'Journalism, History and the Politics of Popular Culture', in Stuart Allan (ed.), *The Routledge Companion to News and Journalism*, London, 2009, p. 14. For a more moderate appraisal, see Louis Dudek, *Literature and the Press: A History of Printing, Printed Media, and Their Relation to Literature*, Toronto, 1960, p. 73.

26. Virginia Berridge, 'Popular Sunday papers and mid-Victorian society', in Boyce, Curran, and Wingate (eds), *Newspaper History*, p. 257 and p. 259.

27. Williams, 'The Press and Popular Culture', pp. 44–45.

28. Ibid., p. 46.

29. Morison, *English Newspaper*, p. 255.

30. 'The Politician', p. 1.

31. 'A Few Words to the Public on the Close of the Year', *NOTW*, 22 December 1844, p. 4.

32. 'The News of the World', p. 79.

33. See 'News of the World', 'Lloyd's Weekly London Newspaper', and 'Reynolds's Weekly Newspaper', *Newspaper Press Directory*, London, 1851, p. 123–24, 116, 133.

34. Grant, *History of the Newspaper Press*, 3, p. 95, p. 97 and p. 87.
35. See 'To Our Readers and the Public', *NOTW*, 11 February 1844, p. 4.
36. For instance, in 1845 the paper boasted it was received in Plymouth by seven o'clock on Saturday evening and so readers could choose which edition they preferred. This suggests that until this point only the first edition was available to readers in Devon and Cornwall. See *NOTW*, 5 January 1845, p. 1.
37. 'To Our Readers and the Public', p. 4.
38. 'The News of the World', *Newspaper Press Directory*, 1846, p. 79–80.
39. '*Lloyd's Weekly London Newspaper*' and '*News of the World*', *Newspaper Press Directory*, London, 1847, p. 106 and pp. 123–24.
40. 'A Few Words to the Public on the Close of the Year', *NOTW*, 22 December 1844, p. 4.
41. They did publish a series of portraits in 1844, and occasional images appeared over the run. See for instance *NOTW*, 14 and 21 July 1844.
42. See *NOTW*, 24 December 1843, p. 1.
43. See *NOTW*, 10 October 1852, p. 4; Griffiths, *Fleet Street*, p. 110. They also announced a fresh set of type from Figgins.
44. See 'Literature', *NOTW*, 16 September 1855, p. 6.
45. *NOTW*, 5 May 1844, p. 1.
46. See for instance, 'Declaration of the Publishers and Printers of the *News of the World*', *NOTW*, 1 September 1844, p. 1.
47. The weekly sales were reported the following week. See 'Declaration of the Publishers and Printers of the *NOTW*', *NOTW*, 29 September 1844, p. 1.
48. 'To Advertisers', *NOTW*, 5 January 1851, p. 4.
49. H.R. Fox Bourne, *English Newspapers: Chapters in the History of Journalism*, 2 vols, 2, London: Chatto and Windus, 1887, pp. 122–23.
50. See 'To Advertisers', *NOTW*, 22 April 1855, p. 4. They claim a circulation of 109,106 a week and compare this to *The Times's* 51,204.
51. Berridge, 'Popular Sunday Newspapers,' p. 253.
52. Ibid., p. 256.
53. Williams, 'The Press and Popular Culture', p. 47. The *NOTW* was set up with £15,000 capital: see Brian Winston, *A Right to Offend*, London: Bloomsbury, 2012, p. 73.
54. 'Notice to the Public', *NOTW*, 1 July 1855, p. 4.

2
Rebranding the *News of the World*: 1856–90

Laurel Brake and Mark W. Turner

'It stands first in point of circulation of all the journals exclusively dedicated to public intelligence and the general business of a newspaper', *NOTW* advert, *Sell's Dictionary of the World's Press*, 1888, vol. 2, p. 1120.

The *News of the World* and newspaper history

The hypothetical model that this chapter and the next interrogate is expounded in the influential volume *Newspaper History* (1978):[1] as the *NOTW* was unaligned with any political party, it was – like all newspapers in 'the middle' – forced to become 'commercial'. Purporting from its inception to be consensual and committed to all classes of reader, it relied increasingly on advertising to remain profitable, an economy that militated against radical politics and ensured its continuation as a 'bourgeois', liberal commodity.[2] We are not alone in our scepticism. Kevin Williams, in *Read all about It!* (2009), also takes issue with this prevalent view of the Sundays, arguing that 'This underestimates their position, and that of popular papers in general'.[3]

The assumptions of the prevailing model – its orientation to a press whose primary function is to serve as a platform for radical politics, its critique of the popular press as a 'decline' from this 'standard' *because of* its cross-class readership and its identification of decline with the onset of commerce and advertising – have been succeeded by a variety of alternative approaches. Recent scholarship has in particular gained much from the critical insights of popular and cultural studies and the theoretical challenges emerging out of poststructuralism. Intertextuality and interdisciplinarity have helped to shape what we understand as the 'text' under scrutiny, and notions of paratext and the 'sociology of text' amount to an extension of bibliographical approaches to those of material culture. A range of overlapping and related fields – from Women's Studies to Business Studies, from Media History to Local History – have generated multiple and productive streams of work on the press. Within the last decade, the analytical tools of digital humanities, digitisation of titles of historic serials and increased access to the range of contents of the press through the circulation of digital surrogates have resulted in a slew of new critical operations on the corpus of the press, and facilitated comparative study of titles and 'big data'.[4]

In summary, the assumptions of much foundational newspaper history have been fundamentally challenged by these major theoretical interventions, across several disciplines. The prevailing 'back story' of the *NOTW* is one of initial success, decline and questionable rejuvenation into a Sunday manifestation of the 'gutter' press.[5] Allegedly reaching the peak of its success in 1855, with its circulation higher than that of its competitors, the *NOTW* lost its dominance of the Sunday market. Having failed to lower its price to 1*d*., and short on innovation in the remainder of the nineteenth century, it languished in stasis until new proprietors, Henry Lascelles Carr and Charles Venn,[6] purchased it in 1891 and, with legal and business management from George Riddell, rejuvenated it under the editorship (1891–1941) of Sir Emsley Carr and made it highly competitive again, by commercialising it. So the story goes.[7] What is generally agreed, however, is that by 1950 the *News of the World* was the UK's biggest-selling newspaper by quite a margin, peaking at a circulation of more than 8.4 million,[8] and that when it closed in 2011 under the ownership of Rupert Murdoch, it still had the highest circulation of the Sunday press, driven largely by a combination of celebrity journalism, scandal and sensationalist investigation.

Mapping the argument – key phases and identity

Against that conventional wisdom, our piece takes a different approach: we examine the nineteenth-century trajectory of the newspaper as a successful title through a closer look at its contents, materiality and interaction with these same characteristics in its competitors, in the midst of the changing legal, social and economic conditions in which the press of the day was embedded. Our methods are qualitative, rather than quantitative, characterised by critical and detailed close reading of the *NOTW* and other titles to form a basis for comparison. We analyse the *NOTW* over 40 years, 1856–95, considering the basis of its survival during lean years and fat ones. The nineteenth-century growth of the paper comprises four phases on which we focus: the 1850s in the paper's initial heyday, 1861–80, in the wake of the paper's decision to remain more expensive than its competitors at 2*d*. and its circulation was considerably reduced, 1880–81 when the price dropped and fiction was introduced and 1891 onwards, when under new ownership the paper changed its look and feel, in sync with the rising New Journalism.

Alterations in newspapers between 1851 and 1861 were prompted by several external factors. The first, in 1850, was the addition to extant weekend prints of *Reynolds's Weekly Newspaper*, which joined *Lloyd's Weekly*

Newspaper, the *Observer,* the *Sunday Times,* the *Weekly Dispatch,* the *Weekly Times* and the *NOTW,* itself a relative newborn (1843 ff).[9] The establishment of the Divorce Courts in 1857 extended the scope for titillating narrative in the form of legal 'reporting'.[10] Change in the press also gathered momentum between 1853 and 1861 from repeals of three long-standing taxes affecting newspapers – on advertisements (1853), 'stamp' duty on every newsprint sheet used in all editions (May 1855) and on paper itself (1861); cumulatively these fostered the formation of a cheap press, both weekly and daily, that multiplied competition in the 'Sunday' sector of the market.

Details of decisions made in the history of the *NOTW* are not always straightforward. For example, for nearly 20 years (1861–80), it elected to remain twice as expensive (at 2*d.*) as the leaders in its market niche. What are the implications of that decision, or indecision?[11] What, other than price, did its distinctiveness comprise? We compare the 2*d.* years with the period May 1880–90, after it became a penny paper.[12] Key changes after 1880 seem entrepreneurial, and coincide with the launch in 1881 of the second wave of New Journalism, manifest in the slightly later penny weekly *Tit-Bits* and the popular daily, the 1/2*d. Evening News. Tit-Bits* dedicated itself *exclusively* to entertainment, by publishing *only* the entertaining paragraphs that the Sundays included inter-alia in their miscellanies; nevertheless, eventually, the *News of the World* – along with the others – responded to the newcomers' extraordinary success by increasing its human interest features such as crime, gossip and illustration, as we argue in detail below. Still, circulation continued to lag, and it was not until 1891 and the arrival of new proprietors that a gradual but wholesale refashioning prepared it for the burgeoning mass market.

Although there are key phases of change, there are salient characteristics that define the paper throughout this extended period: a high proportion of news, national and global, including financial and monetary news and expansive parliamentary and court reporting; breadth of entertainment copy, including early sports coverage; a distinctively unstinting 'Literature' page and theatre reviews. From its first appearance in 1843, the features of its six-column front page indicated its foundations: three columns of adverts, signifying its alliance with commerce, a prominent editorial column 'The Politician', signifying a commitment to political news, and 'Jokes', from *Punch* and the like, announcing its intent to entertain. Neither the contents of the front page nor the tenets of the paper changed perceptibly for over 25 years. With its closely set type, minimal leading and its six columns,[13] the front page (see Figure 2.1) appeared slightly less dense than inside pages, which were unrelieved by illustrations or typographically punctuating headlines except in times of war.[14] Rather, it was happy, like other papers of the day, to publish columns and columns of unrelated paragraphs, with no ornament to distinguish them, and lengthier articles with only the barest title, or initial words in bold face or small capitals. It was, and remained,

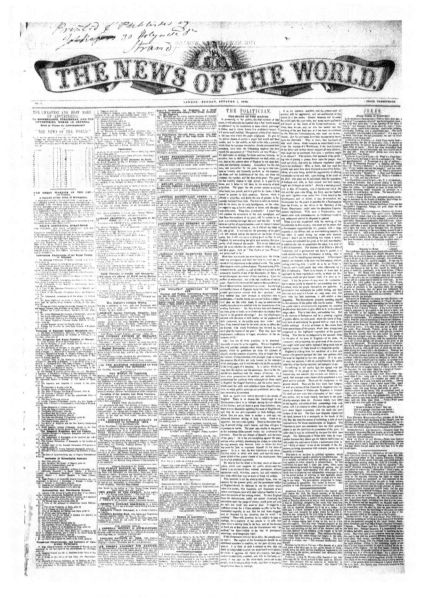

Figure 2.1   News of the World, 1 October 1843, front page

a dense read until more headlines and display advertisements began to appear in the 1870s, and eventually illustrations from 1891 onwards. These lightened the broadsheet pages and, along with other changes of style and layout, were part of the advent of the New Journalism.[15]

In 1880, when it halved its price, and in 1881 when it added fiction to its 'Entertainment' copy, well before its competitors, the *NOTW* echoed New Journalism alterations in the *periodical* press, aiming at cheaper and more alluring contents for a broader base of readership, both economically and with respect to gender. The inclusion of fiction was calculated to attract additional women readers, as well as men. The relatively stable context helped fix the *NOTW*'s identity, but it was, in fact, far from inert. It was attempting to adjust itself to the changing context of publication and competition between 1851–61 and 1891.

Although the *NOTW* was described by press directories as 'ultra liberal' (Mitchell's *Newspaper Press Directory* in 1855) or 'liberal' (Mitchell's in 1863 and *Sell's* in 1889) throughout the nineteenth century, unlike the dailies it was not allied with any political party at this time.[16] Its extensive discussion of political questions was from a liberal perspective that criticised the Liberal Party in and out of government, as well as the Tories. It was *not* radical, unlike the earlier tradition of working-class papers, which has been interpreted to its discredit as prevarication undertaken to appease its avowed target of a broad readership across the political and class spectra. In our reading, its politics were not anodyne.[17] Its two columnists – 'The Politician' and 'Hampden' – and its leaders were not evasive or apolitical, but about political policy and issues. One could argue that against the grain of papers that adhered to a political party, its mode of reporting politics veered toward rationality, if not objectivity. In comparison with the *NOTW*, between 1843 and 1852, the tone, register and selection of what was covered in *Reynolds's* and in *Lloyd's* make the political discourse of the *NOTW* seem nothing more than generally liberal. News *coverage* was notable for its diversity and volume. It included domestic, foreign, parliamentary, financial, court reports, the military, the gazettes and birth, marriages and deaths. Such copy distinctively dominated the columns, in comparison with its other contents, and with other competitive 'Sundays'. This high proportion of broad and deep news copy is perhaps the paper's dominant 'note'. That may account for its reputation throughout the nineteenth century as 'respectable', in contrast with its status in post-war Britain as enjoyable rubbish, with a cross-class readership but dismissed as being outside the boundaries of the serious press. The latter version of its reception ignores the investigative and campaigning copy, rooted in its liberal past, which then and subsequently entertained readers: whether meretricious or worthy, such copy was stylistically sensationalised. Still, in our own day, as Jennifer Egan notes, 'Most of us are desperate for raw experience.'[18]

Sunday/weekend press – *c.* 1855–80

Part of our interest is to disarticulate the 'Sunday' press, to note the different market niches that various titles serve and to identify the likely competitors of the *NOTW* among them.[19] The variety and spread of weekend titles in the nineteenth century are reflected in their broad spectrum of prices, both before and after the repeal of stamp duty took effect in July 1855. Because of this variety, only two titles were direct competitors of the *NOTW* in 1855, rather than all of the Sundays. Both were cheap liberal papers – *Lloyd's* from 1842 preceding the appearance of the *NOTW*, and the *Weekly Times* launched in 1847 as a rival to both *Lloyd's* and the *NOTW*.[20]

How did the *NOTW* manage to survive for 20 years until 1880, when it adopted the 1*d*. tariff? What were its distinctions? While price *was* important, however, it was one among other factors, which included its dual emphasis on breadth and depth of news, lack of party affiliation, early sport reporting, crime as narrative and entertainment – within the borders of respectability, and perhaps its pithy brevity. A notable reliable feature of the *News of the World* up to the 1880s is the breadth and seriousness of its literary reviewing, which usually covered books, journals and often sheet music. For decades, titles selected for review were largely demanding: in February 1870, Froude's *History of England* and Disraeli's speeches, and earlier in its history Dickens's novels. The *Weekly Times* in the same period often omitted reviews of books entirely, and its reviews of journals were consistently of more popular titles than the more strenuous periodicals selected by the *NOTW*. Similarly, comparison of the amount of attention over these decades that the *NOTW* allocates to financial news and the gazettes (on page 8) with coverage of these items in the *Weekly Times* shows differences in character between even those in the same niche that help to distinguish titles from each other for readers. The rest of the Sundays were too different to be counted as competition, with higher prices,[21] and,/or more pronounced (Conservative or Radical) politics,[22] and/or a different balance in the selection of contents.[23]

Throughout the nineteenth century, weekend papers appeared an unstable, experimental genre, in which variations of price, size, content and politics revealed a highly segmented market. It might be that discussion of the Sundays is, in fact, too limited a determination to be helpful. Media historians have tended to talk about the Sunday press mostly in uniform ways, and usually in relation to a very select few papers (*Lloyd's* and *Reynolds's*) that support an argument about print and radical politics.[24] However, the Sunday papers were not only (or even mostly!) published on Sundays, and their editions began as early as Friday, continued throughout Saturday, included special Sunday editions and even extended until Monday.[25] This spread of publication over successive days of the end of the week by nineteenth-century Sundays might have been spurred by the dearth of agents in the trade who operated on Sunday. R. Power Berrey's account of changes in distribution from 1891 makes this gap in infrastructure clear. To fill it, private or 'direct' agents (outside of the trade) were identified and hired by George Riddell.[26]

Traces of the spread of the Sundays may be seen in the routine coverage of 'Yesterday' in the Sunday editions – 'Yesterday' not only as a designation of 'recent' news, but 'Yesterday' hinting at copy in earlier editions, as in the *Weekly Times*'s department on page 1, 'The News of Yesterday' (column c) on 4 Jan 1880. Unfortunately, because the archive normally includes only the latest London edition rather than multiple editions, it is difficult to test this hypothesis properly.[27]

The weekend was a crowded market, including not only the Sunday papers emanating out of London, but also regional weekly papers, increasingly popular and important during the century, alongside other weekly serials. A single notion of the Sundays does not do justice to questions of varying price, the complexity of the multiple editions of most Sunday newspapers or to the ways in which this print form rubbed up alongside other print forms during the weekend. By the 1890s, as Chapter 3 discusses at length, the *NOTW* might not have been in direct competition with print forms other than weekend papers, but it was certainly borrowing from them, making the Sunday more hybrid than ever.

What we have, then, is an evolving genre. Although mid-century Sunday titles had recognisably common aims – to inform and entertain – and certain types of common coverage, they differed in coverage of other topics, such as the frequency and nature of sports and fashion reporting. The type of contents a Sunday miscellany might normally include was a matter of discretion and debate,[28] as was the location of where content might appear in each issue. Sport, fashion and fiction (both original fiction and as the object of reviews) were all sparsely and insecurely present. Most Sunday titles entirely excluded serial fiction during these decades; the type and frequency of sport reporting varied greatly, and topics identified with women – market prices, fashion and religious news – although sparse, appeared to varying degrees, and increasingly, in all Sundays. Even reporting of Parliament was peripatetic, appearing on different pages of the paper before settling for a page that readers might reliably consult with the expectation of finding it.[29]

Stable positions for a section or department in an issue were complicated by a number of variables: Parliament sat only during specific periods, amounting to about half a year;[29] when it was prorogued and in recess, large numbers of newspaper columns were released for different kinds of copy, opening up the movement of departments to accommodate new or expanded categories of material.[30] The development of sport as meriting a 'department' in the *News of the World* can be traced from its coverage on random inside pages to regular appearance on the back page. Furthermore, the routine of multiple editions meant that the first, country or 'Railway' edition,[31] included much of the news, markets and market prices of the previous week's Sunday edition, so the later editions on any single weekend were likely to involve new layout for some pages. When important stories

such as the state of Prince Albert's health and his death, a war or a sensational murder case (or more than one of them at the same time) justified
acres of coverage, then departments might well be moved to accommodate
the extra material. This continued throughout the century as even when
departments looked more stable and regular later in the century they and
their location were never absolutely fixed, as we discuss below.

The contents, price, size and emphasis of the contemporaries of the *NOTW*
were notably tailored to the class, pocket, politics and the frequency of access
to the daily press of its readers. For example, consumers of Sunday titles at
the expensive end of the market in 1854, such as the *Sunday Times* and the
Observer, were more likely to read or take a daily, than artisans, workers
or lower middle-class readers of the *NOTW*. Consumers of dailies did not
require high density reporting of the news of the week. Their Sundays were
more expensive and possessed more space for book and performance reviews
than a title like the *NOTW* with a heavy news remit and commitment to a
different mix of copy for entertainment. Their proportion of literary and
theatrical contents was higher. Like all weekend papers, the *NOTW* included
full coverage of law and crime reports, as well as reviews of the theatres,
music, books and journals, but there was more crime reporting, in a number
of departments across an issue, than reviews and literary copy.[32] For this
weekend sector of the market, crime reports are likely to have had a double
valence – of news *and* entertainment for readers and editors alike. While
such heavy coverage of the variety of courts – Sessions, Police and Central
Criminal – appears as news, and can be justified as news of the realm,
the narratives of illicit behaviour and of colourful characters, now safely
within the confines of the courts and print, also had a high entertainment
value.[33]

So, even after the cheap daily and weekly press developed in the wake of
1855 and 1861, the *NOTW*'s admixture of a news-rich paper with serious
coverage of domestic and foreign politics, and of Parliament as well as entertainment, ensured that it held its own and did not close. It is our contention
then that the *NOTW* stood out as distinctive among its contemporaries, not
only before 1861 but also after, when it continued to combine a cheap price
(although not the cheapest) with wide and capacious news coverage and a
significant element of entertainment.

NOTW – against inertia, *c.* 1861–81

The *News of the World*'s decision in 1861 to retain its 2*d*. price should give
us pause – not to note that it failed to reduce its price, but that it decided
not to. This suggests that it saw a distinction between its type of coverage
and relative gravitas, and the more popular, sensational language of the
penny press found in *Lloyd's*, *Reynolds's*, and the *Weekly Times*. In relation
to *Lloyd's*, one of its main competitors, the *NOTW was* less down market,

and tonally and contents-wise on 'higher ground', which was expressed in the price differential between them for 20 years (1861–80), and in its notably less detailed and graphic crime reporting than *Lloyd's*. Nor did the *NOTW* purport to be a local *London* paper as did *Lloyd's* or its other main rival, the *Weekly Times*, the subtitle of which was *A London Newspaper of History, Politics, Literature, Science and Art*. The perspective of the *NOTW* was more like the London dailies – news of the '*World*'. This orientation to the world beyond London is borne out by its initial circulation patterns,[34] whereby circulation in the counties of the UK proved greater than in London, and its later gravitation to an overseas market to supplement its domestic sales.[35] *Lloyd's* made a point of covering London local government issues, such as elections for the London School Board,[36] while in 1870, for example, the *Weekly Times* includes local London news prominently, on its front page.[37]

However, like *Lloyd's* and the *Weekly Times*, the *NOTW* excluded tales and serial fiction for 40 years. Once it dropped its price to a penny to match theirs in May 1880, it maintained its distinction from them by quickly introducing fiction into the paper in January 1881 – five years before the *Weekly Times* and a decade before *Lloyd's*.[38] In keeping fiction out of their pages and privileging news, the three weeklies had continued their adherence to the news model of the metropolitan daily newspaper press, which resisted, until late in the century, an overlap with the periodical press that the incorporation of fiction would involve.[39] Even in 1893, when W.T. Stead developed his notion of 'journalistic fiction' for his new *Daily Paper*, he introduced his compromise genre gingerly: 'no-first class newspaper demeans its columns by the publication of a novel in instalments'.[40] By adding fiction soon after its new price of a penny, the *NOTW* maintained its distinction from its main rivals – by means of additional content, as well as making a percipient move towards the New Journalism. By including fiction, the *NOTW* aimed at more popular contents to attract women readers and broaden its sales base.

The issue of 4 April 1880 has two telling features in this connection: in the advert announcing the coming price reduction the following month, it refers to the paper as 'a family journal' dedicated to remaining 'UNCONTAMINATED BY IMPROPRIETIES WHICH SO OFTEN MAKE A WEEKLY NEWSPAPER UNACCEPTABLE IN A FAMILY' (page 4, column c). It promises that 'NO OBJECTIONABLE ADVERTS WILL EVER BE INSERTED' (ibid.). These are precisely the faults for which the upmarket *Saturday Review* had denounced *Reynolds's* and *Lloyd's*, above all, in their rant 'Newspaper Cleansing' in 1870: the 'work of public corruption' in which these two titles are allegedly engaged according to the *Saturday Review* includes the insertion of adverts for 'a dirty book or a dirty quack'.[41] Moreover, the contents of page 7 of the 4 April issue of the *NOTW* is *already* aimed at female readers: it contains the gardening column (on the kitchen garden), the monthly fashion column and an advert for feather beds that includes a coupon for five pounds of extra feathers for *NOTW* readers who buy a feather bed.[42] The other copy on the page might also have been adjusted to accommodate women readers: largely non-political news in the 'Country News' department and three columns of court reports – the 'Police Courts' and the 'Sessions'. These particular crimes ('Stealing Postage Stamps', 'Theft of an Overcoat', 'Yielding to Temptation' or 'Found in a Bar After Hours') are not violent, and although they have narrative interest and involve occasional fracas, they are not 'unacceptable'.

Likewise, the fiction that first appears in January 1881 complements the fiction-like narratives of the crime reporting and the quotations from novels in book reviews, an implicit presence of fiction with which *NOTW* readers were long familiar. While the inclusion of fiction began with weekly short stories on the Literature page (9 January 1881, p. 6), they appeared in a novel-like *series*, called 'Life Sketches', unified by a departmental title and the same author, Mrs Adolphus Bell, with each weekly number having a separate, chapter-like title. The characters were apparently different, but melodramatic plots around courtship kept fulfilling the expectations of readers of the series, from one issue to the next. When this series ended, some five months later, it was followed from 15 May 1881 by a novel, *Wrapped in Mystery,* by the Author of 'Life Sketches', and in December 1881 by 'A Life's Episode.' It transpires that 'Mrs Adolphus Bell' is doubly well connected in the world of the Sunday press. Her maiden name, Louise Clarisse Reynolds, would have identified her to readers as a daughter of G.W.M Reynolds, author and founder of that other notable contemporary Sunday penny paper, *Reynolds's*. Less recognisable to readers of the *NOTW* would be the import of her married name, which identifies her as the wife of one of the proprietors of the *NOTW* at the time.[43]

By 1889, literary prose is found even in the opening of the first leader:

> The new year opened in gloom and disquietude. London was immersed in a thick and unwholesome fog; few persons ventured willingly into the open streets and sickly air; business was at a standstill, and an opinion generally expressed was that such another evil-looking New Year's Day had never been seen.[44]

What relieves the gloom is a favourable economic upturn: the Revenue Returns just published for the previous year reveal that 'English trade has been doing very well'. This mixture of accessible, melodramatic and entertaining prose with economic and political analysis indicates the receptivity of the *NOTW* to the mores of the New Journalism, and its aspiration to the wider readership opened up by its penny price. It shows a title already adjusting in the 1880s to the new media of its day, but still without the illustrations and what was to follow after the buy-out of 1891.

As both of the significant changes to the *NOTW* in 1880/81 precede the appearance of *Tit-Bits,* the reasons for their implementation are yet to be understood. According to Bainbridge and Stockdill, they stem from the long tail of the death of John Browne Bell in 1855, at which point ownership of the title was shared among his sons. In 1877 John William Bell, one of the sons died, and the estate was divided between *his* sons, Walter and Adolphus, who eventually persuaded the other shareholders to drop the price to 1*d.*, in an effort to gain more readers; that shareholders had received no dividend for some years helped convince them of the necessity of this policy.[45] This straitened time is reflected in the contents of the paper in 1880, when sports coverage is in abeyance for six weeks at the beginning of the year, and reappears only sporadically, until it regains relatively regular coverage, though still parsimonious, in the summer months. However, from being a staple lure of the popular press, sports coverage is sacrificed for six months by the *NOTW*, which relegates its inclusion to isolated, disparate stories, often not on page 8 where it was expected, nor in its department, 'The Sporting Life.' Even when the department heading is published, there is space for only one or two paragraphs, it is not usually located at the top of a column, *and* when there is room copy is treated as filler: a paragraph of Racing 'Predictions', culled from other named sports journals, might appear in another location, isolated from other sports items.[46] It seems clear that at this point, the *NOTW* has no sports correspondent. At the same time, the number of columns devoted to advertising increases threefold on page 8, crowding out the previously extensive copy on sport (gone or very squeezed), financial news and the gazettes. It might be that the absence of sport results from a combination of more adverts garnered for revenue and the new expense of the employment of a writer of fiction.

In this phase of its existence, then, we find a respectable, popular and successful newspaper with a notable brand of wide news coverage and quality entertainment copy at a low price. Following the shift of the industry to cheap print between 1855 and 1861, the paper is alert to changing market conditions while at the same time undergoing a shift of proprietor in 1855 to a new generation of Bells. Together, these events result in the new proprietors' decision to retain its recently reduced price of 2*d.*, rather than becoming a penny paper, as many of its contemporaries did. We argue through a comparison with other weekend titles that under these conditions, the paper retained a qualitative distinction from cheaper rivals, which kept it afloat, if with declining sales. It took another shift of proprietor to the succeeding generation of Bells in 1877 to respond dramatically to this problem. Halving its price to a penny in 1880 and introducing fiction well before its rivals in 1881, the *News of the World* became a penny paper while still retaining a distinctive element among its peers. A more wholesale rebranding transpired a decade later, when the Bells gradually handed over to a new newspaper dynasty, the Carrs, in 1891, as we explicate in Chapter 3.

Notes

1. See J. Curran and V. Berridge in G. Boyce, J. Curran and P. Wingate (eds). *Newspaper History: from the 17th century to the present day*, London, 1978, p. 70 and pp. 247–64, respectively.
2. See Boyce, Curran and Wingate, p. 36, p. 70 and p. 247.
3. K. Williams, *Read All About It! A History of the British Newspaper*, London, 2009, p. 9.
4. For indicative overviews of the field that emphasise new approaches to press history, see L. Brake, 'Journalism' in D. Felluga, P. Gilbert, L. Hughes (eds), *The Encyclopedia of Victorian Literature*, Maldon, MA, Oxford and Chichester, 2015, pp. 845–54; L. Brake, 'Markets, Genres, Iterations' in A. Easley, A. King (eds), *Ashgate Research Companion to Victorian Periodicals*, Farnham and Burlington, 2015; J. Mussell, *The Nineteenth Century Press in the Digital Age*, Basingstoke, 2012; B. Onslow, *Women of the Press in Nineteenth-Century Britain*, New York, 2000; and M.W. Turner, 'Towards a Cultural Critique of Victorian Periodicals', *Studies in Newspaper and Periodical History*, 1995 (1996), pp. 111–26; See also L. Brake and M. Demoor (eds), *DNCJ: Dictionary of Nineteenth-Century Journalism*, Print: Gent and London, 2009; Online ProQuest, 2009 ff.
5. In his chapter on the *NOTW*, Matthew Engel exemplifies this view. See M. Engel, *Tickle the Public: One Hundred Years of the Popular Press*, London, 1996. The authors are grateful to Matthew Engel for his help in locating an 1890s image, described in a tantalising quotation in his book (p. 208). Representing Sunday titles as yachts in a race for the million mark, it appeared as a hoarding in *c.* 1897 when *Lloyd's* first attained a circulation of a million. Quoted from J. Power Berrey, The *Romance of a Great Newspaper* (London, [1922]), p. 46, Berrey's description from memory in 1922 does not include the *NOTW* in the circulation race in the late 1890s; it appears only on the distant horizon.
6. News of the World Archive: CRP/4/1; News Group Newspapers Ltd Archive, News UK and Ireland Ltd. The News UK archive possesses records of the *NOTW* from 1891, including two about the sale in that year, A Memorandum of Association of the News of the World Ltd (13 May 1891) that refers to an agreement (not in the Archive) between the Bells and Charles Venn (12 May 1891; registered 14 May 1891) and a Purchase Agreement (13 May 1891) between W.J. Bell/Adolphus Bell and Henry Lascelles Carr/J.E. Gunn. Riddell was a signatory to both documents. W.J. Bell was the original Managing Director of the company, but he resigned five months later in October while remaining a director until December 1894, when he was replaced by Charles Jackson. The authors are grateful to Nick Mays, Archivist of News UK, for this information.
7. Sir Charles J. Jackson's name does not appear among those of the directors of the new company in 1891 in the *Stock Exchange Year-Book for 1892*. This states that Jackson became financially involved in the paper in 1893, not 1891. Jackson was Lascelles Carr's brother-in-law and after Carr's death in 1902, Jackson succeeded him in 1903 as a director and Chairman of the Board until his death in 1923. See *Dictionary of Welsh Biography* http://yba.llgc.org.uk/en/s8-JACK-JAM-1849.html?q uery=Charles+Jackson&field=name [accessed 16 May 2015]
8. See C. Bainbridge and R. Stockdill, *The News of the World Story. 150 Years of the World's Bestselling Newspaper*, London, 1993, p. 179; Chapter 17 provides an excellent overview of the many issues that came to determine 'circulation highs and lows' in the mid-twentieth century.

9. The launch of *Reynolds's* was probably not a threat for the more radical portion of the *NOTW*'s 'liberal' readership, as such readers had had a more radical weekly alternative from its inception in the *Northern Star*, which survived until 1852.

10. *Lloyd's*, *Reynolds's* and the *NOTW* often carried stories based on Divorce Court proceedings, either under the category of Court reporting (*NOTW*, 15 December 1861, p. 8; *Reynolds's*, 1 January 1860 p. 7) or in stories developed as stand-alone news items (*NOTW*, 15 December 1861, p. 7; and *Lloyd's* 2 February 1873, p. 4

11. Bainbridge and Stockdill, *The News of the World Story*, p. 24. They attribute the failure to reduce the price to a penny by J.W. Bell, the proprietor who succeeded his father John Browne Bell in 1855, to his feeling 'hampered by family responsibilities'.

12. Ibid, 25. The decision to move to 1*d.* also followed the succession of one proprietor by others in 1877; J.W. Bell's sons – Adolphus and Walter John Bell – prevailed on the family to reduce the price in 1880. The identity of the editor of the paper between 1877 and 1891 remains unclear, in particular whether one or both of the Bells also acted in that capacity before Emsley Carr took over in 1891. Throughout this time, the imprint identified W.J. Bell as printer and publisher. Although both brothers appear in the census records for 1881 and 1891 as solicitors, to date no one else has been identified as editor in this period. The authors are grateful to Nick May for this information about Adolphus and Walter Bell.

13. An additional column was added on 30 August 1891, making each page seven columns, and in May of 1892, four pages were added to the length of the paper, making it twelve pages.

14. See stacked headlines during the Crimean War, *NOTW*, 7 Jan 1855, p. 3, 'Awful News from Sebastapol/Disorganisation/of the British Army'. Such headlines were also deployed to report the death of Prince Albert in Dececember 1861, and for a lurid crime story in the aftermath of his death, *NOTW*, 29 December 1861, p. 5: 'Extraordinary Discovery of the/Bodies of Children Supposed to/Have Been Murdered', and also for 'Execution of Jackson, the Soldier,/for the Murder at Aldershot'.

15. For the transformation of a page by an advert used as an illustration, see 1 January 1893, p. 3 and by a block ad, see 1 January 1893, p. 10. The *NOTW* went tabloid in 1984 (20 May).

16. See Mitchell's *Newspaper Press Directory*, London, 1863, p. 27 and *Sell's Dictionary of the World's Press*, London, 1889, p. 351. By the early twentieth century, however, the paper might be seen as being closely aligned with the Liberal Party, not least because of George Riddell's close friendship with Lloyd George, who granted Riddell his peerage in 1909.

17. See Virginia Berridge, 'Popular Sunday Papers and mid-Victorian Society', in Boyce, Curran and Wingate, pp. 247–64.

18. Jennifer Egan, *Look at Me*, London: Corsair, 2011 [2001], p. 248.

19. This is a tack taken in the nineteenth and twentieth centuries as well as our own: see [J.F. Stephen] in 'The Sunday Papers', *Saturday Review*, 18 April 1856, pp. 493–94; S. Morison, 'The Nineteenth Century Sunday Newspapers', *The English Newspaper*, Cambridge, 1932, p. 225, and D.S. Kamper, 'Popular Sunday Newspapers, respectability and working-class culture in late Victorian Britain', in M. Huggins and J.A. Mangan (eds), *Disreputable Pleasures. Less Virtuous Victorians at Play*, London and New York, 2004, pp. 83–102.

20. The *Weekly Times* in May 1855 changed its format to broadsheet to resemble the *NOTW*, and reduced its pagination from twelve to eight pages to eight; in July it

dropped its price to 2*d.* to match that of the *NOTW,* and *Lloyd's* likewise dropped its price to 2*d.* in 1855. In May 1861, after repeal of the paper tax, *Lloyd's* reduced its cost to 1*d.,* giving it a real price advantage over the *NOTW,* and the *Weekly Times* soon followed. At this juncture, the cheapest price prevailed, with three titles (*Lloyd's,* the *Weekly Times* and *Reynolds's*) costing a penny, the *NOTW* and *Sunday Times* holding out at 2*d,* and the *Observer* and the *Weekly Dispatch* at 5*d.* When the *NOTW* dropped its price to a penny in 1880, its configuration within the Sunday market changed, and in October 1881, when the *Sunday People* was launched at a penny as a Tory 'Weekly Newspaper for all Classes' on the masthead, the Sunday market changed again.

21. For example, the *Sunday Times,* the *Observer,* and the *Weekly Dispatch* cost 6*d* in 1854 (when the *NOTW* cost 3*d.*) and the latter two titles 5*d.* after 1861 (when the *NOTW* – and the *Sunday Times* – cost 2*d.*).

22. Mitchell's *Newspaper Press Directory,* London, 1866, p. 22, describes the *Observer* as 'Whig'.

23. The *Sunday Times,* for example, was strong on literary, dramatic and sporting copy, according to Mitchell's, 1855, rather than the news for which the *NOTW* was renowned. Further, where the *NOTW* covered crime unabashedly, the *Weekly Times* in the 1870s favoured 'Accidents and Offences', a decidedly milder order of event. Much as other Sundays such as the *NOTW* and *Lloyd's* use crime, the *Weekly Times* exhibits a pronounced coverage of accidents in main stories and filler in addition to the department 'Accidents and Offences.' See, for example, the *Weekly Times,* 2 Jan 1870, pp. 3 and 4, where one leader is entitled 'Accidents of the Season'.

24. The most influential work along these lines is Virginia Berridge's seminal essay, 'Popular Sunday Papers and mid-Victorian Society' in Boyce, Curran, and Wingate, pp. 247–264. Berridge's work was pioneering in opening up the category of the Sunday press to media historians.

25. Mitchell's *Newspaper Press Directories* in 1846 (p. 79) and 1847 (p. 113) list *Friday* as the day of publication of the *NOTW,* and in 1862 and 1863 Sunday *and Monday* as the days of publication for the *Observer.* It singles out the multiple editions of the *NOTW* in its 1840s entries: 'the main feature in its management is...the number of its editions – in fact from Friday evening to Sunday morning, there is a perpetual succession of editions, with augmented if not emended intelligence; so as to secure in every post through which it is sent out the latest news from every source' (1846: pp. 79–80; 1847: p. 114). Bainbridge and Stockdill similarly single out the multiple editions of the *NOTW* 50 years later in the 1890s, at the beginning of Emsley Carr's stint as editor in 1891: 'Three editions of the paper were then produced each week: one on Friday, which went abroad and to distant parts of the country and certain other places which had market days on Fridays and Saturdays; a small Saturday edition aimed at places where papers could not be bought on Sundays; and the normal Sunday edition...In addition to the 'specials' that were brought out from time to time from midweek onwards, a big news story occurring on a Sunday would also merit a special edition in those days when there were no agreements between papers not to print after the normal run. Cabs would be dispatched to bring in a 'scratch' staff, who would have the special edition on the streets within hours'. (Bainbridge and Stockdill, pp. 78–79).

26. Berrey, The *Romance of a Great Newspaper,* p. 49. Also, see the account of Riddell's import by Bainbridge and Stockdill, pp. 60–61 in Chapter 3.

27. The British Library normally collected the latest London editions, though there are notable exceptions in their nineteenth-century holdings.
28. Kamper reports alarm in 1889 and 1899 about the prospect of daily papers extending their output to include a Sunday issue ('seven day journalism'), with disapproval focusing on the claim that the kind of material in the dailies was both distinct from what extant Sundays published and inappropriate for publication on the Sabbath (pp. 85–86).
29. For example, in the first half of 1856, Parliamentary reports in the *NOTW* appeared on p. 4 (3 February), p. 2 (1 June); and p. 3 (10, 17 February), before settling on p. 3 during the rest of June and July.[30] See House of Commons Information Factsheet P4, in which 'The Sitting Year' is set out, including recesses, the details of which vary historically. Although times and dates of sitting vary, the patterns in the nineteenth century seem to amount to the same duration as at present, about six and a half months. For the purposes of this paper, it is useful to note that Parliament began with the Queen's Speech in early February, was in recess at Easter and Whitsun for about a week each, and from mid- August until the end of October. The Christmas recess extended to February. After 1858, the pre-Christmas session (October–December) was abandoned!
30. In the *NOTW*, for example, the issues published when Parliament was sitting contained a high number of articles about Parliamentary issues, beside the Parliamentary reports, which occupied typically at least two columns. Even in Parliament's absence, the *NOTW* ran a column 'Topics of the Recess', 2 January 1873, 6e).
31. For the term 'railway edition', see British Library microfilm of the *Dispatch*, 5 January 1851, where it is handwritten on p. 1.
32. Crime appeared in 'Police Courts', 'Central Criminal Court' and 'Middlesex Sessions' departments, but also in leaders, as filler/squibs in 'Miscellany' or 'Our Latest Glance', and as main, stand-alone news stories ('The Child Murder in Stoke Newington' 6 January 1889, p. 4, top of column c) scattered throughout the issue.
33. Compare Adrian Bingham, who writes 'The authority of the judicial process gave legitimacy to the coverage of subjects that would have been considered inappropriate for discussion in other contexts, although journalists had to use a euphemistic style that drew a veil around the most explicit details'. Adrian Bingham, 'Court Reporting', *Family Newspapers? Sex, Private Life, and the British Popular Press 1918–1978*. Oxford, 2009, p. 125.
34. See Bainbridge and Stockdill, *The News of the World Story*, p. 19, in which they argue that Browne communicated directly with country agents for orders for provincial sales to circumvent the London newsagents who were worried about the low price of the paper when it initially appeared.
35. The masthead of the Sunday edition of 4 April 1880 prints in brackets, along with the other vital information on mastheads, 'Registered for Circulation Abroad'. In 1891, Emsley Carr inherited a three-edition production pattern, the first edition of which – on Fridays – went abroad, and to distant parts of the UK. (Bainbridge and Stockdill, p.74).
36. See *Lloyd's*, 13 Nov 1870, which devotes both a leader and an article to this London topic, which continues to get coverage through the end of the year. In the *Weekly Times* as well, in the issue of 2 January 1870, advertisements are notably London based (p. 7), and news stories feature London local fires, accidents, etc. (p. 6). On the page for their regional news, the headings start with

'Metropolis', with 'Scotland' and 'Ireland' always to follow (cf. 2 January 1870, p. 3 column a).

37. See *Weekly Times*, 4 January, 1870, p. 1, columns c and d.
38. See G. Law, Table 1.3 'Major Victorian metropolitan weeklies carrying fiction', *Serialising Fiction in the Victorian Press*, Basingstoke, 2000, pp. 28–29.
39. As Law shows, the provincial press, weekly and daily, carried fiction far earlier than the metropolitan press, ranging from a small number in the 1850s to very large numbers in the 1870s. See Law, Table A.1 'Early serial fiction in provincial newspapers', pp. 215–21.
40. W.T. Stead, *Daily Paper*, November 1893, p. 32. For more on Stead's notion of 'journalistic fiction', see L. Brake, '"Who is 'We'?" The "Daily Paper" Projects and the Journalism Manifestos of W.T. Stead', in M. Demoor (ed.), *Marketing the Author*, Basingstoke, 2004, pp. 54–72.
41. 'Newspaper Cleansing', *Saturday Review*, 9 July 1870, pp. 39–40. Unsurprisingly, the *Saturday Review* prints such a 'dirty' advert about the recruitment of girls for the corps de ballet for the delectation of its readers.
42. Coupons are part of the prize, puzzles and competition features that editors of New Journalism titles inserted to build on features such as the Answers columns in order to entice readers to purchase the journal daily or weekly.
43. Mrs Adolphus Bell is identified in the British Library Catalogue as Louise Clarisse Reynolds, later Mrs Adolphus Bell, the author of two novels only, *The Walton Mystery* (1872) and *Barbara* (1874). None of the *NOTW* fiction seems to have been published in book form, but an advert in *Reynolds's* (3 June 1877, p. 7), indicates that the two novels appear to have been reissued in railway editions at 2s. each. Mrs Bell's husband, Adolphus, was co-proprietor with his brother Walter John from late 1877 to May 1891. We are grateful to Jim Mussell for alerting us to the connection between Mrs Bell and the proprietors.
44. *NOTW*, 6 January 1889, p. 4, column d.
45. Bainbridge and Stockdill, pp. 23–26.
46. Bainbridge and Stockdill's account of Emsley Carr's early days as editor suggests that even in 1891, when he took over, there was a serious shortage of reporters, with extant staff covering diverse types of stories, including sport. See Bainbridge and Stockdill, pp. 73–74: 'it was often a case of all hands on deck. There were no departmental demarcation lines and management staff would not infrequently assist their few editorial colleagues. Even for a normal edition some of them would report on football matches and other sporting events'.

3
Rebranding the *News of the World*: 1891 and After

Laurel Brake and Mark W. Turner

As long noted, and as Chapter 2 suggests, 1891 was a turning point for the *News of the World* (*NOTW*).[1] It was then, in mid-May, that George Riddell, a solicitor acting in association with Henry Lascelles Carr, W.J. Bell, and J. E. Gunn among others, first became involved with the newspaper, which had been lagging in circulation and devoid of financial investment for some years. In its obituary for Riddell in 1934, *The Times* suggested that the *NOTW*'s circulation had plummeted to as low as 30,000, although in its obituary of Emsley Carr in 1941 the figure given was 40,000 and in 1979 Stafford Summerfield, editor of the *NOTW* between 1960 and 1970, estimated it was 'under 50,000' in 1890 and 51,000 in 1891.[2] Whether the figure is 30,000, 40,000 or 50,000, circulation had flatlined in an increasingly crowded market.[3] The new personnel of the 1890s were key to the eventually revived fortunes of the early twentieth century, and their good working relationship clearly owed something to their previous connection through the Cardiff *Western Mail*, of which Lascelles Carr was a co-founder and editor-in-chief and his nephew Emsley Carr, was a journalist, while Riddell was their London-based legal representative. This triumvirate clearly worked well together and proved skilled when it came to overhauling the *NOTW*.[4] Lascelles Carr was a talented chairman who oversaw all changes; Emsley proved an equally talented young editor, taking that position at the age of only 24; Riddell moved from legal advisor to an increasingly important shareholder, eventually becoming managing director in 1903 when the firm became a limited stock company.[5] During this time, the *NOTW* was repackaged and renewed, while remaining consistent with its stated mission to provide a wide range of news, entertainment and business of all kinds. Some of these changes were wrought by the rise of the New Journalism and striking alterations in tone and typography, in which the *NOTW* took a lead in the weekend press; in part this was due to editorial and business acumen. Writing in 1932 former *Daily Express* editor, R.D. Blumenfeld, suggested that the *NOTW*'s 'astonishing progress from poverty to prosperity may be traced distinctly to the moment when Mr. George Riddell (now Lord Riddell), an industrious lawyer, began to take an interest in it.'[6] Drastic overnight refashioning is fairly rare in newspaper history, not least because of the risk in alienating existing readers, and the press is overall a conservative industry. The necessary changes did not occur all at once, in 1891; it took about 18 months for the paper to transform itself visually, and it was not until 1897 that shareholders began to receive dividends consistently.[7] There was an incremental set of new elements, and the paper was refashioned rather than relaunched. There was, for example, surprisingly little fanfare in the wake of new ownership in mid-May 1891 – no acknowledgment within its pages, no announcement or address to readers as frequently appears in the weekly and monthly periodical press, no mention of new editorship or ownership in either the 'Newspaper Happenings' section of *Sell's Dictionary of the World Press* or the other press directories. The only mention that we have found in contemporary journalism was published in a trade paper, the *Journalist*, which records that, 'the *News of the World* has been purchased by a small syndicate, at the head of which is Mr. Lascelles Carr, the managing partner of the Cardiff-based *Western Daily Mail*. One of this gentleman's nephews, Mr. Emsley Carr, has been chosen as sub-editor'.[8] What occurs in 1891 with the new syndicate is the beginning of a *process* of redesign, an initial tidying up of the format and a nod towards the more significant developments that would occur over the next few years. As we have seen, the *NOTW* was never an inert paper and its history, like that of virtually all longstanding papers, is one that includes significant phases of change in the nineteenth century: the 1861 decision to remain at 2*d*., the 1880 decision to move to one penny, the 1881 decision to introduce fiction and the change of direction after 1891 are components of a longstanding history of survival through adjustments to changes in law, technology, markets, and the press.

It is also worth pausing over the nature of Riddell's precise contribution. Blumenfeld suggests that Riddell's particular skill was in 'perfecting the machine, looking after the distribution of the paper, tightening up, expanding, applying methods akin to those of Big Business'.[9] Riddell's obituary in *The Times* precisely remarks on this business savvy: 'The extraordinary progress of Sunday newspapers generally is largely due to the method of distribution through direct agents which he initiated, and which was copied by other Sunday papers'.[10] As Bainbridge and Stockdill recount,

Riddell set about attempting to break the ancient puritan grip on Sundays. He sought to make his newspapers more widely available by initiating a method of selling the paper through direct agents, augmenting those few in the trade who already handled Sunday newspapers. This required a totally new and efficient organization through which the local agents ordered copies direct from the newspaper. The system grew slowly at first but gradually gained momentum until, a year or so after its introduction, he had recruited thousands of *News of the World* agents throughout the country and in Scotland where Sunday newspapers had previously been virtually unknown but were soon circulating in their thousands.[11]

The *NOTW* had long relied on its regional readers; indeed, that seems to have been the basis of its period of strength in the 1840s–50s. Geographical spread along with dedicated selling agents ensured a robust business model, one that perhaps sought to lure some readers away from the regional weekend titles that had become increasingly popular throughout the nineteenth century and helped to expand the market for Sunday reading. However, the circulation boost to the *NOTW* was not immediate.

We get a glimpse of the 'newsroom' at the paper, in a passing recollection from Robert Power Berrey. According to the *Encyclopaedia of the Press* (1992), Berrey had worked with the Carrs at the *Western Mail* since 1885 and was invited by Emsley to join the staff of the *NOTW* in 1893, at first as a crime reporter and then as assistant editor. According to Berrey, the team tasked with providing copy for the paper was remarkably small, just him and Emsley the editor:

'In those days there were only two members of the editorial staff – Emsley and myself. If Sir Emsley happened to be called away suddenly, I found all sorts of queer jobs falling to my lot. I did the book reviews, the leaders, the interviews, the sub editing, the illustrations, and even the racing notes'.[12]

Whether this is strictly accurate – whether others were involved, in more *ad hoc* ways, we do not know – it suggests the fine-tuned nature of the operation in the early years under the new ownership. Bainbridge and Stockdill similarly record Berrey's contribution, 'the editorial man of all trades', as a significant news-gathering force for the paper in the 1890s. Apparently, every week Berrey presented a bottle of whisky to the duty inspector at Scotland Yard, with a view to getting exclusive scoops on the latest crime news.[13] It's a wonderful window on the daily workings of the paper, which at this significant time of renewal relied on a pared-down group of individuals, grafting and multi-tasking across the departments, although like all other daily and weekly papers, it also relied on regular news coming in from the agencies.

During these transformative years in the paper, the gradual alterations completely changed its look and feel, in line with the emerging 'New Journalism.' When the new owners took over, on 14 May 1891,[14] it cost one penny for eight pages of six columns, with four columns of adverts on the front page. Eighteen months later, it was a penny for twelve pages, of seven columns and heavily illustrated. A set of regular departments had been in place since the early 1880s, in some cases much longer (e.g. 'The Politician' and 'Hampden'), and these mostly remained. In the 24 May 1891 issue, the first under the new owners, there was a tidying up of these departments on a slightly cleaner-looking page, with the significant addition of one new column, 'Sporting Notes and Predictions by Pegasus', on page 8, the last page, a key attraction for readers in the future, as we will see below. The only overt notice that a change of ownership had taken place was in the imprint, where the name of a new printer appeared, on the final page, bottom right, 'LONDON:--Printed and Published for the Proprietors by Robert Pearce Humphris, at 19, Exeter-street, Strand, in the parish of St. Paul's, Covent Garden, in the County of Middlesex, Sunday, May 24, 1891'. Gradually thereafter, changes are introduced, sometimes silently, sometimes with a notice to readers:

7 June 1891: the first use of illustration, mostly portrait line drawings

30 August 1891: the newspaper moves to seven columns instead of six, and there is an increased use of illustration

27 March 1892: the first use of a block advert

29 May 1892: linked to new printing presses, the newspaper increases from eight to twelve pages and circulation is said to be in 'half a dozen figures'

17 September 1892: first use of elaborately decorated, visually striking headings for each of the regular departments

24 September 1892: the first use of the banner beneath the masthead, claiming 'Contains More News Than Other Weekly Paper'.

10 September 1893: adverts leave the front page

The development of block advertising and extensive use of illustration changed the look of the paper. The increase in column numbers and experiments with departments, including more sports coverage and literary material, increased the contents and combined news and entertainment.

These key changes were accompanied by a commitment to technological change as well, an important signal to readers of the paper's modernity and forward motion. The move to 12 pages in May 1892 was heavily trailed in the months before, with notices to readers of the new investment in technology that would enable a better service (folding and cutting) and an enlarged issue 'which will make it the Largest Weekly Paper in London'.[15] In the week in which the paper increased its size, 29 May 1892, an article, 'The Machine of the Century', was placed in the very centre of the page, illustrated with an impressively large image of the new Hoe Press, and explaining the full impact of this latest new technology for the paper's print capacity. This bold and confident moment, indicating the fruits of new investment with increased numbers of pages for readers, sought to establish the modernity of the paper, with an emphasis on the speed enabled by cutting-edge technology. This substantial new technological investment, along with the changes in design indicated above, was the foundation of the paper's future success.

Of the new departments created in 1891, the new sports column by 'Pegasus' (the pseudonym of W.J. Innes) was the most significant. While sporting news had been a feature of weekend papers for decades, it was inconsistently covered in the *NOTW* during its lean years, and had focused mostly on racing and the turf. With the rise of the dedicated column, sports became far more prominent, eventually comprising almost the whole of the final page, and often more, with Pegasus consolidating his place as a significant sports writer. Football, which by this time received more coverage than the more traditional racing and the turf in sports columns, was fast becoming the country's most popular sport, not least because of the growth and spread of Association Football in the final decades of the century.

The press was integral to the spread of football in interesting ways. Regional and local newspapers covered local football closely, with 'football specials' or supplements on Saturdays covering the day's results.[16] Furthermore, the daily national and regional press covered football, as did the buoyant specialist daily and weekly sporting press. As David Russell writes, in his history of British football, in addition to the Saturday night football specials:

> the amount of space dedicated to football in the press grew enormously. Overall, it really is difficult to exaggerate the impact of soccer on the contemporary social, cultural and economic environment. In 1875, it was still largely a game for a leisured elite; by 1914, it lay at the heart of much English male culture.[17]

Football was a cultural phenomenon that the press supported vigorously. By 1895, the *NOTW* has a separate 'Football' column by Pegasus, usually of at least a couple of columns in length, in addition to other sporting news by Pegasus on the back page. Football news at this time might be unique in its multivalence, appealing to an exceptionally strong local and regional base (which formed the longstanding foundation of the *NOTW*'s readership) while also attracting wide national interest. It was a national sport made up of local teams and the press fed off the fast-growing popularity for football news. In several press directory advertisements for the *NOTW* in the 1890s, 'Pegasus' is the only writer singled out for particular attention. Pegasus and the sports column mattered. Furthermore, the increase in space afforded sports and football, in particular, was an indication that the new-look *NOTW* was bidding for sports readers from all publications – from the specialist sporting press and from regional papers.[18] The *NOTW* was hoping to lure readers away from other kinds of papers with which it previously had not really been in competition.

Illustration was the next key development in 1891. The placement of illustration on the front page and beyond, introduced somewhat tentatively in the summer of 1891, became a more elaborate and distinct feature of the newspaper over the next year or two. By 1895, the *NOTW* was still the only Sunday paper relying heavily on illustration, and it developed the most visually compelling and varied page. In fact, what is so striking about other weekend papers – *Lloyds's Weekly Newspaper*, *Reynolds's Weekly Newspaper*, the *People*, and the *Weekly Dispatch* – is how little those papers changed graphically between 1890 and 1895. There was occasional use of illustrated portraits in these papers, but nothing more elaborate. The *NOTW* was making a feature of illustration, emphasising the relationship between text and image to tell its interwoven stories, whether news or fiction. Take, for example, the 7 January 1894 issue of the *NOTW*, which was typical of what the paper was doing. There are a whopping 21 illustrations of varying kinds – a cartoon on the front pages related to politics (their version of the *Punch* cut), see Figure 3.1; wood-cut line drawings of heads, connected to various crimes and obituaries, see Figure 3.2; architectural images; maps; seven illustrations of women's fashions on what amounts to a woman's page, see Figure 3.3 and an illustration accompanying an instalment of a serial. These illustrations vary in size: some extend across the width of several columns, some take up several inches in a single column. They are in addition to the regular department titles, each adorned in relatively elaborate ways. 'Our Politician' on page 2 is illustrated with Big Ben, and 'Our Paris Letter' with a depiction of La Madeleine, etc., see Figure 3.4 The extent and variety of visual material, extending to prominent block advertisements, ensure that the eye keeps moving and has a variety of things on which to settle.[19]

Breaking up the page is one of the key features in the weekly press manifest in the New Journalism, which had been gradually emerging since the 1870s. As James Mussell describes it, the characteristics of the New Journalism included 'a set of typographical and textual innovations that transformed the press in the late nineteenth century'.[20] This included material presented often only briefly, in snippets or paragraphs rather than in dense and numerous unbroken columns, as was still the convention in the sober morning dailies. The *NOTW* combined some lengthy material with paragraphs and some news stories extending for more than a column with some paragraphs of only 30 or 50 words. Headlines and sub-headings, which the *NOTW* used more strategically and imaginatively than its competitors at this time, helped to signpost and to demarcate material, breaking up the density of a long column of print and providing ways of trailing the content

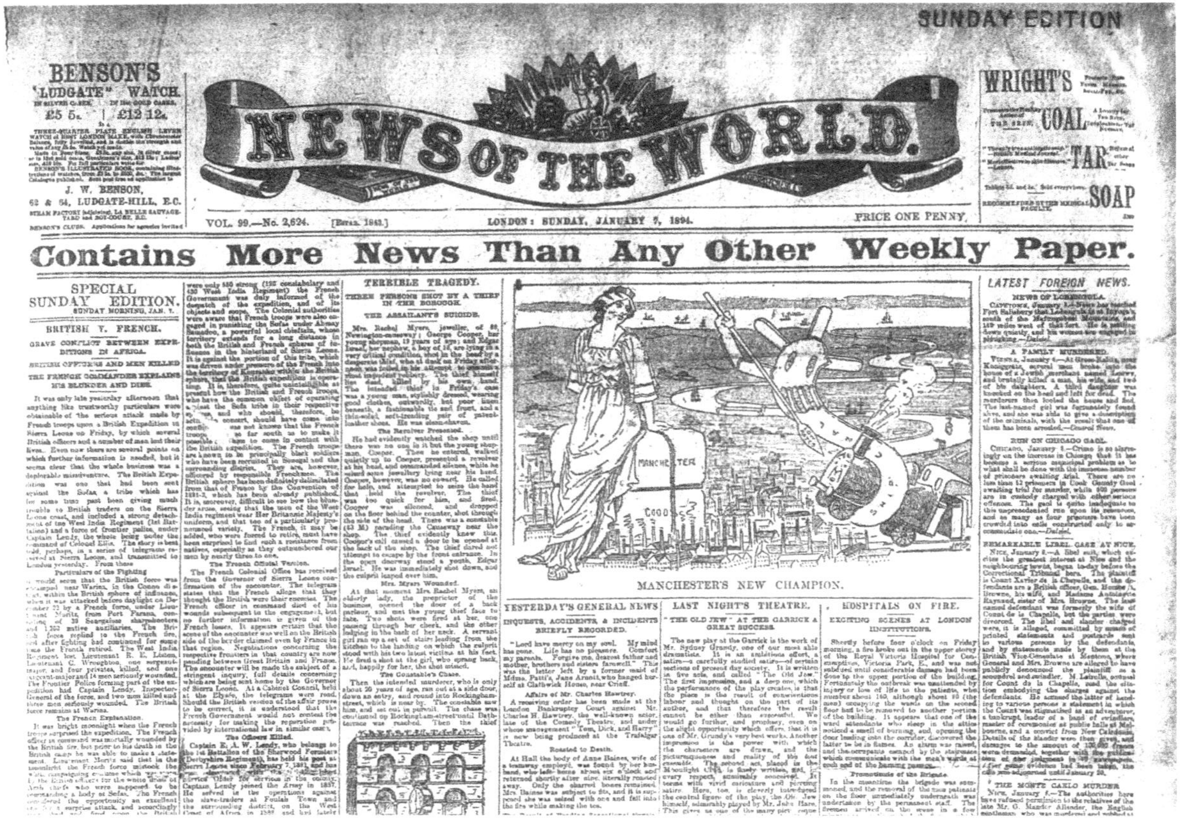
SUNDAY EDITION

BENSON'S "LUDGATE" WATCH.

£5 5s. | £12 12s.

J. W. BENSON, 62 & 64, LUDGATE-HILL, E.C.

NEWS OF THE WORLD.

WRIGHT'S COAL TAR SOAP

VOL. 99.—No. 2,624. [Estab. 1843.] LONDON: SUNDAY, JANUARY 7, 1894. PRICE ONE PENNY.

Contains More News Than Any Other Weekly Paper.

SPECIAL SUNDAY EDITION. SUNDAY MORNING, JAN. 7.

BRITISH v. FRENCH.

GRAVE CONFLICT BETWEEN EXPEDITIONS IN AFRICA.

BRITISH OFFICERS AND MEN KILLED.

THE FRENCH COMMANDER EXPLAINS HIS BLUNDER AND DIES.

TERRIBLE TRAGEDY.

THREE PERSONS SHOT BY A THIEF IN THE BOROUGH.

THE ASSAILANT'S SUICIDE.

MANCHESTER'S NEW CHAMPION.

YESTERDAY'S GENERAL NEWS

INQUESTS, ACCIDENTS, & INCIDENTS BRIEFLY RECORDED.

LAST NIGHT'S THEATRE.

"THE OLD JEW" AT THE GARRICK A GREAT SUCCESS.

HOSPITALS ON FIRE.

EXCITING SCENES AT LONDON INSTITUTIONS.

LATEST FOREIGN NEWS.

A FAMILY MURDERED.

RUN ON CHICAGO GAOL.

REMARKABLE LIBEL CASE AT NICE.

THE MONTE CARLO MURDER.

Figure 3.1 *News of the World*, 7 January 1894, detail of front page

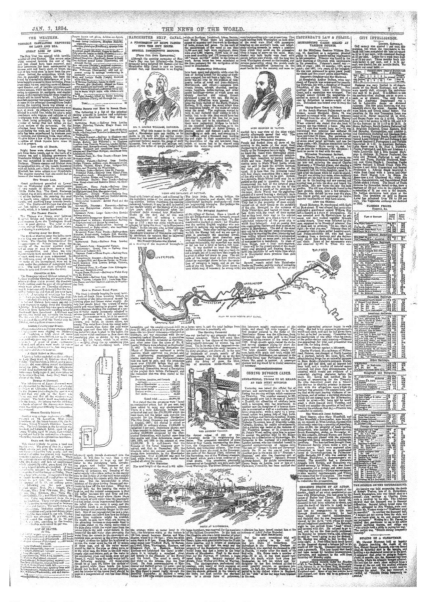

Figure 3.2   News of the World, 7 January 1894, p. 7

Figure 3.3 News of the World, 7 January 1894, p. 9

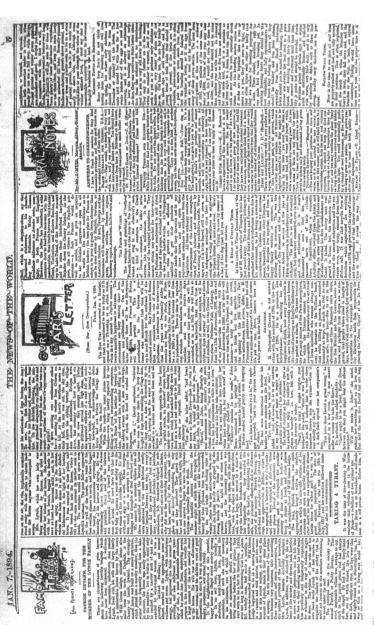

Figure 3.4 News of the World, 7 January 1894, detail of p. 5

of the story that followed. On the front page of 7 January 1894, for example, we see, in different sizes of type:

TERRIBLE TRAGEDY

———

Three Persons Shot By A Thief

In The Borough

———

The Assailant's Suicide

and:

HOSPITALS ON FIRE

———

Exciting Scenes At London Institutions

The variation of headlines, in tandem with the range of illustrations, created a more dynamic page of print than other weekend papers, which used head-lines more modestly and without illustration. The *NOTW* page offered readers choices, different entry points for reading, multiple distillations of content for the glancing eye and a comparatively visually compelling composition. Simply put, in the first half of the 1890s, the *NOTW* increas-ingly looked different from all the other Sunday newspapers. The *NOTW*'s innovations were striking, making it stand out on a crowded newsstand.

The *NOTW*, then, was leading the way when it came to innovative design. In the first half of the 1890s, *Lloyd's* still claimed to be the leading Sunday paper, with its masthead banner announcing the 'largest circulation in the world', a claim that it would keep for several more years. *Lloyds's* front page remains remarkably stable during these years: six columns of dense print with modest use of headlines, but little use of sub-headlines and modest use of illustration. The rest of the paper had a similar mix of departments – combining foreign news, literature, gardening, sports, theatres and amuse-ments with other forms of news. As Mitchell's 1896 *Newspaper Press Directory* described it, *Lloyds's* relied on 'the two great principles of quantity and cheapness' and presented 'an immense mass of matter for the money; with a little of everything, and a good deal of many things'.[21] The density of print on the first page certainly suggests quantity and compression, and the rest of the issue remains generally packed with miscellaneous news, but there is little new or visually engaging about it. Other weekend papers were similarly unadventurous in visual, typographical innovation. The 16-page penny paper, the *People*, 'A Weekly Paper for All Classes', which, according to Mitchell's 1894 *Newspaper and Press Directory*, 'claims to be the biggest Sunday penny paper, and to have a larger sale than any other weekly newspaper',[22] was similarly sober and stable. *Reynolds's* in 1894 was no less restrained, and its seven columns changed relatively little in the first half of the 1890s.

The dynamics of the page are significant because the *NOTW* looked as if it offered an extensive range of material, particularly since it had more columns than most. On front pages of all the Sunday editions of the *NOTW*, there was significant international and domestic political news (wars, major political stories), extending the length of a column and more, and often a 'Latest Foreign News' or 'Foreign Telegrams' column that included crime, disasters and political news in paragraphs provided by news agencies such as Dalziel's, Reuter's and Central News. Also, the front page of the *NOTW* usually included 'Yesterday's General News' – which detailed 'Inquests, Accidents, and Incidents Briefly Recorded', – and perhaps 'Last Night's Theatre' and 'Yesterday's Law and Police.' The Sunday editions of all the papers covered the *weekend* missed by the dailies that were confined to weekdays, and omitted by the Saturday weeklies.[23] In addition, in the *NOTW* there were any number of brief paragraphs about poisonings, imprisonments, divorces and other tit-bits designed to pique interest. Its front-page news is driven by brevity in its delivery – telegraphs, agency dispatches, short records and paragraphs – designed to present the vast array of 'news' quickly. More in-depth coverage of this range of material appears in the departments that follow. 'The Politician', for example, included extensive coverage of Parliamentary and related news, across five columns, covering daily sittings when Parliament was in session. When Parliament was prorogued, 'The Politician' was more usually two columns, and crime, divorce and sensational scandal filled out the page. The banner headline phrase that extended across the front page, which began in 1893 and was used for much of 1894 and also in adverts – 'Contains More News Than Any Other Weekly Paper' – was arguably true, and any given front page might include some 35 different news stories, however brief.

The *NOTW* appeared alone among the Sundays in its graphic innovations, with the look and feel of the broadsheet distinctive in the Sunday market by about 1894–95. However, it might not have been on the other Sunday papers that the *NOTW* had its eye. In fact, it had more in common with the illustrated daily press. It might have been learning from papers such as the new *Daily Graphic* (1890 ff) – a lavishly illustrated penny paper – which combined a range of politics, foreign and domestic news, entertainment and sports in visually compelling pages. For example, the large block advertisements that started to appear in the *NOTW* from 1892 are most visually impressive of all. They are as wide as three columns and nearly half a page in length in some cases, advertising Pear's Soap, Lipton's Tea, Hudson's Soap or Allcock's Plasters, see Figure 3.5. The striking adverts were both a commercial

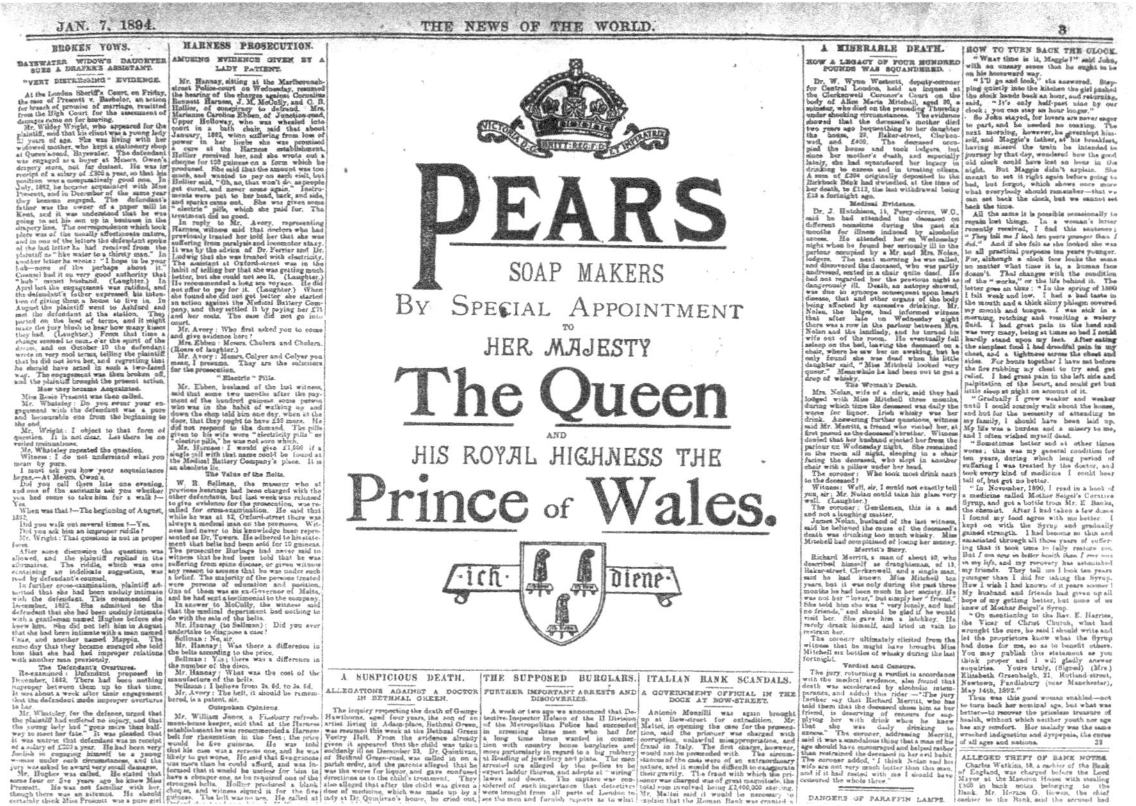

Figure 3.5 News of the World, 7 January 1894, block advertisement, p. 3

innovation and design feature breaking up the page, offering great spaces of white, often with images, in an otherwise fairly densely printed page. These large adverts were distinctly modern looking, signalling the future of print advertisements that were both a form of entertainment and hard sell. They appeared in the illustrated daily and weekly press and weekend magazines, although not in any of the other Sunday newspapers at this time. So, while the *NOTW* still favoured the verbal over the visual, its illustrative material clearly set it apart from other weekend papers.

The *NOTW* was looking in different directions as it sought to reposition itself in a bid for new readers. It distanced itself from other Sundays in its innovative designs, aligning itself more with daily illustrated newspapers among others. It made sport and football more prominent, in a bid to compete with the popular regional papers and it resembled a 'miscellany' in the sheer variety of material that it offered. The front page ranged from politics to theatres to crime to foreign news, all of which continued on subsequent pages in different ways. News, entertainment and commerce all rubbed up against each other on virtually every page. Continuing to examine the 7 January 1894 issue, for example, we find that the regular department on page 4, 'Amusements', with paragraphs about comic opera, exhibitions, farces, etc. is followed by a 'Stabbing at Holloway', 'The Dublin Tragedy', 'Three London Mysteries', in addition to some anarchism and fraud. Page 5 (see Figure 3.4) has three departments – 'Famous Trials', 'Our Paris Letter', and 'Rural Notes' – each offering different kinds of material, whether political, historical, sensational or regional, although sometimes these overlapped. In fact, there were perhaps only three pages of the twelve on 7 January in which the content didn't continually shift across columns: the literary page, which included the ongoing serial fiction, *Moina, A Detective Story* and 'Our Book Taster', a regular column of reviews and literary news; the fashion page, with the regular 'Home Circle' column and numerous fashion illustrations and the sports page, with round-ups of swimming, football, rugby, boxing, skating and athletics, although even here there was some economic news about 'Yesterday's Markets'.

Furthermore, there were echoes across the issue, from one department to another, from one type of copy to another. Stories about crime and detection appeared in the court reports, the news, in serial fiction and in the 'Famous Trials' department; the 'Amusements' department, with reviews and notices of theatre and other entertainments, clearly anticipated two columns of theatre adverts that usually appeared a couple of pages later, also called 'Amusements' but typographically distinct. 'Amusements' was being used in two distinct ways, both a part of the wider culture industry that helped to support the paper through its regular advertisements. No less than crime and politics, business and commerce figured throughout the newspaper, in the frequent 'City Intelligence' column, but also in the block and classified adverts that comprised numerous columns in any given issue. On the one hand, the paper used highly developed visual cues to illustrate the regular departments, in addition to headings and sub-headings to demarcate sections and content; on the other hand, there was a continual blurring of boundaries between types of material. The overlapping nature of the contents of issues might lead us to ask some significant questions about what we're reading: What is news? What is entertainment? Why does it matter? Although departments suggest boundaries, those boundaries are never discrete.

The changes wrought by the Carrs and Riddell made the *NOTW* distinct from other 'Sundays' of the time. In fact, it was as if the *NOTW* was preparing itself for the burgeoning mass market, using the techniques of the New Journalism that were appearing in the daily and periodical press (display adverts, innovative use of typography, use of fiction alongside non-fiction). The arrival of 'mass market' journalism is often considered to date from the launch of the *Daily Mail* in 1896, but the *Daily Mail* was, of course, part of a more nuanced story of the different and uneven ways that various genres of the press – daily, weekly, weekend/Sunday – embraced the New Journalism. As Kevin Williams has noted, it was the Sunday papers, with their combination of entertainment, crime and political analysis that 'provided the basis for the changes that were to take place in the daily press in the last decade of the century',[24] and strict delineations between these different areas of the press occlude the relationships between them. Crime stories were breaking out of the court reporting columns and in the first half of the 1890s both continued to appear – crime as part of 'Yesterday's Law and Police' and crime stories standing on their own, outright. Gradually, court reporting diminished, although the prevalence of crime reporting did not, giving it a greater prominence overall, lending the paper its more overtly sensational tone. If the racy crime and gossip content that arguably came to define the paper and drive circulation in the twentieth century was more muted in the first half of the 1890s, it was pronounced enough in May 1891 for the new editor to find with astonishment 'massives of flimsies piled on my desk' from his penny-a-line staff, who 'had saved up their sensational copy during the week... [and] carefully collected all the sensational police-court news and inquests of the week for Sunday's consumption'.[25] However, the foundations for change were initially graphic and visual, and, in ways that other weekend papers only did to a much lesser degree, the pages of the *NOTW* in, say, 1894–95 closely foretold those later pages of the *Daily Mail*.

Writing retrospectively about 'Old and New Journalists' in the early 1890s, the Fleet Street journalist E.T. Raymond proposed a suggestive model of interdependence between the entirety of the periodical press and the metropolitan dailies: the former were potentially spicy and the latter dull:

> a great deal of licence was given to the comic and the periodical Press, which was, on the whole, much less decorous than that of today. These

publications, indeed, seemed to be tolerated rather on the old respectable principle that, since there must be wickedness, it is well to give it a
definite outlet, so as to avoid the evils of general contamination. These
papers were, so to speak, the journalistic *filles de joie* who, by the sacrifice
of their own reputation, safeguarded the vestal innocence of the responsible sheets. In their pages the reader could, if his tastes lay that way, find
all the spice, suggestiveness, and scandalous piquancy he wanted. In the
great dailies, all was propriety and dullness.[26]

In the first half of the 1890s, the *NOTW* was laying important groundwork
for the direction that paper would take in the early to mid-twentieth century.
There are not strong grounds for arguing that the paper was an especially
more sensational publication than its competitors at this time; its coverage
of the Wilde trials in 1895 – among the most sensational and sensationalised trials of the nineteenth century – was as sensational as other weekend
papers, but no more. However, we can argue that these important graphic
innovations gradually shifted the balance of the newspaper between news
and entertainment towards the latter. News was still important in the 1890s,
but that gradually gave way to more sensational and raucous populism in the
twentieth century. As for entertainment, by the turn of twentieth century,
the paper was pulling out all the stops: serial fiction continued apace but
with much greater emphasis and fanfare, and arguably with a more sensational tone; sheet music was commonplace and pictures, puzzles, games
and competitions were weekly features. By 1902, the weekend newspaper
was a space of entertainment with a more obvious emphasis on commer-
cialism. The boundaries between 'real' sensational news stories and fiction –
focusing attention on blackmail, murder, mystery or assault – were more
blurred than ever; the paper was heavily illustrated and an aggressive use
of straplines and headlines attracted and guided the reader's eye, pointing
out ever new and changing features and developments – a new story, a new
puzzle, a new competition or a new serial. The circulation figures in the
twentieth century – 2 million by the 1910s, 8 million by the 1950s – tell of
the paper's success, a narrative which extends back to the changes wrought
after 1891.[27]

   Looking closely at the *NOTW* across the nineteenth century allows us not
only to explore the particularities of the title, but also to consider more fully
the nature of the 'Sunday', or weekend press. As Chapter 2 above discusses,
newspaper history has tended to consider the Sunday press in ways that
overly unify the genre. Our reading of the *NOTW* here and in Chapter 2
helps to disaggregate the weekend press, a more open and porous category
than scholarship has tended to acknowledge so far. The *NOTW*, which in
the twentieth century was so much defined by its sensationalism, was the
least audacious, most respectable and 'calmest' of the early Sundays. There

is much more work still to be done, to delineate the subtleties of this important market: the relationship of metropolitan to regional identities; patterns of distribution and ownership; wider and more in-depth reading of the breadth of weekend titles; the overlap between the Sunday papers and other weekend press (Saturday weeklies, for example).

While we have begun to exhume some of the business history of the *NOTW,* our emphasis has been on *process.* We examine the decisions made at various points in the paper's nineteenth-century history – in response to market pressures, changes in ownership and editors, new technologies, reading habits and the removal of the taxes on knowledge. We have delineated distinct phases – in Chapter 2, 1851–61, 1861–80 and 1880–91 and in this chapter, 1891 and after – which help us to see the development of the title as it sought to establish, consolidate and claw back its place in a competitive market. For us, they challenge any notion of a singular identity for the paper, or for the category of weekend newspapers more generally. Received wisdom suggests that the Sunday press in the nineteenth century was characterised by radicalism, on the one hand, and sensationalism on the other. These terms do not apply equally to all Sundays, and, as we have indicated, there are significant other characteristics that are consistent in the *NOTW* across the century: a sustained and serious interest in politics and news coverage; an alliance with commerce and business interests; entertainment of various kinds and, perhaps most significant of all, a willingness to innovate, change and respond to new pressures.

After 1891, with a new proprietorial team in place – new owners, editors and printers – we see the importance of that ability to change and develop. The paper expanded its content with additional columns and wholly transformed its visual appearance, leading the way in developing the practices of the New Journalism for the Sunday press in ways that its Sunday competitors were strikingly slow in doing. By 1895, the *NOTW* looked more like some titles in the daily or periodical press than its weekend competitors. These innovations continued throughout the 1890s and by the end of the decade, the title was – certainly in its look, and increasingly in its feel – almost wholly transformed from the paper it was a decade before.

Notes

1. The authors of this chapter want to acknowledge the considerable help that they received from the Archivist at News UK, Nick Mays, whose patient and painstaking replies to queries have contributed substantially to our attempts at business history here, and in other chapters.
2. See 'Lord Riddell, Newspaper Owner and Diarist', *The Times*, 6 December 1934, p. 19; 'Sir Emsley Carr, Editor of the "News of the World"', *The Times*, 1 August 1941, p. 7. and S. Summerfield, *Banner Headlines*. Shoreham-by-Sea, 1979, pp. 18 and 40.

3. See A.P. Wadsworth, 'Newspaper Circulations, 1800–1954', *Transactions of the Manchester Statistical Society 1954–5*, Manchester, 1955, p. 1. Firm circulation figures for newspapers at this time are difficult to ascertain. A.P. Wadsworth characterises the years between the repeal of stamp duty in 1855 and the 1930s as 'the period of secrecy' about circulation, when 'all but a few papers jealously guarded the volume of their sales'. While some of the press directories attempted to include this information, most newspapers would not provide it, and even when they did, it remains uncorroborated. A number of newspapers, in fact, claimed in their adverts or straplines to have the highest circulation, to be the best selling or have the widest readership at this time. Suffice it to say, the circulation of the *NOTW* had declined and it is generally agreed that its reversal of fortune begins with the change of ownership in 1891.

4. See Adrian Smith, 'Carr, Sir (William) Emsley (1867–1941)', *Oxford Dictionary of National Biography*, Oxford, 2004; online edn, October 2006 [http://www.oxforddnb.com/view/article/48272, accessed 20 January 2015]. Smith notes that the link between the Carrs and the *Western Mail* continued, with Emsley acting as chief political correspondent for the Cardiff paper until the 1930s, while simultaneously editing the *NOTW*.

5. See A.J.A. Morris, 'Riddell, George Allardice, Baron Riddell (1865–1934)', *Oxford Dictionary of National Biography*, Oxford, 2004; online edn, October 2006 [http://www.oxforddnb.com/view/article/35749, accessed 20 January 2015]. See also, 'Lord Riddell, Newspaper Owner and Diarist', *The Times*, 6 December 1934, p. 19.

6. R.D. Blumenfeld, *The Press in our Time* London, 1932. p. 161. Summerfield, p. 40.

7. C. Bainbridge and R. Stockdill, *The News of the World Story. 150 Years of the World's Bestselling Newspaper.* London, 1993, p. 62.

8. *Journalist and Newspaper Proprietor*, 6 June 1891, p. 13a.

9. Blumenfeld, *The Press*, p. 161.

10. 'Lord Riddell', p. 19.

11. Bainbridge and Stockdill, *The News of the World*, pp. 60–61.

12. Quoted in D. Griffiths (ed.), *The Encyclopedia of the British Press: 1422–1992*, London and Basingstoke, 1992, p. 104. Regrettably, Griffiths does not provide a source for Power's tantalising quotation. See also Berrey's recollections of this period in R. Power Berrey, *The Romance of a Great Newspaper*, London, 1922, pp. 47–49.

13. Bainbridge and Stockdill, *The News of the World*, p. 79. Later in the 1890s, Berrey was known to tour the music halls looking for stories and songs, the publication of which had by then become a regular feature of the *NOTW* (Bainbridge and Stockdill, pp. 79–80).

14. T. Skinner, 'Miscellaneous Companies' in *The Stock Exchange Year-Book*, London, 1891, pp. 1014–15. The entry lists the Directors as L. Carr (Chairman), W.J. Bell, J.E. Gunn and G.A. Riddell, Secretary E. Fifoot, office 19 Exeter Street, Strand and includes the following description of the company: 'The Company was registered May 14, 1891, to take over the *News of the World* newspaper. The authorised capital is £20,000 in shares of £10, all of which has been subscribed, and £15,900 called up, 1,500 shares being fully paid, and the remainder having £1 16. called. There are also £3,000 5 per cent, first mortgage debentures, and £6,000 6 per cent, second mortgage debentures. The accounts are to be made up to June

30 and December 31. Voting power, one vote for every share. Transfer form, common; fee, 2. 6.'

In the *Directory of Directors* for 1892, by the same author and from the same publisher, Lascelles Carr is listed as a director of five additional companies at the time, being chairman of two (in addition to the *NOTW*), and deputy chair of another. The companies are Cardiff Bill-Posting Company, Ltd; Castle Arcade Company, Ltd; Royal Hotel Co, Ltd; Swansea United Breweries, Ltd, and Thompson and Shackwell. The Cardiff *Western Mail* of which Carr was proprietor and editor is not mentioned, and this is the only time between 1891 and 1896 that the *NOTW* company appears in the Year Books or Directories of Directors.

The authors want to thank Jeanie Smith of the Guildhall Library London for identifying the sources of this elusive information.

15. 'Notice', *NOTW*, 17 April 1892, p. 7 column e. See also Berrey, *The Romance*, p. 47.

16. On the significance of football specials, see M. Taylor, *The Association Game: A History of British Football*. Harlow, 2008, p. 146:

> Press coverage could work both as a supplement to, and in lieu of, an individual's actual attendance at matches. For those who did not watch their team on a regular basis, newspapers offered relatively quick and detailed access to the progress of a favourite team and the fluctuating narrative of a league championship. Football specials, established in most towns and cities during the 1890s and 1900s and flourishing by the 1920s, provided instant news of local and national competition to readers on Saturday evenings.

See also L. James, 'Sporting Journalism', in L. Brake and M. Demoor (eds), *Dictionary of Nineteenth-Century Journalism in Great Britain and Ireland*, Gent and London, 2009, p. 595. In the *Dictionary of Nineteenth Century Journalism* (*DNCJ*) online (in C19, ProQuest), see four entries by S. Tate, 'Betting Coupon Periodicals', 'Football Field and Sports Telegraph', 'Football Programmes' and 'Gambling'. The sports pages were well fed by dedicated agencies providing a daily stream of sporting news, for example 'The Racing Service' offered by the Exchange Telegraphic Company; see an advert for this service in the *Journalist and Newspaper Proprietor*, 20 June 1891, p. 6.

17. D. Russell, *Football and the English: A Social History of Association Football in England, 1863–1995*. Preston, 1997, p. 30.

18. The specialist sporting press has a long history in the nineteenth century, including such important titles as: *Bell's Life in London and Sporting Chronicle* (1822–86), *Sporting Life* (1859–1998), both of which focused largely on racing, and the *Athletic News and Cyclists' Journal* (1875–1931), which was linked to the growth of football.

19. For a discussion of the dynamic relationship between text and images in the early nineteenth-century illustrated press, pre-dating the New Journalism, see P.W. Sinnema, *Dynamics of the Pictured Page: Representing the Nation in the Illustrated London News*, Aldershot, 1998.

20. J. Mussell, 'New Journalism', in Brake and Demoor, *DNCJ*, p. 443.

21. *The Newspaper Press Directory and Advertisers' Guide*, London, 1891, p. 64.

22. *The Newspaper Press Directory and Advertisers' Guide*, London, 1894, p. 69.

23. The *Weekly Times*, a Saturday paper with a Sunday 'special edition' also included 'Yesterday's News' prominently on the front page in 1870 and 1880.

24. K. Williams, *Read All About It! A History of the British Newspaper*, London, 2009, p. 119.
25. Sir Emsley Carr, 'The Sunday Press', *Newspaper World*, 14 March 1931, pp. 1 and 10.
26. Quoted in M. Engel, *Tickle the Public: One Hundred Years of the Popular Press*, London, 1996, p. 207. E.T. Raymond, 'Old and New Journalists', *Portraits of the Nineties*, London, 1921, pp. 290–91. 'E.T. Raymond' was the pseudonym of Ernest Raymond Thompson (1872–1928), a leader writer on the *London Evening Standard* at the time of writing. See his obituary in *The Times*, 11 April 1928, p. 14.
27. See Williams, *Read*, p. 8 and Bainbridge and Stockdill, *The News of the World*, p. 86 and pp. 179 ff.

4
'Child Slavery in England': The *News of the World* and Campaigning for Children (1843–78)

Melissa Score

Introduction

At its demise in July 2011, the *News of the World* (*NOTW*) highlighted its campaigning reputation in its final editorial. It gave just one nineteenth-century example, saying that it had 'crusaded' against child labour. By juxtaposing this cause with its modern-day campaigns, the *NOTW* implied a narrative of children's rights campaigning ranging from the early 1840s to the beginning of the twenty-first century.[1] In this chapter, I examine the *NOTW*'s coverage of child labour between its launch in 1843 and 1878, when workplace legislation began to be consolidated, and argue that it was supportive of reform but cautiously so. Unlike its modern-day equivalent, it did not set the agenda for campaigns about children but instead mapped its coverage of child labour against a programme of legislation.

'Crusading' journalism indicates a concerted effort by a publication to change public opinion and agitate for policy change: it sets the agenda rather than supporting an existing cause. Moreover, it makes space to promote this cause even if it is alone among its competitors in doing so. In a study of the impact of journalism on public policy, Donna Leff, David Protess and Stephen Brooks associated crusading journalism primarily with investigation.[2] Investigative journalism carries risks, being time-consuming, sometimes costly, and with no guaranteed result. It can create a public sensation through exposé and drive a change in policy, but its impact might be short-lived.

The difference between a modern style of crusading journalism and the mid-nineteenth-century practice of reporting and commenting on campaigns is illustrated by a comparison of the *NOTW*'s coverage of child labour reform with what the final editorial termed 'the fight for Sarah's Law, which has introduced 15 pieces of groundbreaking legislation', referring to its anti-paedophile campaign.[3] The *NOTW* claimed ownership of the campaign through vigorous lobbying that persuaded politicians to change the law. In contrast, the mid-nineteenth century *NOTW* never asserted that its support was crucial to child labour reform. One reason was the nature of the reforms: a series of piecemeal and contested trade-specific measures introduced over a long period of time. Such incremental changes had to compete for space in the newspaper with more urgent political news stories.

Furthermore, the issue of factory reform was already before the public in a variety of contemporary print media – novels, Blue Books and pamphlets.[4] By October 1843, when the *NOTW* was launched, Parliament had already investigated the employment of children and women in mining (1842) and in the potteries (1843), and its published reports moved public opinion to demand reforms. The 1844 Factories Act laid down the working hours of children under the age of 13 and of women, instituted the 'fencing in' of fly wheels in mills and stipulated that accidental deaths at work had to be reported to a surgeon and investigated.[5] By the mid-century, the numbers of children employed in factories was falling and would continue to do so, although their involvement in sweated labour proved much harder to regulate. Ginger Frost commented that Parliament concentrated on areas where child labour was most visible, such as the textile industry, or dangerous, e.g. Lucifer matchmaking, because these attracted sensational newspaper coverage.[6] Metropolitan morning newspapers played their part by quoting extensively from Blue Books, and by reporting and commenting on Parliamentary debates. However, this also suggests that the ways in which reforms were covered in newspapers were becoming more fluid, since the *NOTW*'s coverage of the child labour issue was not confined to the Parliamentary coverage and its editorials. Columns and book reviews also played a part, alongside sensational crime stories.

The mid-nineteenth-century *NOTW* did not frame the debate on issues such as children's working hours, rights to education and their health and safety. Nevertheless, it kept these causes before the public through serial coverage of stories about children. As Leff, Protess and Brooks indicate, campaigning can include the frequency with which a paper publishes stories on a particular issue because it signals to the reader the significance that the publication gives it.[7]

Crusading journalism combines investigation with a moral dimension or a sense of righting a social injustice. This model came to be associated with a later form of nineteenth-century journalism and, particularly, with the campaigning editor William Thomas Stead (1849–1912). As editor of the Darlington-based *Northern Echo,* Stead's remit was to campaign for the local Liberal Party interest. However, in 1876, Stead did something quite different: he used his regional paper to highlight Turkish atrocities in Bulgaria and called on Benjamin Disraeli's Conservative government to take action. These articles formed a journalistic crusade as Stead's indignation mobilised public opinion and brought William Ewart Gladstone out of retirement and back to the forefront of British politics. In July 1885, Stead, by then the editor of the daily evening paper, the *Pall Mall Gazette*, created another news event. His exposé of child prostitution in the series entitled 'The Maiden Tribute of Modern Babylon', was written partly in a bid to pressure Parliament to raise the age of consent to 16 years. The *PMG's* shocking revelations appeared in instalments published between 6 July and 10 July 1885. Central to the exposé was a 'sting' operation in which the disguised Stead procured a child to sell to a brothel to illustrate how easily this could be done.

The furore that ensued prompted a dramatic, but short-lived spike in the paper's sales. It deterred advertisers and alienated some of the paper's core upper-class readership. However, there were personal as well as commercial risks: Stead's own involvement in the story led to his imprisonment. In prison, Stead wrote two essays that served as a form of manifesto for his style of campaigning journalism, which was criticised by the critic Matthew Arnold, among others, as the 'New Journalism'.[8]

There are, therefore, significant differences between Stead's combination of evangelical language and prurient detail – the 'crusade' – and the more restrained and subtle campaigning of the *NOTW* before 1878. I argue in this chapter that columns published in the *NOTW* in the 1860s and early 1870s used sensational detail both to persuade readers to support child welfare reforms and to draw in readers. They also emphasised woman's role at home, as the guardian of the domestic sphere.

The *News of the World* and its readers

John Browne Bell's *News of the World* was launched on a platform of political independence and broadly liberal views, seeking readers across political parties and social classes. This helped to set it apart from its rival Sunday newspapers, also priced at 3*d*. – *Lloyd's Weekly News,* launched at the beginning of 1843 and *Reynolds's Weekly Newspaper* (later *Reynolds's Newspaper)*, from 1850. As shown by Virginia Berridge's research into readers, using the types of advertisements that these papers carried, they mainly appealed to skilled working-class and lower-middle-class readers. Berridge specifically discounted the *NOTW* in her unpublished Ph.D. thesis on the working-class Sunday press because of its intention to garner readers across all classes and in rural, as well as urban, districts.[9] In theory, children's employment and its regulation might have been viewed as ideal for the *NOTW's* purposes by marking the paper as moderately liberal but also potentially appealing to paternalist, upper-class Conservatives.

However, advocating the regulation of the hours that children worked implicitly meant criticising another important political grouping: middle-class manufacturers, particularly of the 'Manchester School' of laissez-faire economics. This group, including Richard Cobden and John Bright, campaigned for reforms that the *NOTW* supported, such as repealing the

Corn Laws, but rejected state interference in industry. If the paper intended to spearhead a campaign on child labour in the 1840s, it needed to be careful not to alienate its middle-class readers in the manufacturing cities by appearing to side too closely with their workforce or with the aristocratic rural interests. An example of how it attempted just such a reconciliation, albeit clumsily, can be seen in 'The Politician' in March 1844, which expressed sympathy for two contradictory viewpoints. It supported the aristocratic Tory Lord Ashley's attack on the conditions of women and children in factories, while also sympathising with the Radical MP Richard Cobden – a factory owner – who accused the protectionist Ashley of ignoring the miseries of the agricultural poor. The column's compromise of 'We say to Mr Cobden as we say to Lord Ashley – we believe you both' negated any campaigning impact that it might have had.[10] The column avoided directly criticising Cobden because it strongly supported his campaign for Corn Law repeal to lower bread prices for the poor. Ashley was typical of the rural aristocracy in his support of agricultural protectionism, but the paper supported his position on children's working conditions. By directly addressing both men as notional readers as well as politicians and campaigners, and by appearing to support their chief campaigns, the paper reinforced its commitment to unity. It sidestepped their differing political stances on factory reform to ensure a sympathetic response to the free trade cause.

'The Politician' proceeded to conflate several campaigns with child labour and steered all of them back to the Anti-Corn Law movement. The column linked domestic neglect and unemployment with the Corn Laws, arguing that while unemployed men stayed home to look after children, their wives who worked in factories were becoming 'unwomanly' and neglecting domestic duties. It asserted that legislation historically worked against the poor, and made the link to the price of bread: 'Men are, while seeking their bread, overtaken by premature old age, women are unsexed, children are withered before they can come to maturity, and all for the sake of bread, and on that bread, the landowner lays a monopoly price!'[11] Again, 'The Politician' moved away from Ashley's factory reform and back to the Anti-Corn Law movement, a campaign with greater topicality and resonance among the lower-middle-class and artisan readers of the Sunday press in the 1840s. In order to do this, it foregrounded women's work as the problem, rather than the need to reform working conditions. However, 'The Politician' of the 1840s sympathetically addressed working-class concerns in columns such as 'The Working Classes of England' and 'The Feelings of the Poor – the Ten Hours' Clause', and included a discussion, after the Ten Hours' Clause was dropped, of other practical measures that could improve living conditions.[12]

One challenge for the *NOTW* was that the terms of the child labour campaign constantly shifted: technological changes in factories were reducing demand for child labour there, but the employment of children in unskilled work in smaller workplaces, sweatshops on the streets or within the home continued with little interference. Reforms were not always rigorously enforced since there were too few inspectors and they would not inspect work in domestic establishments.[13] Counter-campaigns were sometimes launched to overturn them. For example, almost as soon as legislation was rushed through Parliament to prohibit the employment of children in mining in 1842, attempts were made to amend it. Similarly, legislation prohibiting the use of 'climbing boys' – children sent up the flues of chimneys to clean them – was passed in 1840, but was not properly enforced, especially outside the main towns.

The historian Clark Nardinelli identifies four main reform tendencies in the factory movement.[14] All four find expression in the *NOTW* at various times. The first group, the alliance of Chartists, trade unionists and radical Tories, led by Richard Oastler and Michael Sadler and known as the Ten Hour Movement, attracted support particularly in 'The Politician' column. The *NOTW* also backed Tory humanitarians such as Lord Ashley, later the Earl of Shaftesbury, who believed children should be protected from child labour by their families, but failing that, private philanthropy and the state should intervene to ameliorate harsh working conditions. Nardinelli's third group was inspired by the Romantic movement and saw child labour as an evil caused by industrialisation, idealising a rural past in which childhood was protected. This view is less explicit in the paper but is evident in the rural settings and nostalgic treatment of family and childhood in poems published in the 'Varieties' section. The final group was that of Liberals, such as Thomas Babington Macaulay, who argued it was sound economics to educate children, protect their health and regulate their hours (but not ban their employment) in order to ensure they grew into healthy, productive adults. This last view emerges at various times, particularly when the 'Hampden' column interrogated the conflicts between the financial needs of the family, including children's wages, and legislation requiring school attendance after 1870.

The *NOTW*'s columnists were particularly assertive of the press's right to champion reform and its role in reminding parliamentarians of their dependence on public support. For example, 'The Politician' of 16 March 1844 cites *The Times*'s exposure of poor law abuses: 'How vain would have been all the labours of the amiable Lord Ashley on that subject, as well as in exposing the horrors to which children are sometimes subject, who are employed in factories, if it were not for the manner in which he was so universally supported by the press.'[15] Nearly 20 years later, 'Hampden' responds in far more melodramatic and less obsequious style to government reform efforts. A report by Sir George Grey acknowledged poorly ventilated workplaces were responsible for high rates of consumption among girls apprenticed to milliners and seamstresses but that nothing could be done because many of these workshops were in the owners' homes. 'Hampden' opined, 'What is government for if it could really do nothing for suffering masses of the people!', putting the paper firmly on the side of state intervention.[16]

The 'Hampden' column made little attempt to court upper-class readers. Where paternalism was clearly failing, 'Hampden' was outspoken in his criticism. The paper did not appear actively to court working-class readers either, at least on price, since it remained at 2*d.* when *Reynolds's* and *Lloyd's* cut their cover prices to 1*d.* after the removal of paper duties in 1861. The *NOTW* also appeared to reject the popular appetite for sensation novels, such as those of Mary Elizabeth Braddon, attacking them in its review section and in the 'Hampden' column. However, it appeared to allow sensationalism in its own reporting, in cases where it attacked an injustice and called for change. This anticipates some of Stead's notions of crusading journalism, since the intention was to provoke the reader into agreeing that reform was needed. It also conformed to Stead's prurient use of sensation to attract the reader's attention. For example, extracts from Nathaniel Hawthorne's account of his experiences of life in England were published in the review section on 4 October 1863. The extract chosen from a long chapter describing the experience of poverty in England (and including examples of the neglect as well as the humane treatment of pauper children) focused solely on a description of a baby presumably infected with syphilis. The passage emphasised disease and transgression: 'Diseased Sin was its father and Sinful Disease its Mother and their offspring lay in the woman's arms like a nursing pestilence'.[17]

A development of this theme by 'Hampden' in the same number makes clear that the paper was addressing its middle-class readers when it wrote about the plight of poor children: clearly 'Hampden' envisaged his reader as a concerned voter, rather than one of the victims of poverty. Under the dramatic title, 'Dying in London', 'Hampden' highlighted wider social problems: that 40 per cent of all children born in England and Wales would not reach their first birthday as a result mainly of poverty.[18] In an attempt to shock his readers, 'Hampden' asserted that working-class children were dying of diseases – from which middle-class children usually recovered – because of poor housing conditions and the lack of light, space, air and food. Current measures were simply an attempt to disguise the problem and completely inadequate to solve it: 'White-washing will not get rid of this poison, sewer-making will not get rid of it.' 'Hampden' then returns to the link between poverty, immorality and disease by citing a recent court case, pointing out the risks of incest in families in crowded accommodation. The column's use of shocking details to illustrate and persuade anticipate New Journalism's use of sensation to highlight campaigns in the 1880s and 1890s, but just as Stead lured readers with graphic accounts of child prostitution, Hampden's reference to incest might have been intended to do something similar. The column makes sublimated links between the book review and the paper's court coverage. The choice of that particular extract from Hawthorne in the book review section performed a dual role of shock and entertainment, as well as highlighting social problems.

The 'Hampden' column often used individual court cases to make a wider social point. In 1864, for example, an inquest into the death of a young seamstress inspired a diatribe against the high rates of consumption reported in the trade. 'Hampden' describes the girl dying of 'apoplexy' caused by the 'foul air of the workroom'.[19] 'Apoplexy' was more often applied to men suffering a fit caused by excessive consumption of food. 'Hampden' exploits its irony when used in the context of tuberculosis. The treatment of this theme is reminiscent of New Journalism in its persuasive style, though less so in the reluctance to personalise the victim in order to dramatise a cause. 'Hampden' expresses his entire argument for government intervention in gender and class terms, drawing on melodrama by using familiar juxtapositions of the wronged working-class girl exploited by the 'thoughtless and reckless females of the aristocracy'. The latter may be conventionally virtuous but are 'bad women' because they are 'heedless of the misery which self gratification occasions'. The opposites of villains and heroines would be recognised by readers of melodrama. Sympathy with the hardworking victim is reinforced in the column by its next image: of orphans and labourers' daughters apprenticed to a trade but dying in the attempt to learn it.

The closest that 'Hampden' came to a Steadian form of crusading journalism was in the column entitled 'Child Slavery in England', published on 3 July 1864. This foreshadowed Stead's combination of moral outrage and social mission, along with a willingness to shock the reader out of complacency. The article appears to follow the conventional pattern of offering an opinion on a current parliamentary debate concerning impending legislation. However, rather than simply lend support to one side or other of a campaign, it becomes crusading in the way in which it makes a direct emotional and moral appeal to the reader. This is evident in the language: child labourers become more than simply a class of worker through the use of emotive diminutives such as 'little labourers' and 'little workpeople'. In particular, the emphasis on the human cost of child labour is explicitly emotional in the vivid image of a little girl too scared to sleep in case she failed to get up in time to work at the factory. Nevertheless, 'Hampden' was aware that he argued from a secure position since he was clearly (and correctly) confident that the Factory Bill before the House of Commons would be passed. The column anticipated the Parliamentary vote, lent support to a resurgent campaign and reminded readers that more remained to be done.

Although the popular Sunday newspapers were often criticised for sensationalism, the *NOTW*'s coverage of children's rights in the 1840s and 1850s largely avoided this, enabling it to negotiate the potential risk of alienating readers and advertisers. Comments on children's work were often framed within discussions of the question of women's work. Hampden's column, couched as a letter to the editor, was the main method of presenting the paper's campaigns in a non-party political way.

The sense of different, but related, conversations taking place in one newspaper – between editorial, opinion column, letters page and news reports – indicates the dialogic nature of newspapers. Although articles were unsigned at this time, different opinions were evident. This tendency existed in daily metropolitan papers such as *The Times,* to which freelance correspondents contributed articles on particular areas of expertise, alongside the paper's own staff reports, letters from readers and leader columns. For the Sunday newspapers, less committed to a daily verbatim record of political debate, there was even greater freedom for diverse opinion and commentary. It was usual for papers such as the *Weekly Dispatch, Lloyd's Weekly News* and *Reynolds's Newspaper* to publish several regular columnists, each with their own view, albeit pseudonymously. Making the case for popular mid-century Sunday newspapers to be regarded as the forerunners of the mass-circulation tabloid papers associated with New Journalism, Raymond Williams noted a combination of lurid crime stories and sensational accidents alongside Parliamentary news, gardening columns, fashion and book reviews in the Sundays, rather than a particularly campaigning style.[20] Overall, however, the *NOTW* prioritised national and international political news; its early intention according to 'The Politician' at the beginning of its run was to appeal to readers of *The Times* as well as those who could not afford a daily paper.[21] It devoted considerable space to reports of the Crimean War in 1854–56, and highlighted the corresponding rise in its sales. It provided detailed coverage on government changes, budget statements and other staples of traditional Parliamentary reporting.

As a weekly paper, and one intended to be read at leisure at the weekend, the *NOTW* was not a paper of record like *The Times*: it necessarily selected the range of political news that it published. Thus, its coverage of the child labour issue suggested that it was of importance to the paper since children's campaigns were vying with other topics for inclusion.

Young seamstresses and milliners

Apart from support for children's work reform, the *News of the World* supported efforts to help apprentice girls, but its efforts were confined to seamstresses and milliners, already a familiar trope for philanthropists. Both *The Times* and the *News Of The World* occasionally published letters from women on the regulation of clothing workshops, such as that published on 26 November 1843 under the heading 'The Poor Needlewomen.' An anonymous seamstress appealed to readers to act on a point of evidence given before the commission appointed by the House of Commons in 1843 to inquire into the condition and employment of children in the garment trades. The issue was the use of poor law inmates to undercut already low wages. The letter almost performs the function of a leader article on the subject, being published immediately after the editorials on page 4. Unlike *The Times,* which published letters without comment, this letter was followed by an editor's note observing that Parliament could prevent this situation by ensuring workhouse inmates made clothes for their own use only.

By publishing the letter in this location along with comment, the paper acknowledged working-class female readers as well as backing their appeal for help. This is particularly significant since women were not counted among metropolitan newspaper readers. In contrast, the Chartist press at this time gave prominence to working women's contributions to political campaigns. The *Northern Star,* for example, regularly portrayed female activism with accounts of fund-raising and petitioning activities. In the early 1850s, the temperance and suffrage campaigner, publisher John Cassell, drew attention to the role working women could play in politics in his *Working Man's Friend.* However, the representation of female activism in the *News of the World* was short lived: demand for space was so tight that the seamstress' letter was dropped from the paper's next edition in favour of the verdict in the case of the Crown versus Daniel O'Connell. The issue thus lost momentum in the paper, even between different editions of the same number, but it was in any case a very rare example of a direct female voice in its pages.

Typically, in its discussion of the needleworkers' plight, the *NOTW* tended to highlight the impact on children and family life rather than on the working women themselves. This is evident in its juxtaposition of stories of poverty with those of violence in the home. On 29 October 1843, the *News of the World* juxtaposed an article headed 'Starving Prices To Needlewomen and Comparison Between Prison and Workhouse Duties' with a crime story entitled 'Horrible Murder of a Child by its Father.' At first sight, the location of these stories on page 3 appears haphazard. However, it also focus the impact of poverty on the home. The emphasis on the horrors of sweated needlework was developed further on page 4, with a leader entitled 'The White Slaves of London.' In this article, the paper was more outspoken in its call on the government to regulate work undertaken by girls (boys apprenticed to tailors are not mentioned). 'White slaves' was a recurring term used about the clothing trades by newspapers and periodicals in this period, and was a nod to the abolition campaign's success in ending slavery within the British Empire in 1838. *Lloyd's* also uses terms such as 'female slavery' to describe the plight of needlewomen in the 1840s but does not highlight the racial aspect, whereas the *NOTW* clearly implies that white female slavery is worse than black female slavery.[22]

Ten years later, the *NOTW* was explicit in its condemnation of aristocratic ladies who sought to improve conditions for working women. This was to be a recurring trope in the 'Hampden' column. In a retrospective view of the early attempt at reform, a column entitled 'White Slavery in London',

(16 July 1854), 'Hampden' referred to the impact newspaper reporting had on public opinion in the 1840s by making a shocking and racially motivated claim: 'Some years ago, the public mind was startled by the disclosure of a kind of white slavery in England – worse than anything suffered by black negresses – the slavery of young women in milliners' and dressmakers' workrooms.' He compares this with the findings of a recent meeting chaired by Lord Shaftesbury (formerly Ashley) to discuss violations of agreements made by various establishments. 'Hampden' comments that the revelations are 'monstrous' and that 'many of the worst evils are now found to be revived'.[23] 'Hampden' rejects Shaftesbury's assertion that he will not be able to legislate because most of the offences occur in private houses. The column unequivocally calls for official measures, though this is not reinforced by an editorial.

'Hampden' was unusual in his insistence to his readers that government must act to reform work carried out in private establishments or in the home. Sheila Blackburn notes that anti-sweating campaigns at this time were constrained by government reluctance to regulate pay and its resistance to the idea of inspecting homes. This was due to a belief that legal control of home working threatened the patriarchal family and the liberty of the individual.[24] The most effective attempts to investigate sweated labour came later in the century and were led by women, such as Beatrice Webb, who could more easily gain access to home workers. Blackburn argues that campaigns against sweated labour were also hindered by a form of fragmentation, as professionals such as doctors and lawyers concentrated on sanitation and disease rather than the issue of low pay. For this reason, problems specific to home working only became recognised as a national political issue in the 1880s.

Workhouse children and chimney sweeps

Outside of the 'Hampden' column, the *NOTW* was more muted in its treatment of the hardships of working and workhouse children, though like *The Times*, it was an implacable opponent of the New Poor Law of 1834 and highly critical of the administration of workhouses. However, its treatment of the notorious cholera outbreak at the Infant Poor Asylum in Tooting, South London, was factual and not sensationalist, in line with the general tone of newspaper coverage at the time. One reason for this was the way in which mid-nineteenth-century newspapers generally reported the third-party investigations into abuses within the confines of specific departments in newspapers, such as the court and legal pages. Moreover, the paper's editorials were largely concerned with political news, commenting upon subjects discussed in Parliament.

The Tooting cholera outbreak was a public scandal. Between 1846 and 1848, the number of pauper children sent by London workhouses to the Tooting institution, run by Bartholomew Peter Drouet, had nearly doubled from 723 to almost 1,400.[25] The epidemic was catastrophic, causing the deaths of 180 children. Drouet's regime initially escaped blame when inspected by the St Pancras Guardians on 2 January 1849. However, subsequent visits by Dr R.D. Grainger, a Board of Health inspector, blamed overcrowding, insanitary conditions and inadequate diet for the spread of the disease, and recommended the school be evacuated immediately. By 10 January, a thousand children had been removed by the parishes responsible.

The deaths and inspection were widely reported and public opinion was outraged by the details that emerged when some of the children's deaths came under the jurisdiction of the Middlesex coroner, Thomas Wakley, editor of the campaigning *Lancet*. The inquest revealed appalling details about Drouet's treatment of the children and the jury found him guilty of manslaughter. As a result, Drouet faced a criminal prosecution on 26 February 1849 on a specimen case. However, the defence successfully argued that there was no absolute proof that the child would have recovered but for Drouet's actions and he was found not guilty on 16 April.

The 1849 Tooting episode tapped into public fears of cholera epidemics and the spread of contagion from overcrowded areas. It highlighted appalling shortcomings in the New Poor Law with respect to the protection of pauper children and the initial attempt to exonerate Drouet of any blame. It demonstrated the power of the reformed inquest system in which an independent coroner conducted the inquiry before a jury. Yet, the *NOTW*'s treatment of the campaign to hold Drouet to account was far from the nature of a moral crusade compared with Dickens's articles in the weekly *Examiner*, which conveyed a strong sense of outrage. The *Examiner*, a politically radical weekly, was not constrained by the need to restrict the inquest news to the legal pages. The details of Dickens's articles are in the *NOTW* reports, but the reader is left to make moral judgments. Nor did the paper initiate any calls for change beyond reporting Wakley's findings. The story was left, in effect, to speak for itself.[26]

Similarly, a famous image of child labour reform in the nineteenth century was relatively neglected by the Sunday papers: that of the 'climbing children' who were employed by chimney sweeps to go into the flues of large houses. Badly treated by their employers, they risked death through suffocation. The worst abuses occurred in the large country houses where the machines were inadequate to clean the huge chimneys. The problem was not a lack of legislation: the ban on the use of climbing boys had already been passed in 1840, three years before the *NOTW* was launched, but it was not always enforced. The worst cases exposed a sharp town-country divide between middle-class homes in urban areas that tended to be designed with flues that could be cleaned by the new machinery and older houses on country estates that could not. As a result, metropolitan readers may have erroneously believed the practice of using climbing boys (or girls) had ended with the introduction of mechanical sweeping brushes 20 years before. Rural magistrates, however, turned a blind eye to the law being flouted in old country houses where the much wider, and angled flues, encouraged some of the gentry to tolerate the use of climbing children.

Jenny Holt has commented that the early nineteenth-century campaign to ban the use of climbing boys was a cause championed by the urban middle classes. Lord Shaftesbury's involvement was somewhat exceptional given his aristocratic and rural background.[27] This is clearly illustrated in an editorial 'Chimney-Sweepers in the House of Lords' published on 7 May 1854 in *Lloyd's,* where Shaftesbury's efforts at reform were contrasted with the attitudes of his fellow peers. *Lloyd's'* editorial unequivocally supported Shaftesbury's efforts to ensure the reforms were reinforced.

There are several reasons why the *NOTW* (like *The Times*) gave so little space to the chimney sweep campaign. There might have been an underlying awareness that the campaign divided rural and urban readers. If the *NOTW* was still attempting to fulfil its original objective of representing the rural gentry as well as the urban reader, it would need to negotiate its position carefully. However, topicality was probably a more significant reason. The story lacked topical bite since failure to implement the law meant an absence of prosecutions, while local magistrates often dismissed those that did take place. Like *The Times* (also with a significant rural readership) the *News of the World* reported cases of cruelty where these were publicly aired.[28] Before Shaftesbury's 1864 Act for the Regulation of Chimney Sweepers, Charles Kingsley published *The Water-Babies: A Fairy Tale for a Land Baby,* the story of the moral education of a young chimney sweep. It was serialised in the monthly *Macmillan's Magazine* between August 1862 and March 1863 and published in (cheap or shilling) volume form in 1863. Kingsley wrote the novel at exactly the same time as the Children's Employment Commission was investigating and writing its report on climbing boys. In the 12 months preceding the 1864 legislation, the *News of the World* made no mention of the campaign to strengthen the law against the use of climbing boys. It did not review Kingsley's novel and omitted any mention of it in his obituary, which instead highlighted *Alton Locke*, a novel about a Chartist tailor.[29] However, this was also true of *The Times*, the paper that had built a reputation in the 1840s for a humane attitude towards the most vulnerable. The final impetus for genuine reform, Shaftesbury's Chimney Sweeps Bill in 1875, resulted not from a newspaper campaign but from the successful prosecution for manslaughter of a sweep, William Wyer, for the death of a climbing boy, George Brewster, in Cambridgeshire. *Reynolds's* noted Shaftesbury's comment that between 1840 and 1864, 23 boys had suffocated in chimneys.[30] *The Times's* editorial of 12 May 1875 was also scathing in its condemnation of Liverpool town hall for flouting the law by allowing the use of climbing boys.

Why, then, was there a hiatus in Parliament's efforts to cement a needed reform relating to child workers accompanied by silence in the press in the early 1860s? The answer most likely lies in the context of the lack of social or political reform legislation in Parliament between 1859 and 1865, when Lord Palmerston was Prime Minister. Cautious attempts by the short-lived Derby administration in 1858–59 to reform the electoral system were shelved until Lord Russell took over after Palmerston's death in 1865. Instead, in the intervening period, the press and the government focused on a series of foreign affairs crises: the 1861–65 American Civil War and its potentially destabilising impact on the economy, Italian unification, war over Maori land rights in New Zealand, the failure of a British expedition against the Ashanti in West Africa in 1864 and the Jamaica uprising in 1865. All of these issues dominated coverage in the British press, until the revival of attempts to reintroduce Parliamentary reform after 1865. As this gained significant momentum, the *NOTW* backed the Reform League and warned in an editorial of January 1867 that it did not matter which party introduced franchise reform, the mood of the country required it.[31]

Overall, the *News of the World*'s discussion of working children between 1843 and 1878 focused on the treatment of children in factories and the abuses of girls in the garment and millinery trades, rather than the plight of working children in rural occupations or in country houses. Coverage in the 1840s closely mapped the reports and the language of Select Committees, legislation before Parliament and other commentaries. However, by the 1860s, its columnists had become more outspoken in defence of the rights of working children, and adopted a more 'crusading', persuasive and sensational style in keeping with the public appetite.

Alongside its discussion of children and work, however, was a strong focus on what it believed most benefitted the home and the family. 'Hampden' was aware of the contradictory impact of reform: while supporting the right of all children to be educated, he responded to an account of a man driven to attempt suicide through lack of food for himself and his family by noting that the requirement for his son to go to school had deprived the family of any income for food. 'Hampden' argued that the law needed to provide for exemptions if a family would otherwise be destitute.[32] This is consistent with the view that children's labour should be regulated but not necessarily ended. Similarly, the columnist supported Shaftesbury's schemes to assist flower girls and watercress sellers with loans to set up coffee and food stalls in the winter, along with soup kitchens and clothing clubs. The paper's only objection was that Shaftesbury planned to include men in his loan scheme.[33]

One of the dominant and most conservative themes of the 'Hampden' column in the 1870s was its insistence of the sanctity of the family, preferring that married women with children concentrated on the home. In the debates over women's roles in the 1870s, the column consistently opposed the extension of the suffrage to women although it supported reform on married women's property rights.[34] 'Hampden', meanwhile, argued that all girls, whatever their social standing, should be trained in cookery, but continued to oppose women training for occupations traditionally undertaken by men since this undercut employment and wages and was a threat to the family unit.[35]

Occasionally 'Hampden' even suggested a conflict of interest between children's and women's rights. Commenting on the rights of poor children to be protected from physical abuse, he wrote 'Surely they have moral rights, if the law has failed to furnish a protection for them?' He acknowledged working-class examples of cruelty to children, which regularly featured in the crime news in the newspaper, but also cited the public-school flogging system as an upper-class example of cruelty. However, the same article argues that women had become too concerned with campaigns for female suffrage to take up the cause of children's rights, something he clearly saw as their role.[36]

Conclusion

In the period from its launch in 1843 to the first major consolidation of factory and workplace legislation in 1878, the *NOTW* neither set the agenda in terms of campaigning against child labour, nor was it particularly consistent in keeping campaigns for reform in the public eye. This was unsurprising since the campaign itself was divided by industry and location – town versus country, workplace versus sweated labour in the home. It also illustrates differences between the popular weekly journalism of this period and the advent of the mass circulation daily press in the twentieth century. The *NOTW*'s final editorial made a connection between children's campaigns across the centuries but unconsciously also drew attention to the huge changes that the paper had undergone since its original ownership by the Bell family.

Close examination of the *NOTW*'s coverage in its early decades shows that it took a nuanced position on children and work, while being wholly supportive of reform, rather than 'crusading'. In particular, rather than using editorials to drive public opinion towards wholesale reform, overt comments in its leader pages were limited and directly related to legislation before Parliament. Yet, the *NOTW*'s opinion columns and news departments nevertheless ensured that debates around workplace and education reforms were aired in the paper. The main vehicle for this was the 'Hampden' column, a letter 'To the Editor' and thus categorically not the words *of* the editor. As the column 'Child Slavery in England' showed, 'Hampden' could write fervently about the treatment of children but more often he inveighed against women, particularly upper-class women, who were blamed for ignoring the plight of their less fortunate sisters. 'Hampden' also criticised working-class women with children for working outside the home since this, he believed, damaged the family unit. Increasingly, 'Hampden' denigrated attempts by middle-class women to enter professions that were hitherto exclusively male, although he supported their education in areas that might be useful in their future lives as homemakers.

Such a nuanced attitude to the debate indicates that the mid-century paper was not yet 'crusading' on the issue of child welfare. To fulfil this role, it would have had to set the agenda for the debate and to have identified the campaign directly with the paper in vigorously worded editorials. It would also have needed to employ its own investigations to expose injustices rather than depending, as did the metropolitan press generally at this time, on third-party investigations, such as Blue Books and on the efforts of philanthropic campaigners and reform-minded novelists. It eschewed the commercially risky aspects of the sensational exposé, although it was prepared to allow the repetition of sensational detail in the 'Hampden' column in the 1860s. Close analysis of the layout of stories and the juxtaposition of news and comment suggests, however, that reforms to children's working and living conditions were taken seriously by the *NOTW* in the mid-century since by reading laterally as well as linearly, the reader could build up a picture of cause and effect in which the domestic abuse of children was linked to poverty, alcoholism, unemployment and the mismanagement of workhouse laws.

Commercially, the *NOTW*'s cautious backing of reform was the most pragmatic course in terms of retaining readers and advertisers. Its support for the reform of children's living and working conditions was undoubtedly sincere, but carried no significant risk, since it fulfilled the paper's aim of securing a broad readership while espousing liberal causes. There was little that could be deemed controversial since children's welfare was a cause that already attracted campaigners from all classes, but it identified the paper with a humanitarian stance on social issues, such as housing reform, sanitation and education.

If Parliament or a prominent campaigner brought the issue in front of public opinion, the paper lent its support but just as quickly dropped the issue if other concerns, such as the Corn Laws, the Crimean War, Ireland or electoral reform were deemed more important. By situating most of its most outspoken comment in a particular opinion column, the paper could continue to claim to be politically independent. The heightened campaigning tone of the 'Hampden' columns of the 1840s and 1860s suggests that at particular times, the paper was prepared to publish strong opinions in favour of reform, as long as these were clearly distinct from the main editorial. This did not amount to a moral crusade for the rights of children but it enabled the *NOTW* to frame arguments in terms of the impact of extreme poverty on public morality. The 'Hampden' column's themes were echoed elsewhere in the paper, for example in book reviews or in the juxta-position of campaign news with crime stories. Such editorial constructs are part of a narrative of campaign rather than a clearly defined crusade but they helped to lodge the narrative of the plight of working children in the readers' minds.

Ultimately, however, in its desire to place home at the centre of family life, the *NOTW* revealed its ambivalence about the role of women outside the home, in work or in politics. The issue of child labour was diverted from campaigning into discussions that promoted a conservative and traditional vision of the domestic unit.

Notes

1. *News of the World*, 7 July 2011.
2. 'Crusading Journalism: Changing Public Attitudes and Policy-Making Agendas' by Donna R. Leff, David L. Protess and Stephen C. Brooks, *The Public Opinion Quarterly*, 50 (3), 1986, 300–15.
3. *News of the World*, 7 July 2011.
4. Examples include Frances Trollope, *Michael Armstrong: Factory Boy* (1840); Charles Dickens, *Oliver Twist* (1837). Two examples from the 1860s reflect the renewed attempt to enforce the prohibition of children used to climb chimneys: Charles Kingsley *The Water-Babies* (1862–63) and James Greenwood's *True History of a Little Ragamuffin* (1866), which contains an episode concerning the illegal use of boys in chimney sweeping. Blue book refers to reports bound in a blue cover, usually containing an official British government publication such as a report issued by Parliament, the Privy Council or a committee.
5. Clark Nardinelli comments that factory owners actually increased the number of children they employed after the act was passed: Clark Nardinelli, 'Child Labor and the Factory Acts', *The Journal of Economic History*, 40 (4), 1980, 739–755, p. 749.
6. Ginger S. Frost, *Victorian Childhoods*, Westport, 2009, p. 68. Frost comments that exposure by muckraking reformers might push the legislature to act, but measures such as the 1871 Brickmaking Act proved similarly difficult to enforce.
7. 'Crusading Journalism', p. 302.
8. Stead, 'Government by Journalism', *Contemporary Review*, 49, 1886, 653–74 and 'The Future of Journalism', *Contemporary Review*, 50, 1886, 663–79. Matthew Arnold, 'Up to Easter', *Nineteenth Century*, 21, 1887, 629–43. For further discussion on Stead's role and influence, see L. Brake (eds), *W.T. Stead, Newspaper Revolutionary*, London, 2012.
9. Virginia Berridge, 'Popular Journalism and Working-Class Attitudes, 1854–1886: A Study of *Reynolds's Newspaper*, *Lloyd's Newspaper* and the *Weekly Times*', unpublished doctoral thesis, University of London, 1972. See also Berridge, 'Popular Sunday Papers and Mid-Victorian Society', in George Boyce, James Curran and Pauline Wingate (eds) *Newspaper History From the Seventeenth Century to the Present Day*, London, 1978, pp. 247–64.
10. 'The Politician', 'The Poor in the Field and the Factory', *NOTW*, 24 March 1844, p. 1.
11. 'The Poor in the Field and the Factory', *NOTW*, 24 March 1844, p. 1.

12. Published respectively on 28 April 1844, 12 May 1844 and 19 May 1844, p. 1.
13. Nardinelli, 'Child Labor and the Factory Acts', p. 747.
14. Clark Nardinelli, *Child Labor and the Industrial Revolution*, Bloomington, 1990.
15. *NOTW*, 16 March 1844, p. 1.
16. *NOTW*, 5 July 1863, p. 2.
17. Review, 'A Frightful Baby' from '*Our Old Home* By Nathaniel Hawthorne', *NOTW*, 25 October 1863, p. 6.
18. 'Hampden', 'Dying in London', *NOTW*, 4 October 1863, p. 2.
19. 'Hampden', 'The Girl's Apoplexy', *NOTW*, 5 July 1863, p. 2.
20. Raymond Williams, *The Long Revolution*, Harmondsworth, 1984 reprinted edition.
21. 'The Politician', *NOTW*, 1 October 1843, p. 1.
22. Under Jerrold, *Lloyd's* also published articles highlighting the horrors of black slavery. See Golding Penrose, 'Letters to a Working Man', *Lloyd's*, 5 June 1853, p. 5.
23. 'Hampden', *NOTW* 16 July 1854, p. 2.
24. Sheila Blackburn, '"To be Poor and to be Honest…is the Hardest Struggle of All": Sweated Needlewomen and Campaigns for Protective Legislation, 1840–1914', in Beth Harris (ed.) *Famine and Fashion: Needlewomen in the Nineteenth Century*, London, 2005, pp. 243–54, p. 244.
25. Peter Higginbotham, 'Mr Drouet's Establishment for Pauper Children, Tooting' http://www.workhouses.org.uk/Drouet [accessed 18 October 2013]
26. Charles Dickens published 'The Paradise at Tooting' in *The Examiner* on 20 January 1849, p. 1, followed by 'The Tooting Farm', *Examiner*, 27 January 1849, pp. 1–2, 'A Recorder's Charge', *Examiner*, 3 March 1849, p. 1 and 'The Verdict for Drouet', *Examiner*, April 23 1849, p. 1. *NOTW* commented in its first report on 14 January 1849 on the insanitary conditions, poor diet and inadequate clothing of the children revealed by inspectors before publishing reports of the inquests, but its reason for doing so appeared to be to warn the rich that unless they took action to help paupers they, too, would be at risk from cholera. The paper's subsequent focus on reporting inquests rather than offering opinion might have reflected the fact that the epidemic was confined to Drouet's establishment and had not spread to the surrounding area. See 'The Tooting Calamity', *NOTW*, 14 January 1849, p. 5; 'The Deaths at Tooting', *NOTW*, 21 January 1849, p. 3; 'The Tooting Calamity', *NOTW*, 28 January 1849, p. 4; 'The Tooting Tragedy' *NOTW*, 4 February 1849, p. 8 and 'The Tooting Tragedy/Trial of Mr Drouet', *NOTW*, 15 April 1849, p. 5.
27. Jenny Holt: '"A Partisan in Defence of Children"? Kingsley's *The Water-Babies* Re-Contextualized', *Nineteenth-Century Contexts: An Interdisciplinary Journal*, 33 (4), 2011, 353–70.
28. For example, *The Times* on 17 February 1857 provided a detailed report of a case of cruelty tried in Chesterfield that resulted in a conviction. The prosecution was only brought because two witnesses – including a wood steward on the Staveley Estate belonging to the Duke of Devonshire – were prepared to pursue the case against the journeyman responsible for beating a climbing boy.
29. 'Senatoriensis', 'Topics of the Recess: Canon Kingsley', *NOTW*, 31 January 1875, p. 6
30. 'Imperial Parliament', *Reynolds's News*, 16 May 1875, p. 3
31. Editorial, *NOTW*, 29 January 1867, p. 4.
32. 'Hampden', 'Dark Scenes of Life', *NOTW*, 25 January 1874, p. 2.

33. 'Hampden', 'The Flower Girls', *NOTW*, 8 March 1874, p. 2.
34. On 2 June 1878, 'Hampden' discussed two bills before Parliament, the Women's Suffrage Bill, which would 'introduce a new and disturbing element into the British Constitution', and the Women's Property Amendment Act Bill, which, he argued, 'would establish a right for married women which cannot be denied upon any ground of justice or equity'. *NOTW*, 2 June 1878, p. 2. This would appear to be an example of 'Hampden' selectively rejecting one feminist campaign for suffrage in favour of another that focused solely on the rights of married women, presumably in keeping with the sympathies of the paper's readers.
35. For example, 'Hampden', 'Woman's Work', *NOTW*, 29 March 1874, p. 2. As Alexis Easley notes in Chapter 5, he made an exception for medicine in 1876. See 'Physicians in Petticoats', *NOTW*, 23 July 1876, p. 2. For Hampden's support for 'useful' education for women, see 'One Million of Girls', *NOTW* 11 August 1878, p. 2.
36. 'Hampden', 'Poor Children', *NOTW*, 4 May 1873, p. 2.

5
Imagining the Mass-market Woman Reader: The *News of the World*, 1843–77

Alexis Easley

When Rupert Murdoch appointed Rebekah Brooks editor of the *News of the World* (*NOTW*) in 2000, one of her first projects was to initiate the sensational 'For Sarah' campaign, which published photos of paedophiles living in local neighbourhoods. The series sparked public outrage, raising the profile of the paper and boosting its flagging circulation.[1] After Brooks became the first female editor of the *Sun* in 2003 and CEO of News International in 2009, it seemed that the so-called 'feminisation' of the British press had finally been realised. Beginning in the 1990s, British media critics argued that the press was becoming increasingly 'feminine' by focusing on publishing personal and confessional content and defining women as the primary producers and consumers of popular print.[2] Today, press historians trace the roots of this 'feminisation' much further back in time – to the end of the nineteenth century, when newspapers associated with the New Journalism began incorporating interviews, investigative journalism, human-interest stories and women's pages in an attempt to reach out to a mass reading audience.[3] In this chapter, I would like to suggest that the construction of the mass-market woman reader begins even earlier, with the Sunday newspapers founded in the 1840s. Using the *NOTW* as a case study, I will demonstrate how these papers imagined women as a key constituency in the market for popular journalism.

Of course, as Rebekah Brooks's career illustrates, it is difficult to interpret the 'feminisation' of the press as being unproblematically 'feminist'.[4] Deborah Chambers, Linda Steinder and Carole Fleming note that the tabloidisation of news works against feminist aims by defining women as sentimental voyeurs, materialist consumers and sexualised objects.[5] Such representations, I argue, take root in the Sunday newspapers of the mid-nineteenth century, when the growth of newspaper advertising defined women alternately as bourgeois consumers of domestic goods and the victims of sensational crimes. While the *NOTW* in its early decades defined women in these narrow terms, often assuming a conservative stance on women's issues, it nevertheless imagined them as an important market segment whose needs must not only be addressed but also created. In this sense, the *NOTW* in its early decades anticipated the paper's later development as a 'feminised', if not 'feminist', vehicle for delivering news and entertainment to a mass audience.

When John Browne Bell founded the *NOTW* in 1843, he claimed to offer 'news for the million'.[6] Although the paper would not command such a large readership until the twentieth century, the paper was nonetheless remarkably successful in its first decade, achieving, according to Altick, a circulation of 110,000 by 1855.[7] Like many other Sunday papers founded after the reduction of the newspaper duty in 1836, the *NOTW* was priced at three pence, was Radical in its political affiliations, and was dedicated to addressing 'all classes of readers'.[8] As Richard Altick points out, the paper most likely appealed to 'artisans and small tradesmen' due to its combination of serious news and sensational crime reportage.[9] However, as a writer for the *London Journal* put it in 1845, the *NOTW* also had a 'tendency to *create* newspaper readers'.[10] In the paper's first few decades, John Browne Bell and his son John William Bell attempted to address the needs of the 'million' – a broad cross-section of readers from all social classes. They did so by providing a potent mixture of useful and entertaining content: political, business and foreign news along with jokes, theatre reviews and scandalous crime reportage. In this way, the Bells, along with G.W.M. Reynolds and other innovators,[11] played an instrumental role in 'creating' the notion of a mass reading public.

From the outset, the *NOTW* imagined women as an important segment of the audience for popular newspapers. Under the successive editor-proprietorships of John Browne Bell (1843–55) and John William Bell (1855–77), the paper actively constructed the woman reader through advertisements for furniture and other domestic goods, as well as through editorial content focused on marriage, family and the domestic realm. Women readers were instrumental in building the circulation of the *NOTW* in its early years and became even more important as the paper struggled to maintain financial viability in the competitive market for weekly newspapers during the 1870s. With increased competition in the newspaper industry brought on by the reduction and eventual elimination of the taxes on knowledge, the *NOTW* relied increasingly on advertising revenue to maintain financial solvency. Since women were more and more defined as domestic consumers, they became an attractive audience for both popular newspapers and their advertisers.[12] Although the *NOTW* did not achieve its goal of reaching 'the million' under its first two proprietors, it nevertheless played an instrumental role in the 'feminisation' of the mass-market press, which later became one of the defining features of the New Journalism.

The News of the World under John Browne Bell, 1843–55

Although John Browne Bell never named women as a target audience for his paper, they were clearly instrumental to his plan of achieving a 'very extensive circulation'.[13] In the first issue of the *NOTW*, published on 1 October 1843, Bell signalled his desire to attract women readers by incorporating a fashion column, 'The Newest London and Paris Fashions for October, 1843: Extracted from the World of Fashion Monthly Magazine.' Located on page 5 of the 8-page paper, the column provided a brief overview of the latest bonnets and dresses. The fashion column was not only used to attract women readers but also to cross-market one of Bell's other publications, the *World of Fashion*.[14] An advertisement for the magazine appears on page 1 of the first issue, promising a 'galaxy of Fashions and Embellishments'.[15] Priced at two shillings and claiming an audience of 'Nobility and Gentry', the *World of Fashion* would seem to have a very different readership than a three-penny newspaper such as the *NOTW*.[16] Even though from the outset Bell claimed to aspire toward a broader 'circulation amongst the poor and the rich',[17] a two-shilling monthly fashion magazine probably would have been out of reach for most readers of the newspaper.[18] The fashion column nonetheless capitalised on women readers' fantasies about up-market purchasing power.[19]

By the time Bell founded the *NOTW*, he already had significant experience publishing women's periodicals. The *World of Fashion* (1824–51) was preceded by *Le Beau Monde* (1806–09), his first periodical publication.[20] The fact that *Le Beau Monde* initially focused on male fashion and eventually incorporated more articles on women's dress suggests the increasing importance of women as consumers of periodicals early in the century.[21] Fashion features and other 'feminine content' were also included in *Bell's New Weekly Messenger* (1832–55), one of John Browne Bell's early contributions to the Sunday newspaper market. As Martin Conboy has pointed out, this sense of gender inclusivity was one of the hallmarks of the Sunday press from its inception in the 1780s.[22] Building upon these earlier publishing ventures, the *NOTW* demonstrates keen awareness of the interests of women readers, not only in its fashion column but also in its other content – in its reviews of domestic novels and plays as well as in its sentimental poetry, humour and kitchen wisdom featured in a regular column titled 'Varieties: Original and Select'. For example, the 'Varieties' column in the first issue includes a tit-bit proclaiming that the love of women 'is an unceasing fountain of delight to a man who has once attained it, and knows how to deserve it'.[23] Further down the column is a poem, 'Morning and Evening Twilight', by Catherine Parr,[24] followed by a 'Hint to Young Ladies', which reads, 'The reason why so few marriages are happy, is because young ladies spend their time in making *nets*, not in making *cages*'.[25]

Such representations of bourgeois femininity stood in stark contrast to depictions of working-class women in the police reports inserted throughout the newspaper. The sensational titles of these police cuttings – 'A Woman Poisoned by Endeavouring to Procure a Miscarriage' or 'Extraordinary Charge of Drugging and Violation' – were most likely aimed at both male and female readers. But the sheer frequency of such news suggests that the emerging conception of a mass reading public involved formulation of the notion of 'women's news' – reports featuring crime against women rendered in highly sentimental language suggestive of melodrama. As Raymond Williams pointed out, the rise of the Sunday paper genre was inseparable from the growth of melodrama as a popular form of entertainment on the metropolitan stage, which similarly emphasised 'crime, adventure and spectacle' and highlighted the travails of 'poor and innocent victim[s]'.[26] Written in this vein, one crime report reads:

> The body of a poor woman, wretchedly clad, was found on Tuesday morning embedded in the mud beneath some logs of timber moored off Marygold stairs, Upper Ground-street. From the appearance of the deceased, coupled with the fact that eleven pawnbrokers' duplicates for various trifling articles were found upon her, there can be no doubt that she committed suicide through distress, and indeed there is too much reason to fear that her child has suffered the same fate. A police-constable named Gawlor, who was on duty on Blackfriars-bridge on Monday night, saw a female with a child in her arms, supposed to have been the deceased, near the water's edge, and on accosting her, she said that she had come out of a workhouse, and had no home to go to.[27]

The sentimental language of the report – describing a 'poor woman, wretchedly clad' with 'no home to go to' – elicits sympathy for the victim of suicide. Indeed, it seems hardly coincidental that adjacent to this crime report is a brief paragraph titled 'Home', which reads, 'The man without a Home is like the man without a Religion. The domestic hearth is as essential to the collection and arrangement of thought and sentiment, as the Altar of Faith is to the regulation of the spiritual part of us.'[28] This brief moral reflection offers indirect commentary on the police report, providing both a justification for and sympathetic response to the woman's crime.

The sentimental depiction of women in police reports resonates with melodramatic representations of female characters in reviews of popular plays published elsewhere in the newspaper. For example, a review of the Queen's Theatre production of *Marie, or the Pearl of Savoy* gushes over Miss Rogers's performance as a heroine who 'discovers that her lover is about to be married to another' and, presumably after a hysterical fit, is 'restored to reason.'[29] Incorporating multiple representations of women – both as paragons of bourgeois morality and as the victims of heart-wrenching crimes – the *NOTW* created a venue through which the emerging concept of the mass-market woman reader could be defined. It is important to note that its 'feminine' content was not separated from the rest of the paper in 'women's pages'; rather, sentimentalised representations of women – wearing the latest fashions, performing on the stage, surviving, instigating or succumbing to crime – were an integral part of the paper as a whole, juxtaposed with columns on politics, sport and foreign news. This fusion of conventionally 'feminine' and 'masculine' content no doubt encouraged both sexes to read eclectically. Such reading practices were of course a source of anxiety elsewhere in the press. When defending Sunday newspapers from their critics in an 1856 article, the *Saturday Review* felt it necessary to claim that the papers contained very little that a 'man would feel inclined to skip if he were reading aloud to his wife or daughter'.[30] Such a statement implies that women's reading is safely under men's control – an assertion intended to assuage worries about the pernicious effects of sensationalist content on feminine morality.[31] In practice, it is hard to imagine that women would not have had the opportunity to read the *NOTW* without masculine supervision. Indeed, the increasing number of advertisements for domestic consumer goods in the paper throughout the 1840s and 1850s suggests that John Browne Bell and his advertisers were counting on women's avid readership.[32] While it may be true that women's periodicals of the period were increasingly defined as apolitical,[33] Sunday papers such as the *NOTW* offered women opportunities to read more omnivorously, consuming political news along with conventionally 'feminine' fare. The front page of the issue published on 23 December 1856, for example, included advertisements for Bijou needle cases, silver watches, cod liver oil and Alfred Fennings's *Every Mother's Book*, as well as a political column summarising the latest news from Switzerland, a selection of jokes reprinted from *Punch* and a police story describing a 'tender passion' between a girl thief and a young artisan. The female reader, like her male counterpart, was thus invited to read across the page in an eclectic way, moving from advertisement to editorial to police report.

The News of the World under John William Bell, 1855–77

The combination of news and entertainment offered by the *NOTW* proved to be a winning formula. By 1854, it claimed to have the largest circulation in the world; however, reductions in the taxes on knowledge presented a host of new challenges.[34] After John Browne Bell's death in 1855, his son, John William Bell, took over as editor in chief and soon after the elimination of the stamp duty that year, lowered the price of the paper to 2*d*. With the removal of the paper duty in 1861, he faced renewed pressure to reduce the price of the paper further in order to compete with other Sunday newspapers priced at one penny.[35] His unwillingness to do so is often assumed to be the major reason for the paper's decline in circulation over the next few years.[36] Indeed, under his editorship, the paper's readership fell from a high of 110,000 in 1855 to just 50,000 in 1870.[37] Yet, in his 1872 report on metropolitan papers, James Grant reports that 'of late the proprietors have made great efforts to increase its circulation'.[38] One of these strategies might have been to position the paper in a more up-market niche alongside the *Sunday Times*, also priced at 2*d*. Indeed, by the mid-1870s, there are indications that the *NOTW* was perceived as differing from its down-market rivals, *Lloyd's Weekly Newspaper* and *Reynolds's Newspaper*. A press directory for 1874 describes *Reynolds's* as a democratic paper containing 'much strong nervous writing, thickly spiced with abuse of the privileged orders' and *Lloyd's* as an 'advanced Liberal and popular progressive' paper 'far more credible … than might be conceived'; in contrast, the *NOTW* is simply described as a Liberal paper addressing 'all classes of readers'.[39] By 1885, the *Saturday Review* notes that the *NOTW* 'takes a more even view than some others of social and political questions' and 'cannot be classed among the unpatriotic journals'.[40]

Redefining the *NOTW* as a more up-market brand of Sunday newspaper might have been a strategy for attracting advertisements aimed at a bourgeois audience. As the number of popular newspapers increased and prices fell, Sunday papers became ever more dependent on advertising revenue. As James Curran put it, 'Advertising exerted pressure for popular papers to move into the middle of the market' in order to remain competitive.[41] Ultimately, this meant incorporating advertisements and editorial content that would appeal to women since they were increasingly defined as primary consumers in 'respectable' working-class and middle-class households. Indeed, the consumer content of the *NOTW* increased markedly between 1843 and 1877, incorporating advertisements for fabric, medicine, domestic magazines, sewing machines and a host of other 'feminine' goods and services.[42]

The rise in the number of advertisements for consumer goods corresponded with John William Bell's most important innovation aimed at attracting female readers: the reformulation of the paper's weekly 'Hampden' column.[43] Established during the 1840s, this series of 'letters to the editor' initially focused on political topics; however, by 1858, its emphasis had changed markedly, focusing instead on domestic and social commentary. Located in the upper-left-hand corner of page 2, the column regularly treated topics related to marriage, family and social life – in a sense functioning as a second editorial following the political leader on page 1 of the paper. By the mid-1870s, women's issues were regular topics in the 'Hampden' column, highlighted with such eye-catching titles as 'The Spinsters' Question', 'Wonderful Works of Woman' and 'Woman's Work.' The column was juxtaposed with other content on page 2 designed to appeal to women readers, for example, brief stories on gardening, the errors of foolish young housekeepers and fashionable shopping in Paris.

During John William Bell's editorship, the fashion column continued to appear, and Hampden's commentary became increasingly focused on women's dress. When writing about fashion, 'Hampden' displayed an insider's knowledge of contemporary style. For example, in an 1876 column on gaudy millinery, he writes, 'As a matter of taste, the little hats are preferable to those imitative coal-scuttles which have once been in vogue' and then proceeds to give a brief history of 'hideous' hairdressing and millinery.[44] Indeed, the language of Hampden's editorials at times seems to have been taken directly from a fashion column: 'Everything that can possibly be yellow, say the ladies' journals, will this season assume that colour, and even such an article of luxury as porcelain is not excepted.'[45] Such a passage adopts the same kind of chatty tone as the fashion column for January that year, which begins, 'Novelties of all kinds, and in every branch of trade, are introduced in compliment to the "Nouvelle Année", some doomed to disappear without ever having entered the world of fashion for which they were destined.'[46] Taken together, the fashion column and Hampden's reinforcing commentary construct the kind of bourgeois woman consumer the newspaper and its advertisers hoped to attract.

Yet Hampden's ideal woman reader was imagined as a very particular kind of consumer: the thrifty and sensible housewife. In several columns, he criticises the tendency of women to indulge in excesses of dress and finery. In an 1876 column, he writes, 'Young women would be a great deal more attractive in really tasteful attire than in the whimsical extravagance of fashion; and if the cost of that extravagance were abolished, young men would cease to console themselves in a bachelor condition with cigars and clubs.'[47] In other words, in order to be a good wife, a woman must be a careful consumer. In a later column, 'Hampden' defines such sensible consumption as a source of female power:

> It is an absurdity to suppose that women have no rights. In the great sanctuary of home they are grand and indisputable. Man being the lord, the loaf-winner, Woman is the lady, the loaf distributor. Man earns and Woman spends. Great and natural is the pride of the man when he places upon the home table the money result of his week's work; and equally great and natural is the pride of the woman when she lays down upon the table the book which shows how well the previous money had been expended.[48]

In order to assume the role of a proper 'loaf-distributor', the woman reader need only look to the advertisements on the front of the paper and at the foot of the page. In this way, advertisements and editorial content worked in tandem, simultaneously promoting the consumption of domestic goods and the *NOTW*.

At times, advertisements seem to acknowledge that the paper appeals to women not only for its 'feminine' content but also for its sensationalist crime reportage. For example, an 1875 advertisement provocatively titled 'Massacre of the Innocents' mimics the kind of sensational headline associated with the newspaper's police reports.[49] In the sentences that follow, it becomes clear that the title does not introduce a shocking case of infanticide but rather an advertisement for Stedman's Teething Powder, which mothers can use to calm their babies instead of employing dangerous opium-based preparations. The advert operates under the assumption that women are the consumers of domestic goods who read Hampden's column at the top of the page as well as the sensationalist crime stories featured throughout the paper. It thus demonstrates in microcosm how the *NOTW* blended sensational, domestic and consumer content as a means of attracting women readers.

'The Massacre of the Innocents' advert, like Hampden's column, suggested that women's habits as wives and mothers were in constant need of guidance and improvement. The woman reader must be cautioned against indulging in finery just as she must be convinced to buy medicine that will not impair her children's health. As Margaret Beetham has observed, early advertising culture was focused on 'persuasive identification of femininity with the body, both potentially pathological and in need of regulation'.[50] Yet, at times the *NOTW* inadvertently gave mixed messages about just how that body should be regulated. For example, in an 1877 column, 'Hampden' attacks women's use of cosmetics, declaring, 'Don't paint, don't disguise yourself. Be true to all (yourself included). If paint-pots and scents be offered, throw them behind the fire. You have not only a soul to be saved ... but a spirit within you, if properly developed, to ensure man's love (your destiny)'.[51] This is a rare case in which 'Hampden' addresses women readers using the second-person pronoun 'you'. In doing so, he assumes the role of a secular preacher who must admonish a wayward flock. For woman to assume her destined role, he asserts, she must above all be authentic – an authenticity that must be 'properly developed' through self-control but presumably also with the guidance of the newspaper's patriarchal authority. Yet, curiously, Hampden's editorial is contradicted by an advertisement for hair dye located at the foot of the page, which promises to 'positively restore, in every case grey or white hair to its original colour'.[52] The advert, like Hampden's column, suggests that readers need to dedicate themselves to self-improvement, but it views such self-regulation in material, rather than moral, terms. The overall message is that women must both value and abhor the cult of beauty and its associated commercial products. Such a message prompts further consumption of the *NOTW*, which promises to address a host of desires that are contradictory and thus can never be fully satisfied.

'Hampden' and the woman question

What is most striking about the 'Hampden' column in the 1870s is its conservatism on women's issues, particularly female enfranchisement. Such a stance was most likely part of the newspaper's marketing strategy. As

Julia Bush demonstrates, most women of the period ascribed to conservative definitions of gender roles, and 'suffragism remained a minority preoccupation across all social classes'.[53] By assuming an anti-suffragist stance, the *NOTW* thus positioned itself within the domestic ideology associated with the 'silent majority' of British men and women.[54] In order to appeal to a broad audience, it needed to assume a conventional stance on women's issues while simultaneously making an argument for the 'power' of women as consumers of journalistic and other commodities.

In 1874, when William Forsyth introduced a suffrage bill in Parliament, 'Hampden' responded in a scathing editorial, arguing that a 'tired husband, father, or brother does not want a companion to chop logic with him or discuss the relative merits of men and manners in Parliament'.[55] He concluded by affirming the domestic ideal, asserting that woman 'was made for a helpmate', which is her 'rightful position'.[56] Three years later, after hearing of Lydia Becker's 1877 pro-suffrage address at the Social Science Congress in Aberdeen, 'Hampden' sharpened his attack, writing, 'Of the ladies whose pride and pleasure it is to attend political meetings and express their sentiments at large, we cherish a hope that a new light may dawn upon their intelligence; a hope that we are sure would be realised by the unmarried if they were to turn their attention to matrimony, abjuring politics, and succeed in obtaining worthy husbands, by whom they would be instructed and convinced of the true rights, the pleasures, the duties, and the enjoyments of home'.[57] By suggesting that political agitation was a misdirection of 'true' female passion and desire, 'Hampden' attempted to affirm the central importance of home and hearth – a recurrent theme in his columns throughout the 1870s.

If suffrage was a chief threat to domestic stability, then women's education and employment were an even greater concern. In an 1874 column, 'Hampden' was willing to acknowledge that bourgeois women might 'earn a little money in a becoming way' as watercolour painters or musicians, but such women were distinct from those 'masculine maidens who want to be great politicians, and fight with men on men's own battle-ground', becoming 'rivals of their fathers and brothers'.[58] The root of the problem, 'Hampden' averred, was the 1870 compulsory education act, which 'adulterated' girls, replacing 'sweetness of temper, liveliness of manner, innocence of thought' with the study of science, mathematics and geography.[59] The 'voluble sisterhood'[60] that encouraged such educational advancement, he argued, stood in stark opposition to the majority of proper domestic women, who worked within their 'allotted sphere'.[61] 'Hampden' was particularly opposed to working-class women's employment outside the home, arguing in an 1877 column, for example, that their participation in the brass manufacturing trade should be 'abolished altogether'.[62] 'What comfort can a working-man have in his home', he asked, 'whose wife is all day employed at the vice and lathe?'[63]

Hampden's belief in marriage as women's natural occupation is reinforced throughout the newspaper in news stories and other features focused on matrimony – for example, updates on royal marriages and descriptions of marriage practices in foreign countries. At the same time, divorce and breach of promise cases were often reported in the paper's back pages, allowing readers the voyeuristic pleasure of peering into the lives of those whose dreams of marital bliss had come to nothing. An 1875 report on a breach of promise case, for example, took up nearly an entire column on page 7, giving a blow-by-blow account of the court proceedings. Most of the report is taken up with a reading of the defendant's letters to his beloved – sentimental effusions that provoked uproarious laughter from the audience.[64] The frequent insertions of (laughter) in the text of the report provide an invitation for readers to imagine themselves in the gallery of the court room or the stalls of a theatre. The newspaper thus provides an opportunity for private enjoyment of a very public entertainment. 'Hampden', meanwhile, had much to say in response to the frequency of such cases: 'Partners for life are taken much as partners are selected to dance with at a ball; but they are not as easily got rid of.'[65] However, as much as 'Hampden' claimed to view breach of promise and divorce cases as 'lamentable', he nevertheless provided amusing excerpts from recent cases, thus capitalising upon the kinds of 'painfully interesting' details usually confined to the paper's back pages.[66] Such cases also provided fodder for an earlier satirical column proposing a stamp tax on proposals of marriage, which 'would establish an unimpeachable ground for an action of "breach of promise" in the event of a change of mind'.[67]

In his running commentary on affairs of the heart, 'Hampden' at one point admits that he does not reject the idea of divorce entirely, arguing in a column titled 'The Quarrelling Couples' that 'English Law wisely severs a tie under particular circumstances of acute suffering'.[68] Such a pronouncement is apt in this particular 1877 issue of the paper, which includes a police report on the front page describing the case of a woman who stabbed her husband in the throat due to jealousy and emotional distress caused by 'frequent wrangles' over relatives.[69] It can be no accident that 'Hampden', in his column on the next page, refers to the pernicious effect of 'small jealousies' and the 'interference of relatives' on marital relationships.[70] This is a rare instance where he seems to comment, however indirectly, on the many representations of domestic violence in the *NOTW*. As previously noted, such sensationalised content was most likely designed to attract both male and female readers, tapping into the conventions of melodrama so ubiquitous in public entertainments of the period. Several crime reports on page 7 of the issue of 23 December 1877, for example, describe in grisly detail women being kicked and beaten by their husbands. One reads:

> Setting a Wife on Fire. – At the Leicester Borough Police Court William White was charged with assaulting his wife. – It appeared that the

prisoner was quarrelling with his wife, and was heard to say he would throw the lamp at her. Immediately afterwards a crash was heard. The neighbour went to the door and saw the complainant standing in the room in flames from head to foot. Her husband was standing close by but made no attempt to extinguish the flames. Defendant, who was under the influence of drink at the time of the occurrence, was remanded. The unfortunate woman was taken to the Leicester Infirmary.[71]

Such reports can be viewed as disciplinary in a Foucauldian sense – serving as warnings for women who would 'quarrel' with their husbands. However, because the crime reports most often featured working-class couples, the upwardly mobile readers of the *NOTW* might have viewed them less as cautionary tales than as sensational entertainment. The disputes of the more 'respectable' classes could be resolved through civilised discussion. Indeed, 'Hampden' concludes his column on divorce by making a plea for clergy to convince quarrelling couples to 'suppress unworthiness of thought and feeling in which the desire of separation originates, and convince the manly husband and the womanly wife that what is really wanted is not divorce, but comfort'.[72] Such a message reaffirmed the importance of conventional gender roles – a 'manly husband' and a 'womanly wife' – for maintaining social stability.

The *NOTW*'s celebration of bourgeois marriage and domestic 'comfort' supported its commercial agenda. A woman must be relegated to the domestic sphere in order to fully realise her 'empowered' role as a domestic consumer. Such an editorial stance was supported by the conservative turn of the Sunday newspaper press more generally. As Virginia Berridge has pointed out, after the 1840s, Sunday papers lost their radical political flavour and became the 'effective means of social control which the Establishment had always hoped the popular press might be'.[73] Indeed, in 1874, 'Hampden' wrote a column extolling the 'purity and the value of English newspapers' as conveyors of national morals;[74] an important aspect of this 'purity' was its reinforcement of conventional gender roles – notions that were undergoing such radical reconsideration elsewhere in the metropolitan press.[75]

Yet, the conservative opinions expressed in Hampden's column did not always go uncontested. After the publication of his column titled 'The Sorrows of the Female Aristocrat', which criticised philanthropic efforts to find work for impoverished noblewomen, the *NOTW* published a rejoinder from 'Mater' in the next issue, which argued that 'lady helpers' were indispensible as nursing assistants.[76] Hampden's conservatism was also indirectly countered by reports on women's activism elsewhere in the paper, which gave details of their efforts with little or no editorial comment. For example, two columns to the right of Hampden's diatribe against the women's temperance movement in America is a short article under 'Foreign News' titled 'The Women's Whisky War', which reports on temperance protests in Ohio, Philadelphia and New York.[77] Although the article echoes Hampden's language by archly referring to the protestors as 'fair crusaders', it is otherwise written as an objective account of the group's activities.[78] The fact that the women's temperance protests are reported alongside other international news suggests that such efforts are newsworthy. Although 'Hampden' attempts to undermine the authority of the protests, warning that American women's activism is likely to inspire 'strong-minded women' in Britain to attempt similar tactics, the juxtaposed report nevertheless functions as a stand-alone piece that readers are invited to interpret in their own way.[79] A later news report recounts recent efforts to organise a women's trade union, without editorial commentary from 'Hampden' or any other source.[80] The subtle ways Hampden's conservative views are placed into dialogue with women's 'news of the world' suggest a complex relationship between editor and reader. Women readers were perhaps entertained and influenced by Hampden's acerbic commentary, yet they still had the opportunity to experience vicariously various facets of the international women's movement by reading the 'women's news' reported elsewhere in the paper.

The News of the World and the Feminisation of the popular press

Even with its efforts to reach out to women readers, the *NOTW* did not achieve great success in the 1870s, ending the decade with an anaemic circulation of 30,000.[81] When John William Bell died in 1877, the *NOTW* not only faced increased competition from cheaper papers but also had to contend with a new competitor at the upper end of the market: society journalism. Sixpenny society newspapers founded in the 1870s, such as Edmund Yates's *World* (1874–1922), Edward Legge's *Whitehall Review* (1876–1912), and Henry Labouchère's *Truth* (1877–1957) shared with the Sunday papers an interest in sensationalism, scandal, gossip and popular theatre. Of course, the society weeklies repackaged this 'down-market' content in an attractive two-column format at a higher cost, creating a brand that on the surface seemed to have little in common with papers such as the *NOTW*. Indeed, in one of its earliest issues, the *World* was careful to distance itself from the 'base and filthy turpitude of certain of the Sunday papers'.[82] Yet, the *World* and other society weeklies owed a great debt to these papers, not only in terms of sensationalist content but narrative voice. Just as the 'Hampden' column set a lively and opinionated tone for the *NOTW*, the carefully crafted editorial personae associated with the society journals assumed a similar 'personal' style. Joseph Hatton's description of Henry Labouchère's editorial voice as 'bitter, personal, brilliant, chatty, impudent, sometimes reckless, always amusing', might have applied just as easily to 'Hampden'.[83]

Perhaps the most striking similarity between the *NOTW* and the society weeklies was their gender inclusivity. The *World* made this audience explicit in its subtitle, *A Journal for Men and Women*, but other society papers simply incorporated content likely to appeal to both male and female readers. The marked success of the weekly society papers at addressing the needs of this mixed-gender audience might have played as a factor in John Bell's decision to maintain the price of the *NOTW* at 2*d.* during the 1870s. By pricing his paper higher than penny Sunday weeklies such as *Lloyd's* and lower than sixpenny society weeklies such as the *World*, Bell was perhaps aiming at an intermediary niche where he would capture the 'better' readers of the penny press while simultaneously attracting middle-class readers who might be in the market for a less expensive newspaper. This middle-class focus of the *NOTW* becomes increasingly well defined throughout the 1870s. For example, it published a regular column titled 'The Magazines', which provided brief summaries of the contents of a variety of middle-brow periodicals, such as *Belgravia*, *Temple Bar* and *St. James's Magazine*, thereby giving the impression that the *NOTW* addressed a similar set of readers.[84]

Reading the society papers alongside the *NOTW* of the 1870s demonstrates a common set of strategies for reaching a broad audience that included women readers. For example, in 1877 the *World* includes articles titled 'Petticoat Politics', 'A Woman's Club', 'Courtship in 1877' and 'The Domestic Male'; *Truth* offers articles on 'Woman's Ambitions', 'Impenitent Bachelors', 'Marrying for Money' and 'Remunerative Employment for Women' and the *NOTW* features columns on 'Political Women', 'Wedlock and Women', 'The New Art of Beauty' and 'The Quarrelling Couples.' At times, the content of the 'Hampden' column echoes the subject matter of the society papers even more directly. For example, in May of 1877, Hampden's column on the fashionable obsession with yellow ('Ladies in Yellow') appears just 11 days after an article on the same topic in the *World* ('Yellow').[85] Likewise, Hampden's December 1877 diatribe against the use of cosmetics in 'The New Art of Beauty', seems to allude to an article published just ten days earlier in *Truth*, which criticised girls' use of 'transparently mysterious little boxes, sold by the Bond-street perfumers'.[86]

The *NOTW* and *Truth* achieved roughly the same circulation by 1880 – 30,000.[87] However, while this was a healthy circulation for a sixpenny weekly, it was a disastrous circulation for a twopenny paper such as the *NOTW*. In 1880, members of the third generation of the Bell family reduced the price of the paper to one penny, thus relocating it to a position beside its original down-market rivals, *Lloyd's* and *Reynolds's*. However, the *NOTW* did not find a foothold in this market until 1891 when Emsley Carr assumed the editorship and, with the help of George Riddell, eventually raised the paper's circulation from 60,000 in 1892 to over 2.5 million by 1917.[88] Finally, it had achieved the mass readership the Bells always imagined. It did so by embracing the New Journalism of W.T. Stead and T.P. O'Connor, which included a change in format and the addition of reader competitions, personalised reporting and serialised fiction.[89] However, in addition to adopting new strategies, it also continued to make good use of the kind of sensationalist material that had characterised the paper from its formation. Thus, rather than interpreting Carr and Riddell's editorial changes as corrections to the Bells' failed strategies, I view them as a realisation of goals that had been many years in the making. If Carr and Riddell successfully courted the kind of mixed-gender mass audience that was the hallmark of the New Journalism, it was as a result of many years' experimentation with miscellaneous content that would provide the combination of news and entertainment a popular audience most desired.

Of course, the subsequent rise and fall of the *NOTW* in our own time is well known. In 2011, when the paper was finally forced to close as a result of the phone hacking scandal, it had achieved a circulation of approximately 2.6 million. Its sudden demise created just the sort of sensation that had fuelled its own success for 168 years. At the centre of the controversy was a woman journalist who represented the opposite of the idealised domestic woman so important to the early history of the newspaper's brand. Described as 'Rupert's Red Menace' or as a 'flame-haired temptress' in the popular press, Rebekah Brooks was the face of a 'feminised' media that had been transformed into a femme fatale or prostitute.[90] On the other side of the frame were her innocent victims, including Sally Dowler, whose murdered daughter's phone was hacked by reporters for the *NOTW*. Her heart-wrenching testimony during the Leveson Inquiry became the emotional focal point of the scandal, sparking widespread public outrage.[91]

The *NOTW* had of course always operated on the knife's edge of respectability. From its inception, the idealised image of the domestic woman so central to its market ambition was presented in opposition to the female victim who haunted the paper's crime reports. The strategy of incorporating 'feminine' news along with sensational crime reportage was an enduringly effective formula but one that could only be sustained within the boundary of the law. The *NOTW* ended by turning in on itself – its former female editor and her 'cut-throat' investigative strategies serving as lucrative fodder for rival tabloids.[92] In a scene that might have been taken from the back pages of the *NOTW* during the nineteenth century, the melodramatic 'temptress' is depicted as killing a newspaper and wounding its innocent victims, leading to a justifiably harsh criminal investigation.[93]

In looking back on the *NOTW* – from its inception in 1843 to its demise in 2011 – it is striking how the paper's innovations were continually defined and redefined as the 'New' Journalism. While in the 1840s, the *NOTW* fashioned itself as a new kind of radical, sensationalist newspaper, it softened this image by incorporating representations of an idealised and sentimentalised femininity. Like the society papers that followed in the 1870s, it mobilised the figure of the domestic woman in order to define itself as a new kind of paper capable of attracting advertisers and the bourgeois readers so essential to the mass-market press. By the *fin de siècle*, the New Journalism emphasised sensation but also employed 'women's pages' and other tactics aimed at attracting and constructing a mass-market reader. Yet, such tactics were far from new. When Alfred Harmsworth asserted that addressing women readers was essential in the New Journalism, he was articulating a principle that had been in force for many years indeed.[94] From the 1990s, the 'feminisation' of the British media was once more imagined as a novel development that must be theorised and worried over. On one hand, newness suggested progress – innovations in journalistic methods and a democratisation of the reading public – but on the other hand it suggested decline: a turn away from bourgeois values of decency, privacy and taste. The woman reader, as an ever-new constituency for popular journalism, thus served as an enduring marker for measuring the achievements and failures of mass-market newspaper publishing.

Notes

1. T. Watson and M. Hickman, *Dial M for Murdoch: News Corporation and the Corruption of Britain*, London, 2012, p. 17.
2. B. McNair, *News and Journalism in the UK: A Textbook*, London, 1999, pp. 18 and 48.
3. See, for example, McNair, *News and Journalism in the UK*; M. Beetham, *A Magazine of Her Own?: Domesticity and Desire in the Woman's Magazine, 1800–1914*, London, 1996, pp. 125–26; and D. Chambers, L. Steiner and C. Fleming, *Women and Journalism*, London, 2004, pp. 217–23.
4. During the 1990s, some commentators lauded the 'feminisation' of the press as a means of humanising news rooms and the papers they produced. See, for example, M.A. Sieghart, 'Woman's Work', *Guardian*, 30 June 1997, p. C2. However, this point was contested by critics such as L. Brooks, 'So Far, So Feminised', *Guardian*, 18 October 1999, p. C4.
5. Chambers, Steiner and Fleming, *Women*, pp. 217–23.
6. From a poster and handbill announcing the first issue of the *NOTW*, as reproduced in First Edition Club, *A Catalogue of Books and Newspapers Printed by John Bell and by John Browne Bell*, London, 1931, p. 4.
7. R. Altick, *The English Common Reader*, Chicago, 1957, p. 394.
8. Anon. 'To the Public', *NOTW*, 1 October 1843, p. 4. On the use of 'Radical' see Altick, p. 356, where he attributes this descriptor to the Tory *Quarterly Review*.
9. Altick, *English Common Reader*, p. 356.
10. Anon., 'The Newspaper Press in London', *London Journal*, 1, 19 July 1845, p. 328. Emphasis in original.
11. See Humpherys, who argues that *Lloyd's* and *Reynolds's* weeklies 'essentially invented the format of the mass media'. A. Humpherys, 'Popular Narrative and Political Discourse in *Reynolds's Weekly Newspaper*,' in L. Brake, A. Jones, and L. Madden (eds), *Investigating Victorian Journalism*, New York, 1990, p. 36.
12. For extended discussion of the ways in which women readers were increasingly targeted by periodical advertisements and constructed as domestic consumers, see Beetham, *A Magazine*, pp. 8 and 142–54.
13. Anon, 'To the Public', p. 4.
14. It is unclear when John Browne Bell first became the proprietor of the *World of Fashion*. In *Women in Print*, Adburgham suggests that he was co-founder in

1824 with 'Mr. Anderson' A. Adburgham, *Women in Print: Writing Women and Women's Magazines from the Restoration to the Accession of Victoria*, London, 1972, p. 228. Certainly, by 1843 the magazine was under Bell's proprietorship. See First Edition Club, *Catalogue*, p. 26.

15. Anon., 'Advertisement for the *World of Fashion*', *NOTW*, 1 October 1843, p. 1.
16. Ibid.
17. Anon., 'The Politician', *NOTW*, 1 October 1843, p. 1.
18. See Ellegård, who argued that the *NOTW* 'appealed to the lower to middle class readers'. A. Ellegård, *The Readership of the Periodical Press in Mid-Victorian Britain*, Göteborg, 1957, p. 20.
19. See Beetham for speculation on the 'aspirational' ways women may have read high-end fashion columns in women's periodicals such as the *Queen*. Beetham, *A Magazine*, pp. 90–91.
20. Bell's interest in women's periodicals might have been sparked his wife Mary Ann's work as a fashionable milliner and dress designer. See First Edition Club, p. 24. John Browne Bell also published the *Magazine of Fashions, Fancy Costumes; and the Regimentals of the Army* (1828–29).
21. Beetham, *A Magazine*, p. 32.
22. M. Conboy, *Journalism: A Critical History*, London, 2004, p. 154.
23. Anon., 'Varieties', *NOTW*, 1 October 1843, p. 6.
24. 'Catherine Parr' was the pen name of Mrs William Henry Kaye.
25. Anon. 'Varieties', p. 6. Emphasis in original.
26. R. Williams, 'The Press and Popular Culture: An Historical Perspective' in G. Boyce, J. Curran and P. Wingate (eds), *Newspaper History from the Seventeenth Century to the Present Day*, London, 1978, p. 44. See also Humpherys.
27. Anon.,'Suicide through Distress', *NOTW*, 1 October 1843, p. 6.
28. Anon. 'Varieties', p. 6.
29. Anon., 'The Theatres', *NOTW*, 1 October 1843, p. 5. The Queen's Theatre on Charlotte Street was commonly referred to as the 'dusthole' due to its shabbiness and its tendency to produce lowbrow melodramas.
30. Anon., 'The Sunday Papers', *Saturday Review*, 19 April 1856, p. 493.
31. See Beetham, *A Magazine*, p. 10; J. Phegley, *Educating the Proper Woman Reader: Victorian Family Literary Magazines and the Cultural Health of the Nation*, Columbus, 2004, pp. 1–30.
32. The front page of the paper's inaugural issue, for example, signalled the inclusion of women readers with advertisements for the *World of Fashion*, light literature and engravings of the royal family. By the issue published on 7 December 1851, the front page included adverts for Rimmel's Perfumed Minature Almanack, Ellen Dawson's *Ladies' Companion; or, Valuable Friend to the Toilet*, William Burton's kitchen stoves, Glenfield Patent Starch and Pears's Rouge and Pearl Powder.
33. Conboy, *Journalism*, p. 135.
34. D. Griffiths, *Fleet Street: Five Hundred Years of the Press*, London, 2006, p. 110.
35. V. Berridge, 'Popular Sunday Papers and Mid-Victorian Society' in Boyce, Curran and Wingate (eds), p. 249. See also Ellegård, *The Readership of the Mid-Victorian Press*, p. 19.
36. See C. Bainbridge and R. Stockdill, *The New of the World Story: 150 Years of the World's Bestselling Newspaper*, New York, 1993, pp. 24–25.
37. J. North, *Waterloo Directory of British Newspapers and Periodicals, 1800–1900*, Waterloo, 2003.

38. J. Grant, *History of the Newspaper Press*, London, 1871–72, 3, p. 87.
39. Anon., *Newspaper Press Directory*, London, 1874, pp. 28, 24, 26.
40. Anon., 'The Sunday Press', *Saturday Review*, 28 February 1885, pp. 275–76.
41. J. Curran,'The Press as an Agency of Social Control: An Historical Perspective' in Boyce, Curran and Wingate (eds), p. 70.
42. For example, in the inaugural issue, published on 1 October 1843, advertisements were limited to two columns on page 1 of the paper. By 16 April 1876, four of the six columns on the front page were devoted to adverts, and additional advertising columns were located near the theatre, police and business news sections of the paper.
43. For convenience, I refer to 'Hampden' as 'he', but the sex and identity of the author of the column are unknown. It was most likely written by various members of the editorial staff, which might have included women. The name 'Hampden' might be an allusion to Renn Dickson Hampden, who in 1847 became the subject of controversy when Prime Minister John Russell appointed him to the see of Hereford, overruling the objections of several prominent bishops. The R.D. Hampden story was reported in the *NOTW* from 19 December to 2 January 1847. Quite possibly, Bell latched on to the name because it suggested the notion of individualism under fire. Alternatively, Melissa Score suggests that the column may have been named after John Hampden, a famous soldier in the English Civil War who died defending Parliament from the exercise of royal privilege (see Chapter 4). In either case, the 'Hampden' column was a regular feature of the newspaper for many years, appearing on page 2 of the paper as late as 1885.
44. 'Hampden', 'The Physician's Warning to Women', *NOTW*, 23 January 1876, p. 2.
45. 'Hampden, 'Ladies in Yellow', *NOTW*, 13 May 1877, p. 2.
46. Anon., 'Ladies' Fashions for January', *NOTW*, 7 January 1877, p. 3.
47. 'Hampden', 'Wife-and-Husband-Question', *NOTW*, 19 November 1876, p. 2.
48. 'Hampden', 'The Ladies' Day at Aberdeen', *NOTW*, 7 October 1877, p. 2.
49. Anon., 'Advertisement', *NOTW*, 17 January 1875, p. 2.
50. Beetham, *A Magazine*, p. 145.
51. 'Hampden', 'The New Art of Beauty', *NOTW*, 23 December 1877, p. 2.
52. Anon., 'Advertisement', *NOTW*, 23 December 1877, p. 2.
53. J. Bush, *Women against the Vote: Female Anti-Suffragism in Britain*, Oxford, 2007, p. 4.
54. Ibid., p. 5.
55. 'Hampden', 'What Would She Do with It?' *NOTW*, 25 April 1875, p. 2.
56. Ibid.
57. 'Hampden', 'The Ladies' Day at Aberdeen', p. 2.
58. 'Hampden', 'Woman's Work', *NOTW*, 29 March 1874, p. 2. The one exception to this rule was the medical profession. In an 1876, 'Hampden' argued that middle-class women could be trained to be competent doctors. After all, he argued, there was a shortage of trained male doctors, and 'a woman may be as skillful in the use of a lancet as in the use of a needle.' Hampden, 'Physicians in Petticoats', *NOTW*, 23 July 1876, p. 2.
59. 'Hampden', 'The Sophistication of Girlhood', *NOTW*, 4 January 1874, p. 2.
60. 'Hampden', 'The Spinsters' Question', *NOTW*, 22 February 1874, p. 2.
61. 'Hampden', 'The Imitation of Men', *NOTW*, 25 October 1874, p. 2.
62. 'Hampden', 'The Ladies' Day at Aberdeen', p. 2.
63. Ibid.

64. Anon., 'The Law Courts', *NOTW*, 25 April 1875, 7.
65. 'Hampden', 'Blighted Affections in the Law Courts', *NOTW*, 18 March 1877, p. 2.
66. Ibid.
67. 'Hampden', 'Proposals of Marriage', *NOTW*, 4 April 1875, p. 2. This proposal followed on his earlier satirical scheme for taxing bachelors and spinsters who refused to marry. 'Hampden', 'A Tax upon Bachelors', *NOTW*, 15 February 1874, p. 2.
68. 'Hampden', 'The Quarrelling Couples', *NOTW*, 14 January 1877, p. 2.
69. Anon., 'Fatal Affray between Husband and Wife', *NOTW*, 14 January 1877, p. 1.
70. 'Hampden', 'The Quarrelling Couples', p. 2.
71. Anon., 'Setting a Wife on Fire', *NOTW*, 23 December 1877, p. 7.
72. 'Hampden', 'The Quarrelling Couples', p. 2.
73. Berridge, 'Popular', p. 256.
74. 'Hampden', 'The Newspapers', *NOTW*, 6 December 1874, p. 2.
75. The mid-Victorian period was of course also a crucial era in the development of the feminist press, which included the *English Woman's Journal* (1858–64), *Victoria Magazine* (1863–80) and *Woman's Suffrage Journal* (1870–90). In addition, groundbreaking essays in the struggle for women's rights – such as Harriet Taylor's "The Enfranchisement of Women" (*Westminster Review*, 1851) and Harriet Martineau's "Female Industry" (*Edinburgh Review*, 1859) – were published in prominent reviews in the mid-century.
76. Mater, 'Lady Superintendents of the Nursery Department', *NOTW*, 24 January 1875, p. 2.
77. 'Hampden', 'Wonderful Works of Women', *NOTW*, 15 March 1874, p. 2.
78. Anon., 'The Women's Whiskey War', *NOTW*, 15 March 1874, p. 2.
79. 'Hampden', 'Wonderful Works of Women', p. 2.
80. Anon., 'The Women's Trade Union', *NOTW*, 18 July 1875, p. 2.
81. North, *Waterloo Directory*, n.p.
82. Anon., 'Very Low Literature', *World*, 15 July 1874, p. 4.
83. J. Hatton, *Journalistic London*, London, 1882, p. 96.
84. See, for example Anon.,'The Magazines', *NOTW*, 5 August 1877, p. 6.
85. 'Hampden', 'Ladies in Yellow', *NOTW*, 13 May 1877, p. 2; Anon., 'Yellow', *World*, 22 May 1877, p. 16.
86. 'Hampden', 'The New Art of Beauty', *NOTW*, 23 December 1877, p. 2; Anon., 'Girls', *Truth*, 13 December 1877, p. 714.
87. North, *Waterloo Directory*, n.p.
88. Griffiths, *Fleet Street*, p. 111.
89. Bainbridge and Stockdill, *The News of the World*, pp. 73–74 and pp. 84–85.
90. W. Underhill et al., 'Rupert's Red Menace', *Newsweek*, 158(4), 2011, pp. 40–44. Of course, the characterisation of the tabloid press as a prostitute precedes the 2011 controversy over the *NOTW*. As journalist Allison Pearson put it in 1999, 'What is the difference between a *NOTW* journalist and a prostitute? Both will screw you for money but at least the prostitute will never claim it was in the public interest.' Quoted in Brooks, 'So Far, So Feminised', p. C4.
91. See S. Simanowitz, 'The Phone-hacking Scandal: British Politics Transformed?' *Contemporary Review*, 293 (2011), pp. 411 and 415.
92. Underhill et al., 'Rupert's', p. 40.
93. Ibid. This view is articulated even more directly in a letter to the editor of the *Irish Times*, which claims that Murdoch and Brooks 'killed a 168-year-old

best-selling British newspaper'. D. O'Donoghue, 'End of the "World"', *Irish Times*, 9 July 2011, p. 15.

94. See R. Pound and G. Harmsworth, *Northcliffe*, London, 1959, p. 200. For further discussion of the earlier roots of the New Journalism, see L. Brake, 'The Old Journalism and the New: Forms of Cultural Production in London in the 1880s' in J. Wiener (ed.), *Papers for the Millions: The New Journalism in Britain, 1850s to 1914*, New York, 1988, pp. 1–24; and J. Wiener, 'How New Was the New Journalism?' in J. Wiener (ed.) *Papers for the Millions*, pp. 47–71.

6
News of the Imperial World: Popular Print Culture, the *News of the World* and India in the late Nineteenth Century

Chandrika Kaul

Introduction

The *News of the World* (*NOTW*) was born into, and incubated within, a cultural environment infused with imperial rhetoric and tales of overseas exploits. From the middle decades of the nineteenth century, and especially following the Great Rebellion in 1857–58, the Indian subcontinent became a key constituent of the British imperial experience. Technological and institutional developments facilitated greater access to the East: the inauguration of the Suez Canal in 1869, the Establishment of Reuters news agency bureaux in India from the late 1860s and the opening of direct telegraph links between Europe and the subcontinent during the 1870s made news more accessible, albeit it remained relatively expensive to procure in both time and money. In recent decades, centripetal, centrifugal and transnational perspectives on empire have gone hand in hand with an emphasis on multi-disciplinarity in pedagogic approaches to its study. Further, it is widely accepted that empire, in its complex and varied manifestations, had a seminal impact upon the socio-cultural milieu of Britain, although there is debate about the nature and extent of such influence. This micro-study aims to situate the *NOTW* and its Indian coverage within the wider discussion on imperialism and popular culture in late nineteenth-century Britain.

The press in Victorian Britain became 'the context within which people lived and worked and thought, and from which they derived their (in most cases quite new) sense of the outside world'.[1] There was an enormous increase in the British market for news about the empire, which offered exciting opportunities for attention-grabbing stories.[2] This process received a fillip from a combination of factors including the removal of government taxes and financial constraints on newspapers by the 1860s, the continuing expansion and diversification of the metropolitan press with the adoption of more popular formats for mass appeal and the increasing access to overseas news resulting from improved communication technologies and the development of international news agencies.[3] Founded in London during 1843, the *NOTW* quickly established itself as the market leader amongst the weekly press. It claimed lineage dating back to 1796 when printer John Bell published a Sunday newspaper titled *Bell's Weekly Messenger.* It was his son, John Browne Bell, who, in addition to continuing *Bell's* as *Bell's New Weekly Messenger,* also established (and edited) the *NOTW*. The paper professed Liberal credentials, was priced (in 1857) at 2*d.*/3*d.* and aimed to compress the news of the week and adapt it for 'the perusal of a class of readers who, though respectable, may be supposed... not to have had much opportunity before the Saturday evening for newspaper reading'.[4] If circulations are any guide, these hard working readers responded enthusiastically to the *NOTW* diet. According to government stamp returns, its sales stood at 674,518 in 1844, rising to 2,926,269 by 1850. During the 1850s, the *NOTW* regularly sold over 3 million copies, reaching its greatest circulation of 5,673,525 during the first year of the Crimean War.[5] Along with *Lloyd's Weekly News* and *Reynolds's Newspaper,* the *NOTW* helped to lay the 'true foundations' of the mass circulation Sunday press in Britain.[6]

As detailed in *Reporting the Raj,* prior to the mid-nineteenth century, *The Times* was the only British newspaper with an extensive system of foreign correspondents in the subcontinent, spending over £10,000 a year on this service.[7] However, with the Crown establishing suzerainty in 1858, increasing space was accorded India in the London press. This chapter aims to shed light on the *NOTW*'s engagement with the core ideologies of militarism and monarchism prevalent in late Victorian Britain, by focusing upon two seminal episodes in the history of the Raj: the Great Rebellion (or the Great Indian Mutiny), which broke out in the spring and summer of 1857 and took 18 months to subdue; and the first tour of India (and Ceylon) by a Prince of Wales (the future Edward VII) during 1875–76, a process that culminated in the staging of a grand Imperial Assemblage in Delhi on New Year's day 1877 to proclaim Queen Victoria, Empress of India. John MacKenzie has argued for the creation of 'an ideological cluster' in late Victorian Britain that infused into and was 'propagated by every organ of British life'. This was an amalgamation of 'a renewed militarism, a devotion to royalty, an identification and worship of national heroes, together with a contemporary cult of personality, and racial ideas associated with Social Darwinism'.[8] What is revealed about British press culture through the lens of the *NOTW*? Given the *NOTW*'s commercial success, what can be suggested about the press-politics nexus and popular imperialism during these decades?

News of the World and the Great Rebellion

The *NOTW* joined the mass of the British press in its preoccupation with the affairs of India during 1857–58, when her fate hung in the balance for several months. Reports of the dramatic struggle in distant lands – the frequent reversals of British fortune, the bloody military encounters and heinous reprisals, the desperate heroism of besieged officers, the suffering of women and children, combined with the supposed religious fanaticism and barbarity of the enemy – all served to provide grist to many a newspaper mill. The line between fact and fiction was often blurred, and, in general, there was little attempt at maintaining impartiality, notwithstanding the sedulous cultivation by the press of its role as the Fourth Estate of the realm. This, again, is not unexpected. Imperial conflict with foreign and non-Anglo-Saxon races allowed the press, both quality and popular, an opportunity to indulge in coverage unrestricted by the conventional dictates of European war reporting. A fundamental lack of knowledge about India and the difficulty of and delay in access to accurate information on the one hand, with the heightened emotions that a call to national patriotism can evoke on the other, combined to inflect popular and journalistic response with a degree of rabidity previously unseen. There were exceptions to this rule in Fleet Street, most prominently from the pen of W.H. Russell, chief foreign and war correspondent of *The Times*, as I have discussed elsewhere.[9] Under these circumstances, what were the main lines of argument advanced by the *NOTW* and how did these alter and develop with the passage of time as well as the fluctuating fortunes of the British?

The *NOTW* did not have permanent correspondents based in India at this juncture, and was dependent on a range of sources including the Anglo-Indian press, official and Reuters telegraphs, Government of India proclamations and first-person accounts. It is from the pages of the Anglo-Indian press – specifically those of the *Bombay Times*, *Bengal Hurkaru* and *Madras Atheneum* – that the *NOTW* published (on 14 June) its first telegraphed extracts from early May 1857, describing the outbreak in Meerut under a suggestive headline: 'Alarming Conspiracy in the Native Army – Intended Murder of all the Europeans in the Country.' Over the following weeks, it provided further information on the unfolding conflict, relaying coverage from Meerut and Delhi: 'Massacre of the British and Preparations for a Terrible Retribution.' The 'bloody scenes' at Meerut, its readers were informed, 'were reproduced in the streets of this ancient Mogul capital'.[10] Additional accounts featured a range of correspondents: thus there is a report titled, 'Frightful Barbarities of the Rebels', based on particulars supplied by the Rev. T.O. Smyth, Chaplain of Meerut, and Mr Greathead, Commissioner at Meerut; reports of 'atrocities' in Allahabad from an American missionary as well as a letter from an unnamed 'gentleman' in Bombay to his brother in London.[11] Other correspondents included 'an eyewitness to the Murders and Pillage' in Delhi and 'An officer in the Bombay army' detailing the grievances in the Bengal army which, was the most severely affected: 'there is no doubt that the seniority system adopted in the Bengal army is shamefully bad'.[12] This formula of detailed coverage of armed encounters, personalised by harrowing accounts from Britons sent unsolicited to its offices, was played out repeatedly in its pages over the following year.

It is not the intention here to recount the military campaigns, as these have been comprehensively covered elsewhere. Instead, we will attempt to gauge a measure of the *NOTW*'s stance from its editorials and leader pages as well as the spin it imparted to the news, highlighting where this diverged from mainstream press opinion. This on-going commentary also helps to provide meaningful insights into the changing nature of popular imperialism during these years. The *NOTW* published weekly editorials beginning with one on 28 June titled: 'The Indian Revolt and Massacre', in which the writer expressed no surprise at the outbreak of revolt given the many blunders committed by the East India Company and its general insensitivity to religious sentiment:

> The setting up [of] a new Mogul proves how injurious have been the half measures which have left some of the dispossessed Princes in a position lingering between disgust and hope. ... the combination of Mahommedan with Hindoo is quite sufficient to show the character of the intrigues that have been going on.[13]

The reference here is to the Governor General Lord Dalhousie (1848–56), who had initiated several unpopular measures against both Hindu and Muslim rulers and unilaterally annexed their kingdoms. Lamenting the bloodshed on all sides, the *NOTW* was consoled by the fact that 'it has happened early; for it will stimulate our rulers, both in India and in England, to take prompt measures' for its suppression. Additional troops, improvement in communications and better management of the armies were all called for. The Rebellion had occurred at an opportune moment in the aftermath of the Crimean War, which had 'drawn attention to the imperfect state of our military resources, and a very great improvement has taken place in the interval. ... We may therefore anticipate nothing but good coming out of this *ill* wind'.[14]

Elaborating over the following months on the causes of disaffection, the *NOTW* displayed a keen sense of perspective at a time when the majority of its compatriots were pandering to hysteria and jingoism. The paper argued that it was 'quite untrue to represent the religious feeling as being sole motive to disaffection. Intrigues on behalf of dispossessed Native Princes, of disinherited heirs, and of border, or even more distant enemies, are the great causes of the outbreak'.[15] Further, military leadership of the Indian armies under the Company did not serve imperial interests. The commanders were drawn

from 'a hybrid class, half soldier, half civilian, but wanting just that soldier-
ship that was necessary to bind them together with their men'.[16] Within the
British army, the regimental officer 'is pleased to cultivate friendly relations
with his men', but unfortunately such camaraderie was absent in India.[17]
Equally damning was the fact that connections, not calibre, determined
appointments, which were based on 'our patronage to the sons of good
men or of political friends, and the army becomes officered by the same
class as the various departments of the civil service'. The weekly underlined
how the 'want of due sympathy between the officer and the private [was]
aggravated by the circumstance that one is the conqueror and the other the
conquered'.[18] On the whole, the qualities that were necessary to inspire and
inculcate loyalty were allegedly largely absent and the consequences of this
'short-sightedness and folly' were now apparent.

Despite a belief in the superiority of Christianity, the *NOTW* nevertheless defended Hindus who were 'strict in the performance of duties...and
although we believe and know that it is a false belief...it is impossible not
to respect them for the devotion with which they cling to the principles
of their faith...These are such men as martyrs are made of'.[19] The weekly
concluded as early as August 1857 that proselytisation should not be the
preserve of the military: 'Let the man of the sword retain the sword, and
the man of the Bible the Bible.' The paper was also convinced that India was
regarded 'too much for the profits that are made there, and not sufficiently
for the actual work that should be done. All this must be reformed'.[20] In
pursuit of its critique, the *NOTW* did not hesitate to disagree with more
experienced minds, for example, the Bishop of Bombay, whose sermon,
delivered in Brighton, emphasised the importance of conversion and reform
of Hinduism. The weekly contended instead that forced conversion would
be counterproductive and was convinced that the government must not be
involved with proselytisation.[21] Similarly, when in October 1857 there was
a call for a National Day of humiliation and prayer in Britain, *NOTW* was
against exploiting the Rebellion for political purposes. 'We cannot regard
them in the light of a national judgement...Sinful as we are, the sins of
misgovernment in India are those of certain individuals, not of the nation'.[22]
Overall, its prescient observations were remarkable and stand out against
the backdrop of journalistic opinion in Fleet Street as well as amongst the
ranks of the Anglo-Indian press, both being divided along racial lines.

Yet, criticism of British military and civilian incompetence did not prevent
the *NOTW* from expressing outrage at the 'appalling' acts perpetrated by
the rebels: 'The imagination can scarcely conceive the fiendish barbarities
perpetrated by the Sepoys'.[23] For instance, it cited the alleged case of the
'daughter of an English clergyman [who] was driven through the streets
of Delhi naked, then subjected to unspeakable outrages by an infuriated
soldiery and afterwards cut to pieces with swords.' Europeans were 'exasperated to madness' by such episodes and the *NOTW* was convinced that they

would inflict 'the most terrible punishments' in reprisal.[24] Nevertheless, what needs to be underscored is that in its pages the use of terminology like 'butchering', 'treason', 'fiendish atrocities' and 'diabolical torture' was juxtaposed with a confident assertion about the 'Loyalty of the Indian people': 'in no part of the country have any symptoms whatever been shown of sympathy with the movement. The disaffection is confined entirely to the army.'[25] These sentiments appear to contradict its enumeration of the main causes of the Rebellion, as referred to earlier. However, we need to emphasise the extenuating circumstances within which events were being reported in Britain due to the slowness of communication (in the absence of direct telegraphic links) and the non-sequential order in which stories were received. Many papers struggled to make sense of unfolding events.

By the end of the summer of 1857, all hopes of a quick victory were lost and a *NOTW* leader writer was forced to acknowledge that the suppression of the rebellion would 'not be accomplished with the ease that was at first supposed'.[26] Citing Benjamin Disraeli's Parliamentary peroration to this effect, the weekly was convinced that 'look where you will, there are indicators of a want of foresight and sad mismanagement, evils which can no longer be denied or neglected'.[27] In keeping with general Fleet Street output, the *NOTW*'s coverage also reflected a preoccupation with the military fortunes of the British, provided detailed description of various campaigns and valorised commanders like Sir James Outram, Sir Henry Lawrence and Sir Colin Campbell, whilst simultaneously decrying the 'ferocity and treachery' of Indian opponents like the Nana Sahib.[28] The long siege and final victory at the Residency in Lucknow, for instance, was one of the most extensively covered episodes of the Rebellion. Apart from capturing the ebb and flow of British fortunes, the *NOTW* also published a double page spread on the 'Narrative of the Fall of Lucknow' by Russell of *The Times* who was accompanying the troops.[29] In one of its leaders titled: 'The British Heroes in India', the paper declared:

The fortitude, the bravery, and the skill of every man there, exposed for three months to a nearly incessant fire from strong and commanding positions held by an overwhelming force, is calculated to excite astonishment, whilst their deliverance is regarded as something almost miraculous, and certainly out of the ordinary character of events... The terrible fire of the enemy was not the only thing to be endured, for pestilence and famine threatened them equally with annihilation. But they were undismayed. They had no fear. They were as calm as they were resolute.[30]

The Rebellion continued to dominate the news agenda in 1858, with mailed news via a combination of land and sea routes, taking on average three-and-a-half weeks to arrive in London. Successive editorials were devoted to the recovering fortunes of the British. In its first leader of the

New Year, the *NOTW* proclaimed how 'the last act of the great Indian drama is being played', and wondered what would follow the suppression of 'this fierce rebellion'.[31] Unless the government resolved to adopt 'a bold, determined, and honourable policy, the mere abolition of the Company's political authority will affect but little good', argued the paper.[32] Contending that Indians understood the difference between right and wrong, it argued that future imperial policy would have to take account of the needs of the governed and would be 'useless for good if it does not secure the confidence of the native population'. In further championing the 'natives', the *NOTW* claimed that they had not been suitably rewarded in the past: 'let the native receive the credit and the profit of his work'.

> Unless a sweeping reform is effected, whereby the peasantry shall be raised from their miserable condition of poverty, the influence of caste reduced, and the whole system of government so framed that it shall be carried on for the advantage of the people, and not for the special benefit of particular persons, there will be a continued undergrowth of discontent that will suddenly spring up some time or other into another rebellion.[33]

As alluded to earlier, the *NOTW* continued to distinguish between the majority of the population and the mutineers: 'The natives of India are not to be confounded with the rascally Sepoys, and the good feeling which has been manifested among them seems to give assurance that a wise, just, and beneficent policy would be appreciated by them'.[34] It supported the Viceroy Lord Canning's proclamation about the future lines of Indian policy based on clemency and justice as well as defending him against Parliamentary attacks. Canning's 'fault' as a statesman was 'not haste, nor want of conscientious study, nor deficiency of moral courage'. Moreover, no individual could govern India without the support of an efficient and devoted cadre of subordinate staff.[35] The *NOTW* was also in favour of the Prime Minister, Lord Palmerston, taking a spirited stance on India, contending that he had become increasingly liberal in his outlook and thus in response to the Rebellion, 'he seems destined to be the man for overcoming it'.[36] The paper approved the details of the proposed new India Bill as presented to Parliament, but was aware that Palmerston would have a battle on his hands to get the measures approved by both Houses given the presence of large numbers of Conservative supporters of the Company.[37] By March 1858, the *NOTW* was able to write with increasing confidence that 'we see daylight after the long storm'.[38] In looking to the future and the need for reform, it cited with approval the sympathetic tenor of Canning's approach and the necessity to combine clemency with practical politics.

> The dawning intellect of India is with us … and while we put down the revolt, we should economise our means of doing so by retaining the

friendship and the enlightened self-interest of loyal Indians... In one sense, this point might be reduced to a question of money; the alliance of the natives is a substitute for an increase of British troops, only at a less rate of cost.[39]

Overall, the *NOTW* was keen to introduce a 'more English mind' into the governance of the subcontinent: 'We have to construct an England in India; and evidently we must throw into that vast dependency a much larger proportion of our own race.'[40]

Royalty, imperialism and the *News of the World*

The second half of the nineteenth century witnessed the consolidation of attempts to make the monarchy effective in an imperial context and to employ its appeal to promote imperial sentiment in the metropolis. Empire enhanced the prestige of monarchy, whilst the symbolism of monarchy validated imperial hierarchies, providing a visible embodiment for an otherwise fragmented entity. As I have analysed elsewhere, a central vehicle of monarchical influence was the royal tour.[41] The Disraelian experiment of associating monarchical influence with imperial power was epitomised by the Prince of Wales's tour as well as the subsequent Imperial Assemblage organised in Delhi by his appointee, the Viceroy, Lord Lytton, son of his friend (and fellow novelist) Edward Bulwer-Lytton of Knebworth. The visit of the future king was a much-anticipated event, as evidenced by the enthusiastic reactions of the British press as well as its Anglo-Indian counterpart. Edward asked Russell of *The Times* to accompany him and write a history of the tour. In addition to detailed narratives carried by most London dailies, the visualisation of his trip through sketches, drawings and photographs also transported the reader to the mysterious Orient. Pictorial journalism in the *Illustrated London News* and the *Graphic*, for instance, laid on a feast of Eastern splendour from the pens of artists William Simpson and Sydney Prior Hall, with the latter, like Russell, also forming part of the royal entourage.[42] Edward's *joie de vivre*, combined with his passion for sport, especially polo, provided a rich palette from which to construct an ebullient image of a vigorous monarchy and by association a confident and strong empire. To the British reader fed on 'Mutiny' propaganda of their countrymen in mortal danger from the 'savage natives', the triumphal celebration of their heir apparent and the warmth of the Indian welcome barely two decades later was widely welcomed.

Within the subcontinent, the response of the intelligentsia, nascent political associations and Indian newspapers was critical, given that the enormous financial outlay associated with the royal spectacle coincided with a famine devastating large swathes of the country. Despite some public protest and newspaper criticism, especially in regions directly affected by the famine, it is instructive to note that the majority of the local press responded to the prince in a cordial and respectful fashion, with large crowds turning up to watch his progress and participate with apparent enthusiasm in the public ceremonies. The Raj ensured that a significant proportion of Edward's itinerary was devoted to sojourns in the Princely States (and Nepal), where he would be assured of a magnificent welcome from India's royalty and his appetite for *shikar* (hunting) and sport abundantly catered for.[43] For Indian rulers, these hunts became 'a prime ceremonial' signifying their prestige and authority.[44] Tigers, panthers, cheetahs, pigs, bears and birds were duly slaughtered in large numbers during carefully stage-managed hunts, with Edward often shooting from atop elephant *howdahs* (palanquins) in time-honoured tradition. Thus readers were informed how the pigs 'showed great courage, fighting fiercely and charging savagely'.[45] What can we discern about the political predilections of the *NOTW* from its coverage of the tour and the state of India at this juncture? Did the popular weekly rise to the challenges of respectful reporting of a royal story amidst the many challenges besetting its empire, or were imperial problems minimised and occasionally airbrushed out of history?

At the departure of the royal party for India in October 1875, the *NOTW*'s leader declared that its 'confidence and esteem' were with the prince: 'We thus express what we believe to be the general feeling of the British public which has been extravagantly rendered by the daily press.'[46] The writer felt that since 'It is among a strange, a great and a magnificent people that the Prince is going', the journey must 'awaken more seriousness than a trip to Margate or a voyage across the Channel'. The British press was generally optimistic, with the *NOTW* quoting *The Times*, which argued that the Prince would be surrounded by 'trusted and experienced counsellors ... so that no anxiety may be felt of the luxurious manners of the East having any baleful influence'. This reference was an unmistakable reminder of the unflattering reputation in Britain of Edward and his popular exploits and of Victoria's disapproval. Within India, the *NOTW* described the fervent preparations afoot in major cities such as Calcutta and Benares. In the latter, inhabitants had even commenced a subscription for 'a permanent memorial' of the visit, in the shape of a hospital, to which the Maharajah had donated £2,500.[47]

A month later, the paper described the Prince's welcome upon landing in Bombay: 'A loyal reception was, of course, expected, but the reality has exceeded expectations.'[48] Attention was directed towards the Indian princes whose presence in Bombay, accompanied by 'brilliant' retinues and representing all shades of religious opinion, displayed a 'magnificence' such that Edward 'could not fail to be delighted with his reception', a view shared by Anglo-Indian newspapers like the *Times of India*. 'The effect was superb and almost beggars description', the paper rhapsodised. The route of the prince through the city was 'lined very deep with natives. This itself was a striking sight to European eyes'. The Indians kept 'absolutely quiet' and maintained the 'most perfect order'.[49] During civil ceremonies, such as a school fête when 7,000 children sang 'God Bless the Prince of Wales', his general 'affability' impressed locals. At night, there were grand illuminations in the city, a pattern repeated throughout his stay especially in the Princely States. Reports from the State of Baroda, for instance, recounted the experiences of Russell and Hall, who observed the common people tending to their daily avocations: 'Nothing could be more quiet, civil, and courteous than the demeanour of the little crowd who gathered round the strangers.'[50] The *NOTW* presciently judged the significance of 'knitting the affections of the Native Princes to the British Empress of Hindostan', as proclaimed in the aftermath of the Great Rebellion. Thus, we learn how the loyal Maharaja of Jaipur was invested with the Star of India, for example. In terms of commercial importance, the imperial cities of Bombay and Calcutta ranked alongside Birmingham and Sheffield and 'it is satisfactory to find a generous friendship strengthening between native populations of India and British rule.' The leader writer was moved to conclude how this 'private tour of pleasure may be regarded now as calculated to have useful political consequences'.[51]

Edward's progress in India 'has had much of the character of a triumph', proclaimed the *NOTW* anticipating the return of the prince in the spring of 1876. The 'geniality of his demeanour and his evident honesty of purpose' were instrumental in 'winning the hearts of all with whom he has been brought into contact'.[52] Public opinion in England, it claimed, was 'satisfied with the result' and the 'old English feeling' that he had taken to India seemed to have found favour with the Indian Princes. In addition, if he 'has really succeeded in getting into the hearts of the Indians, we shall all have cause for satisfaction'.[53] The *NOTW* concluded that 'the true service' that Edward had rendered to the Government of India was in 'presenting to its subjects what they conceive to be a concrete embodiment of the sovereignty exercised over them'.[54] Indians had witnessed the 'unanimity of submission' of 'every man and woman of the white race eager to see the Prince ... profuse in expressions of respect and reverence.' Echoes of the Rebellion also featured in public ceremonial with Edward receiving the survivors of the defence of Lucknow, visiting the well in Kanpur that had been the site of a notorious massacre and hosting a reception to honour Sikh veterans whose loyalty had played a critical role in the final British victory.[55] The paper frankly conceded that in this process, the limited nature of the Prince of Wales's power within the system of Constitutional Monarchy prevalent in Britain had been hidden from Indians. 'The result no doubt has been that the Prince's personal and political position is very extensively believed in India to be considerably different from what it actually is.' However, the *NOTW* was convinced that the end result would be beneficial, since Indians had been given 'a vivid conception of that national unity of which the Monarchy is really a symbol,

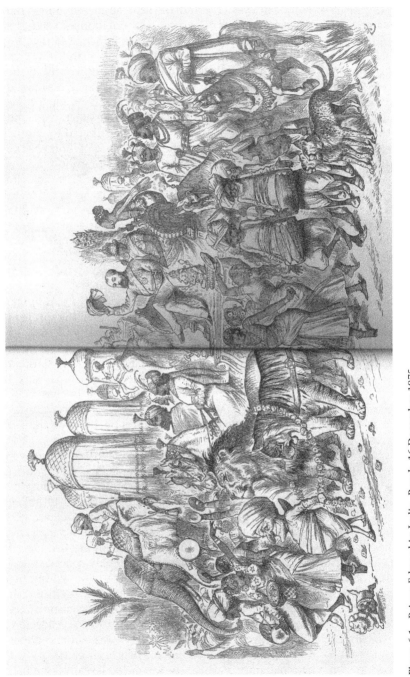

Figure 6.1 Prince Edward in India, *Punch*, 16 December 1875

but which the singular institutions established in India had the strongest tendency to obscure.'[56] Overall, the liberal *NOTW* appeared to be singing from the same hymn sheet as the Tory government.

In sharp contrast, the *NOTW* was critical of the new Royal Titles Bill that was orchestrated through Parliament by Disraeli during 1876, bestowing on the Queen the title of Empress of India, as well as the subsequent formal celebration of this fact at an Imperial Assemblage and royal spectacular in Delhi organised by the Viceroy, Lord Lytton, in 1877. He believed that the Assemblage would appeal to the imagination of both Indian and British masses and further consolidate the enthusiasm of the Indian aristocracy for empire.[57] For Disraeli the amplification of titles would help to 'touch and satisfy the imagination of nations'.[58] Whilst dutifully reporting these proceedings and publishing the text of the Queen's proclamation as well as details of smaller ceremonies in Bombay, Calcutta and Madras,[59] the *NOTW* also utilised its editorial columns to mount a series of spirited attacks against the Prime Minister and government policies both at the time of the passage of the Bill and after the Assemblage. A key element of its offensive was linked to the Indian Famine raging during these months. In an eponymous editorial published barely a few weeks after the Assemblage, the paper accused the government of a cover-up: 'we have not been allowed to know the whole truth until the pageant of the proclamation at Delhi was over.' The *NOTW* proclaimed in no uncertain terms that the 'useless outlay on that costly ceremonial is deeply to be regretted.' *Punch* appeared to share these sentiments as is apparent from the sardonic tone of the ditty addressed to the Indian princes attending the occasion, many of whom had honours bestowed on them by the Raj:

> Think not of cost, nor of the needs that call for it elsewhere;
> The cloud of coming scarcity that darkens the parched air:
> Let not the whiff unmannerly of cyclone-swallowed dead
> Come 'twixt your new nobility, and attar freely shed.[60]

The *NOTW* emphasised how all the resources of India 'will need to be applied to save our new Empire from a scandal so great as our fellow creatures and fellow subjects dying from famine'.[61] The relief works were imperative to ensure that people were fed, in the first instance, but also to support their longer-term economic recovery. In addition, the *NOTW* was convinced that these droughts 'are practically preventable, as are floods [in Britain], only we never learn the lesson nature teaches us in time'. Looking to the future, the paper argued that the Raj 'ought to employ all the engineering skills we have to prevent the calamities which press equally just now on the banks of the Thames and the plains of Madras'. It concluded by expressing confidence in British ability to respond proactively: 'men to whom intellectual power has been given should be ready to convert the warnings into lessons.'[62] Thus, in centre-staging the horrors of the famine and its impact on millions of 'our fellow creatures and subjects', the *NOTW* chose to distance itself from the royal spectacle and highlight where its sympathies lay. By referring to the Delhi Assemblage as a 'useless outlay' and emphasising, instead, the importance of economic development and social welfare policies as critical aspects of imperial obligation, it also voiced the views of both Utilitarian liberals at home and of significant sections of the nascent Indian political intelligentsia.

The second major aspect of the *NOTW*'s critique was directed at 'Disraeli's New Romance'. Disraeli's 'Romance' of the Royal Titles Bill was 'one of the most unfortunate of his productions', ran the opening salvo.[63] The paper

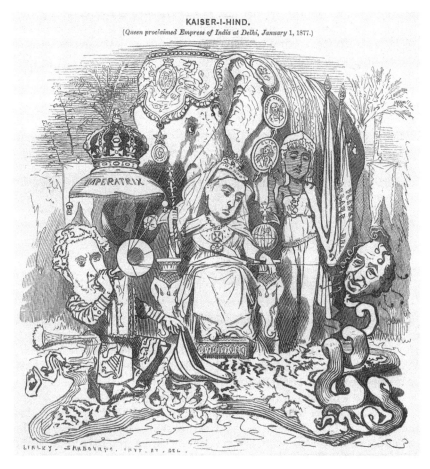

Figure 6.2 Kaiser-I-Hind, Queen Proclaimed Empress of India, *Punch*, 13 January 1877, p. 2

was convinced that the new title would not impart any 'additional significance' to the 'Royal style and dignity', and that it would be 'absurd to allege,
after the loyal manifestations during the Prince of Wales's tour, that the
addition is needed to strengthen the bond of union between the Indian
population and the British Throne'.[64]

> Mr Disraeli's oriental imagination has become fevered under the contem-
> plation of the Prince of Wales's reception by the great Indian chiefs – the
> festivities got up for him, the dances he has danced and the tigers he has
> slain, to the amazement of the natives – and he associates State policy
> with the features of an Eastern tale. We are unable otherwise to account
> for the puerility of the Premier's proposal to Parliament.[65]

It is arguable, given its professed liberal and working-class credentials, that
this attack on the credibility of the Prime Minister was influenced, to a
degree, by the dictates of party political warfare.[66] For, as revealed in the
editorials devoted to analysing the impact of Edward's tour, the journalists
of the popular press clearly appreciated the political potential and role of
royalty in both creating and consolidating imperial sentiment – a conviction that lay at the heart of the Disraelian project *vis-à-vis* India.

Concluding remarks

In 1891, the *NOTW* was acquired by a consortium that included Henry
Lascelles Carr and G.A. Riddell, and later Edgar Fifoot and Sir Charles
Jackson. Emsley Carr, Lascelles's nephew, became editor of the paper and
continued in that post until his death in 1941. Both Carr and Riddell were
knighted for their services during the First World War by the Prime Minister,
Lloyd George. The close association of the paper with the war effort, the
role of its journalists in official propaganda and their support of the Prime
Minister within a tenuous coalition, underlined the incestuous relationship
between press, politicians and political parties.

   However, decades earlier, during the period under review in this chapter,
the *NOTW* had successfully maintained a critical distance from, and stance
upon, imperial policy makers, politicians and military commanders. Through
its editorials and in its response to the stories emanating from India, the
NOTW time and again delivered a balanced and thoughtful critique that
was often at variance with majority opinion in Fleet Street. This was as true
of the weekly's coverage of the military conflagration of the Great Rebellion,
as it was of its response to the spectacle of the royal tour. Imperial wars
abounded during the second half of the nineteenth century, providing the
NOTW and the popular press in general, with an opportunity to display
captivating headlines and graphic images as well as a patriotic fervour, in
their bid to garner wider support from the increasing ranks of newspaper

readers. The monarchical pageant played a similarly facilitating role. Yet, the *NOTW* was not swept along any popular wave of imperial jingoism or royal romance. Its support for political agendas and politicians was subject to constant revision and negotiated at many levels. It was intrepid in criticising the Royal Titles Bill and the Imperial Assemblage devoted to Queen Victoria, arguing that resources would have been better spent in alleviating the lives of millions suffering from famine – not the standard line calculated to appeal to political opinion in Parliament or to significant sections of devout royalists at home. On the other hand, the weekly's editorial perspectives were vindicated, for instance, in the British response to the Rebellion and consequently reflected in the reformist agenda of the Crown in the aftermath of its suppression. The *NOTW* was also sensitive to the imperial idiom, incorporating not simply political might and economic progress but also an element of empathy: 'We are apt to consider material benefits, such as railroads and the like, quite sufficient to reconcile nations to foreign rule ... sympathy would bridge over a greater gulf than any railway bridge could span.'[67] Overall the *NOTW* played an agenda-setting role *vis-à-vis* its reading public and India. Much like Berridge has contended with respect to *Reynolds's*, not every reader would respond to news in the same way but 'their perception was in some way confirmed, reinforced, and molded by what they saw in their chosen paper.'[68] Further, the ambiguities inherent in the party-political landscape in Britain during the late Victorian era also helped to diffuse press allegiances, as effectively argued by Koss.[69] In the process, it allowed papers like the *NOTW* freedom to manoeuvre through the political quicksand with relative ease and maintain an independent line that was to become less conspicuous as the twentieth century unfolded.

Notes

1. J. Shattock and M. Wolff (eds), *The Victorian Periodical Press: Samplings and Soundings*, Leicester 1982, pp. xiv–xv; L. Brown, *Victorian News and Newspapers*, Oxford, 1985.
2. For general coverage of imperialism and popular culture, see books in the Manchester Studies in Imperialism Series.
3. For Indian coverage, see Chandrika Kaul, *Reporting the Raj, The British Press and India*, Manchester, 2003.
4. Mitchell's *Newspaper Press Directory 1857*, London 1857, p. 27.
5. No author, *Through Four Reigns: The Romance of a Great Newspaper*, n.d., pp. 7–9.
6. F. Williams, *Dangerous Estate*, London 1957, p. 103.
7. See Kaul, *Reporting the Raj; History of The Times*, London 1939, Vol II.
8. J.M. MacKenzie, *Propaganda and Empire*, Manchester, 1984, p. 2.
9. See Chandrika Kaul, 'You cannot govern by force alone': W.H. Russell, *The Times'* and the Great Rebellion,' in M. Carter & C. Bates (eds), *Global Perspectives, Mutiny at the Margins: New Perspectives on the Indian Uprising of 1857*, New Delhi & London, 2013, Vol. 3, Chapter 2, pp. 18–35.
10. *NOTW*, 5 July 1857.

11. *NOTW*, 19 July, 20 September, 1857.
12. *NOTW*, 26 July 1857
13. *NOTW*, 28 June 1857.
14. Ibid.
15. *NOTW*, 5 July 1857.
16. *NOTW*, 23 August 1857.
17. *NOTW*, 23 August 1857.
18. *NOTW*, 23 August 1857.
19. *NOTW*, 23 August 1857.
20. *NOTW*, 23 August 1857.
21. *NOTW*, 6 September 1857.
22. *NOTW*, 11 October 1857.
23. *NOTW*, 9 August 1857.
24. Ibid.
25. *NOTW*, 19 July 1857.
26. *NOTW*, 2 August 1857.
27. Ibid.
28. *NOTW*, 11 October 1857; see also 16 August, 27 September, 4 October 1857; 3, 10, 17, 24 January, 7, 14 February, 21 March, 4 April, 2, 16, 23 May 1858.
29. *NOTW*, 2 May 1858.
30. *NOTW*, 17 Jan 1858.
31. *NOTW*, 3 Jan 1858.
32. Ibid.
33. Ibid.
34. Ibid.
35. *NOTW*, 31 January 1858.
36. *NOTW*, 10 January 1858.
37. NOTW, 10 January, 4 April, 16 May 1858.
38. *NOTW*, 21 March 1858.
39. *NOTW*, 7 February 1858.
40. *NOTW* 21 March 1858.
41. See Chandrika Kaul, 'Monarchical Display & the Politics of Empire: Princes of Wales and India, 1870s–1920s', *Twentieth Century British History*, 17 (4), 2006, 464–88. D. Cannadine, *Ornamentalism*, London, 2001.
42. Kaul, 'Monarchical Display and the Politics of Empire.'
43. Ibid.
44. J.M. MacKenzie, *The Empire of Nature*, Manchester, 1988, p. 171.
45. *NOTW*, 16 January 1876.
46. *NOTW*, 17 October 1875.
47. Ibid.
48. *NOTW*, 14 November 1875.
49. Ibid.
50. *NOTW*, 26 December 1875.
51. *NOTW*, 14 November 1875.
52. *NOTW*, 26 March 1876.
53. Ibid.
54. *NOTW*, 2 April 1876.
55. Kanpur and Lucknow were sites of bloody battles between the British and the Indian mutineers. The Sikhs of the Punjab were famed for their martial spirit and remained loyal to the British despite the annexation of their kingdom in the 1840s.

56. Ibid.
57. B.S. Cohn, 'Representing Authority in Victorian India' in E.J. Hobsbawm and T.O. Ranger (eds), *The Invention of Tradition*, London 1983, pp. 185–88.
58. Disraeli in Parliament, cited in W.F. Monypenny and G.E. Buckle, *The Life of Benjamin Disraeli*, London 1929, pp. 805, 827.
59. *NOTW*, 7 January 1877.
60. *Punch*, 13 January 1877, p. 2.
61. *NOTW*, 21 January 1877.
62. Ibid.
63. *NOTW*, 19 March 1876.
64. Ibid.
65. Ibid. See also 26 March 1876.
66. For a general discussion, see A.J. Lee, *The Origins of the Popular Press*, London, 1976.
67. *NOTW*, 19 March 1876.
68. V. Berridge, 'Content Analysis and Historical Research in Newspapers', in M. Harris and A. Lee (eds), *The Press in English Society from the seventeenth to the nineteenth centuries*, London 1986, p. 215.
69. S. Koss, *The Rise and Fall of the Political Press in Britain*, London 1980, Vol. 1.

7
Residual Radicalism as a Popular Commercial Strategy: Beginnings and Endings

Martin Conboy

Introduction

Could it be claimed that the *News of the World* (*NOTW*) demonstrated continuities in appeal across its lifespan? Were there aspects of its appeal to readers in 2011 that drew upon longer traditions of popularity? This chapter will explore some of the background to the rise of Sunday newspapers in the early nineteenth century in order to assess whether the success of the twenty-first-century version of the popular Sunday newspaper had anything in common with its nineteenth-century predecessors. It will argue that it is in its appeal to 'ordinary people', beyond the privileged and the powerful, that the *NOTW* best represented a continuity with Sunday newspapers of the nineteenth century. Over the twentieth century, it had developed a highly nuanced set of rhetorical and stylistic devices that reinforced its claim to be on the side of its readers. Key to this appeal was a particular sort of radicalism: not a politically specific radicalism, rather a position of support for the underdog and a related suspicion of those in power whether that power derived from political office or wealth. This radical tradition had mutated from the earliest stirrings of political publication in England from the late eighteenth century, through the radical unstamped press of the early nineteenth century to become incorporated into a commercially attractive form of appeal to general readerships in the Sunday press of the mid-nineteenth century. Despite all the obvious differences between these various publications, what unites them is this appeal to the politically and economically excluded; we may claim that the *News of the World*' s success was its ability to continue to refine a residual radicalism for the modern age.

Sunday newspapers: the beginnings

Newspaper publishers had tried many profitable permutations during the eighteenth century: the daily, the tri-weekly and the weekly. Despite protests from influential Sabbatarian lobbyists, Sunday newspapers were introduced to extend this range of offerings to the public and needed to provide a distinctive alternative to the more established newspapers if they were to be profitable and moderately attractive to advertisers. The *Observer*, founded in 1791, was the first successful example of a Sunday newspaper and originated a blend of the serious and the sensationalist designed to distinguish it from the daily newspapers, especially at a time when these were characterised by a predominantly political and commercial emphasis.[1] The modest success of the *Observer* prompted rival publications, such as the *New Observer*, from 1821. Despite some disapproval,[2] the first regular Sunday papers were, like most commercial newspaper ventures, aimed at an assumed middle-class readership. The expansion of the Sunday press came as it broke from this exclusively bourgeois model, in the slipstream of increasing working-class readership and the staged reduction of stamp duties from the 1830s onwards. The popular Sunday newspapers that emerged in the mid-century, of which the *News of the World* was one, have proved to be a remarkably resilient periodical genre. Commercially successful Sundays have taken on various styles and forms in order to survive and maximise their market potential and, while they have always been stratified by class division, they have largely been rooted in popular culture.

Newspaper content develops through a process of accretion, and the popular Sunday press was no exception. The components of a commercially popular brand of Sunday journalism were drawn from a variety of existing sources. Sport, crime and sensation provided the base materials for their weekly audiences. As the social and political changes of the early nineteenth century materialised, a particular articulation of social class was to be found in many periodicals that were formed as alternatives to the mainstream daily bourgeois press. The original *Bell's Life in London* for example started out in 1822 as an anti-establishment general weekend newspaper aimed at the working class.[3] As sport became a core component of many weekly and Sunday experiments at the start of the nineteenth century *Bell's Life* moved quickly to incorporate sporting news, adding *'and Sporting Chronicle'* to its title within months of its launch. In 1824, *Pierce Egan's Life in London and Sporting Guide* was published for the first time and became attractive enough as a commercial proposition to become incorporated into *Bell's Life* in 1827. From the early 1830s, *Bell's Life* gave increasing coverage to horse racing and this feature soon began to dominate the paper. As a contribution to the shaping of popular Sunday fare, the sporting contacts cultivated by the paper provided a useful way of gaining information about scandal among the wealthy, a topic that was eagerly seized upon by lower-class readers. *Bell's Life* managed to extend its appeal to the literate poor as well as to the more affluent classes because of its concentration on the cross-class appeal of sports such as racing and boxing, and the equally popular practice of betting on both.[4]

Unstamped newspapers, such as *Cleave's Weekly Police Gazette* despite its relatively short lifespan (1834–36), provided evidence that a combination of prurience and populism could be a profitable one. Stories emanating from the police and the courts could inflame popular prejudice about the arrogance of the well-heeled as well as highlighting the squalor and desperation of the urban poor. Cleave's Saturday paper has been estimated to have had a circulation of 20,000 per week,[5] and its success led to more commercially oriented publications developing this model for a wider public.

The tendency to concentrate on material, often ignored by the mainstream press, which exposed aristocratic corruption and the exploitation of the poor, prompted an inevitable shift in the address of Sunday newspapers to a predominantly working-class readership through the middle part of the nineteenth century. A combination of increasing literacy rates and the greater affordability of cheap material, produced by more efficient printing technology, meant that working people had better access to cheap, printed material although they had little opportunity to read except on Sundays. Yet, despite their commercial success, as Wiener has noted,[6] Sunday newspaper reading remained disreputable.

The three Sunday newspapers launched in the mid-century that were to acquire long-term significance were *Lloyd's Illustrated London Newspaper* (1842) the *News of the World* (1843) and *Reynolds's Weekly Newspaper* (1850). *Lloyd's Illustrated Weekly Paper*, as it was called until its eighth issue in Jan 1843, was a blend of populist politics and what were to become twin Victorian obsessions in periodical form – sensationalism and illustration – although both illustration and fiction were dropped on its renaming as *Lloyd's Weekly Newspaper* in 1843. It emerged from Edward Lloyd's successful early publishing career, during which he had specialised in 'Penny Dreadfuls', therefore, quite logically, drawing upon a narrative tradition of the gruesome and the shocking.[7] Lloyd launched it in the guise of a weekly fiction newspaper, but as the fiction was often too closely mapped onto the sensational occurrences of London's streets it was soon required to pay stamps as a newspaper. Once it had established its editorial identity, *Lloyd's* provided a liberal-commercial approach to newspaper content rather than any radical outlook, with an appeal across class boundaries to lower-middle and working-class readers.

Almost as quick out of the publishers' stalls, in 1843, the *NOTW* became the best selling weekly newspaper of the age. It reached an impressive circulation of 200,000 within a few months of its launch, based largely on its courting of provincial readerships. However, its ascent to world-leading circulation was neither swift nor even – it prospered initially only until the death of its publisher and owner John Browne Bell in 1855.[8]

Reynolds's Weekly Newspaper was first published as *Reynolds's Weekly Newspaper* in 1850 and changed its title in 1851; it was another good example of the appeal of a finely judged blend of the political and the commercial.

The owner, G.W.M. Reynolds, was a republican by conviction and had been a leading figure in the Chartist movement.[9] Although he wrote signed front-page political pieces, he gradually tempered these to furnish a combination that would appeal to the widest possible readership as well as to advertisers. He provided a newspaper that was full of populist, crowd-pleasing sensation, written with an ear for the sympathies and assumed prejudices of its readers. Police news, court news and general gossip were all accentuated if there was any connection with either the plight of the poor or the foibles or vices of the aristocracy. Furthermore, the melodrama that was a key to his news reporting, drew on the style and success of the publisher's own commercially successful novels.[10]

Let us now consider in detail how the *NOTW* placed itself within the developing traditions of Sunday newspapers. Newspapers are always launched in hyperbole and the *NOTW* was no exception. 'The Novelty of the Nation and the Wonder of the World' was how it announced its arrival to the British public on 1 October 1843, demonstrating an early example of the alliteration that would remain a characteristic of the headlines of the later tabloid genre,[11] and which stemmed from the discourse of public entertainments in the Victorian era such as melodrama and the Music Hall. It is also worth noting that its stress on providing news of the world is all the more remarkable given that its launch predated the development of the telegraph.[12] The paper entered an expanding market for popular print, optimistic that it would be able to establish a wide readership among those who had been drawn to the unstamped publications of the 1830s, as well as those keen to be informed about general news on a weekly basis. In terms of its market, this new paper seemed convinced that it had hit on a new trick. Hitherto, it claimed, in its first edition, there had been two forms of journalism: 'Journalism for the rich man and journalism for the poor', while the *NOTW* intended to span that divide adding, in a phrase that would identify its editorial ambition up to its closure, that it would: 'tell the truth to all and of all.' As pointed out, newspapers discussed so far in this chapter were directed predominantly at the working and lower-middle classes; it was not really until Harmsworth's *Daily Mail* that we would see a commercial newspaper product that could successfully harness the mass market across both the political and social range.

However, the culturally and socially inclusive aspects of the opening editorial claims of the *NOTW* did have a resonance that in retrospect is worth exploring in greater detail. The word 'journalism' had only been recently imported into the English language and, according to one commentator, it was precisely to encompass the yoking together of the high and the low that this new word was coined. Journalism was setting out to combine popular culture and political information in a commercially driven, generic experiment.[13] The lived experience of newspaper owners and other periodical publishers would have told them that there was a distinct appetite for such a blend,[14] and this newly coined word would begin to provide a name for this successful brew.

From 1843, the *NOTW* quickly established itself as a liberal critic of government policy, with the Crimean War providing an early opportunity to practise this stance.[15] In their provision of news from abroad, Sunday newspapers could be at an advantage as they had more time to collect, synthesise and process a variety of reports from their own and other news sources in the pre-telegraph era.

The context of its launch was as important for the long-standing place that it eventually secured at the heart of British popular culture as it was initially a Sunday newspaper devoted to a blend of news from the criminal courts, the bankruptcy courts, society and the military establishment, together with accounts of sensational events such as fires and criminal activity as well as translations and summaries of sensational literature, trading on the commercial and populist tradition of the radical press of the late eighteenth and early nineteenth centuries. In addition, it managed to incorporate within this blend ample coverage of parliamentary and foreign news, and non-sensational aspects of domestic news such as financial information, gazettes and markets well into the 1870s. Like its imitators and rivals, the *NOTW* had to develop a cautionary approach to public affairs holding its balance on the high wire between the boundaries of public tolerance and profitability; delivering sensational material while moralising on behalf of its readers.

Victorian Sunday newspapers – generic patterns

Berridge claimed in 1978 that the popular Sunday papers of the second half of the nineteenth century are an 'important and – in general – neglected area of the press'.[16] This remains the case, by and large, 37 years later. This neglect is a significant loss to cultural and scholarly debate since the Sunday newspapers provide many important indicators of how popular newspaper culture developed into the tabloid era. Beyond their content, they provide an illustration of how social class and politics became structured for mass markets in the press, in a characteristically British fashion. She claimed that mass-circulation Sunday newspapers, 'marked a synthesis between the old non-political traditions of chap-book and last dying speech and the political radicalism of the unstamped and the Chartist papers'.[17] Furthermore, they extended the cultural tradition of a 'close relationship between the reader and the read',[18] which was transmitted across from the earlier unstamped and Chartist papers to the new working-class Sunday press. In fact, this sense of intimacy would form an essential feature of Newnes's popular publications as the New Journalism began to reshape popular periodical consumption from the early 1880s,[19] and became a familiar strategy in attracting and retaining readers in the tabloid tradition later in the twentieth century.[20]

The new popular Sunday papers provided much direct advice to their readers, sometimes in direct editorial exhortations but particularly in responding to letters on politics, class action and voting. They also ran editorial campaigns on behalf of issues that they knew would resonate with their audience. However, despite their association with the political concerns of their readers, these publications were not political enterprises in themselves. On the contrary, they were clearly much more pragmatically based on a 'Shrewd assessment of the possibilities of an expanding working-class market.'[21] This ensured that content was matched to market, and the papers gave both readers and advertisers what the publishers were convinced would maximise circulation and profit. Nevertheless, each title had its own criteria for the selection of news content, which meant that the audience for sensation was understood slightly differently in each paper's assessment of the market. *Lloyd's* was pro-Protestant and anti-Catholic, *Reynolds's* selection of 'news' and features was governed by anti-aristocracy and pro-republican sentiments and the *NOTW* was notably news rich in comparison. The structural similarities of sensation contributed to a safety first experiment in the construction of audience taste that led to a common denominator approach that Hampton has described as providing a 'representational ideal'.[22]

From a political perspective, Sunday papers were still attracting hostility in 1880, from a veteran Tory quarterly, the *Quarterly Review*, as being full of a radical sounding yet unfocused discontent:

> The staple of the leading articles is discontent – discontent with the laws, with the Constitution, with the governing classes, with the employers of labour, with everything, in short, which is not of the lowest working-man level. Socialism and Republicanism are not indistinctly indicated as the objects to be aimed at in modern politics, and so no opportunity is lost of comparing the virtues of the working-classes with the vices of an 'effete aristocracy.'[23]

Sensation, crime and social status had been regularly and explicitly linked as a means of satirising the corruption, hypocrisies and cruelty of the ruling classes and clergy in France in the years before the French Revolution,[24] and this tradition had its counterpart in the radical press of the early nineteenth century in England. The popular Sundays, directed as they were to the Sunday-reading artisan and working classes, carried the resentments characteristic of these classes at that period, meaning that they were in tone, radical by default.

Key to this radical tone was the style and structure of the stories, which drew on previous scandalous storytelling conventions and which began to shape the political orientation of these narratives for readers. There were clear political consequences in the commercialising of the radical impulse. David Vincent has argued that this emergent popular press played a large part in developing a commercial genre that: 'in translating the discrimination of news into a completely new category of popular leisure coincided with the virtual disappearance of working class politics.'[25]

Peter Brooks has provided a perspective that allows us to consider the structure of stories within these popular newspapers.[26] His interpretation of the dynamics of melodrama is highly relevant for our study. He sees melodrama as a cultural successor, in secular form, to some of the binary divisions of Christianity. It presents a world in which characters take their place unproblematically within one camp or the other: good or evil. In such a simplified, yet emotionally appealing, pattern of narration there is not much potential for exploration of the causes of antisocial or criminal behaviour and even less space for examining any complexity of motivation. The deceptive appeal of this sort of presentation has been described as substituting the 'genuine arousal' of true radicalism with the 'apparent arousal as a cover for eventual if temporary satisfaction'.[27]

Melodramatic narratives tend to be limited to apportioning blame to the inherent weakness or vulnerability of individuals, and represent the world as a narrative of contrasts between good and evil, without much in the way of analysis. Although Judith Knelman argued that melodramatic tropes acted to reveal the darker side to social life in the Victorian era, they did so without any systematic analysis of the causes of injustice and were often used simply to reinforce prevailing standards of behaviour, making them a fundamentally conservative strand of information provision.[28]

Melodrama is an ideal vehicle for what Patricia Hollis has described as a rhetoric rooted in the analytical model of 'old corruption' within the unstamped press.[29] It is a rhetoric that highlights the individual as the primary cause of injustice. Melodramatic form in popular Sunday newspapers did little to incorporate what she identified as a new rhetoric in the 1830s that had begun to articulate analyses of the plight of working people within industrial capitalism. Taking this point further, Anne Humphreys explored how popular narratives actually helped to form early understandings of political discourse for the emerging working class, claiming that, among other features, melodrama helped to structure a political sensitivity that foregrounds personal, exaggerated scenarios and presents them with little in the way of analysis as it is the sensational that predominates for effect.[30] Within the evolving social experiences of the early and mid-nineteenth century, melodrama provided closure around the potential contradictions between capital and community and enabled solutions such as provisional individual escape or punishment, rather than analytical explorations of the times. The success of the two leading exponents of popular Sunday journalism, as the century neared its end, could be explained thus:

> By purveying a mild brand of liberalism with a pro-working class and anti-aristocratic tinge (as did *Lloyd's*), or by the continuation of the type

of outdated radical analysis which appeared in *Reynolds's*... the papers were the effective form of social control that the Establishment had always hoped the popular press might be.[31]

News of the World – the story continues

By 1891, the *NOTW*'s circulation had slumped to approximately 40,000.[32] At this point, it was sold to Henry Lascelles Carr who had a much clearer idea of the potential for the paper. Not only did he turn around the paper's fortunes, he also began a period of stability of ownership, with the paper remaining in the family until 1969; this was probably one of the reasons why it maintained its identity and vigour. It steadily climbed to become a commercial success with 2 million sales a week by the outbreak of the First World War.[33]

What enabled such a triumph in this period of a truly mass market press? How was it different? For a start, it was one of a handful of national Sunday newspapers that continued to span the generality of news and a high degree of sporting expertise. Beyond this, and key to its prominence, was its provision of a sort of investigative journalism that a weekly newspaper had time to research: the sensational and the sordid. It developed from the turn of the twentieth century into a newspaper that specialised in insider stories, digging under the surface and pushing closer to and even beyond the borders of good taste, professional ethics and legal limits. The heroics of undercover investigations added to the reputation of the paper. The *Sunday People* was its main rival at the start of the newspaper circulation wars of the 1920s and 1930s but it fought off this competition, meaning that the position of its main rival was taken over by the *Sunday Pictorial*.[34] At this point, it had become once again, as in the 1840s, the market-leading Sunday newspaper with a distinctively modern identity. This, the newspaper continued to burnish, highly dependent as it was on a skilfully maintained appeal to the residual radicalism of its working-class readership.

It offered cash rewards for information leading to the conviction of criminals and saucy stories about celebrities. It ushered in the journalistic procedures that would evolve into paparazzi culture. It developed, through the 1930s and 1940s, a close set of relationships with nightclub bouncers, policemen, hostesses, nightclub owners, approachable members of the criminal underworld and court employees to guarantee a reliable stream of information on activities from an alternative world to that of its readers. Vicarious excitement was the magical ingredient but it was able, in this blend of crime and punishment, to position itself as a very moral newspaper to both the Establishment and to its paying audience.[35]

It established and maintained a literal bond with its readers, as well as a rhetorical and thematic commonality of interest. For example, from 1942, it ran an advisory bureau to respond to questions from readers on work, legal, educational, medical and marital problems. By 1972, the paper claimed to have responded to 3 million letters.[36] This service was supplanted by the hugely successful agony aunt, Unity Hall. Although other newspapers provided similar services, it was the combination of these features and other aspects of its appeal to a core identity among its readers as part of their weekly lives that provided the special alchemy of its commercial success over its rivals.

What it managed to weave through its content was a consistent and strong common identity across the nation. It was very much in this combination of content, appeal and its specific timing as a Sunday newspaper that it was able to profile itself as a truly national phenomenon and, in terms of commercial success, a unique product: 'as British as roast beef and Yorkshire pudding', as its editor, Stafford Somerfield, phrased it on its front page on 20 October 1968. Its place in national popular culture, evidenced by its huge circulation, bringing it into the majority of homes, was as undeniable as it was problematic for all it revealed about the nation's obsession with sexual gossip and tittle-tattle about the great and the good, enveloped within a newspaper that provided a digest of all the important news of the day. This meant that Orwell could give it pride of place in his account of a typical and nostalgic view of life before the Second World War:

> It is Sunday afternoon before the war. The wife is already asleep in the armchair and the children have been sent out for a nice long walk. You put your feet up on the sofa, settle your spectacles on your nose and open the *News of the World*.[37]

During the Second World War, it had reached a circulation of almost 4.5 million and continued after the war to power ahead of its rivals – both daily and weekly – in achieving a circulation of 8.44 million by June 1950 (Audit Bureau of Circulation). Its combination of sport, celebrity gossip, sordid tales of the rich and even the not-so rich and infamous, meant that by 1950 it had no serious competitor, especially as the most successful daily newspaper at that point, the *Daily Mirror* was increasingly repositioning itself as a more seriously political newspaper. By this time, the *NOTW* had established a tangible and cosy place in the affections of the nation, as an intrinsic and widely recognised part of the national narrative. Its populist, innuendo-driven ribaldry was a perfect complement to two other character-istic British entertainments of the twentieth century: McGill's saucy seaside postcards (1902–62) and the *Carry On* films (1958–79).

What made it distinct was that not only did it report crime but it also successfully involved itself and its readers as lead protagonists in editorial-ised investigations. In these collaborations and elsewhere in the newspaper, it championed the 'little people' and provided them with the vicarious pleas-ures of seeing the high and mighty brought down to Earth with as comical and sensational a flourish as possible: twisting the populist knife. Yet, such residual radicalism as it might claim as a legacy from nineteenth-century tradition had become as much a parody as any realistic social critique. By the late 1950s, it had adopted a sales slogan with an echo of its opening ambitions and an ambivalent promise of an all-exposing populist eye: 'All human life is there.' The high point of this notoriety was the Profumo affair of 1963 and the publication of Christine Keeler's memoirs.

For all its vulgarity and sensationalism, it was at its peak before it was transformed into a tabloid, and its transformation into the compact formula was not as swift as might have been expected. From 1969, Rupert Murdoch, the new owner of both the *Sun* and the *NOTW*, charged editor Larry Lamb with the task of making the former a daily version of the latter.[38] As soon as this process was underway, the position of the weekly paper as a distinctively vulgar contribution to British periodical culture was challenged, by its own stable mate and by rival newspapers striving to test the lower reaches of public tolerance. The *Sun* perfected a 'blue-collar ventriloquism' combining right-wing populist politics, sex, sport and an increasing symbiosis with the world of television that the *NOTW* found difficult to match.[39]

In 1984, perhaps looking to his strategic move to Wapping, Murdoch agreed to shift the weekly to a tabloid format. Relinquishing its popular broadsheet identity sacrificed its last element of distinctiveness in the popular market, when the other tabloids were already catching up fast on the *Sun's* version of sex, sport and sensation. Post-1960s, the audience took a lot more to shock. This meant that as a tabloid the weekly would have to push things much further to maintain its market. By the 1980s, publications such as the *Daily Star* and the *Sunday Sport* had extended the borders of acceptable taste much further than the titillating but relatively domesticated journalism of the *NOTW*. These developments meant that the latter was forced to step too far beyond the tastes of even its most hardened readers, as in the tabloid excesses that led to the Calcutt Enquiry and later the scandal that led to the imprisonment of Royal Editor, Clive Goodman in 2007.[40] It had finally stopped being the family newspaper – spurred on by the newer excesses of the *Sunday Sport* in particular, which seemed to go out of its way to parody the whole popular Sunday newspaper genre.

The shift of popular Sunday newspapers to a tabloid format might have been a survival strategy or, in the case of the *NOTW*, it might have signalled the first stage of its eventual demise. The popular Sunday newspaper and the tabloid genre are not, ultimately, an ideal coupling. As the *Sun* continued on its rise in circulation, a daily version of the *NOTW*, the Sunday stable mate entered a period of relative decline. Paradoxically perhaps, its continued success might have been predicated upon an older image of the role of the Sunday genre, particularly the newspaper's radical, populist rhetoric and its editorial advocacy of ordinary people. Perhaps the restyling of the newspaper in 1984 was an early indication that tabloidisation was not necessarily a one-way street to success, and that at this point the seeds of the destruction of the modern popular Sunday newspaper were sown. At that moment, it began the logic of pushing the boundaries of public taste still further in order to continue to survive in a media marketplace dominated by a daily onslaught of sensation, gossip and tabloid news in most media forms and increasingly, into the twenty-first century, in wider socially mediated formats.

Examining continuities at the end of the line

We will now focus on the final edition of the *NOTW*. Most newspapers dwindle into obscurity before finally being swept out of the circulation tallies of the day. The *NOTW* was different in that it blazed out in a trail of infamy while still the highest selling Sunday newspaper in the country. In fact, its success as a popular Sunday newspaper, a genre so dependent historically on disreputable behaviour, had always been most remarkable when it had been acting at its most reprehensible. It closed, ironically, despite being relatively successful in adapting to a new era in which the boundaries of good taste are being stretched ever further by established media forms competing to keep pace with the new populism of social media and related online forums. However, in attempting to maintain this competitive success, it felt compelled to transgress the acceptable political and cultural norms of the day with catastrophic results for the paper and continuing ramifications for popular newspapers in general.

Despite the many editorial changes down the years, one thing that had retained its prominence was the residual radicalism of the newspaper, siding with the 'ordinary' reader and contributing to a rhetorical support of the underdog rather than in any substantial or political engagement in the underlying causes of the plight of poor or disadvantaged people. Such superficial and emotive sympathy with the superficial circumstances of poverty or misfortune is a common feature across popular commercial periodicals in general. Often this rhetoric was extended to campaigning as, for example, from 1990 when the heroic figure of 'Captain Cash' 'helped the needy and bashed the greedy' in a continuing commitment to the needs of the deserving poor and as a scourge of those masquerading as the 'needy' in a comic-book version of good Samaritanism. Increasingly, from the 1980s onwards, the paper moved from the traditional prurience of the lower classes concerning the affairs of their social betters, as best exemplified in the Profumo affair of 1963, into a more general exploitation of celebrity and eventually came to define celebrity as simply people who were in the paper. The problematic aspect of such a desperate drive to follow the lives of those in their pages reached a nadir in the hacking into the mobile phone of the abducted teenager Milly Dowler, which ultimately led to the *NOTW*'s closure. As a tragic illustration of the logic of this editorial endgame, Milly

Dowler was not a celebrity but a missing teenager who happened to be in the newspaper.

To close the historical loop of this particular newspaper's contribution to popular media culture, what we now need is a brief examination of the narratives that the *NOTW* relates of itself in its closing edition – a self-composed epitaph to a genre. We need to pay particular attention to its explicit assessment of its tradition and its display of the top stories that had made it commercially so successful and culturally so significant. In exploring the *NOTW*'s own editorial account of its contribution to journalism, we will consider the continuities of the established narratives of the popular Sunday press from the early nineteenth century onwards and the extent to which the demise of · this tabloid was a sign that its particular discursive appeal had reached the end of the line. Approaching its closure, it had an average sale of 2.6 million (Audit Bureau of Circulation) but boosted by its notoriety, its final copy sold 3.8 million as a souvenir commemoration issue (Audit Bureau of Circulation). It comprised the newspaper plus a 48-page souvenir pull-out. The newspaper itself is enveloped by front and back page crammed with images of famous, recent front-page scoops. The front page is adorned with the slogan: 'The world's greatest newspaper', while the back page places, in a vernacular reflection of the great Orwell quotation that is reproduced alongside it, the following testimony of a reader, once again stressing the life-long place of the newspaper within the lived reading experiences of ordinary people:

> I have read this paper since I was old enough to read newspapers. I'm 68 now. I cannot imagine Sundays without you. I will always remember the *News of the World* for the good things you have brought to light. I'm sad to say goodbye to my Sunday favourite.[41]

The personalisation of this tribute is matched by the author's repetition of the word 'you' in reference to the newspaper. The reader is literally saying goodbye to a life-long friend.

The Orwell quotation from 1946 is deployed once again and its place on the editorial page of this final edition is justified:

> These are the words of the great author George Orwell. They were written in 1946 but they have been the sentiments of most of the nation for well over a century and a half as this astonishing paper became part of the fabric of Britain, as central to Sunday as a roast dinner. [42]

This same leading article moves quickly to an implicit claim that the newspaper, despite its populist credentials, is very much within the tradition of the 'newspaper of record' most often claimed by the elite politically oriented press:

> We recorded history and we've made history.[43]

It continues its well-crafted, emotional engagement with readers as it employs explicit personalisation and the language of overt sentimentality, continuing a tradition well trodden by the founders of the New Journalism in the 1880s:

> But most of all, on this historic day, after 8,674 editions we'll miss you, our 7.5 million readers.
>
> You've been our life. We've made you laugh, made you cry, made your jaw drop in amazement, informed you, enthralled you and enraged you.
>
> You have been our family, and for years we have been yours, visiting every weekend.
>
> Thank you for your support. We'll miss you more than words can express.
>
> Farewell'.[44]

The final editorial gives a pageant of historical campaigning successes in the same tradition that it had once embraced in support of the soldiers in the Crimean in the 1850s. Its recent Military Covenant and its sending of toys to the children of service men and women in Afghanistan at Christmas are highlighted as particular demonstrations of its unswerving loyalty to the ordinary soldier and his/her family as part of a national community of readers.

Next there comes a double-page spread of recent successful campaigns, which all chime with the self-selected identity of the newspaper. It does this, listing its greatest recent moments very much in binary, melodramatic mode:

> Heroes and Villains
> We've saved children from paedos & nailed 250 evil crooks.[45]

This is accompanied as an insert on the same page on the activities of its celebrated investigative reporter, Mazheer Mahmood:

> Dirty dozen
> CRIMEBUSTER MAZ FINGERS HIS TOP 12 COURT VICTORIES.[46]

It refers to itself as: 'The world's greatest investigative newspaper', while Mazheer Mahmood, otherwise known in characteristically humorous fashion as 'The fake sheikh' is the notable figure in the story. In a world where newspapers and broadcasters have been running scared from both the expense and the fall-out from genuine investigations and veering towards safe and formulaic journalism, there was something both journalistically distinctive and commercially attractive about the *NOTW*'s tenacity in maintaining investigations within the contours of its own traditions. Mahmood's victories might have had sensation and celebrity culture written through their heart but they were well within the established editorial traditions of the paper and they were genuinely of interest to the public and served often to present the Establishment with uncomfortable truths.

One of its most treasured memories of itself is the claim that it helped shape law surrounding parents' rights to know the whereabouts of child sex offenders that became popularised in the paper under the campaign for 'Sarah's Law' after the abduction and murder of Sarah Payne. The appeal of this campaign lies in its combination of the paper's self-appointed role as the protector of the vulnerable in the form of abused children and its complementary role as the scourge of the abusers themselves. Furthermore, it allows the paper to continue to style itself as making law on behalf of the weak and wresting power to legislate from a complacent Establishment. The campaign for 'Sarah's Law' was clearly a modern, pivotal moment of self-rationalisation, carrying all of the paper's claims and maintaining much of the logic of the radical rhetoric that stretched from Reynolds to Stead and beyond within the commercial popular press. To reinforce the populist support generated by this campaign and its demonstration of an actual bond between paper and its readers, the mother of the child provides a moving testimonial to the *NOTW* as part of the final edition. In an article entitled, '*NEWS OF THE WORLD* proved it is a force for good', she explains:

> God only knows why the *News of the World* has stuck by me for so long and for that you'd have to ask them but the reason I have stayed with them is that they have always been a paper that cares and a voice for the people …. It is easy to forget in these dark times that the *News of the World* has often been a force for good and that has more than anything to do with the people that work on it … … they have been as much a part of our Sundays as the roast over the years.[47]

While it is not inconceivable that this piece may have been 'tweaked' by a sub-editor or even written outright by a staffer on the newspaper, the sympathetic tone fits well with the newspaper's projected image and surely at such a moment, in the wake of public disgust at the Milly Dowler phone hacking exposure, we must assume that the piece had at the very least, strong support from the named author. In the article, commissioned especially for this final edition, Sarah Payne, the mother of the murdered child, is drawn to the familiar imagery of the paper's history, repeated in so many of the other articles: a voice for the people, a force for good and as traditional as Sunday roast. These images reinforce longer narratives of the Sunday newspaper as a representative of the views of the ordinary against those in power and an actor in a melodramatic universe that sometimes enables good to triumph after the darkest of days, as well as the location of such rhetoric at the heart of popular narratives of national identification.

The souvenir edition is heralded by a facsimile of the first front page of the *NOTW* with an additional humorous punning: 'Old the front page', which indicates that this historical account is certainly to be read within the irreverent tone of the contemporary paper.

The 48-page souvenir pullout gives a timeline from 1843 to the present displayed in historic front pages.

Not all of these pageants are of serious scoops or the breaking of important political news. In keeping with its other more sexualised tradition, it cheekily but knowingly inserts a celebration of its own Murdoch-inspired page three tradition.[48] Throughout the paper there are billboard-style inserts entitled 'Why I'll miss my News of the World' with readers' comments inserted, further reinforcing the idea, visually this time, that this was a paper that had actually bonded in a meaningful and demonstrable way with its readers, a paper that even in its demise was in receipt of its readers' best wishes, in communication with them in a set of vernacular funeral orations.

The champion of the people is also defensive of the tabloid genre itself, which it claims is under attack from people who disregard these sorts of newspapers because they have no respect for their readers. Carole Malone expresses her concerns thus:

> So, it's the End – a cruel, terrible, excruciating end for this journalistic giant which is so much more than just a newspaper.
>
> And, even as I write, I cannot believe this will be the last ever edition of what, for decades, has been one of the great British institutions...
>
> I know there have always been those who hate the *News of the World*, who hated our politics, our power, the kind of stories we ran.
>
> But they're the people who hate the existence of **ALL** tabloids, who sneer at the people who read them, who dismiss everything they do as irresponsible and fatuous...
>
> This has always been a paper for the working man and woman, a loud-mouthed, never-give-up campaigner that could always be counted on to be on the side of those that needed it to be.[49]

The narrative style that its stories represent to its community of readers presents a world exposed to the vagaries of 'existential anarchy',[50] and the *NOTW* takes on the mantle as the conduit for at least rhetorical support for the victims of the world's arbitrariness or simply supplies howls of outrage. Away from the eulogies, self-congratulation and reminiscences, the final stories of the paper proper are still drawn from the Sunday tabloid catalogue, from the xenophobic to the grotesque to the downright bizarre.

Describing a sex trafficker allows the newspaper to deploy its alliterative lexicon to make its point better:

MR PIG

The bulging Bulgarian growing fat selling sex slaves to Britain.[51]

The celebrity column 'XS' contains a characteristic range of soap opera stories, spin-offs from other television shows such as *The Apprentice* and speculation about the Royal family all straining to be a little more risqué or intrusive than its rivals. There is a familiar tabloid top-ten feature on Britain's greatest inventions, and a punningly grotesque story of a tiny baby which both in their complemetary ways illustrate the tabloid pattern:

Cream of Britain

CUSTARD BISCUIT, FISH FINGERS & SMILEY POTATO FACES NAMED AS OUR GREATEST INVENTIONS.[52]

EXCLUSIVE: THE 1-IN-A-100 tot

Miracle of the living Barbie doll [with actual size photo at birth 19 cms].[53]

S.J. Taylor, writing presciently of a longer cultural process in 1992, bemoaned the demise of a vibrant American popular press, which had disintegrated because it became too respectable for its readers' tastes in the face of competition from television and celebrity periodical formats, leaving the supermarket tabloids as the only home for the sort of racy and sensational coverage that readers had sought in their newspapers over the years:

The lesson from America is that, without the tabloids and their spirit of irreverence, the press becomes a bastion of conformity dedicated to lofty purposes understood only by a few, an instrument for and by the élite – a danger sign for any society.

The lesson for Britain is that when the tabloids go too far, society seeks to control them, and press freedom for one and all comes under threat.

This book celebrates the tabloid press, its nervy, irreverent and frequently outrageous sensationalizing of the news.

For America, it's an elegy; for Britain, an apology.

It's a record of the last of the good old days.[54]

The *NOTW* is gone. It is possible that, under pressure to compete in a media-saturated world where social media provide a level of intrusion on a scale unimaginable even ten years ago, it was inevitably going to be found stretching itself too far in pandering to a taste that it had to helped establish for the sensational, and for the hidden inside of a story revealed on behalf of its readers. What it maintained to the end, however, is an insistence that within that muckraking tradition, no matter how badly it ended, there was an appeal to, and a representation of, the interests of ordinary people against those of the Establishment. Its opening promise from 1843: 'tell the truth to all and of all' was still echoed in its final edition. Residual radicalism had had its day.

Notes

1. S. Koss, *The Rise and Fall of the Political Press in Britain. Volume 1: The Nineteenth Century*, London, 1981.
2. D.S. Kamper, 'Popular Sunday Newspapers: respectability and working class culture in late Victorian Britain', in M. Huggins and J. Mangan (eds), *Disreputable Pleasures*, London, 2004, pp. 83–102.
3. D. Harvey, *The Beginnings of a Commercial Sporting Culture in Britain, 1793–1850*. Aldershot, 2004.
4. Harvey.
5. J.H. Wiener, *The War of the Unstamped: The Movement to Repeal the British Newspaper Tax, 1830–1836*, Ithaca, NY, 1969, pp. 175–76.
6. J.H. Wiener, *The Americanization of the British Press, 1830s–1914: Speed in the Age of Transatlantic Journalism*, Basingstoke, 2011, p. 45.
7. P.R. Hoggart, 'Edward Lloyd, the father of the cheap press', the *Dickensian*, 80, 1984, 33–38.
8. C. Bainbridge. and R. Stockdill, *The News of the World Story: 150 Years 1843–1993*, London, 1993.
9. L. James, 'Reynolds, George William MacArthur (1814–1879),' *Oxford Dictionary of National Biography*, Oxford, 2004; online edn, May 2008 [http://www.oxforddnb.com/view/article/23414, accessed 25 Feb 2015]
10. A. Humpherys and L. James, *G.W.M. Reynolds, Nineteenth Century Fiction, Politics and the Press*, Aldershot, 2008.
11. M. Conboy, *Tabloid Britain Constructing a Community Through Language*, Abingdon, 2006, pp. 14–45.
12. A. Jones, *Powers of the Press: Newspapers, Power and the Public in Nineteenth Century England*, Aldershot, 1996, pp. 28–46.
13. K. Campbell, 'Journalistic discourses and constructions of modern knowledge', in L. Brake, B. Bell and D. Finkelstein (eds), *Nineteenth Century Media and the Construction of Identities*, 2000, pp. 40–53.
14. D. Vincent, *Literacy and Popular Culture*, Cambridge, 1993, p. 246.
15. Bainbridge and Stockdill, *The News of the World*, p. 72.
16. V. Berridge, 'Popular Sunday papers and mid-Victorian society', in G. Boyce, J. Curran and P. Wingate (eds), *Newspaper History: from the seventeenth century to the present day*, London, 1978, pp. 247–64.
17. Ibid., p. 247.
18. Ibid., p. 251.
19. K. Jackson, *George Newnes and the New Journalism in Britain, 1880–1910: Culture and Profit*, Aldershot, 2001, p. 13.

20. A. Bingham and M. Conboy, 'The *Daily Mirror* and the creation of a commercial popular language: a people's war and a people's paper?', *Journalism Studies*. 10 (5), 2009, 639–54; P. Chippendale and C. Horrie, *Stick It Up Your Punter: The Rise and fall of the* Sun, London, 1992, pp. 147–48.
21. Berridge, 'Popular', p. 253.
22. M. Hampton, *Visions of the Press in Britain, 1850–1950*, Champaign, IL, 2004, pp. 1–18.
23. T. Catling,'The Newspaper Press', *Quarterly Review*, 150, 1880, pp. 521–22.
24. R. Darnton, *The Forbidden Bestsellers of Pre-Revolutionary France*, London, 1997.
25. Vincent, *Literacy*, p. 252.
26. P. Brooks, *The Melodramatic Imagination*, New York, 1984, p. 16.
27. R. Williams, 'Radical/respectable', in *The Press We Deserve*, London, 1970, p. 21.
28. J. Knelman, 'Subtly sensational: a study of early Victorian crime reporting,' *Journal of Newspaper and Periodical History* 8 (1), 1992, 35.
29. P. Hollis, *The Pauper Press*, Oxford, 1970, p. vii.
30. A. Humpherys, 'Popular narrative and popular discourse in *Reynolds's Weekly Newspaper,'* in L. Brake, A. Jones and L. Madden (eds.), *Investigating Victorian Journalism*, Basingstoke, 1990, p. 42.
31. Berridge, 'Popular', p. 256.
32. Bainbridge and Stockdill, *The News of the World*, p. 72.
33. Ibid., p. 86.
34. Ibid.
35. A. Bingham, *Family Newspapers? Sex, Private Life and the British Popular Press 1918–1978* Oxford, 2009, pp. 127–133.
36. Bainbridge and Stockdill, *The News of the World*, p. 133.
37. G. Orwell, 'Decline of the English Murder', *Tribune*, 15 February 1946, p. 48
38. Chippendale and Horrie, *Stick It*, p. 7.
39. M. Conboy, *The Language of Newspapers: socio-historical perspectives,* London, 2010 p. 127.
40. R. Snoddy, *The Good, The Bad and the Unacceptable*, London, 1993.
41. *News of the World*, 10 July 2011, p. 17
42. Ibid., p. 3.
43. Ibid., p. 3.
44. Ibid., p. 3.
45. Ibid., pp. 4–5.
46. Ibid., p. 5.
47. Ibid., p. 6.
48. Ibid., p. 9.
49. Ibid., p. 19.
50. J. Langer, *Tabloid Television: Popular Journalism and the 'Other News'*, London, 1998, p. 157.
51. *News of the World*, 10 July 2011, p. 17.
52. Ibid., p. 33.
53. Ibid., p. 21.
54. S.J. Taylor, *Shock! Horror! The Tabloids in Action*, London, 1992, pp. 17–18.

8
Passports to Oblivion: J.M. Staniforth's Political Cartoons for the *News of the World,* 1893–1921

Chris Williams

> Mr. J.M. Staniforth, caricaturist of the News of the World and the Western Mail, occupies the probably unique position of a draughtsman whose work circulates in millions of copies and is seen by many millions of people each week.
>
> The *Strand Magazine*, May 1914[1]

> For 30 years, cartoons by 'J.M.S.' have appeared in the 'News of the World,' and his familiar initials are known wherever the 'News of the World' circulates – that is to say, throughout the world. We know from many a reader living in the outposts of Empire how keenly these cartoons have been appreciated and that many a shack and cabin in the back blocks of the world are decorated with them.
>
> *News of the World*, 18 December 1921

Joseph Morewood Staniforth was born at Gloucester on 16 May 1863 to a saw repairer/cutler and his wife. Staniforth grew up in Cardiff, and left school at 15 to become a printer's apprentice with the *Western Mail*.[2] His emerging talent as an illustrator led to his transfer to the paper's editorial team and his employment as an occasional and then a regular cartoonist, both for the *Western Mail* and its sister paper the *Evening Express* and, from 1893 onwards, for the *News of the World* (*NOTW*). Although occasionally interrupted by illness (he suffered from tuberculosis and heart problems), Staniforth's work appeared very regularly for both the Cardiff daily and the British Sunday until his death on 17 December 1921. Many cartoons were also republished in stand-alone volumes – examples include *The General Election, 1895* (1895), *Cartoons of the Welsh Coal Strike* (1898), *Cartoons of the Boer War* (two volumes, 1900, 1902) and *Cartoons of the War* (seven volumes,

1914–15) – and other work appeared in the form of picture postcards and illustrations for magazines, pamphlets and books.[3]

Contemporary appreciation of Staniforth's talents was considerable. The polymath Thomas Henry Thomas ranked the cartoonist alongside more conventional artists Goscombe John and Christopher Williams, going on to suggest that 'in power of instant characterisation and insight, and skill of artistic touch, he hardly cedes to that acknowledged master in this quality – the late Phil May.'[4] *Wales* magazine considered Staniforth's cartoons 'one of the most popular features in British journalism',[5] and when, in 1919, the *Western Mail* celebrated its fiftieth anniversary, a host of contributors, including Labour MPs and trade unionists, paid their tributes to 'Staniforth's genius'.[6] On his death comparisons were drawn between this 'doyen of British cartoonists' and (variously) Hogarth, Gillray, Leech and Tenniel. Staniforth, it was suggested, possessed 'incomparable genius as the portrayer and critic of public men and public events'. For Prime Minister David Lloyd George, Staniforth was 'one of the most distinguished cartoonists of his generation', who had rendered 'great national service'.[7]

Sir Osbert Lancaster, cartoonist of the *Daily Express*, once said that '[a] professional preoccupation with the topical is the surest passport to oblivion',[8] and, despite the high repute in which he was held during his lifetime, for many decades after his death J.M. Staniforth was largely forgotten. Since the 1970s, a number of biographers of Lloyd George and historians of (mainly) Wales have used the cartoons purely for illustrative purposes: that is, without discussing their intrinsic qualities and usually failing to acknowledge the identity of the cartoonist himself. Occasionally examples of Staniforth's work have been included in anthologies of cartoons such as Frank E. Huggett's *Cartoonists at War* (1981) but without any sustained assessment of his contribution.

This situation began to change with Joanne Cayford's Ph.D. thesis on the *Western Mail*, and Hywel Teifi Edwards's work on images of the Welsh collier.[9] The first sustained evaluation of Staniforth's artistic contribution was subsequently provided by Peter Lord, who termed 'J.M.S.' 'the most important visual commentator on Welsh affairs ever to work in the country', whose cartoons 'reflected, perhaps more accurately than any other visual source, the diversity of Welsh life in the period'.[10]

If historians of Wales have slowly begun to take notice of 'J.M.S.', and especially of his work in the most successful Welsh daily newspaper of the period, the *Western Mail*, it is fair to say that his 'British' cartooning has been subject to comparatively meagre investigation. Timothy Benson does use a number of Staniforth's *NOTW* cartoons in his *The Cartoon Century*, and Glenn Wilkinson, in his work on depictions of war in Edwardian newspapers, also considers the *NOTW*, although like many before him, he shows no interest in the identity of the cartoonist responsible for the images that he analyses.[11] Historians of the *NOTW* itself have only rarely touched upon the topic: Matthew Engel mentions the revamp of the 1890s (on which more below) as putting a cartoon on the front page,[12] and Cyril Bainbridge and Roy Stockdill refer in passing to 'a history of the Boer War, told in a hundred cartoons' (there were two volumes).[13]

This chapter, then, is the first attempt to survey and analyse the entire cartoon corpus of 'J.M.S.' as it appeared in the *NOTW*. It does so within the context of an understanding of the cartoonist's entire career, and the relationship that he had with the *Western Mail* as well as that with the Sunday paper. It begins by establishing the parameters of Staniforth's contribution, and by tabulating the key characteristics of his approach as a political cartoonist. Some attention is then paid to the largely invisible nature of the editorial process by which original artwork was transformed into printed cartoon, and the extent to which the artist's original intentions may have been mediated or influenced by other editorial personnel. A third avenue of investigation is afforded by the artistic, cultural, literary and musical references carried by the cartoons, which may tell us something not only of the intellectual horizons of the cartoonist himself, but also of his readers. A final section then examines in greater depth Staniforth's approach to the central topic of political choice (as amplified through cartoons produced during the six General Election campaigns of his *NOTW* career).

There are limitations – imposed by the nature of the surviving sources – on what may be stated with confidence about Staniforth's cartooning. The artist himself left virtually no personal papers. The newspapers in which the cartoons appeared hardly ever made explicit reference to the artwork itself. The News International Record Office contains only fragmentary archival material that sheds very limited light on the editorial process by which the cartoons were handled, although the nominal ledgers do tell us that he was the best paid visual artist working for the paper, earning £19 10s. every quarter from 1910, rising to £54 12s. a quarter by the end of his life.[14] Of necessity, the analysis contained here relies predominantly on the corpus of published cartoons, set within the context of the editions of the newspapers themselves.

J.M. Staniforth's first cartoon to appear in the *NOTW* was published on 9 July 1893. 'Britannia's Blessings' celebrated the marriage of Prince George, Duke of York, and Princess Mary of Teck (later King George V and Queen Mary). The first few cartoons appeared on inside pages, but from 'The Modern Laocoön' (commenting on industrial strife, 10 September 1893) they moved to the front page.[15] This was part of a significant recasting of the newspaper's 'look' by its new proprietorial team (Henry Lascelles Carr, George Riddell, Emsley Carr and Edgar Fifoot) who, according to R. Power Berrey, 'by their enterprise, initiative and ingenuity' turned what had been an ailing prospect 'into a virile attractive news sheet' in the course of a few years.[16] Prior to this date the front page had been divided between four columns of advertisements and three of political news – short pieces of usually no more than one paragraph. However, from 10 September the front page was given over entirely to news. Below the newspaper's title was a banner, that changed regularly, drawing attention to prizes, competitions or the fact that (as was stated many times in the autumn of 1893) the *NOTW* 'Contains More News Than Any Other Weekly Paper.' Below the banner, centrally placed, were the cartoons. There they stayed throughout Staniforth's career – only two (additional) cartoons appearing anywhere else[17] – his last cartoon ('The Prodigal's Return', about the Irish Free State's acceptance of Dominion Status within the British Empire: see Figure 8.1) being published on 11 December 1921, the Sunday before his death.[18]

Figure 8.1   'The Prodigal's Return', 11 December 1921

John Bull: 'The Fatted Calf won't have a dog's chance, my boy.' Almost the identical image, with the exception of the lettering on the bag ('Canadian 2nd Regiment Queen's Own Rifles' instead of 'The Prodigal Son'), on the door ('London' instead of 'British Empire'), and the hat worn by the cub (a military cap) had appeared under the title 'A Cub From Over The Seas' in the *News of the World* on 18 September 1910. Caption: The Old 'Un: 'Ah! my boy, I am delighted to see you! I only wish more of your brother-cubs would follow your example'

Table 8.1 provides precise information on the total number and frequency of Staniforth cartoons appearing in the *NOTW* between July 1893 and December 1921. The pattern has its inconsistencies – there were years (1897, 1898, 1913, 1914) when rather fewer Staniforths appeared than was common for most of his career – but the overall record of more than 1,200 cartoons means that the work of 'J.M.S.' appeared on the front page of what became Britain's biggest-selling Sunday approximately four weeks out of every five.[19] In three cases (1900, 1904 and 1906), he produced a cartoon for every Sunday of the year. This is a remarkable record that allows for a longevity and consistency of analysis that is rarely possible with political cartoonists. When Staniforth's *NOTW* cartoons are considered alongside over 6,000 *Western Mail* cartoons (1889–1921) and nearly 3,000 *Evening*

Table 8.1 Number and frequency of Staniforth cartoons in the *News of the World*, 1893–1921

Year	Number of cartoons	Frequency of cartoons (%)
1893	26	100
1894	52	100
1895	46	88.5
1896	51	98.1
1897	20	38.5
1898	15	28.8
1899	49	92.5
1900	52	100
1901	49	94.2
1902	44	84.6
1903	50	96.2
1904	52	100
1905	51	96.2
1906	52	100
1907	48	92.3
1908	48	92.3
1909	47	90.4
1910	39	75.0
1911	38	71.7
1912	35	67.3
1913	22	42.3
1914	20	38.5
1915	34	65.4
1916	41	77.4
1917	39	75.0
1918	50	96.2
1919	49	94.2
1920	45	86.5
1921	49	94.2
Total	1213	81.6

Note: Frequency: the number of cartoons divided by the number of Sundays in the year (or part year, for 1893 and 1921).

Express illustrations (1887–1901) then it is possible to agree with the *NOTW* obituarist who judged that '[p]robably no other cartoonist has ever drawn so many or has been so fertile in ideas'.[20]

Staniforth was, overwhelmingly, a political cartoonist. That is, he sought to comment on the great and pressing issues of the day, and only occasionally allowed himself to be diverted by sport, fashion or (even, in the *NOTW*) scandal. Table 8.2 presents an attempt to categorise Staniforth's cartoons according to their subject matter. Few of these categories are watertight, and some cartoons have to be included under more than one heading, but the general pattern is clear enough. Politics, diplomacy and war constituted the staple diet of this cartoonist, with economic and industrial issues also looming large. Even the label of 'social and cultural issues' is here applied to matters that often had political resonance: education policy, the demand for better housing, old age pensions and proposals for temperance legislation or for measures to soak up unemployment. 'Miscellaneous' covers generalised comment on the seasons, the weather and on sport (rugby football, yachting and boxing appeared most frequently).

Given the prominence of the two major wars of the period, as well as the generalised peacetime threat to Britain's global security that was a staple of public discussion in Edwardian (if not late Victorian) Britain, it should come as no surprise that Table 8.3 shows that Kaiser Wilhelm II of Germany was the

Table 8.2   Subjects of cartoons, 1893–1921

Subject	Total number of cartoons	Percentage of total
British domestic politics	206	16.7
International affairs and conflicts*	201	16.3
First World War and its aftermath	186	15.1
South African War and its aftermath	151	12.2
British economy and industrial relations	135	10.9
British Empire, monarchy, armed forces	110	8.9
Social and cultural issues	94	7.6
Ireland	56	4.5
Miscellaneous	96	7.8

Note: *Not including either the First World War or the South African War.

Table 8.3   International leaders caricatured

	Total number of caricatures
Kaiser Wilhelm II	107
Tsar Nicholas II	34
Paul Kruger	33
Woodrow Wilson	10

Table 8.4 National stereotypes caricatured

National stereotype	Total number of caricatures
John Bull	375
Cousin Jonathan/Uncle Sam	72
Marianne	58
Russia	40
Britannia	37
Herr Fritz	34
France	33
Turkey	33
Italy	27
Austria-Hungary	23
Japan	19
Russian Bear	16
Germania	15
Erin/Ireland	14
Greece	13
British Lion	12
Bulgaria	11
Serbia	9
British Bulldog	8
China	8
Dame Wales	7

Table 8.5 British and Irish politicians/public figures caricatured

	Total number of caricatures
David Lloyd George	130
Herbert Henry Asquith	104
Arthur Balfour	97
Sir Henry Campbell-Bannerman	76
Lord Rosebery	71
Joseph Chamberlain	66
William Harcourt	63
Lord Salisbury	45
John Redmond	25
John Morley	23
Austen Chamberlain	22
Lord Kitchener	17
Lord Roberts	16
King Edward VII	16
Winston Churchill	15
Andrew Bonar Law	13
King George V	12
Edward Grey	12
William Ewart Gladstone	11
William Hicks-Beach	10

Figure 8.2   'Steady Pressure', 30 July 1899

This cartoon first appeared in the *Evening Express* of 24 July 1899 titled 'Time For A Rest', and with the following caption:

OUTLANDER: 'Can't you squeeze him a little more, we don't think that's enough.'

JOE, THE OPERATOR: 'No, I think you ought to be satisfied. I've squeezed him as much as ever he'll stand at present.'

When it appeared in the *News of the World* under its revised title, it carried the following caption:

OUTLANDER: 'Can't you squeeze him a little more, we don't think that's enough.'

JOE, THE OPERATOR: 'He'll have to "give" a lot more, 'ere I've done with him.'

Figure 8.3   'Preparing for the New Session', 8 February 1914

The cartoon was uncaptioned, but for today's readers the politicians are (clockwise, from top left): Asquith, Bonar Law, Lloyd George, Churchill, Edward Carson, John Redmond.

Figure 8.4 'The Pied Piper of South Africa', 1 February 1903

This cartoon appeared first in the *Western Mail*, on 28 January 1903. The captioning for both newspapers was identical.

'All the little boys and girls ...
Tripping and skipping, ran merrily after
The wonderful music, with shouting and laughter.
     For he led us, he said, to a joyous land,
Where waters gushed and fruit trees grew,
And flowers put forth a fairer hue,
And everything was strange and new.'

(Robert Browning)

'I, who have seen so much of the war, could never have believed it possible that the man who was execrated a year ago would be welcomed so heartily to-day. He seems to exercise a curious fascination over the rough sons of the veldt.' – Press Correspondent at Ventersdorp.

This image was republished in *Cartoons* (Cardiff, 1908), p. 27, with the additional caption 'Remarkable enthusiasm was raised amongst all sections in South Africa by Mr Chamberlain's conciliatory speeches, and by his promises on behalf of the Government during his tour through the country.'

most frequently drawn international leader, with Tsar Nicholas II of Russia and President Paul Kruger of the Transvaal (who features in Figures 8.2 and 8.9) some considerable distance behind. Readers of the *NOTW* might well be expected to recognise such individuals, but in common with existing traditions of Victorian cartooning, Staniforth also made heavy use of national stereotypes, as reflected in Table 8.4. A number of nations and states might be represented by a cluster of different images: in addition to the Kaiser, therefore, Germany also took the form of the moustachioed Herr Fritz, the usually matronly Germania and (though not shown in the table) animals such as the eagle and the Dachshund. John Bull was by far and away the most popular stereotypical character employed (see Figure 8.10), but he might be complemented (or replaced) occasionally by Britannia, a lion (as in Figure 8.1) or a bulldog. France appeared as Marianne, as a uniformed male (here simply 'France') and elsewhere as a cockerel or a poodle.

Other non-national stereotypes were also employed. Most frequently drawn was the goddess 'Peace' (31 appearances), rivalled by her opposites 'Bellona' and 'Mars' (together 12 appearances). Father Christmas's advent was seasonal (17 appearances) and Father Time has been spotted on 10 occasions. Other abstract concepts used included 'Justice', 'Civilisation', 'Victory' and 'Humanity'.

Staniforth's preoccupation with politics and statesmanship, both domestic and international, also emerges strongly from Table 8.5, which lists the frequency with which recognisable politicians and other public figures appear, Figure 8.3 being a favourite ensemble portrait by the cartoonist himself. Prime Ministers (or politicians who became Prime Minister at some point during Staniforth's lifetime) occupy seven of the top eight places, Joseph Chamberlain (who made, broke and sired prime ministers) being the understandable exception (see Figure 8.4, and also Figures 8.2, 8.5, 8.6 and 8.7). The prevalence of Irish issues, especially Home Rule, accounts for the high profile of John Redmond, and the South African and First World Wars put Lords Kitchener (see Figure 8.7) and Roberts in the limelight. Chancellors of the Exchequer, responsible of course for the imposition and adjustment of direct and indirect taxation, were often caricatured – Austen Chamberlain, Andrew Bonar Law and William Hicks-Beach ran into double figures (although Bonar Law's claims to fame ran beyond No. 11 Downing Street), and others who were drawn included Reginald McKenna and Charles Ritchie. There is, inevitably, a very long list of those who were drawn on fewer than ten occasions, and honourable mentions should go to Henry Labouchère, Keir Hardie, Cecil Rhodes and Sir Douglas Haig. Individuals who were neither politicians, generals nor monarchs but who were sufficiently well known to be caricatured included the fraudster Jabez Balfour (admittedly also a politician), nurse Edith Cavell and Oscar Wilde. Historic personalities were rarely drawn, but exceptions were made for William Shakespeare, Horatio Nelson and Napoleon Bonaparte. Jesus Christ made just one appearance in 'Heaping up Wrath' – on 13 September 1896 – the topic being the Armenian massacres.

Staniforth's visual style was of its time – to a modern reader the cartoons can appear cluttered, text heavy and sometimes painfully heavy handed. They were rarely subtle, although they could contain ambiguities, intended or not.[21] Their value is to be found not so much in their (generally highly competent) draughtsmanship, even less in their (only occasional) artistic originality, but in the political and cultural messages that they embodied. To understand those messages, however, it is first necessary to say some-thing about the creative process and the editorial transformations to which it may have been subject.

For the bulk of his career, J.M. Staniforth worked from his home in north Cardiff, moving to Lynton in Devon in 1919. One may suggest with reasonable confidence that any direct contact with *NOTW* editorial staff in London would have been no more than occasional. There is nothing to indicate that he received any instruction or guidance on what to draw, either from the editors of the *Western Mail* or from Emsley Carr at the *NOTW*. His cartoons were drawn, titled, captioned and then sent to the newspapers' offices in Cardiff and London. Largely, Staniforth drew sepa-rate cartoons for the *NOTW* and the *Western Mail* or *Evening Express*. But in several years at least some of what appeared in the *NOTW* had already appeared in (normally) the *Western Mail*. This happened on 20 occasions in 1894, on 11 in 1895 and a further 11 in 1896. Then for almost three years (from the end of September 1896) there was no duplication at all, but from 3 September 1899 until the end of 1903 all but 17 Staniforth cartoons that found their way into the Sunday paper had already appeared the previous week in a Cardiff publication. Then, suddenly, this duplica-tion stopped, and it hardly ever happened again during the remainder of Staniforth's career.

It is difficult to explain such a pattern, although the death of Lascelles Carr in 1902 might have given his nephew Emsley the opportunity to review the custom of duplicating *Western Mail* cartoons in the Sunday paper. Where duplication occurred it facilitates some insight into the degree to which the *NOTW* editorial team might have subjected Staniforth's originals to revi-sion. There is no evidence of any artwork being modified. Rather, titles and captions were sometimes changed, usually with the object of making the cartoon's meaning more obvious to what was presumably thought to be a less sophisticated audience.[22] To take an example, on 2 September 1903 the *Western Mail* carried a Staniforth cartoon – 'A Mirth-Provoking Document' – that purported to reflect German hilarity at the revelations contained in the Royal Commission on the War in the South Africa. This appeared with caption unchanged under the title 'As Others See Us' in the *NOTW* on 6 September 1903.[23]

Such transformations might be considered relatively innocuous, but there were three examples where the change of a title and caption transforms the original cartoon's putative meaning. One is provided in Figure 8.2 (above). 'Time for a Rest' in the *Evening Express* on 24 July 1899 clearly suggests that it would now be advisable to allow Paul Kruger to reflect on the crisis between Britain and the Transvaal. However, the same cartoon appeared in the *NOTW* six days later entitled 'Steady Pressure', with Colonial Secretary Joseph Chamberlain determined to force more concessions from the Boer leader. Almost certainly, any changes to the title and caption had been made in London, presumably without Staniforth's consent. What makes disentangling this process more complicated is that the diplomatic context for the two cartoons was fluid. Thus, on 19 July, it was widely reported in the press that the Transvaal Volksraad was about to enfranchise Uitlanders (non-Boer settlers) who had been resident there for seven years. Chamberlain believed that, on the basis of this concession, war could be avoided, and issued a brief statement that 'the crisis in the relations between Great Britain and the Transvaal may be regarded as ended.' The Council of the Uitlanders in Johannesburg responded by imploring the Colonial Office to stick to the demand for a shorter – five-year – term of residence. This is, presumably, an explanation for the first version of the cartoon.[24] However, by the time the same image appeared in the *NOTW* Chamberlain's position had shifted, and in a speech in the House of Commons on 28 July he stated that the 'humiliating inferiority' of British subjects in the Transvaal could not remain unremedied, irrespective of the precise terms of enfranchisement.[25] Such a statement, at least, goes some of the way to explain the retitling and recaptioning of the image, and the consequent transformation of its meaning.

A later cartoon from the South African War offers an example of a much blunter transformation. 'Poor Luck' (*Western Mail*, 16 May 1901) depicted Kitchener as master of a fishing smack, bemoaning the fact that he had caught only a dozen 'Boer commando' fish. When the same cartoon (with no more fish in the net) appeared under the title 'Gathering Them In' in the *NOTW* on 19 May Kitchener was suddenly optimistic: 'A few more of these hauls and there'll be none left.'[26]

A third example is provided by Figure 8.5, which appeared as 'But – ' in the *NOTW* on 11 October 1903, and shows both an agricultural and an industrial worker responding with scepticism to a speech made by Joseph Chamberlain at Glasgow on 7 October in which he set out his proposals for preferential tariffs.[27] The *NOTW* editorial that Sunday was of similar mind:

> He proposes to tax such necessaries as bread and meat, and to reduce taxes on tea, coffee and similar foodstuffs…. He adduces certain figures…to show the net result of this shuffling of tariffs. These figures…are not proofs of anything. It will require a vast array of statistics to prove to the people of England that there is any advantage in reducing the size of their loaf and leg of mutton, in order to enlarge the teapot.[28]

Figure 8.5   'But –', 11 October 1903

This cartoon first appeared in the *Western Mail* of 8 October 1903 titled 'Beyond All Expectations' and with the following caption:

PROFESSOR CHAMBERLAIN: 'And now, gentlemen, I have explained how the feat is done. By putting a tax on food you naturally expect to be losers, but I have clearly demonstrated that instead of losing you will be gainers by the transaction. Out of the hat I have drawn a united, prosperous and glorious Empire, together with twopence's a week profit for you, Mr Hodge, and twopence halfpenny profit for you, Mr Artisan!'

When it appeared in the *News of the World* under its revised title, it carried the following caption:

PROFESSOR CHAMBERLAIN: 'And now, gentlemen, as you see, out of this wonderful hat comes a little profit for each of you!'

MESSRS HODGE AND ARTISAN: 'Ah! yes, guv'nor, but have you got anything up your sleeve?'

Yet the original *Western Mail* cartoon, 'Beyond All Expectations', may be read in a much more positive light, for out of the hat 'Professor Chamberlain' draws not just 'a little profit' (as in 'But –') but 'a united, prosperous and glorious Empire' as well. In general 'J.M.S.' was, in his cartoons, a strong (if not unequivocal) supporter of Chamberlain over the issue of tariff reform, and it seems probable that the first incarnation of this image represented his response to the Glasgow speech, a response evidently not shared by the editorial staff of the *NOTW*.

The non-appearance of *Western Mail* cartoons in the *NOTW* after 1903 makes the only other source of information on the editorial process a small collection of 11 original drawings held in the News International Record Office.[29] These have Staniforth's own suggestions for title and caption on the back with, in seven cases, amendments in blue pencil to a greater or lesser degree. None has the transformative qualities of the examples given above. Two of the cartoons never appeared in the *NOTW*: on the Sundays intended (in 1915 and 1917), the work of other cartoonists appeared instead. Generalisation about the editorial process from such a small sample (the provenance of which is unknown) is problematic, but it does suggest at least some mediation of the cartoonist's intent by the London staff of the paper. Whether similar processes were also in place in Cardiff is unknown, although the rapid turn-round between the cartoon being drawn and it appearing in the next morning's paper might have made this less likely.

Whatever occasional level of interference Staniforth might have anticipated, tolerated or suffered in the conversion of his cartoons from pen and ink to newsprint, the images appear to have remained inviolate. Many of his drawings carried with them cultural references of one kind or another that might tell us something about the cartoonist's intellectual horizons, as well as the extent to which he anticipated that his audience would comprehend the reference. At a basic level, there were those cartoons that referenced nursery rhymes, pantomimes, fables and myths.[30] An example of a well-known story is found in Figure 8.4, in which Joseph Chamberlain is characterised as the Pied Piper, leading enthusiastic South Africans (mostly Afrikaners) in the direction of 'unity' and 'prosperity'. The fate of those the Pied Piper led away would appear to be an irony not appreciated on this occasion by the cartoonist, although whether or not his audience perceived ambiguity here we can only speculate. Elsewhere there are references to Jack and the Beanstalk and Cinderella, to many of Aesop's Fables, and to the Arabian Nights. Popular song and music hall inspired some cartoons: from 'Goodbye, Dolly Gray' to Gus Elen's 'E Dunno Where 'E Are' and from H.F. Chorley's 'The Brave Old Oak' to Charles Dibdin's 'Farewell My Trim Built Wherry.'[31]

Classical myths and legends were another staple of Staniforth cartoons. 'The Modern Theseus' (6 September 1914) presented Germany as the terrible Minotaur and the Allies in the guise of the hero, with the drawing adorned by some lines from one-time President of the USA, John Quincy Adams. Elsewhere Lord Rosebery appeared as Perseus, David Lloyd George as Odysseus and Orpheus and the Irish Nationalists John Redmond, John Dillon and William O'Brien as ('The Doubtful') Cerberus. Ajax, Damocles, Diogenes, Galatea, Hercules and Icarus also made appearances. The story of St George and the Dragon provided inspiration on no fewer than five occasions with David Lloyd George playing the hero three times.

It is in the realms of literature and art that one might find the most interest. The novels of Charles Dickens (*David Copperfield, Great Expectations, Oliver*

Figure 8.6 'Don Quixote and the Windmill', 26 January 1902

This cartoon appeared first in the *Western Mail* on 23 January 1902. Originally the caption was simply: Sancho Panza (Mr Lloyd-George): 'It jolly well serves you right! This comes of shuffling.' For the *News of the World* edition the following additional information was inserted above:

'By a majority of 210, the House of Parliament once more ratified the South Africa policy of the Government, and to the delight of Mr Lloyd-George and other pro-Boers, left "C.B." and his followers stranded and helpless. – Morning Paper.'

Twist and *The Old Curiosity Shop*) inspired seven cartoons, Miguel Cervantes's *Don Quixote* two (see Figure 8.6). Favourite poems included Samuel Taylor Coleridge's 'The Rime of the Ancient Mariner' (five), and Thomas Babington Macaulay's 'The Lays of Ancient Rome' (three), but many others featured. Lines from Robert Browning's 'The Pied Piper' have already been seen accompanying Figure 8.4, and other poets cited included S.J. Arnold, Oliver Goldsmith, Felicia Dorothea Hemans, Robert Herrick, Thomas Hood, Thomas Ingoldsby, Rudyard Kipling, Henry Wadsworth Longfellow, Thomas Moore, Edgar Allan Poe, William Robert Spencer, Alfred Lord Tennyson, James Thomson and Charles Wolfe. The single most popular source of all was of course William Shakespeare, responsible for twenty-eight references: six each for *Hamlet* and *Macbeth*, four for the *Merchant of Venice* and two each for *King Henry VIII*, *King John* and *The Tempest*. Other dramatists whose work is featured included William Barnes Rhodes (three for *Bombastes Furioso*) and Sir Charles Henry Hawtrey (*The Private Secretary*).

Staniforth himself was a keen amateur artist and something of an art critic. On 28 occasions, he deliberately copied or parodied some of the major artists of the Victorian and Edwardian periods. One example is given in Figure 8.7 – 'Crusaders Sighting Jerusalem' which took its inspiration from Edwin Austen Abbey's painting of the same name in commenting on the progress of the South African War. Whether Staniforth was simply happy parading his expertise in art or whether some of his readers would have recognised the reference it is difficult to say, but other artists whose work proved a fertile source included Frank Bramley, John Collier, Arthur John Elsley, John Gilbert, Arthur Hacker, John Hassall, William Holman Hunt, Thomas Benjamin Kennington, Edwin Henry Landseer, Edmund Blair Leighton, Lord Frederic Leighton, John Seymour Lucas, John Millais, John Pettie, William Quiller Orchardson, Edward John Poynter, Solomon Joseph Solomon, Marcus Stone, John William Waterhouse, William Lionel Wyllie and William Frederick Yeames. Moreover, Staniforth was not immune to the temptation to respond to the work of other cartoonists, including Frederick Carruthers Gould and the collective efforts of *Punch*.

A final consideration is that of the nature of the relationship between the political stance adopted by the cartoonist and that taken by the newspaper through its editorials. There has already been some discussion (above) of those occasions when the intent of Staniforth's original artwork was clearly and substantially modified by his colleagues at the *NOTW* so as to communicate a very different message from that which he might have first intended (whether about the diplomatic course to be pursued in relation to the Transvaal, the success or otherwise of Kitchener's 'scorched earth' policy during the South African War or the persuasiveness of the case made by Joseph Chamberlain for tariff reform). It has been argued by other scholars that the *NOTW*'s politics were hardly material to its appeal: Matthew Engel suggests that 'the politics was there only for form's sake: it did not look as

Figure 8.7 'Crusaders Sighting Jerusalem', 8 December 1901

This cartoon appeared first in the *Western Mail*, on 4 December 1901, 'with apologies to Mr E. A. Abbey, R.A.', and with the caption: 'It appears to be certain that the Boers are tired of the war, and the latest reports received by Mr Kruger from South Africa are said to show an increasing want of ammunition, arms, and provisions. It is not impossible, I am assured, that negotiations will be entered on seriously before the end of the year is reached. – *Morning Post* Brussels Correspondent.' The *News of the World* edition retained the apologies to Abbey, but the caption read: 'It appears to be certain that the Boers are tired of the war, and the latest reports received by Mr Kruger from South Africa are said to show an increasing want of ammunition, arms, and provisions. – Morning Paper.' Below: 'S-L-SB-RY and CH-MB-RL-N: "Another effort, Kitchener, and our long-troubled journey is at an end"' though it was meant to be read', and Alan J. Lee has noted that the Sunday press in general was not seen as particularly important politically.[32] That said, there were editorials to be read and, as already noted, the vast bulk of cartoons by 'J.M.S.' were on political subjects. Interestingly, Engel and Lee disagree on the paper's essential politics: for Engel it is 'usually of what might be called a right-wing nature', whereas Lee sees it as clearly Liberal.[33] If Lee is right (and some of the evidence cited below suggests that he is), then that may have presented a further challenge for a cartoonist the bulk of whose work appeared in the explicitly Tory *Western Mail*.

General election campaigns provide the most appropriate laboratory for testing the political direction being offered by leader column and political cartoon, as both usually set out to instruct voters on the choices they should make (or to abstain from so instructing, which was just as significant). During Staniforth's career with the *NOTW* there were six elections: 1895, 1900, 1906, January and December 1910 and 1918. On 7 July 1895, the editorial line was clear enough: 'We hope...that the country will give [the Government] the sanction of a massive majority.' Staniforth's 'The New Skipper' (30 June) had already endorsed Salisbury, Balfour and Chamberlain while criticising Rosebery and Harcourt. Now his 'No Connection with the Shop Next Door' (Figure 8.8) aligned him fully with the issue's editorial.[34]

The 1900 general election took place during the South African War, and there was little doubt as to the outcome given the fact that the war appeared to have been won and its imminent end was anticipated. The *NOTW* editorial of 23 September argued that 'the question for every elector' was 'the dominant importance of upholding the honour of Great Britain abroad', and that the 'political settlement of the South African trouble' should be left in the hands of the Unionists rather than be 'handed over to the tender mercies' of the Radicals. Such action would 'set at naught the valuable lives which have been lost, and the vast amount of treasure which has been expended in asserting the rights of this country and in placing the British nation supreme in the councils of Empire'. Staniforth was in agreement: a whole series of cartoons from mid-September through to the end of the election endorsed Salisbury's Unionist government and the cartoon of 7 October – 'Electors Have Chosen The Empire' (Figure 8.9) – made it appear that a vote against the incumbent administration would be little less than 'treachery'.

By the general election of 1906 the political context had altered substantially, and the Liberals swept to a landslide victory. None of the editorials in the *NOTW* during the campaign was prepared to advise voters on which party should be endorsed, and this studied neutrality was characteristic of Staniforth's cartoons. 'Arrival of Aliens' (7 January 1906) showed John Bull puzzled as to which of the politicians clamouring for admittance to Parliament were 'desirables' and which 'undesirables', a theme that was repeated the following week with 'Opposition Shops'. 'Uncertain' (28 January

Figure 8.8 'No Connection with the Shop Next Door!' 7 July 1895

1906) was equally hesitant as to the faith that might be invested in Campbell-Bannerman's government.

The January 1910 election evoked a different response. Although Staniforth's 'The Commencement of a New Act' (2 January 1910) presented it as a 'free trade v. tariff reform' pantomime, by 9 January cartoonist and editorial were in alignment and the message, if not exactly unambiguous, was discernible. The leader stated that 'one question... easily overshadows the others... the question of Imperial, of National defence, of which the first and last line is, and ever must be, the Navy.' After referring to a speech by Balfour that had 'created a profound disquiet' by raising the question of the 'inevitableness' of war between Britain and Germany, it went on to state that Asquith's 'statement of hard facts as to what has been done to maintain our naval supremacy' was 'far more reassuring to the country', and praised the naval building programme of the incumbent administration. Staniforth's cartoon of the same date – 'The Chief Item of Interest' (Figure 8.10) – showed John Bull absorbed in a newspaper headlined 'British Programme of Building Dreadnoughts', with his back turned to two circus ringmasters (Asquith and Balfour) proclaiming the relative benefits of 'free trade' and 'tariff reform'. Here we have a cartoon not quite in alignment with its editorial, but equally far closer to the *NOTW*'s (covert?) Liberalism than the unashamedly pro-Tory cartoons that Staniforth was drawing for

Figure 8.9　'Electors May Have Chosen The Empire', 7 October 1900

This cartoon appeared in the *Western Mail* on 3 October with the title 'Which Will You Vote For?'

the *Western Mail* at the same time. By contrast, the December 1910 election evoked largely neutral responses from both leader-writer and cartoonist, focusing on the questions of the House of Lords veto and the proposal for a referendum.

The last general election that J.M. Staniforth cartooned – that of December 1918 – was, like that of 1900, a 'khaki' election. The choice was, if anything, even more clear cut in the eyes of the *NOTW*. Lloyd George was, according to the editorial of 8 December, 'The Man Who Gets Things Done':

> The Prime Minister is the Minister without a failure on his record. To whatever work he has set his hand, he has carried it through with a courage and enthusiasm which has set its mark upon our history. There is still great work to be done. With a united nation at his back he is the man to complete the arch of victory.

Staniforth's 'The Road Mender' (1 December 1918) and 'The First Favourite' (8 December 1918) both showed John Bull endorsing Lloyd George, and his 'A Finishing Touch' (15 December 1918) had John Bull emerging from the

Figure 8.10 'The Chief Item of Interest', 9 January 1910

polling station with a 'Coalition Government' in one hand and a 'League of Nations' in his coat pocket, indicating to the (ex-)Kaiser and Crown Prince that he had 'settled' their 'hash'.[35]

The evidence of six general election campaigns suggests, therefore, that Staniforth's art was by and large aligned with the *NOTW*'s editorial position (it would have been unusual had this not been the case), but that the cartoons that appeared in the British Sunday may not have been a completely accurate representation at all times of his political views, which were on the whole (and most obviously in 1906 and 1910) further to the right. Only a comprehensive survey of all editorials, cross-referenced to all 1,200-plus *NOTW* cartoons and systematically compared with, at least, the 6,000-plus *Western Mail* cartoons, would allow more definite conclusions that took into account all political issues and not just those that were highlighted in the crucible of a general election.

J.M. Staniforth's cartoons were an integral part of the revamping of the *NOTW* in the early 1890s, and they remained a central and prominent feature of the newspaper's political coverage until the cartoonist's death. The assessment here of both cartoons and cartoonist contributes significantly to our understanding of the political and cultural character of both the *NOTW* and its readership from the late Victorian era through to the immediate aftermath of the First World War. The *NOTW*'s successful search for a mass audience was assisted by its employment of a skilled and popular cartoonist whose visual editorialising constituted a complementary (and occasionally alternative) pole of interpretation and comment to that offered in the more conventional leader columns. Indeed, just perhaps, J.M. Staniforth's cartoons reached not only millions of ordinary readers, but also one very famous amateur sleuth. For, according to Dorothy L. Sayers:

> to Lord Peter [Wimsey] the world presented itself as an entertaining labyrinth of side-issues. He was a respectable scholar in five or six languages, a musician of some skill and more understanding, something of an expert in toxicology, a collector of rare editions, an entertaining man-about-town, and a common sensationalist. He had been seen at half-past twelve on a Sunday morning walking in Hyde Park in a top-hat and frock-coat, reading the *News of the World*.[36]

Notes

I should like to thank the British Academy for awarding me Small Research Grant SG-47830, 'J.M. Staniforth and the *News of the World*, 1893–1921'; the Heritage Lottery Fund for supporting the Your Heritage application YH-12–00264, 'Cartooning the First World War in Wales'; the Research Institute for Arts and Humanities at Swansea University and the School of History, Archaeology and Religion at Cardiff University, both of which provided vital support for the work that underpins this contribution and Dr Elaine Canning (Swansea University) and Dr Angela Gaffney (Amgueddfa Cymru: National Museum Wales) for their invaluable advice and input.

1. This tribute appeared as part of an article 'My best caricature', which featured a number of contemporary cartoonists. The Staniforth that appeared was 'Preparing for the New Session', *NOTW*, 8 February 1914 (Figure 8.3 above).
2. For more on Staniforth's life and on other aspects of his work, see Chris Williams, 'Staniforth, Joseph Morewood (1863–1921)', *Oxford Dictionary of National Biography*, Oxford, 2011; idem, 'Contesting radical cultures: the cartoons of J.M. Staniforth of the *Western Mail*', in Krista Cowman and Ian Packer (eds), *Radical Cultures and Local Identities*, Newcastle-upon-Tyne, 2010; idem, 'Picturing "the member for humanity": J.M. Staniforth's cartoons of Keir Hardie, 1894–1914', *Merthyr Historian*, 24, 2012, 25–51; idem, '"Our war history in cartoons is unique": J.M. Staniforth, British public opinion and the South African war, 1899–1902', *War in History*, 20, 2013, 491–525; idem, 'Cartooning the rise of Labour, 1900–1921', in Chris Williams and Andrew Edwards (eds), *The Art of the Possible: Politics and Governance in Modern British History, 1885–1997: Essays in Memory of Duncan Tanner*, Manchester, 2015.
3. All of Staniforth's First World War cartoons may be accessed via the 'Cartooning the First World War in Wales' website: www.cartoonww1.org. Other important volumes were *Cartoons of the Welsh Revolt* (1905 – referring to the opposition to the Education Act of 1902) and two 'deluxe' volumes of selected cartoons – titled simply *Cartoons by J M. Staniforth* – in 1908 and 1910.

4. T.H. Thomas, 'Art in Wales', in Thomas Stephens (ed.), *Wales: To-Day and To-Morrow: 80 writers, 80 portraits*, Cardiff, 1907, p. 356. For Phil May see Simon Houfe, *Phil May: His Life and Work, 1864–1903*, Aldershot, 2002.
5. W.E. Pegg, 'Makers of Welsh opinion II: the conductors of the *Western Mail*', *Wales*, 1 (1911), pp. 62–65, 65.
6. *Western Mail*, 1 May 1919.
7. *NOTW*, 18 Dec 1921; *Western Mail*, 19 December 1921.
8. Mark Bryant, *Dictionary of Twentieth-Century British Cartoonists and Caricaturists*, Aldershot, 2000, p. vii.
9. Joanne Mary Cayford, 'The *Western Mail* 1869–1914: a study in the politics and management of a provincial newspaper', unpublished Ph.D. thesis, University of Wales, 1992; Hywel Teifi Edwards, *Arwr Glew Erwau'r Glod: Delwedd y Glöwr yn Llenyddiaeth y Gymraeg, 1850–1950*, Llandysul, 1994; idem, 'The Welsh collier as hero: 1850–1950', *Welsh Writing in English*, 2 (1996), pp. 22–48; idem, *The National Pageant of Wales, 1909*, Llandysul, 2009.
10. Peter Lord, *The Visual Culture of Wales: Industrial Society*, Cardiff, 1998, pp. 163–70: p. 164. See also idem, *The Visual Culture of Wales: Imaging the Nation*, Cardiff, 2000, pp. 318–19.
11. Timothy S. Benson, *The Cartoon Century*, London, 2007; Glenn R. Wilkinson, '"There is no more stirring story": the press depiction and images of war during the Tibet expedition 1903–1904', *War & Society*, 9 (1991), pp. 1–16; idem, '"The blessings of war": the depiction of military force in Edwardian newspapers', *Journal of Contemporary History*, 33 (1998), pp. 97–115; idem, '"To the front": British newspaper advertising and the Boer War', in John Gooch (ed.), *The Boer War: Direction, Experience and Image*, London, 2000; idem, 'Literary images of vicarious warfare: British newspapers and the origin of the First World War, 1899–1914', in Patrick J. Quinn and Stephen Trout (eds), *Beyond Modern Memory: The Literature of the Great War Reconsidered*, Houndmills, 2001; idem, *Depictions and Images of War in Edwardian Newspapers, 1899–1914*, Houndmills, 2002.
12. Matthew Engel, *Tickle the Public: One Hundred Years of the Popular Press*, London, 1996, p. 212.
13. Cyril Bainbridge and Roy Stockdill, *The News of the World Story: 150 Years of the World's Bestselling Newspaper*, London, 1993, p. 43.
14. News International Record Office, *NOTW*, Nominal Ledgers, Reels 101–104 (1900–23).
15. See '"Our War History in Cartoons is Unique"', Figure 2, p. 497.
16. R. Power Berrey, *The Romance of a Great Newspaper*, London, 1922, p. 47.
17. One ('The Old Love and the New', about the end of the cricket season and the beginning of that of rugby football) in the same issue, 10 September 1893, the other ('Shot by a Friend') on 18 March 1894.
18. This is the only cartoon in Staniforth's entire career that was obviously 'recycled' from another.
19. On the 'missing' Sundays, cartoons were usually supplied by other artists.
20. *NOTW*, 18 December 1921.
21. For a discussion of the ambiguities of Staniforth's cartoons of the South African War, see '"Our War History in Cartoons Is Unique"', pp. 510–24.
22. '"Our War History in Cartoons is Unique"', Table 3, contains a list of all such retitlings of cartoons dealing with the South African War, discussed pp. 503–05.
23. A second example is provided by Figure 8.6, where the title remained unchanged but additional contextual information was provided in the caption.

24. J.L. Garvin, *The Life of Joseph Chamberlain, Volume Three: 1895–1900 – Empire and World Policy*, London, 1934, pp. 418–21.
25. Ibid., pp. 424–25.
26. This example is discussed at greater length, with the image provided, in '"Our War History in Cartoons is Unique"', p. 505.
27. Julian Amery, *The Life of Joseph Chamberlain, Volume Six: Joseph Chamberlain and the Tariff Reform Campaign, 1903–1968*, London, 1969, p. 466.
28. The *NOTW* editorial on 4 October was equally uncompromising, depicting Chamberlain as 'an apostle apart from his old party and colleagues', and commending the Unionists for having 'no palate for a violent reversal of Free Trade doctrines'.
29. News International Record Office, A335-A345: 11 drawings for cartoons published in the *NOTW*, 1910–19.
30. Staniforth had published an illustrated volume on *Nursery Rhymes* in 1903.
31. 'E Dunno Where 'E Are' was the title of the *NOTW* cartoon of 23 September 1900. See '"Our War History in Cartoons is Unique"', figure 10, and pp. 515–17.
32. Engel, *Tickle The Public*, p. 220; Alan J. Lee, *The Origins of the Popular Press in England, 1855–1914*, London, 1976, p. 166.
33. Engel, *Tickle the Public*, p. 220; Lee, *Origins of the Popular Press*, pp. 166, 207.
34. 'With The Flowing Tide', *NOTW*, 28 July 1895 celebrated the Unionist victory: a contented Lord Salisbury pilots his 'Union' boat back to Westminster, while Lord Rosebery's vessel has capsised.
35. 'The Road Mender' is one of the originals (A341) in the News International collection. Staniforth's title was 'The Road Maker.'
36. Dorothy L. Sayers, *Clouds of Witness*, London, 2003 edition: originally published 1926, p. 92.

9
'Woman as Husband': Gender, Sexuality and Humour in the *News of the World* 1910–50s

Alison Oram

In April 1912, the *News of the World* (*NOTW*) published the sensational story of how a young working-class woman had passed as a man, under the head-line: 'Woman As Husband. Amazing Romance of Two Chiswick Girls':

> People will do much for friendship's sake, but not often does it happen that a girl, for love of another girl, will put on men's clothes and live and work as a man, playing 'husband' to her friend's 'wife'. Yet this is the bold escapade in which a Chiswick girl has just been detected. Since last August Adelaide Dallamore, 23, a servant, has been working in West London as a plumber's mate in workman's clothes, and during a large part of that period her girl chum has been sharing her lodgings as 'Mrs Dallamore.' They are such devoted 'pals' that, rather than yield to a threat to separate them, they adopted this startling device.[1]

The two-column article, which featured a photograph of Adelaide Dallamore in her men's clothing, explained how she had successfully passed as a young workman among other men. Through interviews with Adelaide and her 'wife', the newspaper described their home life together. Her disguise was revealed when she was arrested, following a fracas in the street, after her wife's family had tracked them down.

This was a story of gender crossing and same-sex love. The tone of the story changed frequently throughout its coverage, switching between aston-ishment, puzzlement and sentimentality, with a good deal of humour and joking through the voices of the two young women. Only part of it appeared in the style of a police court report. Although the magistrate was critical and patronising, 'telling [Dallamore] she had acted very foolishly', this was passed over swiftly in the report, and Adelaide was represented by the newspaper as someone to be admired for her skill in successfully living as a man. The *NOTW* slid uneasily between the terms love and friendship in describing the emotional bond between Adelaide and her girlfriend Jessie Mann, as the quote shows, but at no point was it suggested that their decision to live together as husband and wife was morally reprehensible.

This was not an isolated instance. Stories of women's cross-dressing (or passing as men), always termed *masquerading*, appeared regularly in the human interest and crime pages of the *NOTW*, as they did in other mass market newspapers.[2] The subject was popular before and after the First World War, and there was a regular run of such coverage in the 1920s and 1930s. From the Second World War these reports began to fade away.

What can these stories of women's cross-dressing tell us about the changing ways in which the *NOTW* negotiated gender, sexuality and modernity during the early to mid-twentieth century? This chapter emphasises the role of humour and the 'marvellous' in the human interest story, as elements of newspaper sensationalism that enabled multiple readings of sexual and gender transgression to continue to flourish into the 1950s.

Cross-dressing stories appeared across the popular press, but the *NOTW*'s were generally lengthier and more detailed than those in other newspapers, reflecting its marketing claim to be an entertaining Sunday read. Accounts of women's masquerading were sufficiently common to merit a consistent formula, creating a minor genre familiar to readers, which was maintained over many decades to the 1950s. Signalled by headlines such as 'a remarkable masquerade', the narrative begins with the sensational discovery – that a man had been found to be a woman, and the mechanism through which this had been revealed. Often this was via the police and court room,[3] at a hospital when the cross-dresser had been seriously ill, or after death. The report reconstructs her journey across gender boundaries, and assesses the cross-dresser's appearance as a man, her skills in performing masculinity and her relationships with workmates and neighbours. The masquerader usually had a girlfriend or wife, or at least enjoyed flirting with women, details of whom and which were elaborated as part of the amazing story. These accounts were full of humour – how did she get away with that? – humour derived from fooling employers, peers and the authorities, but never at the expense of the cross-dressing woman herself. She was positioned as a boundary-crossing *trickster*, in charge of the whole event, and was admired for her skill in passing as a man.[4] The passing woman was not condemned for being socially transgressive, but celebrated for her boldness, success and her near-magical achievement.

These stories of women's 'masquerading' were part of modern mass market newspaper publishing. Journalists took up reports from the local courts and rapidly wrote and presented them within this familiar generic formula, which nevertheless changed over this period. This was a commercial popular genre, not a 'traditional' or 'folk' genre, accidentally left over from earlier cultural understandings.[5] The cross-dressing story remained ubiquitous during a period when popular newspapers were fiercely competing for readers, by using modern technological methods, introducing more illustrations, the bolder presentation of headlines and more colloquial styles of writing.

The significance of the NOTW lies in both its pre-eminent circulation – 4 million by 1939, the highest in the world and far ahead of its nearest Sunday rival, the People – and in its reputation for the most titillating reporting of sensation, sex and scandal that could be published in a respectable family newspaper.[6] The NOTW was famed for its detailed court reporting, especially of divorce cases and sexual crimes.[7] However, its sensationalism encompassed all kinds of drama and excess – shocking and gory crime, thrilling and tragic accidents, suicides and the deaths of children – as well as bizarre and astonishing stories that flouted the assumptions of everyday life. Cross-dressing accounts appealed to and entertained audiences on many levels. These female masqueraders were appearing in the everyday world of the public house, workplace and household, familiar territory to the working- and lower middle-class reader. With their parallels to the male impersonator on the music hall stage (often reviewed on other pages of the NOTW), they could also be understood in relation to popular entertainment. Moreover, through their dramatic uncovering and the attempts to regulate the cross-dressing woman, these stories had links to court room reports and to potential criminality and immorality. These human-interest stories provided weekend entertainment and spectacle for the reader, alongside pages of sport, light serial fiction, reviews of music hall, theatre and cinema and show-business gossip.[8]

Sexual modernity in the popular press

In their intense competition for readers, mass market newspapers both magnified and evaded 'sex', as Adrian Bingham has demonstrated.[9] The NOTW was particularly adept at promising titillation while avoiding offence to its audience and advertisers. Some newspapers mobilised 'modern' justifications for increasing sexual content and frankness, reporting debates on birth control in the 1920s, while others replayed traditional moral crusades.[10] The NOTW did not, in this period, follow the sexual enlightenment agenda of some of its competitors. Rather, the NOTW gained notoriety for salaciousness in the first half of the twentieth century primarily through its court reporting, as the 'squalid recorder of squalid crime',[11] and its wider coverage and more detailed reporting of sexual crime and immorality than other papers.

Despite its reputation, the NOTW, like the rest of the mass circulation press of this period, was opaque in the way it reported sexual transgression. Even in lengthy court reports it self-censored, omitting specific details of sexual offences or adultery.[12] It used indirect, euphemistic and moralistic language to allude to sex. A 'grave' or 'serious' offence might refer to abortion, rape or male homosexuality, depending on the context. Even when used in the court room, scientific and medical terms for sexual practices or parts of the body were rarely repeated in the press, though the *NOTW* did go slightly further than other papers.[13]

Stories of women's cross-dressing repeatedly focused on the masquerader's relationships with her wife or girlfriends, offering readers a discourse on (as it turned out) same-sex love and partnerships. By the late twentieth century, stories of passing women would come to be read in terms of modern sexual identities as being about lesbianism or transgender desire. However, before the 1950s, the concept of female homosexuality had little or no currency in mainstream popular culture.[14] A female husband's marriage might be seen as 'a strange menage' but not as sexually immoral.[15]

Historians of sexuality have argued that the categorising and labelling of sexual practices such as transvestism and homosexuality in the medical and scientific literature were gradually filtering into the British courts by the 1930s.[16] The 1928 prosecution for obscenity of the lesbian novel *The Well of Loneliness*, and the reporting in the press of the trial have been claimed as the beginning of increased public knowledge of lesbianism.[17] Further historical work has challenged this model, especially its timing and reach in popular culture. Even male homosexuality (reported more enthusiastically in the *NOTW* than in other papers) was barely named as a sexual practice, identity or crime, the most direct language used being 'perversion'.[18] Looking at the spectrum of cross-dressing reports over time in this newspaper challenges the focus on key turning points in the history of sexuality. Women's masquerading, as a newspaper story with a particular celebratory and humorous format, survived *The Well of Loneliness* trial and continued to appear in the popular press until after the Second World War.[19]

Readers did not require court room discussion reported in any detail, nor sexual activities named, to enjoy the frisson of reading about 'sex'. Newspaper reports of sensational divorce court hearings, for example, which inevitably involved accusations of adultery (as the only grounds for divorce in this period), avoided direct discussion of sex or the sexual body in order to maintain public decency while ostensibly shaming the individuals involved. Yet, as Lucy Bland and Gail Savage show, these euphemistic reports were understood as entertaining and erotic by many readers, and drew establishment criticism and eventual reporting constraints through the 1926 Judicial Proceedings (Regulation of Reports) Act.[20] There was widespread sexual ignorance among the general public of all classes, and especially among women, which meant that oblique language and euphemism in the press could be read as suggestive and created an aura of eroticism and secret sexual knowledge, even when the meaning was open-ended and only vaguely understood.[21] Kate Fisher writes that popular printed material and entertainment were often highly sexualised in the first half of the twentieth century, but, nevertheless, difficult for individuals to decipher.[22]

Cross-dressing reports must be seen in the context of these wider sexual languages of popular culture and entertainment, especially the narrative styles of humour and mystery. Taking three examples from 1912, 1929 and 1946, this chapter will go on to show that gender transgression and sexual possibilities were communicated not only through press censorship, portentous codes and moralism, but also via comedy, puzzles and enchantment. These threads of newspaper sensationalism were developed to a high art in the *NOTW*. Mass market newspapers draw from working-class entertainment traditions and mimic the idiom of everyday banter in order to connect with their readers.[23] Perhaps the most significant source of popular humour, playfulness and excess was the music hall, as Andy Medhurst argues.[24] Mainstream print cultures were obliged to be less vulgar than live entertainment, but drew on similar forms of knowingness, comedy and licence. Stage and screen performance was charged with erotic appeal, whether straightforwardly heterosexual or the more complex address of the male impersonator, whose songs and patter were laced with innuendo and double entendre.[25] Many variety performers' acts were suffused with 'knowingness', an interaction that created sexual, saucy and other meanings between the audience and performer.[26] A similar, if more sedate, process operated in popular journalism, in the associations made between the male impersonator on stage and the cross-dressing woman on the streets.[27]

Sex was a significant theme but not, of course, the only one in popular entertainment and humour. Within the cross-dressing story, as in wider popular comedy, the amusement turns on several elements: the fooling of other people (the comedy of superiority), the incongruity of gender-swapping, the carnivalesque – the astonishment at the unexpected physical body and its vulgar implications – and the inversion of normal hierarchies. As a trickster, the cross-dressing woman reinvents the familiar humorous trope of the individual – the 'little man' – subverting not only the immediate authority of employer, vicar or police but also the broader regulatory structures and institutions of modern life. The humour in the masquerading stories certainly renders acceptable the enormity of challenging gender boundaries. It also light-heartedly refers to anxieties about women's capabilities and public roles during a long period of tension in gender relations. In its reference to the male impersonator, the amusing cross-dressing story makes sex and desire visible through saucy suggestiveness while at the same time deflecting them through knowing jokiness.[28]

The playful incongruity of the passing woman and her carnivalesque success in escaping gender boundaries add a marvellous quality to these reports. The language of mystery and surprise is strong in the cross-dressing story. It exercises the 'magical imagination' of the reader, and emphasises a sense of wonder, reminding us that the sensational human-interest story often aimed to puzzle and enchant, in order to entertain.[29] A number of scholars have recently argued for the continuing place of enchantment and marvel within modern popular culture: secular rationality by no means forced out older pleasures of wonder, magic and fantasy.[30] Part of the enchanting mystery of the cross-dressing narrative was the acting out of marvellous desires – the desire to be of the opposite sex, the desire (as a woman) to have a wife – making ordinary life appear open to new possibilities and unsettling existing ways of understanding sex, gender and the self.

The amazing romance of Adelaide Dallamore

How do the 'marvellous' and the comedic work in the cross-dressing story, and how do they change during this period? For Adelaide Dallamore and others, they certainly included the mystery of their successful passing as men. The language of the press signalled this to readers from the first paragraph, where 'the bold escapade' of Dallamore's gender crossing and 'this strange romance' of the two girls are introduced. The question of 'how did she get away with it?' was central to the puzzle and dissected in its various elements; how she managed to look like a man, work in a masculine job, pass muster with her workmates and neighbours and pose as a married man. As Adelaide Dallamore recounted, she often went fishing with one of the plumbers. 'No-one ever suspected me. I even played football with men, and went rowing on the Thames.'[31]

Most of the cross-dressing women reported in the *NOTW* and other newspapers came to light through the police, courts or hospitals. These official institutions not only had the power to view their bodies and reveal their 'true' sex, but also to regulate and comment upon their gender-crossing activities. This could have offered an opportunity for the newspapers to moralise about their gender transgression or deride them. However, until the late 1940s, the *NOTW* avoided this narrative, preferring to describe masqueraders as skilful and admirable, as we see with Dallamore, who explained confidently to the newspaper why she had dressed and worked as a man, representing it as a rational choice to obtain higher pay and thus set up home with her girlfriend. 'Last August I decided to experiment as a man to see if I should "do".' The amusing qualities of the story depended upon the incongruity of a 'Woman as Husband', which was emphasised by the photograph below it, apparently of a young man but entitled 'Miss Adelaide Dallamore.' After various odd jobs, Dallamore applied for a position as a plumber's mate. 'It wasn't difficult. A plumber's mate has only to wait on the plumber at his job, handing him his tools and just doing what he's told, and I got on all right.' She was clear about the advantages gained by reversing the gender order: masculinity meant earning power, more comfortable clothes and social autonomy. 'It is so much easier to live as a man than a girl. For one thing I could earn better money. I was free to go anywhere I liked and do what I pleased. ... and in my male attire I was free from annoyances.'[32] By annoyances, Dallamore meant sexual harassment.

Like other cross-dressing women, Dallamore was characterised as an audacious and successful trickster. A key quality of the trickster figure is their capacity for boundary crossing of all kinds, between high and low culture, between fantasy and reality and between masculinity and femininity. As a trickster, the passing woman wins out, escaping social censure despite her rule-breaking, while creating humour at others' expense.[33] Dallamore subsequently worked for a large firm of plumbers, employing 20 pairs of men, where:

> nobody suspected that I was a woman. They just looked on me as an unusually well-behaved young man, because when work was over I didn't use [sic] to hang about drinking and smoking, but went straight home, like a good young married man should.[34]

This is the comedy of superiority: the trickster and the reader enjoy having the better of the workmates, who never guessed. It was one thing to fool your peers – other working people – but there is an added edge to the comedy when authority figures, representing everyday power structures, become the butt of the humour. Dallamore's employers 'never suspected the sex of this exemplary "young man"' and the police initially believed she was a man when they arrested her for disorderly conduct.

The absurdity of gendered clothing was a comic theme returned to repeatedly. 'Adelaide for the first time for eight months was walking out with her "wife" in skirts instead of trousers. "I haven't got used to skirts yet," she grumbled. "The awkward things!"' Later in the account they joked again about clothing, this time making fun of the formality of masculine clothes as well as drawing attention to the rigidity of normal gender boundaries: '"Do you remember what an awful job we had tying your first necktie?" The girl plumber burst out laughing at the recollection,' and explained that it had taken an hour and a half to get it tied properly. The reported laughter signals to the reader that this is a funny story about the comedy of dressing up and swapping gender roles. It also links women's real-life gender crossing to male impersonation on the music hall stage, which continued to be a robust and popular type of variety act through to the 1930s. Like contemporary male impersonators such as Vesta Tilley or Ella Shields, Adelaide Dallamore and others learned that with a little practice, faking gender was possible. Yet, there are many levels to this humour. Dallamore's 'escapade' was physically positioned on the newspaper page next to a short report that Mrs Pankhurst had been given bail by Bow Street magistrates. The contemporary struggle for women's suffrage threatened the security of masculine public privileges. The role of humour in mediating sexual politics is particularly apparent in this 1912 cross-dressing story.

The joking and light-hearted exchanges between Adelaide Dallamore and her wife Jessie might have sought to divert attention from their transgressive flouting of heterosexual family life in favour of passionate same-sex love, but it also emphasised the warmth of the relationship. The homoerotic appeal of the male impersonator was suggested in Jessie's flirtatious appraisal of Adelaide Dallamore's appearance: 'And you looked so nice in men's clothes! Better than in skirts!' Their same-sex partnership was introduced in the *NOTW* report as 'the weird story of their "married" life'. However, the interview allowed the Dallamores to assert their passionate attachment and respectable working-class marriage:

> 'We have always been very fond of one another,' [Adelaide] said, explaining the reason of [sic] the escapade. 'We've felt more like lovers to each other than friends, haven't we, dear?' The 'wife' readily assented; it was plain even to a stranger that the affection between the two girls was much more than common.

Jessie's family were urging her to marry a man she did not like and so 'we agreed that the only way out of the difficulty was for me to become "a man," take Jessie away quietly, and live with her as a 'husband".'[35]

Notions of, and a language for, female homosexuality were almost entirely absent from mainstream popular culture and the popular press before the First World War.[36] The *NOTW*, through its interview with the couple, treated the Dallamore marriage as an unusually strong but not unacceptable bond between two women. The language of love and romance suggested a parallel with heterosexual marriage, which was primarily understood as a social and kinship institution in this period, and only secondarily as a location for sexual activity. Adelaide Dallamore invoked honourable reasons for her conduct, and described her female marriage in respectable and virtuous terms: 'We were supremely happy together ... We never quarrelled once. We were a sort of model couple.'[37] Yet the humour and strength of emotional feeling, combined with the aura of 'knowingness' signalled by the music hall male impersonator context, could indicate that there might be something deliciously saucy going on, even if it could not be identified. This is a 'twilight moment', Anna Clark's term for the large conceptual gap between socially approved behaviour and that explicitly named as forbidden, within which lie sexual desires only half-understood by individuals or only partly acknowledged in culture.[38]

Adelaide Dallamore is a trickster who has not been daunted by her chastisement in court. The long interview celebrated her skilful overturning of the natural gender order as an amusing and carnivalesque marvel. Dallamore's masquerade did, of course, reinforce the normative ideals of working-class masculinity – she was a good worker and respectable breadwinning husband – as did most of the gender-crossing stories. Yet her success in exploding assumptions about gender differences, and in conveying the pleasures of cross-dressing and same-sex love, meant the world was not quite returned to normal. There was no conventional closure to this or other masquerading stories.

The astonishing paternity of William Holton

The next story to be explored in detail was published in the late 1920s. The meaning of gender and the position of women continued to be a major point of negotiation in interwar popular culture at a time of intense competition for markets among the popular press.[39] Historians of sexuality debate whether the years 1928–29 should be seen as a key moment for the 'scientific' discourses naming female homosexuality to cross over into mainstream knowledge in Britain. The lesbian novel *The Well of Loneliness* was successfully prosecuted for obscenity in 1928 and many historians have argued that this event created a widely recognised cultural connection between mannishness in women and lesbianism.[40] The *NOTW* published only a short piece on the trial and reported to readers that the book was found obscene because it dealt favourably with the subject of 'unnatural practices between women'.[41] In the following year, the masquerading case of Colonel Barker – who had actually married another woman – was widely reported across the press. She was condemned by the judge in court for 'perverted conduct' that had 'profaned the House of God, outraged the decencies of nature, and broken the laws of man'.[42] Despite the significance awarded to them by historians, however, these two cases did not produce a sea change in the popular press reporting of other cross-dressing stories, and the tone of marvel and playfulness continued.

In May 1929, hard on the heels of the Colonel Barker case, the *NOTW* reported the story of William Holton, a woman discovered to be passing as a man on admission to the Evesham Poor Law hospital.[43] Forty-two-year-old Holton had been living for some years with another woman who had two children, one of whom she believed had been fathered by Holton. The *NOTW*'s story and interview with Holton's 'wife' contained stronger sexual allusions than earlier reports, but maintained the magical qualities of masquerading, developing a tone of playful wonder around the extraordinary and astonishing feat of producing a baby. The language of marvel and sensation was used to set up the story from the beginning, with the headlines: 'Another Man-Woman: Amazing Fortitude of Masquerader: Illness Betrays Secret.'[44] It published two photographs, one of Holton, the other of her wife and child, and devoted two lengthy columns to detailed discussion of the 'perplexing' features of this 'remarkable instance of sex impersonation'.

[S]he worked as a timber haulier, a coal heaver, a cow-man, a road-mender, and a navvy, drank heavily and smoked black twist, and, most astonishingly of all, claimed paternity of a child born to a woman with whom she had lived for over four years. Exposure came when, stricken with a grievous illness, she was admitted to a Poor Law infirmary in a Midland town. Only this sudden affliction could have betrayed the secret of her sex, for until physical breakdown came she had cheerfully undertaken heavy manual labour of a kind which would have taxed the endurance of the strongest of men ... Meanwhile the woman whose life was linked to hers in a strange association is bewildered by the startling turn of events.[45]

The mystery was heightened by Holton's refusal to speak to anyone,[46] and the story was told through interviews with Mabel Hinton, Holton's common-law wife, and his/her neighbours and workmates. The account followed the classic form of the genre, tracking Holton's work record, masculine appearance and habits and the nature of his/her married life. Admiration was expressed for her skill in passing as a man for so long, and humour around his/her capacity to fool so many of his/her associates.

The *NOTW* pursued the intimate details of her physical disguise, marriage and parenthood a little more closely than in earlier masquerading stories. There was a light-hearted dynamic around expectations of gender, as individuals tried to rationalise their new knowledge of Holton. Much of the humour turns on their having been taken in for so long as they 'frankly confessed their astonishment'. A woman who had known Holton for some 15 years said: 'I have always remarked that he had a squeaky voice, but I never suspected the truth.'[47] Intense curiosity was displayed about the physicality of his/her disguise. The *NOTW* reported that on discovery at the hospital 'her chest was bound with wrapping.'[48] The report revelled in the evidence of Holton's pronounced masculinity. 'As a navvy she was as strong as any of the men, and could sling a bag of cement about as easily as any of the others.' In a period when women smoked mild cigarettes if they smoked at all, much was made of his/her love of strong tobacco, including a sub-heading 'Bogus Man Who Smoked Black Twist.'[49] The tobacconist recalled that: 'at her request a brand of light flake tobacco of a strength that only the most inveterate smokers could tackle, was specially stocked for her.' The humorous incongruity of Holton's gender crossing was emphasised by this excess. Holton had passed as a man for about 20 years, during which time she/he had fooled many employers as she/he worked in various heavy labouring jobs around the west Midlands.[50]

The central section of the report described the ups and downs of Holton's 'marriage' to Mabel Hinton. Hinton gave the *NOTW* 'some astonishing details of their life together', much of this in romantic and histrionic style, but, of course, these did not include any intimate details. They had met five years earlier when Holton was working at a coal wharf in Birmingham. '[S]he became enamoured of "him",' despite the fact that Holton refused to go through a wedding ceremony with her. Some time after settling down together they quarrelled, 'but the nature of the rift is still their secret.' Holton left Hinton for several months, which she described in dramatic and sentimental terms. '"It was one of the blackest times in my life...for I had grown to love my "man" with all the love in my heart and soul. I worshipped him.' Reverting to more pragmatic measurements of successful working-class marriage, she added: 'Never once did he beat me or spank the children.' Neighbours corroborated Holton's respectable masculinity: he had 'worked hard for the "wife" and children...[and] was devoted to the baby.' He had sympathised with his wife about the heavy nature of domestic work. '"You must be tired, my girl," Holton would say, after she had done a day's washing. "I always thought that women's work was the hardest."' This is a typical trickster jest that can be appreciated by the reader, now also in the know. Holton had successfully won Mabel Hinton as his/her wife, and she/he was a jealous husband: she/he 'would not permit her to go near other men'. Holton's own attractiveness – 'Undoubtedly she made a handsome man and had a way with the women' – suggests the powerful sexual desires that coalesced around the cross-dressing woman, both in his/her everyday life and as signalled to the newspaper reader.

Holton was a particularly accomplished trickster, subverting the laws of reproduction as well as those of social gender. His/her achievement in fathering a child capped all previous cross-dressing stories and added further layers to the sexual readings of the story. Mabel Hinton continued to claim that he was the father of her child. She protested:

'I never once suspected anything but what my husband was a man. ... My boy .... was born 18 months ago, and ....I believe him to be the father...Our life together was then quite happy and perfectly normal.'[51]

Mabel's story of bewildered innocence is contradicted by her own history; she already had one illegitimate child when she first met Holton. Whether seen as a fool, or as complicit in the mystery, Mabel Hinton holds many of the secrets of this unusual queer family. There was, indeed, a baby, yet the claim for Holton's fatherhood is positively absurd. Readings of cross-dressing stories continued to owe a lot to the entertainment tradition of male impersonators on stage and in film into the 1920s and 1930s. Suggestive jokes and the eroticised body were rendered acceptable in mainstream culture through humour and the designation of the stage as a licensed space. In this context, one reading of the Holton scenario is as farce, as one big joke. However, as well as still having cultural links to the male impersonator figure, Holton is also the stage conjuror, in her mysterious paternity, magically begetting the baby with a theatrical flourish.

William Holton's baby was an unsolvable, irrational puzzle of the highest order. The reporting of this case retained the classic formula of cross-dressing stories, in its admiration of the trickster's skill. Holton had had very few brushes with any regulatory authorities during approximately 20 years of passing as a man. It was falling critically ill – effectively, bad luck – that had led to her unmasking. There was no courtroom appearance, and thus no repetition of the language briefly reported in the Colonel Barker or *The Well of Loneliness* trials, nor official condemnation of his/her actions. However there were stronger allusions to, and pointed humour around, sexuality in Holton's appropriation of heterosexual paternity.

Ellen Young: 'a form of perversion'

This classic type of cross-dressing story continued to feature in the *NOTW* during the 1930s and it was only after the Second World War that the idea of sex between women was explicitly introduced into the cross-dressing narrative in the *NOTW*, and labelled as 'perversion'. In November 1946 Ellen (or Allan) Young, aged 26, was prosecuted for making false declarations for the purpose of procuring a marriage, and also for forging an identity card, following her wedding to Irene Palmer, also 26, at Baddesley Clinton Catholic Church in Warwickshire. There is a sharp contrast between the two reports of this case published in the *NOTW*. The first, an account of evidence from the committal proceedings, was structured as a classic masquerading story, full of humorous and entertaining elements.[52] The second report of the formal trial, one month later, took a very different tone, quoting the cod-psychological arguments used by Young's defence counsel.[53]

At the first hearing, readers of the *NOTW* heard that Young had been 'posing as an ex-RAF pilot' and wore men's clothes in court.[54] Some familiar trickster jokes appear, as Young fooled her girlfriend, her girlfriend's family and various young men into accepting her masculinity. In a 'confession' to the police read to the court Young said she had been working at a factory in Guildford in 1943: 'I wore slacks for convenience. I got into the habit, and consequently I took to wearing men's clothes.' She was in men's clothes when she met Irene Palmer at Waterloo station late in 1944; they 'became friendly' and went to the pictures together. Irene Palmer assumed Young was a man and the relationship flourished. They corresponded, met up occasionally and 18 months later, 'more or less jokingly', Allan/Ellen Young asked Irene Palmer to marry her.

The engagement and Warwickshire wedding were presented as a comedy of compounding errors. Young was received at Palmer's home as a man, and other relatives regarded her as 'a very likeable young man'. She tried to maintain her pose as a former RAF flight-lieutenant by finding some young servicemen to be her best man and guard of honour. In the week before the wedding, two of these young men shared beds with Young, without being aware she was a woman. This was a classic joke in the cross-dressing genre, and when recounted in the courtroom it provoked amusement in the public gallery and the *NOTW* sub-heading 'Laughing Women Rebuked.' In her post-arrest 'confession', Young offered convoluted explanations of how she had thought better of going through with the wedding. She asked another girl friend to write to Palmer to say she was pregnant by Young. Young's mother had also written to Irene Palmer's mother to say it was her daughter and not a son who was intending to wed Irene. In this confusion, Ellen Young reassured Palmer that 'None of it is true'; she was in fact a man.[55]

Despite the humour, Young appears a less confident trickster than earlier cross-dressers. The *NOTW* published two contrasting photographs, one of Young 'in male attire', the other of her in women's clothing, demystifying her gender-crossing. Earlier masqueraders had almost all been pictured only in their male persona. During this committal hearing, the prosecutor deconstructed her disguise as a man. Allan/Ellen Young had sent Palmer a photograph of herself in Home Guard uniform. '"You may well come to the conclusion", [he] commented, "that the moustache which Young is showing in the picture has been pencilled in after the picture was taken".'[56] At this point, the joke is moving against Young.

The *NOTW* fostered some knowing humour around sexuality in this female husband scenario. The prosecution described Irene Palmer as 'a simple village girl'. Her protestations of innocence evoke those of Holton's wife in the 1929 story, but are clearly more believable. Palmer was 'infatuated' with Young, and the reported evidence showed a strong loving attachment between the two young women. Young had written over 50 'passionate letters' to Palmer, extracts from which were read out in court and quoted in the *NOTW*: 'With all my love to the sweetest girl in the world. My love is yours, and yours alone, darling sweetheart.' After the wedding, the pair had gone on honeymoon. Young stated: 'for the first week we stayed at some rooms Irene had obtained. We slept together...' The *NOTW* did not normally indicate what had been cut from court proceedings, so the ellipsis in this report emphasises that some material had been omitted. For her part, Palmer said from the witness box: 'So far as I knew I lived with the defendant as man and wife... [sic]' Young promised her a baby. 'Young always made a point of undressing in the dark, but at no time had I any reason to think that the defendant was other than a man.'[57]

The second report of the trial, published four weeks later, dropped this light-hearted tone and had more explicit references to sex between women. Still presented as a sensational story, it was now also framed as a courtroom morality tale. Ellen Young, now 'smartly dressed in women's clothes', pleaded guilty, and her defence lawyer made what he presumably thought was the best interpretation of her actions.[58] He noted several factors in Young's history. The case 'arose out of something deep in Miss Young's nature'. Her hair was cut short at the age of 14 for an operation and she had never worn it long since. 'She had been greatly affected by the fact that a soldier of whom she was fond disappeared at Singapore.'[59] After this, she had begun to steal and had acquired four previous convictions. Her lawyer explained: 'When she was serving a sentence in Holloway prison she was brought into contact with a form of perversion through an older woman', and he asked Young's mother: '"Do you realise your daughter is not quite normal?" "Yes, sir," replied Mrs Young.'[60]

Young's defence counsel was painting a picture – presumably now recognisable to at least some readers, and certainly within the court – of gender and sexual abnormality, in which Young was largely a victim. The traumatic crushing of romantic hope focused on her soldier boyfriend had disrupted the usual path of femininity and had been compounded by lesbian contagion, through the older predatory women Young had met in prison; a concept which here appeared for the first time in popular as opposed to middlebrow literature. New medico-legal discourses of psychology and sexual deviance were used in this trial although the terminology was not at all precise – 'certain incidents took place in Holloway prison' – and were now reported at length by the *NOTW*.[61]

Two-thirds of the newspaper's story was taken up by an interview with Ellen Young, presented to gain the reader's sympathy alongside their prurient interest in her wrongdoing. Following the line of explanation offered by her lawyer, she described at length how she had played sports with boys when a child, including football, cricket and boxing. The loss of her boyfriend in the war had left her broken-hearted. She had fraudulently obtained a suit because during the war, 'slacks were the fashion' and this, together with her previous convictions, led to her sentence in Holloway prison with 'women of every class. Vice was the usual topic of conversation of many of them. I was young, and some of them set out to corrupt me.' Some humour remained in her tale, but it was self-deprecating and slightly desperate.

> I carried a pipe, but no one ever saw me smoke it. I used to swagger with a pint of beer in my hand... But I am not a beer drinker, and it seems strange to-day to me that no one seemed to notice that I was the perfect "heeltapper".[62]

The second report still carried a homo-erotic charge. Young described in her interview how: 'I found that when I was dressed in men's clothes.... some girls seemed attracted to me and at first I thought it a lark to pretend to make dates with them.' However, now, this same-sex desire is pathologised by association with her sexual experiences in prison, creating a marked shift from the buoyant cross-dressing jokers of the earlier stories. Ellen Young disowned her trickster self, and backtracked rapidly. She 'sat sobbing in the dock' and, having been sentenced to 9 months imprisonment, told readers that she was 'thoroughly ashamed of the whole episode in my life which has just ended'.[63]

The cross-dressing story, as a tale of magical masquerade and comedy, was rapidly running out of time in the late 1940s. How can we explain the nature and timing of this shift? The Ellen Young case demonstrates the influence of the new psychologisation of offending that spread rapidly in the post-war criminal justice system. The search for motives, particularly for young offenders, drew on psychoanalysis and sexual science. This new approach was also fanned by a widespread social anxiety about the family after the war that led to debates on how to deal with youth delinquency, strengthen marriage and encourage motherhood. In the Young case, it was her own lawyer who thought it best to defend her through contemporary psychological discourses and, although explicitly citing her same-sex desires, suggested that she could still be saved. The *NOTW* did not stand out as the only newspaper that discussed sexual 'perversion' in reporting the Young trial. Both the *Daily Mirror* and the *Daily Herald* used the phrases 'form of perversion'[64] or 'contact with older perverted woman',[65] though their reports were considerably shorter. The *Daily Express* reported the trial with no reference to perversion or sexuality, while the *People* (the main competing Sunday paper) did not report the case at all. While the language of 'perversion' was not completely clear, many readers were likely to understand the meaning, especially as this term was frequently applied to male homosexuality.

Since the *NOTW* recorded court reports in more detail than other papers, it relayed these new approaches and concepts to its readers. We can also see a conventional narrative of court room drama now being applied to the cross-dressing story. Despite the comedy in the first story, the second *NOTW* report follows the explanation voiced in the court room and describes a morality tale of the downward path. In this context, the cross-dressing story as a marvel of trickster success and joking starts to break down. The process was aided by the decreasing familiarity of male impersonation as a strand of popular entertainment. While some famous practitioners on stage and screen were still performing, it was largely disappearing, or shrinking into the feminine principal boy act after the Second World War, moving away from the knowing, risqué and sexually alluring male impersonators of the 1920s and 1930s.[66]

However, despite the shift illustrated in this 1946 female marriage story, the process of change in the use of humour was a protracted one. In the *NOTW* there was a long period during which women's cross-dressing and female marriage could still be seen as marvellous and astonishing, despite the deployment of psychology in the courtroom. New terminology that seemed to pathologise love between women in a cross-dressing case had appeared in the paper in 1937, when two young women who had married in Harrogate were condemned in court for their 'unhealthy friendship'.[67] While this begins to foreshadow the more emphatic post-war naming of love between women as perverted, elements of the humorous cross-dressing trickster remain in other stories into the 1950s. The tale of Pearl Brown and Margaret Haworth offered several kinds of comic performance. 'Teaming up on release from prison, the two girls went to Blackburn, where, covered with confetti, they posed as a honeymoon couple.' Over several days of thieving and deception they tricked many people in London and the north-west. There was no moral narrative to this cross-dressing story, just simple, criminal fun.[68] Queer female behaviours, such as passing as a man, gender crossing, close female friendship and female marriage were not necessarily pathologised or named as perverted until the end of the 1950s.[69]

Conclusions

Newspaper stories of women's cross-dressing or masquerading are an important thread in the development of late twentieth-century sexual identities. However, rather than imposing contemporary categories of lesbianism and transgender back onto the gender-crossing woman, we need to see how these newspaper narratives actively constructed a range of queer possibilities. Such press reports were not simply a modern way of communicating 'traditional' popular meanings. Media modernity and sexual modernity were intersecting processes, moving between marvellous formulations of gender crossing and rationalist scientific models. The popular press both promoted and avoided 'sex', and the *NOTW* did both magnificently. These stories of women's masquerading demonstrate the persistence of humorous and magical understandings of sex and gender in the press and their usefulness. The deployment of enchantment and the marvellous to tell complex and disruptive human-interest stories is an under-appreciated component of media modernity.

Humour needs to be taken more seriously as a narrative style in analysing the history of popular culture and the media.[70] This chapter has shown something of its role in the *NOTW* in mediating contentious understandings of gender and sexuality, albeit in a very specific type of story. Many of the jokes were straightforward enough, some less so: the trickster who fools her superiors, the music hall suggestiveness about the sharing of beds, the questions over how babies were made, the secrets of married life and the excitement of same-sex flirtation. The cross-reference to the music hall permits a wealth of 'knowing' possibilities and meanings to be drawn.

For historians of sexuality, the highly intricate forms of sensation, humour and novelty that pervaded the popular press contribute to our understanding of same-sex relationships, especially before the 1960s, in all their complexity.

For historians of the media, the shifting negotiation of cross-dressing stories demonstrates the many registers with which the popular press worked. Genres of commercial performance were mixed with popular ideas and imaginaries, enabling the *NOTW* to maintain its reputation for risqué reporting and engaging amusement.

Notes

1. *News of the World* (hereafter *NOTW*), 7 April 1912, p. 9. Unusually for a cross-dressing story, the report never gives the masculine name used by Adelaide Dallamore.
2. Between 1910 and 1960, over 150 different stories of cross-dressing and gender-crossing were published in the *NOTW*. This is an approximate total of 'real life' reports. It excludes theatrical cross-dressing.
3. Cross-dressing was not itself against the law but the man-woman might be prosecuted for offences such as theft or (rarely) for fraudulently contracting a marriage.
4. For useful discussions of tricksters see William J. Hynes and William G. Doty (eds), *Mythical Trickster Figures: Contours, Contexts, and Criticisms*, Tuscaloosa and London, 1993.
5. It is possible to trace the antecedents of the cross-dressing genre back to eight-eenth-century ballads.
6. For circulation figures, see Matthew Engel, *Tickle the Public: One Hundred Years of the Popular Press*, London, 1996, pp. 221 and 228. Political and Economic Planning, *Report on the British Press*, London 1938, p. 84, p. 243 and p. 247.
7. Until the 1926 Judicial Proceedings (Regulation of Reports) Act curtailed detailed divorce court reporting.
8. For the narrative styles of sensation, see Martin Conboy, *The Language of Newspapers: Socio-Historical Perspectives*, London, 2010, Chapters 5 and 6; Kevin Williams, *Read All About It! A History of the British Newspaper*, London, 2010, pp. 143–44.
9. Adrian Bingham, *Family Newspapers? Sex, Private Life and the British Popular Press, 1918–1978*, Oxford, 2009, p. 263.
10. Bingham, *Family Newspapers*.
11. Cyril Bainbridge and Roy Stockdill, *The News of the World Story: 150 Years of the World's Bestselling Newspaper*, London, 1993, p. 13.
12. Lucy Bland, *Modern Women on Trial: Sexual Transgression in the Age of the Flapper*, Manchester, 2013, esp. Chapters 1 and 5, pp. 215–16; Bingham, *Family Newspapers*, Chapter 4; Gail Savage, 'Erotic Stories and Public Decency: Newspaper Reporting of divorce proceedings in England', *The Historical Journal* 41(2), 1998, pp. 511–28.
13. Bingham, *Family Newspapers*, pp. 174–76.
14. Alison Oram, *Her Husband was a Woman! Women's Gender-crossing in Modern British Popular Culture*, London, 2007.
15. *NOTW*, 7 April 1912, p. 9.
16. Chris Waters, 'Havelock Ellis, Sigmund Freud and the State: Discourses of Homosexual Identity in Interwar Britain', in Lucy Bland and Laura Doan (eds), *Sexology in Culture: Labelling Bodies and Desires*, Cambridge, 1998. Angus McLaren, *The Trials of Masculinity: Policing Sexual Boundaries 1870–1930*, Chicago, 1997, Chapter 9.

17. Emily Hamer, *Britannia's Glory: A History of Twentieth-Century Lesbians*, London, 1996. See Laura Doan, *Fashioning Sapphism: The Origins of a Modern English Lesbian Culture*, New York, 2001, for a more nuanced account. Also discussed in Rebecca Jennings, *A Lesbian History of Britain: Love and Sex between Women since 1500*, Oxford, 2007.
18. Bingham, *Family Newspapers*, p. 194.
19. The case studies discussed below have also been analysed in my book (Oram, *Her Husband was a Woman!*), but this chapter builds on that work to make a new argument about the deployment of humour and marvel in the *NOTW*.
20. Bland, *Modern Women on Trial*, esp. Chapter 5. Savage, 'Erotic Stories', pp. 522–26 Bingham, *Family Newspapers*, pp. 133–44.
21. For sexual ignorance see Kate Fisher, *Birth Control, Sex and Marriage in Britain 1918–1960*, Oxford, 2006, Chapter 1. Lisa Z. Sigel, *Making Modern Love: Sexual Narratives and Identities in Interwar Britain*, Philadelphia, 2012, pp. 34–36 and 52–54.
22. Fisher, *Birth Control*, pp. 55–56.
23. Conboy, *Language of Newspapers*, Chapter 6.
24. Andy Medhurst, *A National Joke: Popular Comedy and English Cultural Identities*, London, 2007, Chapter 5.
25. Male impersonators (including, in this period, Vesta Tilley and Ella Shields) varied from the restrained to more rumbustious acts. J.S. Bratton, 'Beating the bounds: gender play and role reversal in the Edwardian music hall,' in M. Booth and J. Caplan (eds), *The Edwardian Theatre: Essays on Performance and the Stage*, Cambridge, 1996.
26. Peter Bailey, *Popular Culture and Performance in the Victorian City*, Cambridge, 1998, Chapter 6.
27. For a more extended discussion of this point see Oram, *Her Husband was a Woman!*, pp. 12–13 and 43–45.
28. For theories of humour and its functions see: Medhurst, *A National Joke*, Chapters 2 and 5; Noel Carroll, *Humour: A Very Short Introduction*, Oxford, 2014; Andrew Stott, *Comedy*, New York, 2005; J. Palmer, *Taking Humour Seriously*, London, 1994; C. Powell and G. Paton (eds), *Humour in Society: Resistance and Control*, Basingstoke, UK, 1988.
29. For the magical imagination see Karl Bell, *The Magical Imagination: Magic and Modernity in Urban England 1780–1914*, Cambridge, 2012.
30. Michael Saler, *As If: Modern Enchantment and the Literary Prehistory of Virtual Reality*, Oxford, 2012. Michael Saler, 'Modernity and Enchantment: A Historiographical Review,' *American Historical Review* 111(3), June 2006, 692–716. Owen Davies, 'Newspapers and the Popular Belief in Witchcraft and Magic in the Modern Period,' *Journal of British Studies* 37, April 1998, 139–65.
31. *NOTW*, 7 April 1912, p. 9. A word on pronouns: there is considerable discussion about how to refer to gender-crossing individuals who might have strongly self-identified in the past as being of a particular gender, but some of whom might have identified as transgender in a later era. In discussing these newspaper stories I have generally followed the usage of the contemporary press and referred to cross-dressing women as 'she', partly because their words are mediated by the newspaper and court room so we cannot be certain of their self-identity, and partly because it emphasises the dissonance and sensationalism of these reports.
32. Ibid.

33. W.J. Hynes and W.G. Doty, 'Introducing the Fascinating and Perplexing Trickster Figure', and W.J. Hynes, 'Inconclusive Conclusions: Tricksters – Metaplayers and Revealers', both chapters in Hynes and Doty, *Mythical Trickster Figures*. Stott, *Comedy*, pp. 51–55.

34. *NOTW*, 7 April 1912, p. 9.

35. Ibid.

36. Oram, *Her Husband was a Woman!*, pp. 54–59.

37. *NOTW*, 7 April 1912, p. 9.

38. Anna Clark, 'Twilight Moments,' *Journal of the History of Sexuality*, 14 (1–2), 2005, 140–56.

39. Adrian Bingham, *Gender, Modernity and the Popular Press in Inter-War Britain*, Oxford, 2004.

40. Doan, *Fashioning Sapphism*.

41. *NOTW*, 18 November 1928, p. 3. See Oram, *Her Husband was a Woman!*, pp. 79–81. Bingham, *Family Newspapers*, p. 179.

42. *NOTW*, 28 April 1929, p. 6. See Oram, *Her Husband was a Woman!*, pp. 64–67. James Vernon, '"For Some Queer Reason": The Trials and Tribulations of Colonel Barker's Masquerade in Interwar Britain', *Signs* 26 (11), 2000, 37–62.

43. *NOTW*, 12 May 1929, p. 5. Any earlier female name of Holton's was never reported in the press.

44. *NOTW*, 12 May 1929, p. 5.

45. Ibid.

46. At this point; Holton was later interviewed by the local paper. *Cheltenham Chronicle and Gloucestershire Graphic*, 27 Aug 1932, p. 3.

47. *NOTW*, 12 May 1929, p. 5.

48. Ibid. This is the only cross-dressing story across the whole period in which the binding of breasts was directly referred to.

49. Penny Tinkler, *Smoke Signals: Women, Smoking and Visual Culture in Britain*, Oxford, 2006.

50. *NOTW*, 12 May 1929, p. 5.

51. Ibid.

52. *NOTW*, 3 November 1946, p. 3.

53. *NOTW*, 1 December 1946, p. 3.

54. *NOTW*, 3 November 1946, p. 3.

55. Ibid.

56. Ibid.

57. Ibid.

58. *NOTW*, 1 December 1946, p. 3.

59. The fall of Singapore in 1942.

60. *NOTW*, 1 December 1946, p. 3.

61. Ibid.

62. This phrase refers to the etiquette of buying drinks in a working men's bar, when the first man to finish bought the next round. It was considered shameful to be a heel-tapper, to avoid buying a round of drinks by always leaving a little at the bottom of your glass. The beer left in the glass recalls the shape of the metal tip used to save wear on shoes. World Wide Words Newsletter: 29 Mar 2014 www.worldwidewords.org/nl/xmcr.htm Accessed 10 July 2014.

63. *NOTW*, 1 December 1946, p. 3.

64. *Daily Mirror*, 29 November 1946, p. 5.

65. *Daily Herald*, 29 November 1946, p. 2.

66. Oram, *Her Husband was a Woman!*, pp. 151–53.

67. *NOTW*, 13 June 1937, p. 8.

68. *NOTW*, 8 February 1948, p. 3; 15 February 1948, p. 3. For 1950s cases see Oram, *Her Husband was a Woman!*, pp. 146–51.

69. Alison Oram, '"Love Off The Rails" or "Over the Teacups"?: Lesbian Desire and Female Sexualities in the 1950s British Popular Press' in Heike Bauer and Matt Cook (eds), *Queer 1950s: Rethinking Sexuality in the Postwar Years*, London, 2012, pp. 41–57.

70. See, for example, Lucy Delap, *Knowing their place: domestic service in twentieth-century Britain*, Oxford, 2011.

10
The Irish Edition – From 'Filthy Scandal Sheet' to 'Old Friend' of the Taoiseach

Kevin Rafter

Introduction

When the *News of the World* (*NOTW*) closed in 2011, the title was the third best selling publication in the Sunday newspaper market in Ireland with a circulation level of just over 115,000 copies that accounted for some 12 per cent of all Irish Sunday sales. The overlap between the Irish and British newspaper markets – and the role of Irish editions of British titles – are an underwritten aspect of the histories of media and journalism in the two juris-dictions. By examining the history of the *NOTW* in Ireland, this chapter, in one specific but important area, assists in redressing this weakness.

The *NOTW* might have been, in the words of former editor Stafford Somerfield, 'as British as roast beef and Yorkshire pudding' but the news-paper had a history beyond Britain, and a full appreciation of the *NOTW* requires wider consideration beyond its core placement in British media history.[1] Indeed, as this chapter demonstrates, the history of the popular British title is very much intertwined with twentieth-century Irish history. Drawing on a number of different archive sources this chapter shows how the *NOTW* in Ireland from the 1920s to its demise in 2011 moved from having an 'outsider' status to eventually acquiring a type of semi-official status.

This Irish history of the *NOTW* is divided into three distinct phases. First, the lobby to promote a distinctly Catholic ethos in the newly independent Irish Free State in the 1920s led to legislation directly intended to ban the *NOTW* in Ireland. Second, the conflicts and contradictions of nascent modernisation and secularisation in Ireland in 1960s are clearly evident in the reappearance of the *NOTW* in the Irish market. Third, the commercial drive to capture increased Irish market share from the mid-1990s onwards saw the newspaper promote partisan and uncritical political coverage, and assist in the electoral and political achievements of one political party.

Phase 1: 'that diabolical publication'

One of the features of the newspaper market in Ireland at the creation of the Irish Free State in 1922 was strong Catholic Church opposition to imported British Sunday newspapers.[2] This opposition was motivated primarily by the prominence in popular Sunday titles of crime reports and coverage of divorce proceedings.[3] The primary focus of Catholic campaigners was a desire to protect their specific ideological outlook from 'being swamped by voices, music, words and images from all over the world'.[4] An earlier campaign of opposition to British popular newspapers on sale in Ireland – marked by newspaper burnings and intimidation of retailers – had ultimately been unsuccessful.

The popular British Sunday newspapers were reportedly selling between 80,000 and 120,000 copies every week in Ireland by 1910 with the *NOTW* 'the clear market leader and pacesetter'.[5] It was claimed in 1926 that the *NOTW* was selling more than 130,000 copies in Ireland every week, which would have made it the dominant newspaper among all the British editions on sale in the Irish Free State in this period with a total sale that was larger than that of all the Irish morning newspapers combined.[6]

The priority of those campaigning for a stricter censorship regime – and lobbying for legislative change – was firmly directed at certain British popular newspapers. The editor of the Christian Brothers magazine, *Our Boys*, Brother J.C. Craven explained why censorship was needed:

> And let me tell you that the reading of such papers as the *News of the World* has depraved the minds of the younger section of our community to such a degree that they are copying the manner of the robber, the murder, the scoundrel and the filthy beast, as recorded in that diabolical publication.[7]

The *NOTW* was a specific target not just because of its extensive coverage of crime, sexual crime and divorce proceedings in Britain. The newspaper also carried birth control advertisements, which obviously clashed with Catholic Church teaching and sensibilities. This critical reception to the *NOTW* and similar titles was not unique to Ireland. In the same period, there was 'an ongoing public debate' in the United Kingdom about the content of the popular press.[8] Advocates for press restriction were, however, more successful in the new Irish Free State, and they ultimately got their way when the Irish government established the Committee on Evil Literature in February 1926. The committee was tasked with determining, 'whether it is necessary or advisable in the interest of the public morality to extend the existing powers of the state to prohibit or restrict the sale and circulation of printed matter'.[9]

The committee sat from February to December 1926 and in both written submissions received and in oral evidence taken the *NOTW* was the main target.[10] The Christian Brothers in Dublin submitted a list of 38 'objectionable papers & periodicals' with the *NOTW* first on the list. The submission referred to 'gilded filth; papers that publish answers to the letters of young men and women relating to sexual intercourse; papers and books containing advertisement of certain drugs and instruments which urge people to the most monstrous crime.'[11] The Catholic Writers Guild singled out two titles – the *Sunday Chronicle* and *NOTW* – that 'cater mainly for the morbid tastes and the unhealthy curiosity of the semi-illiterate by retailing the week's most unsavoury tales of crime, most especially sexual crime and also the most unpleasant revelations made in the public courts and the divorce courts'.[12]

The report of the Committee on Evil Literature led to subsequent legislation, the Censorship of Publications Act, 1929. This legislation sanctioned the banning of printed works that contained indecent or obscene content as well as publications that advocated birth control or devoted 'an unduly large proportion of space to the matter of crime'.[13]

It did not take long for the *NOTW* to come to the attention of the newly established Censorship Board. In a parliamentary reply in November 1930 it was revealed that several imported newspapers had been banned for publishing content that was 'usually and frequent indecent'; for publishing advertisements promoting 'the unnatural prevention of conception'; and for having 'unduly large proportion of space devoted to the publication of matter reliant to crime'.[14] The *NOTW* was on this list for carrying too much crime reportage, although in truth, it was the nature of the crime coverage (and its focus on sexual crimes) that deeply worried the Catholic leadership. The *NOTW* received its first prohibition order on 2 June 1930; the ban lasted for three months.[15]

The *NOTW* had been selling 130,000 copies every week in Ireland. The loss of this revenue stream was an obvious setback to its owners. When news of the first ban was confirmed, wholesaler Charles Eason was immediately contacted to facilitate meetings with the authorities in Dublin. However, as Eason informed the circulation manger of the *NOTW*, 'considering the history of the whole movement I think it would have been a very extraordinary situation if the *NOTW* had escaped. Rightly or wrongly your paper was selected for years as target of attack'.[16]

Nevertheless, representatives of the *NOTW* travelled to Dublin to meet the Minister for Justice and the Censorship Board in July 1930. They wanted the ban to be revoked but their lobbying was to no avail. The newspaper reappeared in September 1930 when the initial three-month ban lapsed but a second prohibition order was issued on 4 November 1930.[17] The censorship legislation stipulated that when a newspaper was banned a second time, the prohibition became permanent unless revoked by the Minister for Justice.

The 1929 legislation is generally referenced in the context of bans on birth control advertisements and on works of literary fiction by authors including Samuel Beckett, Thomas Wolfe and Edna O'Brien, among many others. This latter concentration is hardly surprising, given that, 'the proscribed list read like an alphabet of modern literature'.[18] However, the censorship campaign's initial target was to outlaw British popular titles such as the *NOTW*. With the banning of the newspaper in 1930 the Catholic Church-backed censorship lobby had achieved its objective.

Phase 2: 'Pretty girls in bathing suits'

In the 30-year period between the banning of the *NOTW* in 1930 and the variation of the prohibition order in 1961, allowing an edition of the newspaper officially to be sold again, Ireland underwent considerable transformation. After the country had adopted a policy of neutrality during the Second World War – called the Emergency in Ireland – the 1950s were very much defined by continuity with previous decades especially in relation to Catholic Church authority but, as John Whyte has argued, in other respects 'even at that time, there were signs of resistance'.[19] A process of modernisation and secularisation was slowly underway, 'with a kind of underground struggle over culture and politics that was eventually to change the face of the country'.[20] The pace of change quickened dramatically in the 1960s, although Ireland was engaged in a process that was 'complex, confused and very far from a linear narrative'.[21] The history of the *NOTW*'s second phase in Ireland provides a very good illustration of what J.J. Lee has labelled a 'mood of questioning'.[22]

In a parliamentary reply in May 1949 the Minister for Justice confirmed that the *NOTW* continued to be subject to a prohibition order under the Censorship of Publications Acts, 1929 and 1946.[23] It was put to the minister that regardless of the legal ban, copies of the *NOTW* were still arriving in Ireland – 'through the post in ordinary newspaper wrappers' – to which he replied: 'I have not received any complaints that copies are coming through the post but I have brought the matter to the notice of the Minister for Posts and Telegraphs.'[24]

Legally the *NOTW* should not have been available for Irish readers, although possession of the newspaper was not a crime in itself. There is sufficient evidence, however, to show that – just as in the case of some banned novels – this reading material was available to some members of the public in Ireland. Interestingly, in light of its legal status the *NOTW* was also mentioned in parliamentary exchanges in March 1947, March 1951 and May 1952.[25] It seems that, somehow, some politicians had access to the weekly title.

Order sheets maintained by Eason's, the newspaper distributor, contain the word 'banned' for 1931 along with another entry, 'not distributing in Eire'.[26] The company does not appear to have had any distribution dealings with the newspaper until 1938. The *NOTW* was obviously keen to tackle the commercial loss arising from its Irish exclusion. According to Peter Martin, in 1938 the London publishers – on the advice of J.C.M. Eason – received 'unofficial permission from the Minister for Justice to sell a sanitized Irish edition'.[27] The legal status of this new Irish edition title in 1938 was uncertain.

The national edition of the *NOTW* had been banned in Ireland but it was unclear if the prohibition order would extend to a 'new' Irish edition. The 1938 move seems to have been an exercise in 'testing the waters' to gauge local reaction. Sales numbers were relatively small. Eason's distributed 903 copies of a new weekly Irish edition in 1938, reaching 2,990 in 1941. By way of contrast, two other British imports, the *Express* and the *People*, had sales of 2,609 and 1,164 in April 1941 alone, while in the same month the *Sunday Independent* sold 23,565 copies.[28] Eason's also distributed the *NOTW* in Northern Ireland, although again the bulk of sales were for a local weekly edition as indicated in Table 10.1. Interestingly, Eason's also imported a small number of copies of the national Sunday edition of the *NOTW*. The wholesaler's archives list 52 copies in 1939 and 39 in 1940, before importation was cancelled due to transport difficulties across the Irish Sea during the Second World War. There is no explanation as to why Eason's imported this banned publication or to whom the copies were supplied.

Restrictions imposed on the importation of British newspapers and magazines during the Second World War were eventually lifted in 1950. There was a rush to regain lost market share. One leading Catholic Church figure claimed that, 'some British Sunday papers have appointed whole-time Irish representatives to push the sales of these tariff-free papers here.'[29] Despite the reappearance of British titles, the main newspaper distributor Eason's still did not handle the *NOTW* for the market in the Irish Republic. During the 1950s, the newspaper was not listed on Eason's printed order sheets south of the border although it was listed on similar printed order sheets prepared by the company for Northern Ireland.[30]

Throughout this period Catholic Church criticism of British titles continued with language familiar from the previous half century. Yet,

Table 10.1   Eason's distribution of the *News of the World*, Northern Ireland

	Sunday edition	Weekly edition
1936	40	2,258
1937	36	1,876
1938	55	1,709
1939	125	1,644
1940	102	1,351
1941	179	1,385

Source: *Eason's Archive, EAS/A1/6/1/4(8).*

despite the legal ban and the absence of an official distributor, there were sufficient copies of the *NOTW* in circulation in the mid-1950s to cause concern for John Charles McQuaid, the Catholic Archbishop of Dublin.[31] On 1 March 1955, McQuaid was advised by Fr. Joseph Deery, a member of the Censorship Board, that the *NOTW* was 'being imported surreptitiously in increased quantities ... [and that] ... this banned paper was being sold in Dublin on Sunday afternoons'. The suspicion was that the newspaper was not coming through the postal system but rather 'by rail or road from Belfast'. The matter was to be raised with the most senior civil servant in the Department of Posts and Telegraph – unfortunately no correspondence survives – but Deery informed the Archbishop that, 'At your Grace's suggestion, I shall see if the Custom's Officers at the Border can help to block the "News of the World." It may well, however, be smuggled through.'

It was clearly becoming more difficult to keep the newspaper out of the Irish Republic and by the late 1950s, the *NOTW* was 'unofficially' on sale. The management in London was cautiously exploring the possibility of having the prohibition order lifted. Archive copies of the newspapers from 1958 and 1959 at the British Library show that at least eight different editions of the *NOTW* were printed every week including separate editions for Northern Ireland and, occasionally, the Irish Republic.[32] Towards the end of 1950s the *NOTW* was publishing articles under the by line 'From our special correspondent in Eire' and, like other British newspapers, was a source of 'extra cash for local freelance journalists'.[33]

At that stage, the differences between editions consisted primarily of changes to the front page. For example, the Irish edition of 5 October 1958 contained a front-page story on the Pope that did not feature in any other edition. Similarly, on 1 February 1959 the Irish edition published a short front-page story under the headline 'Eire President for U.S.' and the following week the front-page contained a prominent photograph of the wedding of the daughter of Dublin's Lord Mayor. The gradual re-emergence of the newspaper – amid moves to deal with the prohibition order in place for the national edition – was not without some difficulty:

> it became something of a production nightmare because complicated changes had to be made to make the contents acceptable to the Irish authorities. Large, offensive pictures and bland stories replaced the more racy pin-ups and court cases of the normal editions.[34]

Newspaper staff in the UK also had to ensure that advertisements for contraceptives were removed from the Irish edition given the legal position in Ireland while 'at one stage, an artist was employed full-time in the Manchester office whose principal role was painting bras on pictures of topless women.'[35] Despite the continued strength of conservative attitudes and values, the *NOTW* was re-emerging into a changing Ireland. The media landscape was changing. The arrival of a domestic television service – and its potential role as a forum for discussion and debate – was greeted by senior religious leaders 'with a degree of trepidation'.[36] Against this background, the publisher of the *NOTW* applied for a 'variation order' to the original censorship ban in June 1961. The order essentially left the original ban in place but excluded 'from application of Prohibition Order all issues of a new special Irish Edition published after that date'.[37]

There was, however, a degree of caution about a full-scale return to the Irish market including a belief in London that many Irish people saw the newspaper as 'a filthy scandal sheet' and that the Catholic Church judged the title as 'nothing but pornographic literature'. Internal caution was ultimately reflected in a decision to publish 'toned down' content in the Irish edition. Despite good sales in its first three months 'officially' back in the Irish market, circulation figures declined dramatically after initial curiosity fell away. Journalist Gerard Fairlie was sent to Ireland to meet wholesalers and newsagents, as well as senior government and industry figures including the head of the Government Information Service and deputy head of the Irish Tourism Board.[38]

Fairlie found that the rigid Catholic conservative dominance of previous decades was diminishing. In a report prepared for *NOTW* management in September 1961, he argued that they had been over-cautious in seeking to stay on the right side of the censor and the Catholic Church. The strategy had created a newspaper seen locally as 'dull', and one that was too conscious of the censor: 'we have leant over far too far backwards in trying not to offend.' Fairlie concluded that caution had left Irish readers 'not merely disappointed, but cheated by the absence of pretty girls in bathing suits, and the occasional sensational story.' He advised that, 'we must brighten the paper and take chances. It is better to be banned than just fade away.' The Irish edition was also at disadvantage in being printed early on Saturday, with the result that it arrived in Ireland without the football or racing results.

Drawing on the views heard from local sales agents, Fairlie recommended giving Irish readers what they wanted: the latest football and racing results and 'bright pictures of pretty girls, freely sprinkled about the paper'. The feedback that he received during his visit convinced Fairlie of the importance of this strategy, and he was not shy about advocating a bolder editorial approach that jettisoned the toned down content in the Irish edition:

> The Chairman of the Censorship Board has stated that he has no objection to girls in bathing suits. Objection could – and would – come to pictures featuring breasts or stressing posed bare legs. But a lovely female figure is perfectly all right as such, provided it is not too provocatively posed. In fact, lovely female forms are a necessity for our circulation. I stress this is a MUST.

According to Bainbridge and Stockdill, who recorded the development of the Irish edition in this period: 'the Irish, having perfectly good newspapers of their own, didn't buy English newspapers to read Irish news. They wanted English news and sport, photos of pretty girls and only nominal "fig leaf" coverage of Irish affairs.'[39] However, aside from agreeing on the need for greater titillation, Fairlie actually concluded the opposite on Irish content, arguing to management in London for investment to recruit local freelance commentators for sport and news as well as employing a local news reporter. The recommendation was to 'brighten the Irish edition, and make it more like the real *News of the World*'. A deliberate policy was subsequently pursued to increase Irish content. George McIntosh, a news and features writer, was assigned to Dublin during the week while a second journalist, Charles Orr, was sent outside the capital to seek out interesting news stories.

A typical Irish edition, from 2 August 1964, contained a social column – 'An Irishman's Diary' by Charles Grattan – on page 4 as well as extensive local sports coverage including reports on Gaelic games, Irish horse racing results and the national athletic championships held that weekend in Co. Wexford. Football news from the League of Ireland featured prominently on the back page in place of English league football from the national edition. The final pages of the Irish edition were printed late enough on Saturday afternoon to carry the results of the last horse race at the Curragh (23 August 1964). The newspaper also started carrying RTÉ television and radio listings in its Irish editions but not, given political sensitivities, in its separate Northern Ireland edition.

Irish readers were increasingly given the type of story favoured in the national edition as a sample of headlines from the 9 August 1964 edition illustrates: 'Threesome in a country cottage' (page 4); 'Wife may forgive ex-Soccer star' (page 4). The same edition also included what was billed as a 'searching investigation into the menace of homosexuality in Britain' in which the writer, Noyes Thomas, posed the question, 'Is there a cure for this scourge?' (page 8). As Bingham has shown, 'prejudice against homosexuals was firmly entrenched in the popular press.'[40] This type of moralistic crusade was, however, insufficient to counter the discomfort for many Irish Catholics at the reappearance of the *NOTW*. On 1 June 1962, three women co-signed a letter to the Archbishop of Dublin's office, which was sent along with copies of the *NOTW* dated 13 May and 27 May 1962.

> It has come to our notice that the enclosed paper is on sale in the shops of Dublin and throughout the country. We are of opinion [sic] that the articles, and one article in particular, as well as a photograph in the issue of 28th May [sic] are offensive and could, in our opinion, be constituted as dangerous to the morals of young people. Is there any action which can be taken about this matter?[41]

What followed clearly shows the close connections between Church hierarchy and state leaders in Ireland even in this period of emerging modernisation in the early 1960s. On receipt of the letter, the Archbishop's Secretary – the Rev. James Ardle McMahon – spoke by telephone with Peter Berry, the Secretary of the Department of Justice, and one of the country's most senior civil servants. Eight days after the initial complaint was sent to the Archbishop (on 9 June) Berry replied by post. He judged that the complaint was 'well founded' but ultimately – with some regret – determined: 'As a personal view I doubt if the offensive matter in the issues in question would be regarded by the Censorship Board as <u>indecent</u>...I do not think that a police prosecution would be successful.'[42]

Berry did not, however, conclude matters at this point. In his correspondence, the Secretary of the Department of Justice assured the Archbishop's staff that he himself would arrange for an examination of subsequent issues of the *NOTW*, and would arrange for a complaint to be made to the Censorship Board 'if I feel that a complaint would stand up'.

Berry asked his staff to investigate the matter of a prohibition order. Two officials assessed issues of the *NOTW* from May and June 1962. One replied that there were no grounds to 'sustain a complaint' while the second official through the Censorship Board '<u>might possibly</u>' ban the newspaper based on some content in the editions reviewed specifically 'the cheese cakes photographs' and an account of 'a person who changed his sex'. Interestingly, the latter official concluded in a handwritten addition to his official typed note: 'in so far as the facts could be said to be sensational (or 'sordid' or 'indecent') the [same sex story] story could not be objected to; its treatment of the facts was not lurid.'[43]

Berry replied on 6 July 1962. The senior official noted that he had 'read (distasteful task)' the issues of the *NOTW*. And while concluding that the newspaper contained 'offensive, vulgar matter', he observed that he had 'come to the conclusion that the Censorship Board would not regard the publications as meriting the issue of a prohibition order'.[44] Even at that stage in 1962, the Catholic Church's dominance was under challenge and, as this episode illustrates, its ability to impose its will without question was starting to diminish.[45]

The longstanding censorship regime was significantly dismantled in 1967, although what seems as a final unsuccessful attempt to ban the *NOTW* was actually made in April 1969. Nevertheless, the Catholic Church was still a hugely influential institution that even an emboldened *NOTW* management in London could not ignore. In the first instance, Ireland's laws prohibiting the promotion of contraception still had to be respected with contentious advertisements removed from the Irish edition. Moreover, from the few surviving issues of the Irish edition from this period it is clear that editors in London were as late as 1970 still conscious of not pushing too far with content and, in particular, with photographs.

A two-page spread on a British legal case about sex change identity was illustrated in the national edition with a topless photograph but this image was replaced in the Irish edition with a swimsuit photograph (8 February 1970). Similarly, a feature article on the actress Raquel Welsh was illustrated with far less suggestive photographs in the Irish edition when compared with the national edition, although again the text was left unchanged (22 February 1970). The Irish edition was commercially important in London – adding to circulation and profits for its national parent – but four decades after it was first banned sensitivity still existed about what local content was acceptable in the edition of the *NOTW* sold in Ireland.

Phase 3: 'Now Printed in Ireland for Ireland'

The media landscape in Ireland changed dramatically in the two decades after 1970. Near the end of this period, legislative change effectively deregulated the local broadcast market, particularly in the radio sector. During these years, competition also intensified in the newspaper market with a variety of new local entrants and greater visibility for British titles.[46] Indeed, by the early 1990s, British newspapers had a high circulation in Ireland. In the Sunday market at the end of 1991, the combined sales of the *NOTW*, the *Sunday Mirror* and the *Sunday People* were in the region of 300,000 copies or 32 per cent of the entire Sunday newspaper market. Figures supplied in a parliamentary debate on the newspaper industry in May 1995 indicated that since 1975 sales of all British titles in Ireland had grown by 40 per cent.[47]

In the context of an underlying decline in newspaper sales in the United Kingdom in the 1990s one of the countermeasures adopted by several British publishers was 'to move into the Irish market'.[48] The decision made commercial sense, not just to acquire more sales but also to win a larger slice of the local print advertising market. British publishers including News International with the *Sun*, the *Sunday Times* and the *NOTW* sought to further expand their commercial presence in Ireland with a focus on publishing even more substantial 'Irish editions' of selected titles.

The National Library of Ireland first commenced holding copies of the *NOTW* in December 1996, based on the publication of a new separate Irish edition. In this period the banner below the title's front-page masthead proclaimed: 'Now Printed in Ireland for Ireland.' Policies pursued in the United Kingdom including cover price reductions, and scratch card games were also introduced. Unlike in the earlier era, the 'Irish editions' of first, the *Sunday Times* – and eventually the *Sun* – involved significant investment in permanent and freelance editorial – and commercial – staff in Dublin and the creation of highly localised editions of the national newspaper. During this period, British newspapers benefited not just from sales in Ireland but also through selling local advertising, which further increased revenue from Ireland. For example, when the Euro was introduced in Ireland in 2001 the public awareness campaign included an 'advertorial feature' in several newspapers, including the *NOTW*, costing €18,400.[49]

The newspaper was selling in a much-changed Ireland where in a few short years in the 1990s legislation was introduced to liberalise the sale of contraceptives and to decriminalise homosexuality while a constitutional amendment was passed allowing for the introduction of divorce laws.[50] The *NOTW* was, in many respects, now a far less important priority for those championing the preservation of 'traditional values'.

The newspaper was producing two Irish editions, one targeted at readers in the Irish Republic, another for those in Northern Ireland. Very occasionally, a single Irish edition appeared, as on 4 May 1997 when the masthead strapline changed to 'Your Sunday Best for all Ireland.' During this period, the most significant difference between the Irish edition and the national edition was on the front page and a two-page inside opinion section. The Irish edition contained a commissioned local opinion article, a local editorial and a weekly column by Pat Buckley, a controversial former member of the Catholic Church. The visibility of Irish content in the *NOTW* increased through 1997 based on a mix of crime and sex stories, which would have provoked a 'told you so' response from those who agitated for prohibition in an earlier era.

For example, on 16 March 1997, both story preferences were combined in an Irish edition front page 'exclusive' that proclaimed 'Attack Victim Tells of Gardai Ordeal – Scandal of Cop's Sick Sex Quiz.' The banner strap under the title masthead changed for that week to wish readers, 'Have a great St. Patrick's Weekend.' In a similar vein, on 11 May 1997, a front-page photograph was accompanied by the headline; 'Exposed: Ex-Miss Ireland in sexy frolics' with the promise of more details on pages 12 and 13. When not concentrating on crime and stories of a sexual nature, the content in the Irish edition favoured reports on immigration with a distinct slant as typified by the following headlines: 'Irish race riot fear' (1 June 1997), 'Scoundrels plotting to flood Ireland' (22 June 1997) and 'Bogus Bride Gang Smashed' (29 June 1997).

The newspaper was attracting increasing attention, but not always for the right reason. For example, during 1996, a series of *NOTW* articles on the detrimental impact of Spanish fishing practices on the Irish industry was raised in Dáil Éireann. While the government acknowledged concerns about illegal fishing it also observed that 'much of what appeared recently in the *News of the World* was hyped up and highly inaccurate'.[51] Nevertheless, with greater local reporting, the *NOTW* increased the editorial credibility of its Irish edition. The newspaper's biggest 'scoop' in this period concerned the 1970 arms crisis when two ministers were dismissed from government amid allegations of illegal arms importation in the context of the nascent conflict in Northern Ireland. The allegation in the 2001 story that witness statements had been tampered with was described as 'significant and requiring investigation' by the then Minister for Justice.[52]

The *NOTW* had essentially filled a role as 'outsider' in terms of the elite and political establishment in the first half-century following independence. However, from the mid-1990s the newspaper aligned itself with the traditionally dominant Fianna Fáil party. In the post-1994 period, when Bertie Ahern was leader of Fianna Fáil in opposition, his media strategy targeted the tabloid press and, in particular, the *NOTW*. While maintaining some sense of balance in the first four months of 1997, the newspaper's political preference became more obvious once that year's election campaign got underway. On 18 May 1997, a prominent two-page interview with Ahern also delivered a front-page story under the headline, 'Ahern in secret peace mission'. The Fianna Fáil leader was applauded for his proposed initiatives to restore peace in Northern Ireland. An Irish edition editorial in the same issue dramatically observed: 'Ahern has the makings of greatness. He could become a statesman to equal the legendry Eamon De Valera... A vote for Ahern would be a vote for all Ireland.'

The newspaper ran a dubious anti-Labour Party front-page story on 25 May 1997, which prominently featured quotes – and a photograph – of Fianna Fáil's justice spokesman. The editorial in the same edition featured a strongly worded attack on the incumbent Rainbow coalition, said without any supporting evidence to have been 'riddled with divisions', while welcoming pledges from Fianna Fáil and the Progressive Democrats to cut income taxes and crime rates. The newspaper's Irish edition on the eve of polling day in June 1997 led with an immigration story – and followed it up with an editorial – that laid the blame for the 'growing invasion of refugees from abroad' with the outgoing government. The *NOTW* did not explicitly advise its Irish readers who to back in the ballot box in 1997, but the message was clear – through the juxtaposition of an editorial calling for strong government to fight crime and cut taxes alongside an opinion article by Bertie Ahern headlined with his promise, 'We'll go to war over jobs, crimes and taxes'.

This policy continued after Ahern was elected Taoiseach (Prime Minister) with the *NOTW* essentially providing unmediated access to voters. Overall, the Irish edition published 120 political editorials between March 1997 and December 2000, of which 88 (73 per cent) were written by Fianna Fáil politicians.[53] In May 1998, following the publication of a gushing *NOTW* editorial praising Ahern, one of his media advisors wrote a note, which was subsequently released under a Freedom of Information request. Alongside the clipping from the *NOTW* the advisor wrote: 'Taoiseach, our old friends in the News of the World like you, I think! I would suggest that you might drop them a note and thank them for their support.'[54] That note from 1998 was – as this chapter has shown – a very long way from those written about the *NOTW* in Ireland in the 1920s and 1930s. Backing for Ahern continued through into the 2002 general election. Ahern maintained a very close relationship with the newspaper. He attended the newspaper's Christmas party in Dublin every year. Indeed, following his exit from power Ahern wrote a sports column for the Irish edition of the newspaper and featured in a controversial *NOTW* television advertising campaign.[55]

Conclusion

Under its various owners, the *NOTW* maintained commercial interests in Ireland. As the ownership battle between Rupert Murdoch and Robert Maxwell was underway in the late 1960s, it was reported that the newspaper's long-time owner was in the process of acquiring a majority stake in a leading printing and publishing group in Dublin.[56] Just over 30 years later it was reported that News Corp was considering a £70 million investment in a printing press for its Irish editions, which across all titles had a combined weekly circulation of 600,000 copies.[57] When this printing facility opened in 2002, Bertie Ahern – in the company of Rupert Murdoch – was invited to officiate at the official opening.[58]

As this chapter has shown the Irish history of the *NOTW* is very much associated with three distinct periods in twentieth-century Ireland: its prohibition in the post-independence period as a facet of attempts to merge Catholic ideology into the governance of the new Irish Free State; its re-emergence in 1961 coincided with the start of a new openness in the Irish Republic and its promotion of Fianna Fáil under the leadership of Bertie Ahern in the 1990s. During these phases the newspaper also responded to the requirements of the Irish market by altering its content – and it did so with remarkable sensitivity in the 1960s, possibly to ensure no repeat of its earlier prohibition.

The Irish market has long been a source of revenue for British media companies through circulation sales and, in more recent times, advertising. Throughout the twentieth century, Ireland was important commercially to the *NOTW* management. We find evidence of this importance in attempts to overturn the prohibition ban in 1930 – and subsequent moves to re-enter the Irish market – as well as the considerable effort made to ensure the new Irish edition in the 1960s was a success and later still the significant investment in a new Irish edition in the 1990s.

Until its demise in 2011, the *NOTW* remained one of Ireland's biggest selling Sunday tabloids. In 1981, the newspaper had combined weekly sales in the Irish Republic and Northern Ireland of 148,000 copies.[59] Sales in the Irish Republic alone reached 169,000 copies in 1990. These figures were maintained during Ireland's post-1997 economic boom, even with greater competition in the Sunday tabloid market. Like all other newspapers in the Irish market, there was a decline in circulation following the collapse of Ireland's economy in 2008. The final set of recorded circulation figures show that the *NOTW* was selling 115,577 copies of its Irish edition when it was closed in 2011. Claims were made that phone hacking was used in the newspaper's Dublin newsroom to research some stories for the Irish edition, but, unlike in an earlier era, the authorities in Ireland did not pursue the issue.[60]

Notes

The author would like to thank Cormac Kennedy, Head of Group Property at Eason's, for his assistance in accessing the company's archives; Nicholas R. Mays for supplying Irish material in the *NOTW* Archive at News International; Stewart Gillies at the British Library for locating the handful of surviving copies of Irish editions of the *NOTW* at Colindale; Noelle Dowling at the Archdiocese of Dublin archives for assistance with John Charles McQuaid's papers; and the staff at the National Library of Ireland and the National Archives of Ireland.

1. Cyril Bainbridge and Roy Stockdill, *The News of the World Story: 150 Years of the World's Bestselling Newspaper*, London, 1993, p. 217.
2. For a wider consideration of the newspaper in Ireland in the period up to 1930 see Kevin Rafter, 'Evil Literature: The banning of the News of the World in Ireland,' *Media History*, 19 (4), 2013, pp. 408–20.
3. See Michael Adams, *Censorship: the Irish Experience*, Dublin, 1968; Peter Martin, *Censorship in the Two Irelands 1922–1939*, Dublin, 2006.
4. Christopher Morash, *A History of the Media in Ireland*, Cambridge, 2010, p. 39.
5. L.M. Cullen, *Eason & Son A History*, Dublin, 1989, p. 9.
6. Catholic Truth Society. *The Problem of Undesirable Printer Matter*, Dublin, 1920.
7. Letter to Minister for Justice, 10 December 1926, National Archives of Ireland (NAI): Committee of Evil Literature (CEL): JUS 7/1/5.
8. Adrian Bingham, *Family Newspapers? Sex, Private Life and the British Popular Press 1918–1978*, Oxford, 2009, p. 9.
9. 'Documents circulated to Members of the Committee', NAI: CEL: JUS 7/1/2.
10. See for example 'Catholic Headmasters Association Submission and Evidence' NAI CEL, JUS 7/2/3: 'A start might be made by putting the "Sporting Times" and the "News of the World" on a black list.' See also 'Summary of evidence, Irish Vigilance Association', NAI: CEL: JUS 7/1/2 where newspapers considered 'objectionable and as unsuited morally to the people of this country' included the *Sporting Times*; the *NOTW*; the *Empire News*; *London Mail*; and *Health and Efficiency*.
11. 'Submission of Christian Brothers April 1926', NAI: CEL: JUS 7/2/7.
12. The Guild was an organisation representing Catholic writers and artists.
13. Censorship of Publications Act, 1929.
14. Dáil Éireann, vol. 36, column 720, 28 November 1930.
15. Ibid.
16. See Cullen, *Eason & Son*, p. 272.
17. Dáil Éireann vol. 36 col. 720, 28 November 1930.
18. John A. Murphy, 'Censorship and Moral Community,' in Brian Farrell (ed.), *Communications and Community in Ireland*, Dublin and Cork, 1984, p. 53.
19. John Whyte, *Church and State in Modern Ireland, 1923–1970*, Dublin, 1980 edn, p. 330.
20. Tom Garvin, *News from a New Republic: Ireland in the 1950s*, Dublin, 2011 edn, p. 9.

21. Roy Foster, *Modern Ireland 1600–1972*, London, 1989. p. 596.
22. J.J. Lee, *Ireland 1912–1985 Politics and Society*, Cambridge, 1989, p. 479.
23. Amendments to the original legislation introduced in 1946 included establishing an appeals mechanism.
24. Dáil Éireann, 19 May 1949, vol. 115, column 1567.
25. Dáil Éireann, 14 March 1947, vol. 104, column 2202; 8 March 1951, 124, colulm 1517; 18 May 1952, vol. 131, column 1867.
26. Eason's archive, EAS/A1/6/1/5.
27. Peter Martin, *Censorship in the Two Irelands 1922–1939*, Dublin, 2006. p.190.
28. Eason's archive, EAS/A1/6/1/5.
29. Devane, 1950, p. 3.
30. Eason's archives, EAS/A1/6/1/5/2.
31. These exchanges are taken from McQuaid Archive DDA/AB8/B/XXV and include correspondence from Fr. Joseph Deery to Archbishop John Charles McQuaid, 1 March 1955; McQuaid's reply to Deery, 3 March 1955; correspondence from Deery to McQuaid, 4 March 1955.
32. For example, the newspaper dated 11 January 1959 was printed as different editions including the Manchester Edition, stamped early morning edition; the Lancashire Edition L, stamped 'late morning edition'; Sunday Special, stamped 'north western edition' NW; the Sunday Special, stamped 'NW' and containing Welsh soccer reports; the Sunday Special Scotland, stamped 'S'; a Sunday Special Irish edition stamped 'I' and a Northern Irish edition. From 1964, the Irish edition was on occasions stamped 'EI' on the front page with the Ulster edition marked 'U' although 'E' sometimes replaced these for the 'Eire edition' and 'I' for the edition sent to Northern Ireland. Unfortunately, only a selection of these local editions has been preserved at the British Library. The National Library of Ireland only commenced holding copies of the paper in December 1996 based on the publication of a new separate Irish edition.
33. Charles Orr, *Splash! Drama and Comedy in a Newspaperman's Career*, Devon, UK, 1989, p. 22.
34. Bainbridge and Stockdill, *The News of the World*, pp. 212–14.
35. Ibid., p. 213.
36. Robert Savage, *A Loss of Innocence: Television and Irish society 1960–72*, Manchester, 2010, p. 163.
37. Annual Report of the Censorship of Publications Appeal Board, 1961 Department of Justice (National Library of Ireland, J.60/7).
38. Gerard Fairlie, 'Report on the Irish Edition by Gerard Fairlie following his visit to Eire, 4–8 September, 1961.' Provided to the author by News International from the *NOTW* Archive.
39. Bainbridge and Stockdill, *The News of the World*, p. 214.
40. Bingham, *Family Newspapers?*, p. 161.
41. Correspondence in John Charles McQuaid archives, Dublin. Ref DDA/AB8/B/XXV.
42. NAI, Department of Justice 2006/148/8.
43. NAI, Department of Justice. 2006/148/8.
44. NAI 2006/148/8. Peter Berry to Rev. James McMahon, 6 July 1962.
45. See also Savage, 2010 for relations between the new television service and church authorities.
46. See John Horgan, *Irish Media A Critical History Since 1922*, London, 2010.
47. Dáil Éireann, Vol. 143, column 727, 16 May 1995.

48. Roy Greenslade, *Press Gang: How Newspapers Make Profits from Propaganda*, London, 2003, p. 625.
49. Dáil Éireann, Vol. 546, column 448, 11 December 2001.
50. See Diarmaid Ferriter, *Occasions of Sin: Sex and Society in Modern Ireland*, London, 2009.
51. Dáil Éireann, Vol. 460, column 2209, 1 February 1996.
52. Dáil Éireann, Vol. 540, column 1047, 6 July 2001.
53. Kevin Rafter, 'Run out of the Gallery: The changing nature of Irish political journalism,' *Irish Communications Review* 11, 2009. p. 100.
54. Freedom of Information documentation released to *The Sunday Times*, 28 March 1999.
55. As Taoiseach, Ahern also officiated at the opening of new News International offices in Dublin but following his retirement and subsequent corruption controversies, the plaque marking the event was removed from the entrance to the building.
56. 'Pergamon bids £26m for The News of the World Organisation,' *The Irish Times*, 17 October 1968.
57. Frank Mulrennan and David Murphy, 'Murdoch eyes £70m Irish printing site,' *Irish Independent*, 12 February 2000.
58. 'Taoiseach opens Murdoch print plant,' breakingnews.ie., 7 June 2002. http://www.breakingnews.ie/ireland/taoiseach-opens-murdoch-print-plant-53829.html (19 August 2015).
59. 'Pub's case against the "News of the World" is postponed,' *The Irish Times*, 3 December 1981.
60. Conor Lally, 'Former journalist says newspaper in Ireland also hacked phones for stories,' *The Irish Times*, 8 July 2011.

11
'One in Every Two Households': The *News of the World* in the 1950s

John Stokes

In 1949, the writer Rodney Ackland had a play on in London's West End entitled *Before the Party*. Its plot involved a middle-class family, headed by a solicitor determined to better himself in the local community, thrown into a panic when a young but widowed daughter confesses to having murdered her drunken husband. Set in the post-war present, the story gave the widow a romantic ex-war-hero lover, and featured that staple of British drama – a loyal but perceptive nanny, in this case an inveterate reader of the *News of the World*. Discovering Nanny's copy of the paper, the solicitor erupts to the effect that that he has forbidden it in the house since it is 'full of the most intimate details of divorce'. Challenged with the fact that he handles divorce cases himself, he explains that they are never of this particular type:

> I try to confine myself to clean ones. Cruelty, lunacy or drunkenness for instance – something I would not be ashamed of my daughters hearing in court. The only sexual divorces we handle are those where the misconduct has been performed purely as a formality.[1]

Later on, asked why she reads about 'awful murder and divorce cases', Nanny counters that she likes 'to know what's going on in the world' since she has 'quite enough of fairy tales' in her job. She prefers 'to read about real life for a change', refusing to 'spend the whole time in rosy spectacles with my head in the clouds'.[2] The solicitor has meanwhile crumpled the offending object and thrown it in a bin.

A small but resonant detail in Ackland's post-war drama, the Sunday newspaper, which must have been immediately recognisable to everyone in the audience, serves as a portable prop. Even the members of the family are happy to browse Nanny's copy when no one else is around. It stands for a version of British society – Nanny's 'real life' with its 'murder and divorce cases' – that they simultaneously demonstrate and deny.

Ackland was a skilled writer with leftist leanings and he knew what he was doing: *Before the Party* ran for 100 performances from October.

In June the following year Nanny's favourite would break all records by selling 8,443,000 copies. By the mid-1950s the figure was still over 8,000,000,[3] in a period that saw, on the international stage the outbreak of the Korean war, the development of the 'H bomb', the invasion of Suez in 1956, the Hungarian uprising in the same year and the cold war 'space race'. At home, there would be concern about the economy, about fading military strength, 'race-riots' and planned increases in higher education. However, more importantly, as far as newspaper readership was concerned, these would be the years of Conservative success, with the party winning consecutive elections in 1951, 1955 and 1959 and feeling entitled to boast – Harold Macmillan's 'never had it so good' – that affluence now permeated all levels of society. Tory publicity successfully created a mood that the papers would strive to reflect. When Reginald Cudlipp was appointed editor of the *NOTWs* in 1953 he recognised the social change, took advantage of the lifting of wartime restrictions on paper to increase the number of pages and set about entertaining his readership with occasional short stories, sponsored foreign adventures and reports of celebrity activities.

Throughout these years, when the paper was at the very height of its popularity, it covered all the major events, both national and international. Nevertheless, a typical front page would feature, in addition to bold crisis headlines, smaller notices of royal events, society weddings, show business announcements, freak weather conditions (when is the weather not freakish?) and, with great frequency, stories involving outrageous acts of cruelty to children and animals. Few of these subsidiary items were likely in themselves to disturb a settled view of the United Kingdom as a morally concerned and essentially stable society, although there was often a hint of what lay deeper inside the paper with a court-based story about sinister 'offences' or other scandalous goings-on. On 30 July 1950, page 4, for example, a piece on the atomic bomb is juxtaposed with a report of a nudist marriage.

The front page of the *News of the World* contrasts strongly with that of its rival the *Sunday Pictorial*, where the headlines typically concentrate upon national scandals, and are rarely political. There is some similarity with the front page of the *People*, although the *NOTW* tends to pay much more attention to events of obvious international significance. Inside the paper, however, the more titillating kind of story takes over. Features on children and animals persist, but here we find more of the court reports that the paper had long relied upon, articles about violent criminals of the past (such as Kitty Byron who stabbed her lover back in 1902)[4] and of the present (John Christie, Derek Bentley, Ruth Ellis, John Bodkins Adams). Here, too, among the murders and 'cosh-boy' break-ins, between the ads that promise relief from piles, ruptures, dandruff and itchy skin, sex finds its prurient home. Reports of the sex trade in London's West End are sometimes so coy that they read like the inadvertent discoveries of an unusually ingenuous tourist. ('I Didn't Know Places Like This Existed In London' runs the head-line for a story about a gay coffee bar off Piccadilly Circus on 5 January 1958, page 9). When the streets were largely cleared of prostitutes following the Street Offences Act of 1959 the paper even managed to make capital out of their absence: 'The painted dolls, the scared novices, the seasoned, haggard harpies who for years have plagued the lives of decent citizens have vanished'.[5]

At the very centre of the paper the leader column is surrounded by opinion pieces specially commissioned, mainly from the right-wing pundits of the day such as Lord Boothby and Randolph Churchill although some left-wingers such as the up-and-coming Labour politician Harold Wilson are allowed their say.[6] Douglas Bader, the disabled war hero, is a regular commentator. Even on the leader page, the sentiments are more to do with threats to the national stability than with calls for structural change. Topics range from cruelty to animals (yet again) to 'parasites in the Welfare State', from flogging to hanging. Special features to complement the criminals might include the memoirs of Scotland Yard detectives. The paper's take on the 'real life', so much admired by Ackland's Nanny, is balanced throughout by an optimism based on tradition and the past: the royal family obviously, the heroic achievements of the Second World War, which carry over into the political rhetoric of the present – the fight against monetary inflation is a 'new Battle of Britain',[7] at the time of the Suez crisis General Nasser becomes the 'Hitler of the Nile'.[8] All through the decade the decline of the Empire, though now to be known as the Commonwealth, is reported as it might have been in the nineteenth century, as primarily a series of brutal 'terrorist uprisings' – the Mau Mau in Kenya, EOKA in Cyprus.

In subsequent pages, while high culture is notably absent (no book reviews, for instance), there are notices of current variety shows and new films. Importantly, there are competitions – a fashion challenge in which one has to place garments in the order of their attractiveness (judged by an expert in the field) and crossword puzzles. Both, with their relatively high cash prizes (upwards of £2,000 overall), remained essentially unchanged for many years. On the other hand, sports coverage increased steadily until it usually took up three pages: one for darts, snooker, horse and dog racing, two for either mainly football (listed results geared to the pools) or mainly cricket, depending on the season. Equally significantly, it becomes apparent on turning the pages now that the number of pin-ups increased over the years (the bikini was becoming commonplace) as did the number of column inches devoted to women's issues – which meant, though not exclusively, clothes and food. By the end of 1959 there was actually a page headed 'Woman's World' and a diary feature with a female journalist's name attached.

Perhaps the best way of describing the character of the paper in the course of the 1950s is as an 'entertainment' (admittedly some of it of a dubious nature). This might, in turn, go some way to explain its extraordinary popularity. In the course of a decade, the paper became fully identified with a brand of modern conservatism that was happy to endorse the future when it involved pleasure and material improvement but otherwise judged the present by setting it against a selective version of the past. As an ideological stance, this could be offered to the country as whole, purportedly without claiming any special interests. At the time of the General Election in 1951, the paper featured on a single page statements by the leaders of all three main parties (Clement Atlee, Winston Churchill and Clement Davies) and a non-committal editorial entitled 'Let Conscience Decide.'[9] It is noticeable now, though, that by 1958 the Conservative Party has by far the largest and most commanding advertisements and that these are based on a campaign idea that anyone, whatever their background, profession or, indeed, gender, could and should vote Tory.

The historian Peter Hennessy has described the late 1950s as 'a moment of intermingling for notions of identity, faith, morals, crime and punishment.'[10] This 'intermingling' is only partially apparent in the pages of the *NOTW* although religious leaders including the Archbishop of Canterbury, Geoffrey Fisher, and Donald Soper, the prominent Methodist minister, did write for it. There was some intermittent recognition that the ethnic composition of the country was changing – all the way from an article headed 'Let's welcome the Jamaicans. They belong here'[11] to some deceptively 'neutral' reports following the so-called 'race riots' of 1958: 'One Coloured to Every 257 Whites' ran the eye-catching headline above figures about relative unemployment among the 'coloured' population and a description of housing conditions among those who had '"colonised", or formed small close pockets in certain areas.'[12] Attitudes to situations far from home could afford to be more outspoken. 'Apartheid is wrong' was the front-page headline in 1960 quoting the statement made by Selwyn Lloyd, Conservative Home Secretary, that 'Britain rejects the idea of any inherent superiority of one race over another.'[13] Nevertheless, the paper's leaders did, as Hennessy also says, tend to support the views of the more right-wing party activists on such issues as 'trade union power and what was then called "coloured immigration"'.[14]

Back in 1943, when the paper celebrated its centenary, Winston Churchill whose political triumphs, vicissitudes and visible ill health were to be recorded throughout the post-war years and who, earlier in his career, had been an assiduous contributor, had sent a message to the editor hoping that 'long might it continue to educate and amuse the British race'.[15] Of precisely whom 'the British race' might now be composed, whether the phrase might carry any meaning at all, were to become in the 1950s, and after, the underlying, sometimes buried, questions of the day, not least in the *News of the World*, long concerned in one way or another with insidious threats to the national status quo and Churchillian concepts. Immediately post-war attitudes survived far into the mid-century and were profitable.

Circulation figures certainly seem to prove the point. In 1931–32 the paper had been selling some 24.32 million copies a year; by 1950 this was 47.6 million, which was more than 10 million ahead of its nearest rival, the *People*, and 10 times the number of copies sold of the *Observer*.[16] Put another way, this means that it can be claimed that in 1950 'one in every two households in Britain had a copy.'[17] That was in a context in which, according to Richard Hoggart in his *The Uses of Literacy* of 1957, 'two out of three in the adult population read more than one Sunday newspaper, and more than one out of four read three or more Sunday papers'[18] or, as another radical literary critic who came to the fore in the 1950s, Raymond Williams, chose to express it, 'by 1947 every ten adults read twelve daily and twenty-three Sunday papers.'[19] Multiple readership, perhaps somewhere between two-and-a-half and three readers per copy, whether within the same household or not, would even suggest that more than half the population as a whole now read the *NOTW* on a regular basis.

The most intriguing implication of such captivating – if mathematically challenging – statistics is that what is often represented, then as now, as a 'working-class' newspaper must have reached far more readers than made up the class with which it was most closely associated. A report prepared by Mass Observation in 1949 noted, 'the majority of the *NOTW* readers are buying a paper whose editorial politics come into direct conflict with their own,'[20] but explained the paradox by claiming that 'the *News of the World* is read almost entirely for its gossip features, so that it is not surprising that its readers (the majority of whom themselves have Labour sympathies) remain out of touch with its political views.'[21] However one explained this fact, it was clear that the paper's appeal reached beyond simple party and class allegiances

The situation becomes yet more complex if we take precise demographics into account. The 1950s saw the coming of age for consumer surveys, usually produced for the benefit of advertising agencies and those manufacturers who might take advantage of what they had to offer. Circulation figures were frequently broken down into alphabetised socio-economic groupings. The prominent *Hulton Readership Survey* of 1950 (which many later historians have relied upon) divides the social classes into five reasonably distinct categories: A, the well-to-do, usual income level of head of household: over £1,000 a year; B, the middle class, usual income level: £650–£1,000; C, the lower-middle class, usual income level: £400–£649; D, the working class, usual income level: £225–£329; E, the poor, usual income level: under £225 a year. A table in the *Hulton Survey* shows that 'of all classes 50.00% read the *News of the World*; of Class A 22.7%; of Class B 26.4%; of Class C 38.7%; of Class DE 57.4%.'[22]

This summary would seem to confirm that the *NOTW* sold to an exceptionally wide socio-economic range. The *Hulton Survey*, however, prefaces its tables with some cautionary warnings. An increase in print runs, made possible by the greater availability of newsprint after the end of the war, should not be directly correlated to readership; it might simply mean that there were more copies to go around. Nor, of course, should it be assumed that individual readers always paid the same degree of attention to what was in front of them – a salutary reminder for prospective advertisers. In addition, recent social change might have skewed traditional class divisions:

> Considerable thought has been given, and is being given, to the question of whether these distinctions should be in economic or in social terms. Prior to 1939 the question was largely immaterial, for the economic and the social hierarchies were the same: the lower-middle-class were better off than the working class, and the middle class than the lower-middle class. But the violent changes which have occurred since then in the income-structure of Great Britain have thrown the two out of gear, so that 'spending power' is no longer in line with social class.
>
> The family of a coal-face worker, for example, or a stevedore, may well have an income of £500 or £600 a year: the family income of the local schoolmaster, or curate, or bank clerk, may easily be as low as £300. But the miner and the stevedore remain essentially 'working class' in their living patterns and thought processes, just as the schoolmaster and the curate remain middle class or lower-middle class.
>
> The discrepancy becomes worse if we consider 'spending power' – or, rather, 'free' spending power. The curate will normally refuse to live in a council house, and may insist on sending his children to 'private' schools, so that even if his income were as high as the stevedore's £500 the amount he would have available for the purchase of such things as television sets would be very much less.

As the authors of the survey were eventually forced to concede, any system that attempted to take so many differentials into account would be 'so heterogeneous as to be quite useless as a guide to marketing policy'.[23] Similarly, what might have served as a warning to advertisers at the time is equally relevant to cultural historians writing about popular newspapers, such as the *NOTW*, long after the event.

Nor do statistics of the kind provided by the *Hulton Survey* tell us very much about how a newspaper was actually read. The problem is recognised by Adrian Bingham in his excellent *Family Newspapers? Sex, Private Life, and the British Popular Press, 1918–1978*. Bingham notes not only the sketchiness of archival evidence but also the fact that 'bald' circulation figures do not 'indicate to which particular aspects of a newspaper readers are responding' and that even correspondence columns are subject to editorial intervention and selection.[24]

This is surely true of the *NOTW*. Newspapers might be instantly recognisable in terms of visual appearance and public identity but they are heterogeneous in content and multi-vocal in tone. Even the front page of the *NOTW*, although usually dominated by a headline of national or international significance, allowed multiple choice. So, for example, on 28 October 1956, it offered as its main story the Russian invasion of Hungary, but this was flanked by a picture of Princess Margaret at Covent Garden on one side and a highly insinuating story about the apparent suicide of a Canvey Island clergyman (in the habit of going sailing with choir boys, 'was married but had no children') on the other.

Like most newspaper historians Bingham, although he does acknowledge that surveys such as the one carried out by Mass Observation can be useful, pays no attention to the texts that we call 'literary'. Yet, while evidence of the kind provided by memoirs, by novels and plays might not be straightforwardly 'empirical', it can direct us to other kinds of truth and to the subjectivity involved in what sociologists tend to categorise simply as 'reception'. At the very least, literary texts can tell us how imprints were deployed as cultural symptoms. Here, for instance, is a passage from George Orwell's famous 'Decline of the English Murder' essay of 1946 that purports to provide sociological evidence but with its combination of detailed precision and atmospheric colour obviously goes beyond the bounds of the simply observed:

> It is Sunday afternoon, preferably before the war. The wife is already asleep in the armchair, and the children have been sent out for a nice long walk. You put your feet up on the sofa. Settle your spectacles on your nose, and open up the *News of the World*. Roast beef and Yorkshire pudding, or roast pork and apple sauce, followed up by suet pudding and driven home, as it were by cup of mahogany-brown tea, have put you in just the mood. Your pipe is drawing sweetly, the sofa cushions are soft beneath you, the fire is well alight, the air is warm and stagnant. In these blissful circumstances, what it that you want to read about?
>
> Naturally about a murder.[25]

In fact, Orwell had already used this memorable moment (twice) in his novel *Coming up for Air* (1939) when the hero recalls his upbringing, presumably in the early 1900s.

> On Sunday afternoons, the only time when he really took things easy, he'd settle down by the parlour fireplace to have what he called a 'good read' at the Sunday paper. His favourite paper was *The People* – Mother preferred the *News of the World*, which she considered had more murders

in it. I can see them now. A Sunday afternoon – summer, of course, always summer – a smell of roast pork and greens still floating in the air, and mother on one side of the fireplace, starting off to read the latest murder but gradually falling asleep with her mouth open, and father in the other, in slippers and spectacles, working his way slowly through yards of smudgy print.[26]

A fixed generic distinction between factual reportage and imaginative reconstruction is often hard to maintain. It is for that very reason that we should not be greatly surprised to find a not dissimilar scenario, again involving the *NOTW*, occurring as one of Richard Hoggart's memories of his own 1930s boyhood in *The Uses of Literacy*:

I could continue almost endlessly recalling other individual details which give this kind of domestic life a recognisable quality of its own; the steam-and-soda-and-hashed-meat smell of wash-day, or the smell of clothes drying by the fireside; the Sunday smell of the *News of the World*-mingled-with-roast-beef; the intermittent reading of pieces of old newspaper in the lavatory; the waste of Sunday afternoon, relieved by occasional visits of relatives or to the cemetery, whose gates are flanked by the stalls of flower-sellers and by the workshops of those who sell expensive headstones.[27]

Does the repeated appearance of the olfactory Sunday lunch, with its specific newspaper accompaniment, prove its historical veracity? Or is this a literary template conveniently to hand? An inherited folk trace of familial security? A personal recollection of particular occasions, nonetheless? If the last, how can we be sure? Hoggart's passage is couched in the first person whereas Orwell's is generalised (which is why it transfers so easily from avowed fiction), yet the important point is that both authors lay claim to a particular kind of class authenticity.

As Stefan Collini, along with others, has noted, 'the question of "authentic" working-class voices acquired a sudden prominence in metropolitan literary and intellectual circles in the late 1950s in Britain.'[28] Although frequently presented as an essential element in working-class life, there was nevertheless more than one way of viewing the 'authentic' significance of the *NOTW*. The young and self-consciously 'deracinated' male protagonists of novels by Kingsley Amis and John Wain seem to have been particularly anxious to distinguish themselves from its shabbily naïve readers, left-overs from pre-war days. *Lucky Jim* provides a succinct example when Amis has Bill Atkinson, a down at heel insurance salesman some years older than the novel's hero, Jim Dixon, the well-educated university lecturer, put in his place with a single glancing sentence: 'Atkinson, unexpectedly garrulous, described a case he'd been reading about in the *NOTW*, asked Dixon's opinion on a clue in its prize crossword....'[29] Nothing more needs be said.

Charles Lumley in Wain's *Hurry on Down* of 1953, among the first of a string of post-war novels by and about well-educated young men disenchanted with an inherited culture, is even more dismayed by the unprepossessing world he finds himself sharing. Unemployed and broke, confronted by a landlady anxious for rent, he is obliged to bluff his way out by pretending to be a private detective:

> Did she remember the Evans case, the one that got so much space in the *News of the World*? But then, she did not read the *News of the World*, of course, she would not have seen it: anyway, he, Charles had been responsible for bringing that man to justice.[30]

The flattering implication that the landlady is too genteel to read the paper almost works, although a reverse strategy is required later on when Charles has to deal with the family of Rosa, a would-be girlfriend:

> The invaluable *News of the World* provided them with topics; first what Rosa's father thought about the burning issue raised by their football correspondent, then the slightly less burning, but still urgent, controversy on the boxing page. Finally the murders, and how disgracefully easy it was to escape from Broadmoor and these places. Twice during the fifteen minutes, Rosa's father spat into the fire, and the second time he did so, Charles decided to co-operate and spat too. He could not decide whether this had been the right move.[31]

Shaken by this (surely unlikely) performance Charles ruminates that 'Nothing ever happened in houses like this, nothing except things people could understand. No problems, no art, no discussions and perplexities, just birth, death, eating, resting, sitting in front of the fire on Sunday afternoons with the *NOTW*.'[32]

A similar vision of the typical *NOTW* reader, his or her experience confined to the most basic of human events with 'no problems, no art', is implied by Angus Wilson's Mrs Wrigley, the ex-East Ender who epitomises aspirational vulgarity in his novel *Hemlock and After* of 1952.

> 'Children are that ungrateful,' grumbled Mrs Wrigley. 'I got eleven of them. Won the *News of the World* tray for it. But much good it's done me. Three's in Aussie, and my daughter over Ipswich way's got television. I might be dead for all they care.'[33]

We might note that all three representations of working-class life are conceived by middle-class Oxbridge graduates. However comically presented, social advance entails near contempt for what is left behind, or gratefully avoided, and what often seems like a dismissive response to the materialism of people who hadn't got much in the first place. However, there is also what we might think of as the view from inside; given the patrician hold on publishing in the period, it is less easily found. In Alan Sillitoe's novel *Saturday Night and Sunday Morning* (1958) the hero, Arthur Seaton, in bed with his best friend's wife, sends her young son to the parlour to get 'the *News of the World* that's just been pushed in the letterbox'.[34] The importantly 'authentic' point here is not only that Arthur is well positioned for any sexual stimulation that the paper might offer, but that it is Sunday, so he actually has time to browse its delights. It is hard to imagine that Arthur would take anything other than pleasure in reading about the secret pleasures and public exposures of his weekday bosses.

That endlessly recycled journalistic trope, the 'double life', was invariably expressed in the form of the one literary reference that everyone can recognise: 'Jekyll and Hyde.'[35] The pages of the *NOTW* are packed with disclosures of one kind or another: truth-revealing reports from the law courts, 'confessions' freely volunteered by stars of stage and screen (and more and more often of TV), 'investigations' into corruption carried out by fearless journalists much as in the late nineteenth century. Together they constitute a picture of a society in which everything is and is not what it seems, its imperial façade is still just about in place but constantly threatened by new back-door, back-stage revelations. The selling point would seem to be that the pleasure to be gained from reading about other people's duplicity is accompanied by confirmation that one is not alone in practicing deception. In fact – a cultural factor that the satirical novels exploit – there is often an amused knowingness about the whole prurient process that simultaneously mocks the class distinctions upon which such voyeurism depends.

Perhaps because it typically occupies a space between public and private appearance, transvestitism seems to have been particularly noteworthy form of the double life, for example, 'An Eerie Half-World Between the Sexes.'[36] Bigamy, too, gets plenty of attention, while age difference is invariably of interest, (e.g. 'The Parson aged 64 Marries Girl of 19', a front page feature on 6 October 1957). Although the basic strategy of appearing non-judgmental while specifying, and thereby tacitly agreeing with, the 'punishment' remained unchanged, there were nevertheless some seemingly anomalous, even superficially 'liberal', contributions. Writing in October 1955 in the light of the Magistrate's Association's recent rejection of a recommendation that homosexual conduct between consenting adults be decriminalised, an Old Bailey judge confessed to his deep dismay at having been obliged to send offenders, predominantly clergymen, to gaol:

> In 1553 an Act was passed which made homosexual offences punishable by death, and so the law remained until the Offences Against the Person

Act 1861 which made the maximum punishment penal servitude (now imprisonment) for life.

The provision of such a severe punishment, however, has produced no abatement of the vice. Indeed, those in authority are agreed that it has spread and continues to spread alarmingly.[37]

What was to be done? Prison only condemned the offender to spend time with men like himself; segregation would obviously only confirm that risk. Yet 'there is the dark shadow of the ever-increasing indulgence in this type of vice. The number of detected cases must be infinitesimal compared with the number that pass without detection.' Important though it was to display a charitable concern for the 'tragedy' of individual lives, there was, in short, nothing to be done except wring one's hands in public. The sanctimonious contradictions of this position, widely held in the 1950s, are obvious and have subsequently been much remarked upon. Homosexuality is somehow both hidden and visible, usually under the all-purpose word 'offence', (although that may to some extent simply reflect the language of the courts); the effeminate, facially debauched,and often 'foreign', figures increasingly to be seen on the streets of the West End nevertheless need to be 'exposed'. Homosexuality is a minority preference that is socially threatening – because it is deemed to be contagious and addictive.

An already ominous mood climaxed with the arrest of Lord Montagu and others in 1953 followed by their trials, including for conspiracy to commit sexual 'offences', and their eventual conviction in March 1954. The cumulative coverage given by the press to the Montagu affair has provoked some debate among social historians as to the exact nature – and, indeed, the actuality – of a homosexual 'witch hunt' in the period. While some assume this to be the result of a deliberate and well-considered government policy, others have argued that the virulent innuendo of the press campaign was quite separate from whatever was being discussed and concluded at Westminster.[38]

However one chooses to estimate its power, the *NOTW* certainly played its part in the onslaught, with full reports of not only the Montagu case but also many other hearings that involved homosexual incidents. (Inevitably these were interposed with features on the Coronation including the Archbishop of Canterbury's message to the readership on 31 May 1953, page 6). Unapologetic and unashamed as ever, the paper published on 6 June 1954, page 4, under the heading 'What Goes On in Britain's Gaols?', a leader protesting against the kind of prison conditions that Montagu and his friends had endured. A week later, it ran an article with a heading invoking the aftermath of the Wilde scandal of the late 1890s: 'The Ballad of Reading Gaol rings true today' (13 June 1954, page 4). By combining its traditional claim to be a voice for humanitarian reform with a contemporary mission to rid society of a 'contagious' vice, the paper helped to reinforce a repressive climate, condescending yet punitive, in which gay men could be viewed as the pathetic victims of their own desires and therefore deserving of better treatment, but 'treatment' nonetheless.

What also counted for the *NOTW*, perhaps more than for any other paper, was the class context of sexual behaviour since the Montagu case had involved a peer of the realm consorting with junior aircraftsmen. Although it may not have been the major perpetrator of homophobic hate speech at the time – a distinction that probably belongs to the *Sunday Pictorial* – the *NOTW* brought to the situation a characteristic emphasis on abuses of class privilege signalled by references to fashionable addresses (not just Montagu's estate at Beaulieu where the offences were said to have been committed, but his flat in Mount Street),[39] expensive clothes (the inevitable 'suede shoes'),[40] and impressive vehicles (Montagu leaves the court driven in ' a high-powered low-built grey sports car').[41]

The implication here is that the masculine virtues most recently demonstrated in the war against Hitler are corrupted not by an outdated hierarchy so much as by decadent and irresponsible weaknesses within the class system that threaten to infect society altogether. This, again, was in line with the paper's social conservatism – for all its careful use of popular idioms. Seen from this perspective, the fictional representations of the paper's readership in Amis, Wain, et al. might be judged rather more generously as implying a vulnerable constituency at the mercy of manipulative forces determined to maintain compliance. The novelists' satire could even be seen as a literary way of questioning the unearned authority of the press as a whole, a major topic of the day and the ostensible concern of the Royal Press Commission convened in 1949 to investigate, among other things, contemporary concerns about monopolistic control.[42] Although the *NOTW* was not owned by a press baron until Rupert Murdoch took it over in 1969, it was inevitably associated with the concentrated power and wealth increasingly based on media resources. It existed, thrived and ultimately began to decline in the context not just of the newspaper business as a whole but in the larger field of 'communications', which had begun most obviously to include television and the popular music industry. Sir William Carr, who took over as Chairman of the News of the World Organisation in 1952, had soon set about diversifying its investments into provincial papers and commercial TV.[43]

The 1950s saw the arrival not just of rock and roll, and relative (if partial) prosperity, but intellectual reactions to technological innovation. Given the size of their readership, their association with established ways of life and yet the visible evidence that they were undergoing quite dramatic processes of change, it is not at all remarkable that Sunday newspapers should have attracted the attention of the newly developing academic field we now know as Cultural Studies. The task that lay before the new discipline was to identify the factors that had brought the expansion about, to broaden the field of enquiry so that journalism came under the broad banner of 'communications', which didn't simply dismiss 'mass' popularity as depersonalised 'consumption' but explored the specific nature, indeed, the 'value' of a product or mode of behaviour. Cultural Studies would enquire into the true meaning of the 'popular'.

Documentary evidence of the close link between developments in the media and the growth of Cultural Studies is provided by a rarely remarked upon collection of essays entitled *Your Sunday Paper* that Richard Hoggart published in 1967. Here the aim was to demonstrate the extent to which the formal changes that were taking place within a particular publishing genre were by no means confined to the demands of a single niche market. A key example was the re-emergence of the traditional 'investigative' piece, in various newly professionalised forms, in all manner of Sunday papers whether 'quality' (the *Sunday Times*, in particular) or 'popular' – and which seemed in itself to have little to do with the questioning of class difference. As Hoggart announced in his introduction:

> Again, some longstanding characteristics of British social life – for instance, the relationship or assumed relationship between differences in social class and different kinds and degrees of literacy – decide many of the qualities of the Sundays; such assumptions run through the newspapers like the ribs of a ship.[44]

Among his contributors, the journalist and sociologist Paul Barker, later to become editor of *New Society*, noted that most newspaper investigations were 'timeless' and to that extent toothless, in that they related to topics that could be current at any moment.[45] Stuart Hall, a founding father of the 'New Left', connected conservatism with the contents of the typical gossip column – 'inconsequential stories about consequential people'. It was, he said, 'a selective microcosm of the newspaper's social universe', which, nevertheless, acts as 'a sort of "gate-keeper" between the readers and the fictional social world of the newspaper...a world we would not otherwise know.'[46] The lack of serious arts coverage ('no problems, no art', John Wain's fictional hero had complained in 1953) was lamented by several, and Raymond Williams made the point, to be fully borne out in the following years, that Sunday paper criticism increasingly tended towards 'what is in effect publicity material.'[47]

The *NOTW* was only one of the papers inspected by the academic monitors associated with Cultural Studies, but it was undoubtedly the most charismatic and it could hardly escape the severity of their judgements. Politically and socially conservative, sexually prurient and morally censorious, homophobic beyond even the accepted standards of the day, exploitative of women and their bodies – all of these things the paper undoubtedly could be. Yet, at the same time and rather less acknowledged by intellectuals, it offered practical advice on legal and other matters, usually quite sound, via its 'John Hilton' feature, and it served several other useful social functions. A character in a short story by Shelagh Delaney, whose play *A Taste of Honey* (1958) had signalled a major shift in the 'authenticity' of modern English drama, takes it for granted that the obvious place to put a notice about a missing relative is the *NOTW*.[48] The paper's competitive entertainment (*pace* the pathetic tea tray, awarded for fecundity in Angus Wilson's *Hemlock and After*) was probably no more weighted against the punter than the large-scale forms of gambling such as the dogs, the horses and the football pools that were endemic throughout the country. The paper had what was by the 1950s generally agreed to be the finest sports coverage in the business. In all these respects, as Rodney Ackland's play, *Before the Party*, recognised and the novelists chose to downplay, it contributed to the national culture of which it was a part with an enlivened view of reality. Hoggart, not known for his enthusiasm for the beguiling face of contemporary capitalism, acknowledged as much when he wrote in *The Uses of Literacy*:

> those special favourites of working-class people, the Sunday gossip-with-sensation papers, the papers for the free day, assiduously collect from throughout the British Isles all the suitable material they can find, for the benefit of almost the whole of the adult working-class population...One should think first of the photographically detailed aspect; the staple fare is not something which suggests an escape from ordinary life, but rather it assumes that ordinary life is intrinsically interesting.[49]

By the start of the 1960s, with circulation now down to the 6 million mark,[50] and fierce rivalry from the *People* and other more up-to-date papers, it was time for the *NOTW* once again to rejuvenate itself by exploiting even more ruthlessly some tried and tested formulas – specifically the sensational possibilities of those celebrity lives that were unashamedly 'extraordinary' in their sexual dimensions or that could, at least, be made to seem so. At the same time, it was important to stress the 'ordinary' origins of the glamorous individual in question. A new editor, Stafford Somerfield, who had formerly overseen foreign affairs, was appointed in place of Cudlipp and he turned to the actress Diana Dors, whose exploits, factual and fictional, the paper was already in the habit of recording.[51] Serialisation of her 'memoirs', *Swinging Dors*, started on 24 January 1960 (pages 4–5) and ran throughout the spring. Sexual scandal had already proved to be the ideal accompaniment to an increasingly theatrical nationalism – an irony not lost on the Irish republican author Brendan Behan who, in his play *The Hostage* (1958), has his unquestioningly Anglophile, royalist, lady social worker, Miss Gilchrist, rely on the *NOTW* for her information about the way of life she so much admires across the water. On learning that a young British soldier has been taken prisoner by the IRA, she exclaims:

'Poor boy! Do you know, I think they ought to put his story in the *News of the World*. Ah, we'll be seeing you on the telly yet. He'll be famous like that Diana Dors, or the one who cut up his victim and threw the bits out of an aeroplane. I think he has a serial running somewhere.'[52]

Crime and sex had always gone well together, and Dors had had some dubious associates, but sex would now unquestionably take the lead. With the publication of the Dors memoirs the paper took a significant step towards becoming known almost exclusively for its lubricious content: the *News of the Screws* as the satirical magazine *Private Eye* (which ironically enough has always shared many of its gossipy predilections) would now have it. The paper would nevertheless have difficulty in keeping up with changing mores and with contemporary views of class.

Evidence of how far it had come, and intended to go on, is offered by the full page announcements it placed in the *Newspaper Directory* describing its own advertising team. In 1949, this claimed that the paper had 'a readership of over 17,000,000 copies per issue' and that 'Its increasing influence amongst all classes in the United Kingdom is fully appreciated by National Advertisers.'[53] In 1960 a similar glossy page reads rather differently:

> More men and women read the *News of the World* than any other newspaper – including the young people in the 16–24 age group. Sell to all age groups in every social grade through the most potent and cheapest advertising medium.[54]

We should note the emphasis on youth – teenagers now have considerable buying power and in reality, the paper was increasingly worried about losing the younger generation. There is also a shift from the word 'class' to the word 'grade', and a stress on the cheapness of the newspaper medium – which is probably designed to make a silent comparison with commercial TV.

Later in the same year, 1960, Penguin Books published *Lady Chatterley's Lover* and the *News of the World* responded by reporting the views of the Anglican church which predictably played it both ways, with the Bishop of Woolwich defending Lawrence's sexually frank novel only to be reprimanded by his senior, the Archbishop of Canterbury.[55] Conveniently enough, the demands of sexual description and moral censure were both served in a manner that reflected the traditional ambiguities of the *News of the World* itself.

A decade earlier, on Sunday 1 January 1950, the paper had reported the hopes of various show business personalities for the year ahead. The singer Vera Lynn wanted for her newly acquired house in Finchley, 'one of those shiny, labour-saving American style kitchens one sees on the films and in the magazines'; Annette Mills, first star of children's television, wanted an end to vivisection and other forms of cruelty. Overall she hoped to see 'the first young fresh shoots of a newer and better way of life growing out of the muckheap of this decaying civilization of ours, so that before it quite disappears, a new one will be strong enough to take its place.'[56] These are extraordinary words for someone who had made her name singing to a wooden puppet, but the sound of the war against fascism can still be heard in them. In December 1959 when the paper repeated the formula, there were twenty-three rather than four 'personalities' and they were almost all involved in television. Following in the tradition of Vera Lynn many had moved into a new house in the previous year, several simply wanted a new series or a film role in the year to come. No one mentioned 'civilization' or the war, although a leader on the same page made a firm connection between prosperity and peace. It announced:

> Farewell to the Frustrating, Frightening Fifties. Why frustrating? And why frightening? Because of the dreadful shadow of the H-bomb. Because of the uneasy years of the 'cold peace'. Because of the rough, tough climb back from the crippling aftermath of war.
>
> Forget it now. On to the Successful Soaring Sixties. Why successful? Why soaring? Well, it looks as if we left a lot of the gloom behind. There's an air of goodwill around that isn't only due to the festive season.
>
> At last! The Summit seems to loom nearer. At last there's some jam on the bread today instead of being promised for tomorrow. At last a good many of the 'have-nots' are beginning to become the 'haves'.[57]

This, then, was to be the future: a peaceful, property-owning democracy, with the emphasis on property, where entertainment offered one of the best investments around, underwritten by sex whenever possible. It was, in its way, an accurate prophecy of the 1960s although it made no mention of the impact of new media that the paper was already in the process of acknowledging with, for instance, the actor Richard Attenborough's weekly review of record releases: LPs from the likes of Herbert von Karajan conducting the Philharmonia Orchestra alongside 45 r.p.m. discs from Bill Haley and Lonnie Donegan. Nor does this euphoric leader mention the changing face of what Churchill had once called, without embarrassment, 'the British race'.[58]

Notes

1. Rodney Ackland, *Before the Party*, London, 2013, p. 34. The play adapted a short story written by Somerset Maugham in the 1920s.
2. Ackland, *Before the Party*, p. 44.
3. Cyril Bainbridge and Roy Stockdill, *The News of the World Story: 150 Years of the World's Bestselling Newspaper*, London, 1993, pp.178–79.
4. *NOTW*, 10 February 1952, p. 6.

5. *NOTW*, 16 August 1959, p. 1.
6. E.g. *NOTW*, 9 December 1956, p. 8.
7. *NOTW*, 15 July 1956, p. 1.
8. *NOTW*, 29 July 1956, p. 6.
9. *NOTW*, 21 October 1951, p. 6.
10. Peter Hennessy, *Having it so Good. Britain in the Fifties*, London, 2006, p. 501.
11. *NOTW*, 14 November 1954, p. 6.
12. *NOTW*, 7 September 1958, p. 1.
13. *NOTW*, 3 April 1960, p. 1.
14. Hennessy, *Having it so Good*, p. 360.
15. Stafford Somerfield, *Banner Headlines*, Shoreham-by-Sea, 1979, pp. 84–85. For Churchill's involvement with the paper also see Matthew Engel, *Tickle the Public. One Hundred Years of the Popular Press*, London, 1996, p. 227 and p. 229, and Bainbridge and Stockdill, *The News of the World*, pp. 105–08.
16. Hennessy, *Having it so Good*, pp. 105–06.
17. Engel, *Tickle the Public*, London, 1996, p. 230.
18. Richard Hoggart, *The Uses of Literacy*, London, 1957, p. 331.
19. Raymond Williams, *Communications*, Harmondsworth, 1976 third edn, reprinted 1977, p. 20.
20. *The Press and its Readers*. A report prepared by Mass-Observation for The Advertising Service Guild, London. 1949, p. 114.
21. Ibid., p. 86.
22. *The Hulton Readership Survey, 1950*, London, 1950, p. 8.
23. Ibid., p. 5.
24. Adrian Bingham, *Family Newspapers? Sex, Private Life, and the British Popular Press, 1918–1978*, Oxford, 2009.
25. 'Decline of the English Murder', first published in *Tribune*, 15 February 1946, in *The Collected Essays, Journalism and Letters of George Orwell*, Harmondsworth, 4, pp. 124–8, p. 124.
26. George Orwell, *Coming Up For Air*, London, repr. 1948, p. 47, repeated on p. 189.
27. Hoggart, *Uses*, pp. 36–37.
28. Stefan Collini, *English Pasts. Essays in History and Culture*, Oxford and New York, 1999, p. 215.
29. Kingsley Amis, *Lucky Jim*, London, 1953, p. 301.
30. John Wain, *Hurry on Down*, London, 1953, p. 3.
31. Ibid., p. 177.
32. Ibid., p. 181.
33. Angus Wilson, *Hemlock and After*, London, 1952, p. 178.
34. *Saturday Night and Sunday Morning*, London, 1958, p. 18.
35. E.g. *NOTW*, 23 November 1952, p. 2; *NOTW*, 5 April 1953, p. 3; *NOTW*, 19 June 1955, p. 7; *NOTW*, 24 February 1957, p. 2; *NOTW*, 28 July 1957, p. 5.
36. *NOTW* 3 Nov. 1957, 3. Also see, for example, *NOTW* 26 Nov., 1950, 1.
37. His Honour J. Tudor Rees, 'What Can Be Done With These Problem Men?', *NOTW*, 22 October 1955, p. 6.
38. Patrick Higgins, *Heterosexual Dictatorship. Male Homosexuality in Postwar Britain*, London, 1996, esp. pp. 241–50 and pp. 267–82. Also see S. Cohen and J. Young eds, *The Manufacture of News: Social Problems, Deviance and the Mass Media*, London, 1981; Richard Davenport-Hines, *An English Affair. Sex, Class and Power in the Age of Profumo*, London, 2013; Richard Hornsey, *The Spiv and the Architect. Unruly Life in Postwar London*, Minneapolis and London, 2012; Matt Houlbrook,

Queer London. Perils and Pleasures in the Sexual Metropolis, 1918–1957, Chicago and London, 2005; S. Jeffery-Poulter, *Peers, Queers and Commons: The struggle for gay law reform from 1950 to the present*, London, 1991; Chris Waters, 'Disorders of the Mind, Disorders of the Body Social: Peter Wildeblood and the Making of the Modern Homosexual' in Becky Conekin, Frank Mort, Chris Waters (eds), *Moments of Modernity. Reconstructing Britain 1945–1964*, London and New York, 1999, pp. 134–52.

39. *NOTW*, 31 January 1954, p. 2.
40. *NOTW*, 8 November 1953, p. 1.
41. *NOTW*, 10 January 1954, p. 1.
42. It is surely impossible in 2015 to read the commission's report without being struck by the complacency of its conclusions: 'It is generally agreed that the British press is inferior to none in the world. It is free from corruption: both those who own the Press and those who are employed on it would universally condemn the acceptance or soliciting of bribes.' (*Royal Commission on the Press*, 1947–1949, London: HMSO, 1949, p. 149.)
43. Bainbridge and Stockdill, *The News of the World*, p. 175.
44. Richard Hoggart (ed.), *Your Sunday Paper*, London, 1967, p. 12. The book was originally commissioned to relate to a series of adult education programmes to be put out by ABC TV.
45. Hoggart, *Your Sunday Paper*, p. 33
46. Ibid., p. 80.
47. Ibid., p. 154.
48. S. Delaney, 'My Uncle the Spy', in *Sweetly Sings the Donkey*, London, 1964, p. 78.
49. p. 100.
50. Bainbridge and Stockdill, *The News of the World*, pp. 178–79.
51. E.g. *NOTW*, 28 August 1955, p. 7.
52. 'The Hostage', in Brendan Behan, *Complete Plays*, London, p. 217.
53. *The Newspaper Press Directory*, London, 1949, p. 22.
54. *The Newspaper Press Directory*, London, 1960, np.
55. *NOTW*, 6 November 1960, p. 1.
56. *NOTW*, 1 January 1950, p. 4.
57. *NOTW*. 27 December 1959, p. 8.
58. More than half a century after the leader of 27 December 1959 had predicted a bright future, Zadie Smith's brilliantly authentic novel *N-W*, published in 2012, would itemise some of the papers currently available on a London High Street: 'Polish paper, Turkish paper, Arabic, Irish, French, Russian, Spanish, *News of the World*.' Like all such lists this both separates and combines. The presence of the *News of the World* serves as testimony to the welcome wonders and inevitable stresses of the multi-cultural Britain that had emerged since the 1950s. Was its supplementary function in Zadie Smith's novel an acknowledgment of the survival of the white working-class or was her point that – even towards its inglorious end in 2011 – it could still claim, as it had in the 1950s, to be the only paper read by the nation as a whole?

12
Bringing Popular Journalism into Disrepute: The *News of the World*, the Public and Politics 1953–2011

Kevin Williams

Introduction

The closure of the *News of the World* (*NOTW*) in 2011 was the culmination of a debate about the paper's journalistic methods that stretched back over the post-war period. The newsgathering practices deployed by the *NOTW* had resulted in clashes between the paper, politicians and the public over its methods and their consequences for individuals, society and the state of the press. These clashes were more acute as the pressure to find exclusive stories became more intense and the capacity to unearth information was enhanced by new technology. The journey that led to the newspaper's eventual demise started with a series of decisions at the beginning of the 1960s, the most noticeable of which was the serialisation of the Diana Dors memoirs in January 1960. This story 'set popular journalism on a course that would end with the phone-tapping scandals of today'.[1]

Concerns about the *NOTW*'s reporting practices were part of a struggle to ensure that the British press operated responsibly and avoided the worst excesses of irresponsible and intrusive journalism. The struggle revolved around self-regulation and the increasing inability of the popular press to police its own practices and methods. Changes in the *NOTW*'s newsgathering methods were brought about by a number of factors, the most important of which were ownership and competition. Murdoch's takeover in 1969 contributed to a significant shift in the organisational culture of the newspaper. Days after the hacking revelations, one anonymous senior News Corp executive told investigative journalist Carl Bernstein where blame rested: 'more than anyone, Murdoch invented and established this culture in the newsroom, where you do whatever it takes to get the story, take no prisoners, destroy the competition, and the end will justify the means.'[2] The question of ownership is closely tied to the changing nature of competition. More intense competition in the Sunday newspaper market from the late 1950s created the conditions that led the paper to push back further the boundaries of acceptable reporting. Greater competition led to a more aggressive style of journalism and more emphasis on crime, celebrity, sex and sensation.

Changes in the commercial environment have to be located in the radical transformation of post-war British society. Editors, owners and reporters found it more difficult to interpret public taste and to understand the expectations of their readers. A *NOTW* representative in evidence to the Royal Commission on the Press in 1948 stated that the paper had 'never' conducted a readership survey.[3] The editor, Arthur Waters, simply knew what his audience wanted – sex, crime, beer and cricket in the summer, football in the winter.[4] Unlike Waters, who died suddenly in 1953, subsequent editors of the *NOTW* were recipients of a vast and ever-increasing amount of data about people's views, tastes and preferences. The *NOTW* was also struggling to satisfy readers for whom newspaper reading was now a secondary activity. However, changes in newsgathering methods were attributed to an increase in public demand for prurient stories about the private lives of celebrities.

This chapter examines the *NOTW*'s voyage from being an institution that was a bastion of everyday life in Britain in 1945 to its closure in 2011 amidst public opprobrium of its methods. This journey is characterised by the intensification of the battle to maintain circulation, the changing nature of ownership and editorial policy, the regularisation of payments for information, the growing collusion between sources and journalists in the generation of news and the long-term disenchantment with the press brought about by changes in patterns of work and life. Post-war practices of editors and reporters became the subject of public scrutiny and debate. Despite many people's reservations about self-regulation ensuring that the newspaper industry acted responsibly – and self-regulation since 1953 can hardly be described as a success – bodies such as the Press Council played an important role in facilitating public debate.

A very British institution

The *NOTW* was deeply embedded in British life at the end of the Second World War. By 1950, the newspaper sold more copies on Sunday than its competitors, with average weekly sales peaking at 8,436,000 during that year.[5] This figure was artificially enhanced by the conditions of austerity and rationing that prevailed in Britain, but sales remained around the 8 million mark until 1953, the year press regulation appeared. The *NOTW* was Britain's most read newspaper with nearly one issue for every six people in the country and in that year Reginald Cudlipp, elder brother of the *Daily Mirror*'s Hugh Cudlipp, stepped up from the position of deputy editor of the *NOTW* – as his predecessor had done – to inherit the editor's chair.

This succession cemented the perception that the newspaper was 'one of the nation's great unchanging institutions.'[6]

1953, however, was a turning point in the newspaper's history. The paper's circulation began steadily to fall, a decline that became more precipitous as the 1950s turned into the 1960s.[7] Between 1954 and 1959, the newspaper lost over 1.5 million sales, a greater decrease than any newspaper has suffered within the same length of time since the war. The *NOTW*'s decline was accompanied by the successful circulation drives of its main rivals,[8] the *People* and the *Sunday Pictorial*, which accentuated concerns inside the paper about its standing as Britain's best-selling newspaper. Sir William Carr, following a long struggle, became chairman of the Board in 1952.[9] He perceived the newspaper to be in a state of crisis. Cudlipp departed in late 1959 and his successor Stafford Somerfield embarked on radical measures to arrest the decline. Somerfield wanted stories that 'will make your hair curl' and introduced 'two new forms of provocative content: kiss-and-tell memoirs and saucy investigations'.[10] His approach had a short term impact on sales but it brought the newspaper into conflict with the newly formed General Council of the Press.

Post-war press regulation

The General Council was recommended by the First Royal Commission on the Press in 1949 in response to disquiet about the threat posed to freedom of expression by the increasing concentration of ownership of newspapers and the perceived influence of advertisers on their editorial content. The Commission's deliberations centred more on ownership and political bias than prurient reporting and invasions of privacy. This was manifest in the parliamentary debate to set up the Commission,[11] the evidence given to the Commission and the deliberations on a private members bill in 1952 to set up a statutory press council.[12] Reporting standards were primarily conceived of in political terms. Intrusive journalism was described as an example of 'undesirable types of journalistic conduct' particularly in relation to reporting intimate details of ordinary people who are in the news accidentally but the thrust of the Commission's scrutiny was on interventions into the lives of political figures.[13]

It took four years to establish the General Press Council and the body that emerged was a long way from what was envisaged. Run by the industry, it had no lay members and was chaired by the owner of *The Times*. By 1953, concerns about ownership and political bias had been superseded by unease about 'mass circulations based upon vice, squalor, rape and sex crimes of every sort'.[14] The bill that forced the Conservative government to act on the commission's recommendations was introduced with 'the object of maintaining and improving the moral, ethical and technical standards of British journalism'. The moral dimension was picked up by MPs who condemned the popular press for 'not contributing to the national welfare or national edification at all', but rather creating 'a cesspool of crime and sex'.[15]

Concerns about the prurience of the press had been fuelled by what Labour MP Douglas Houghton described as 'the sordid, squalid and revolting accounts of the Christie case' in the press.[16] The 1950s was the 'decade of sensational murder' with 1953 memorable for two notorious cases, The Thames Towpath Murders and the Christie murder spree at 10 Rillington Place.[17] Fleet Street reporters in the latter case competed ferociously to acquire the rights to Christie's life story. The reporting of Christie's murders, and in particular of his sexual peccadilloes, was 'significantly more direct' than it would have been prior to the war.[18] This shift was a threat to the *NOTW*, which specialised in the sensational reporting of courtroom accounts of crime. The tone and style of its coverage were beginning to appear 'rather dated'.[19]

The search for circulation set the post-war agenda for popular Sunday journalism. The newspaper industry was emerging from a long period of austerity, and the artificial barriers that had protected many papers were removed. The result was that several major newspaper titles such as the *News Chronicle*, *Empire News* and *Sunday Dispatch* disappeared. The cold winds of competition again blowing through the market accentuated concerns about the consequences of a renewed circulation war. Launching a debate about the state of the press in 1957, Anthony Kershaw, the new Conservative MP for Stroud, alleged that newspapers 'can only stay in business by selling entertainment and excitement' and 'there is consequently little room for serious news in the papers.'[20] Kershaw's view was echoed across the political spectrum, including by some of the leading practitioners of popular journalism in this period. Harry Procter was the doyen of Fleet Street investigative reporters and worked for various papers including the *Daily Mirror*, *Daily Mail* and *Sunday Pictorial* (renamed the *Sunday Mirror* in 1963) and in his memoir in 1958, he confessed that owners and editors simply wanted to make money and were willing to use sex to sell their newspapers. He was particularly critical of the *Mirror* which 'was perfectly honest' that 'Sex ... sold papers ... by the million. Hard news was merely the third course.'[21]

As Britain's best-selling newspaper, the *NOTW* was at the forefront of the concerns about growing triviality and sensationalism. Criticisms of the paper's methods often focused on the activities of Norman 'Jock' Rae, the paper's chief crime correspondent, who did 'everything and anything' to acquire his stories.[22] This involved paying sources including murderers and their families as well as police officers and court officials. Prior to changes in the law, in the 1950s newspapers could pay criminals for the inside stories of their exploits by covering their legal defence costs. The *NOTW* made substantial payments to murderers such as John Haigh and Herbert Mills, as well as the families of convicted killers after they were executed. Such 'confessions' added circulation, but Rae's methods went beyond chequebook journalism when he arranged to meet with the serial killer John Christie to get his story while he was on the run and eluding every police force in the country.[23] Such efforts by Rae and his crime colleagues in Fleet Street – collectively labelled the 'Murder Gang' – to 'push the envelope' and deploy any method to get an exclusive displayed an approach to news reporting that was increasingly to characterise the *NOTW* in the post-war period.

Public responsibility

Rae and his colleagues justified their approach by stating they were 'giving millions of readers what they craved'.[24] Large circulations raised the question of the public's responsibility for the sordid and salacious nature of the reporting. Beverley Baxter, the Conservative MP for Southgate, believed that 'the whole responsibility does not lie with those who edit and write for the newspapers.'[25] Readers, he stated, had to take some responsibility. Baxter expressed his opinion in 1953, a time when the public was trying to be heard. Previously the public was 'helpless' in getting its views listened to by the press: 'letters of criticism to the newspapers are frequently not printed, and letters correcting inaccurate information are frequently ignored.'[26] Editors were able to manage criticism. Change was partly attributable to the General Press Council, despite its obvious weaknesses in speaking for the public.[27] However, the Council was one component of a growing public debate on the press in the 1950s. Television provided a new platform for public comment. In 1956, Granada TV launched the programme *What the Papers Say*, which presented a wry look at newspaper reporting while BBC programmes such as *The Editors* and *In the News* put editors and correspondents in the public limelight. Regular commentaries on the press, such as Randolph Churchill's column in the *Spectator*, appeared in newspapers and magazines. Editors and owners were increasingly sensitive to efforts to discuss their newspapers' performance.

The relationship between popular newspapers and their readers had been evolving since the war. The desire to know more about the readers was anchored in a variety of commercial, cultural and political needs. Understanding the views of ordinary people was crucial to the reconstruction of post-war British society and the press played its role in campaigns to increase public information – a continuation of their wartime propaganda role. The *NOTW* had realised that people at war wanted to read news other than official communiqués and public announcements.[28] The paper had continued to provide accounts of court reports documenting people's sexual misdemeanours, but it also pioneered other forms of interactions with readers. This was in part a response to the limited space allowed by newsprint rationing. The most significant innovation was Jack Hilton's advice bureau.

Advice columns had appeared in newspapers in a variety of shapes and forms in the nineteenth century but during the Second World War a number of newspapers including the *NOTW*, *Daily Mirror* and *People* used the format to develop a new relationship with their readers.[29] Hilton's bureau was an advice service that dealt with 150,000 cases per year.[30] Like the Citizen's Advice Bureau, which had started in 1939, Hilton's bureau offered readers personal, legal and consumer advice connected with the war. The bureau was one of a number of subsidiary activities that also included competitions and mail order schemes established by the *NOTW* to help promote reader loyalty. The bureau continued into the post-war period and cost the paper up to £100,000 per annum. Most of the responses to readers' queries were not published but Hilton's bureau enabled the *NOTW* to develop 'a form of personal connection with readers' and acquire 'the potential to know more about what was happening in their lives.'[31] Enquiries were used to identify patterns of interest or concern amongst readers that sometimes contributed to the editorial pages in the form of stories, such as the Rachman slum housing scandal of the 1960s.

The development of the non-commercial aspect of the paper's relationship with readers was in keeping with how the *NOTW*'s owners, the Carr family, understood the business. They had run the *NOTW* as a family concern since 1891. Staff members were part of the family. Under Sir William Carr, they were not paid very much and were not required to work very hard.[32] He rarely sacked his employees,[33] and parties and get-togethers that representatives of the family attended characterised employment at his paper.[34] In a period of austerity when people were encouraged to pull together, such practices were reinforced. Adrian Bingham draws attention to the conception of the British popular press as 'family newspapers'.[35] Popular Sunday newspapers appear more influenced by this notion than their daily counterparts. This conceptualisation was imposed on them in the nineteenth century through their publication on the Sabbath and the part they played in the struggle around the diffusion of useful knowledge to working people. In their role as family newspapers they had 'to maintain a careful balance between sensation and sobriety' and avoid printing anything 'too outrageous'.[36] This balancing act was acutely felt by the *NOTW* because of the association with the Carr family. Maintaining family values in the content and operation of the newspaper faced greater difficulties once Britain moved out of austerity. The cost-cutting culture associated with Rupert Murdoch's ownership from 1969 of the paper was first introduced in the latter days of Carr's ownership. As sales declined and competition intensified, services such as the Hilton bureau's activities were curtailed. Mark Chapman Walker, the paper's managing director, was not eager to close the bureau,[37] but its operation was not compatible with the search for sales and profits and under Murdoch it was shut down in 1974. The 'demand for the service had not gone away, but the Bureau simply did not make money for the newspaper.'[38]

Profit and privacy

The *NOTW*'s efforts to revitalise its fortunes first found success in the serial-isation of Diana Dors's private life from 24 January 1960, immediately after Stafford Somerfield was appointed as editor. A film star, model and pin-up girl, Dors sold her story of crime, adult sex parties, her jealous husband and her relationships to the newspaper for around £35,000. The paper had beaten off competition from its rivals, in particular the *Sunday Pictorial,* to present a 12-week series of articles which according to their subject took 'all the mucky bits' to tell a story of a scandalous, violent and seedy life.[39] The Dors payout was a critical moment in the development of the *NOTW* and popular Sunday journalism. Serials had always played a role in the Sunday press; during the war, weeklies such as *Reveille* regularly provided glimpses into the private lives of the famous. The Dors serialisation introduced a new 'nastiness' into popular journalism.[40] Somerfield transformed the paper with an emphasis on buy-ups and a more vulgar treatment of sex. Coy descrip-tions of infidelity and inappropriate behaviour were replaced by salacious details of the sex lives of celebrities. In Matthew Engel's words, 'hysterical hypocrisy' replaced the 'old measured prurience'.[41]

The crucial aspect of the Dors story was the response of other newspapers. Traditionally, Sunday newspapers had responded to their rivals' exclusives by taking the moral high ground. Writing in the *Spectator,*[42] Bernard Levin described how the *Sunday Pictorial*, which had been outbid by the *NOTW* for the rights of Dors's story, eschewed the regular Fleet Street response by adopting a 'more vigorous counter-action'. It serialised the story of a couple called Patrick Holt and Sandra Dorne under the title 'The Shocking Mr. Dors.' Ostensibly about Dors's late husband, the articles closely resem-bled what appeared in the *NOTW*. Holt and Dorne were not participants in the sex parties at the heart of the stories but had allegedly been told about them later. The resemblances between the stories reflected the *Pictorial* story's by-line 'as told to Bernard McElwaine'. Levin highlighted the 'cascade' of stories 'stepped up, week by week, in both papers, until it...reached a level which even by British newspaper standards – as far as pornography is concerned...– is almost past believing'. The *Pictorial* attempted to outdo its rival in revealing the sordid details of Dors's story and initiated a more overt form of competition between Sunday papers.

Greater intensity in the search for scoops led to the 'stealing of stories and the art of the "spoiler", the practice of running material designed to fool readers into thinking they had an inside track on the exclusive paid for by a rival'.[43] Two newspapers, the *Sunday Pictorial* and the *People* set the pace in the late 1950s. For example, the *People* paid £200,000 for the rights to run a series of articles in late 1959 based on Hollywood icon Errol Flynn's autobi-ography *My Wicked, Wicked Ways*. The serialisation added 200,000 readers to the *People*'s sales.[44] The pressures to buy up exclusive stories of celebrities, criminals and those caught up in scandal led to the departure of journalists from the industry including Harry Procter who left, 'ashamed' of his profession. Disapproval was also registered by the General Press Council, which criticised the Dors serialisation as 'grossly lewd and salacious...a disgrace to British journalism'.[45] The Council, however, was condemned for being too soft on the press. Its adjudication of complaints was seen as shaped by the line that newspapers had 'to take the blame for the sins of society'.[46] Editors such as Somerfield believed that Council adjudications, mild as they were and steeped in the industry's perspective, were having an impact on the news agenda of popular newspapers.[47] He accused the Council of 'trying to exercise control on the contents' of the *NOTW* over the Dors serialisation.[48] This view did not accord with the Council's critics who describe its decisions as 'overly sensitive to government', 'faintly ridiculous'[49] and doing 'little to influence the development of professional standards'.[50] However, the Council, which was reconstituted as the Press Council in 1962, helped to develop public scrutiny of the press and although imperfect – every enquiry into the press since 1961 has found the Council's representation of the public wanting[51] – this was an important contribution.

Christine Keeler and chequebook journalism

In the early 1960s kiss and tell stories acquired a serious political dimension. The Profumo affair in 1963 was another 'defining moment' in press history.[52] The involvement of the *NOTW* in what is seen as 'a classic illustration of press misconduct' revolves primarily around the serialisation of Christine Keeler's story – twice. Her relations with the War Minister and a Russian naval officer caused a political crisis for Harold Macmillan's government. The *NOTW* bought Keeler's story and its combination of sex, espionage, crime, political intrigue and passion ensured that the paper enjoyed a huge increase in circulation.[53] The Council censured the *NOTW* for publication of the 'sordid details' of Keeler's life, which it considered as 'particularly damaging to the morals of young people'. It believed that by 'exploiting vice and sex for commercial reward the *News of the World* does a disservice both to public welfare and to the Press'.[54] Six years later, the Council took the extraordinary step of taking out its own complaint to censure the newspaper when it decided to re-run Keeler's account of the scandal.

The hysterical and intrusive nature of the reporting of the Profumo affair was a response to the pressures on the press. Relations between Fleet Street and the government were at a long time low as a result of the jailing of two reporters from the *Daily Mail* and the *Daily Sketch* for not revealing their sources in the reporting of the Vassall spy case in the autumn of 1962.[55] In 1963, they had been called before the Radcliffe Tribunal, which had been set up to examine potential breaches of security in the case and ministers were particularly sensitive to leaks about confidential matters.[56] The tribunal was highly critical of the reporting of Vassall stating, that there was no truth in more than 250 articles that it reviewed about the affair.[57] The press in turn accused Radcliffe of a whitewash about spies in Whitehall, and the *NOTW*'s reporting of Profumo in the summer of 1963 was steeped in Fleet Street's belief that the Establishment had something to hide. Somerfield believed that the efforts to restrict the paper printing Keeler's version of events were motivated by political expediency and social snobbery.[58] The *NOTW* coverage was also a response to the imposition of restrictions in 1962 on the reporting from magistrates' courts of committal proceedings, which deprived the paper of one of its main sources of crime news. Further limitations followed the tightening up on payments to criminals following the *NOTW*'s payments to the chief prosecution witness in the Moors Murder trial in 1965. The squeezing of traditional news sources led the paper to look for new ways of generating stories.

A further impetus to the frenzied reporting was the change in the management of the newspaper as the Carr's old-fashioned newspaper operation fell apart. A 'great flabby beast of an organisation',[59] Carr's *NOTW* succumbed to the post-austerity newspaper market. Shares in the *NOTW* were divided between family members; the two main shareholders were Carr and his cousin Professor Derek Jackson. A long running feud and the circulation crisis led Jackson to sell up in 1968; the Carr family did not have enough money to buy Jackson out and the way was paved for Murdoch to take control. William Carr's personal life was chaotic and in a well-documented moment of miscalculation he was outmanoeuvred by Murdoch.[60] Under Murdoch the shift in the balance between sales and sobriety detectable in the early 1960s simply accelerated.

Editorial change

Change in the editorial approach of the *NOTW* in the 1970s was not initiated by Murdoch but grew out of the internal realignment inside the paper following the Profumo affair and external pressures such as the competition from television, a new medium that contributed to the decline in public deference. MPs who voted against the Establishment of commercial television in 1954 had expressed worries about the 'sexing-up' of news and entertainment.[61] Satirical programmes and investigative journalism helped to undermine the authority of Britain's elites, and the popularity accruing to those appearing on television fuelled the extension of celebrity culture. The *NOTW* thrived in an environment of declining deference and celebrity culture. Exposés of people in power and celebrities increased as the news hole diminished with competition from TV news. In 1973, the secret filming of Lord Lambton, Under-Secretary at the Ministry of Defence, smoking cannabis with two prostitutes brought the paper into dispute with the government, Parliament and the Press Council, which condemned the methods used and the payment promised to those who had set up the illicit shots.[62] Murdoch defended the reporting, believing it was in keeping with the tradition of muck-raking journalism, but for many the Lambton revelations were an example of excessive press intrusion into people's private affairs. A number of 'right to privacy' bills introduced in the late 1960s lead to the setting up of the Younger Committee in 1970. It opposed a statutory right to privacy in 1972, but its deliberations highlighted the growing intensity of public concern. On a number of aspects of privacy the Committee chose to listen to the views of special interests such as the press, police and Magistrates Association rather than public attitudes.[63] This disposition was a reflection of politicians' increasing eagerness to use the media to promote their interests and careers.

The growth of salacious reporting of the private lives of politicians and celebrities in the *NOTW* was at first tentative. Somerfield's departure in September 1970 was followed by a series of editors more cautious in embracing the new reporting culture.[64] Cyril Lear, the immediate replacement, was a careful editor who shied away from Somerfield's 'publish and be damned' approach. He delayed publication of the Lambton story to the chagrin of some of his colleagues and the owner.[65] It was in 1984 when the paper went tabloid that a radical shift in editorial policy was apparent. A 'burgeoning trade in personal information' took place under editors whose background was in the field of celebrity journalism.[66] There was a monetisation of the gathering of doubtfully gained information. Payment for unauthorised information became a 'well established' procedure at the *NOTW*.[67] Journalists were allowed regular access to cash to pay sources including police officers, public officials and private detectives without reference to editors other than for large one-off transactions. Such payments were not new but their normalisation was. The practice, according to Roy Greenslade who has called attention to the transformation in payment culture at the *NOTW*, 'led to the "monster of phone hacking".' He believes the *NOTW* and the Murdoch press 'should take the blame for having helped to foster an expectation ... that money can be made from the sale of private information, personal records, tip-offs, snatched mobile phone pictures and the like'.[68]

The road to closure

Throughout the 1980s, money talked as more sordid details of the private lives of politicians appeared in the *NOTW*. In 1989, politics and sex combined again in the paper's revelations that Pamella Bordes conducted an escort business in the House of Commons with a security pass provided by two Tory MPs. In circumstances reminiscent of the Keeler affair, a security enquiry was conducted by the Thatcher government, which found no breaches of security but showed that the story had not been acquired by traditional journalistic endeavour. The publicity agent Max Clifford had sold the story to the *NOTW* as part of a campaign to promote Bordes. Selling 'kiss and tell' stories to Fleet Street became a highly profitable business for a variety of media and PR agencies, many of which were set up by former newspaper editors and reporters.[69]

The 'bonk journalism' of the 1980s also reflected the pressure on the popular press to go further down market with the arrival of the *Daily Star* and the *Sunday Sport*. Politicians from all parties, members of the public and even sections of the press called for statutory regulation. Several private members bills to provide protection to victims of press intrusion were introduced and an outpouring of anti-tabloid invective followed the revelations about the royal family and Prince Charles and Princess Diana's divorce, which had figured prominently in the *NOTW*. Broadsheet editors were convinced that privacy legislation was necessary to protect traditional investigative journalism. Despite this, the Press Council appeared impotent in the face of the increasing 'recklessness' of the British press. It was no surprise in 1990 that the Calcutt Report recommended replacing the Council with a statutory body. As with Younger, ministers shied away from taking on the press, and the industry was allowed 'one last chance' to make self-regulation work.[70] A new body, the Press Complaints Commission (PCC), was given 18 months to do this and, in 1993, the government 'reprieved' the PCC from the demise recommended by Calcutt and prevented an increase in its powers proposed by the National Heritage Select Committee.

Escaping the 'last chance saloon', the *NOTW* was emboldened. Now it had to create the news by searching for stories that would provide it with a competitive edge. Entrapment was a feature of the paper's journalism from the 1990s with reporters such as Mazher Mahmood deploying subterfuge and secret video filming in a series of stings to expose public figures. The 'Fake Sheikh' won awards from the industry for revealing malpractice in the public interest, but as the subterfuge employed became more elaborate and the incentives used to encourage law breaking more dubious, criticism mounted. Court cases fell apart and the public interest justification questioned. The collapse of the Victoria Beckham kidnap case in 2003, as a result of the discovery that the *NOTW* had made a large payment to the chief prosecution witness, led the judge to express his concern about the 'temptations to which money being offered in return for stories, in particular about celebrities, gives rise to'.[71] This comment is to be seen in the context of the Lord Chancellor's decision the previous year not to ban such payments in return for a toughening up of the PCC's code of practice. The unwillingness of the PCC to examine the method of entrapment deployed by the *NOTW* was reinforced in later years by the reticence of the PCC to explore malpractice around phone hacking.[72] This reflected an increasing caution in face of the influence and power of News Corp and its owner.

The *NOTW* was robust in its support of Mahmood and his methods. Mahmood was cast as part of the newspaper's traditional commitment to exposing wrongdoing: 'We believe it is our duty to shine our spotlight into the darker corners of everyday life. That tradition is 160 years old. And lest there be any doubt, we have no intention of giving up.'[73] Commercial reasons played their part: 'at a time of falling circulations and editorial financial restrictions (entrapment) is a comparatively cheap form of journalism with a quick result.'[74] The intensity of the newspaper business in the early 2000s was highlighted by a number of newspaper executives at the Leveson Inquiry.[75] Falling circulations and declining advertising revenue were accompanied by new forms of competition from the web and a collapse in the global economy. The *NOTW* moved on to more dubious methods to obtain information. Private investigators were employed to gather confidential personal information by hacking mobile phones and computers and the 'blagging' of personal data.[76] These methods, along with entrapment and payments to public officials, became part of the *NOTW*'s newsgathering operation.

This was encouraged by a newsroom culture at the paper in which intimidation was rife and cut-throat competition between colleagues encouraged.[77] Harassment characterised the reporting culture in which the commitment to the story was everything; how it was obtained and whether it was accurate were of less concern.[78] But what was happening at the *NOTW* was part of a 'far deeper crisis' in British journalism – a 'decline in traditional news gathering and original reporting'.[79] Professional journalism, with commitment to checking facts, standing up stories and protecting the integrity of sources was increasingly undermined. Editors encouraged the new practices at the *NOTW* and executives disregarded the ethical and legal considerations these generated.[80] The growing treatment of readers as consumers, highlighted in the use of the term 'punters' to describe them, marginalised the public's voice in the practice of popular journalism. It was almost inevitable that the increasing reliance on hacking and payments at the *NOTW* in an environment, in which professional checks and balances had been removed or denigrated, combined with a growing contempt for the readers, would end in a disaster.

Conclusion

The post-war history of the *NOTW* is characterised by growing intrusion into individual privacy. Diana Dors's one-off remuneration in 1960 morphed into a system in which the intrusion into private lives of celebrities was carried out on an extensive scale. The regularisation of payments for information was the cement that held the system together exemplified by the *NOTW* carrying ads offering readers 'big money' for 'a celebrity, a scandal, a human interest story, or any other great tip'.[81] Leveson revealed the extent to which payments were made to a network of officials across public life for gossip and information about celebrities and people in the news. Many of these practices were apparent prior to Murdoch's takeover, but under his ownership and in the face of increasing competitive pressures they became embedded in the culture of the newspaper.

Notes

1. A. Curtis, http://www.bbc.co.uk/blogs/adamcurtis/posts/WHAT-THE-FLUCK (accessed 9 June 2014).
2. Quoted in P. Jukes, *The Fall of the House of Murdoch* London, 2012, p. 12.
3. Royal Commission on the Press, minutes of evidence, 19th February 1948, 7406, House of Commons Parliamentary Papers online. http://parlipapers.chadwyck. co.uk/marketing/index.jsp
4. Quoted in S. Somerfield, *Banner Headlines*, Shoreham-by-Sea, 1979, p. 106.
5. 'News of the World 1843–2011' *Press Gazette*, 8 July 2011.
6. M. Engel, *Tickle the Public: One Hundred Years of the Popular Press* London, 1996, p. 225.
7. For discussion of trends in newspaper circulation in the post war period see J. Tunstall, *Newspaper Power: The New National Press in Britain* London, 1996; C. Seymour-Ure, *The Press and Broadcasting since 1945* Oxford, 2nd edn, 1996.
8. See R. Greenslade, *Press Gang: How Newspapers make Profits from Propaganda*, London, 2003, pp. 126–29.
9. Sir William Carr was 'not the natural heir to the Carr empire'. He is described as a 'relatively junior and unimportant member of the family'. His two twin brothers were the heirs apparent and their untimely deaths during the war thrust him to the fore. He is said to have had 'no literary skills' and occupied a 'minor post of the business side of the newspaper'. He had to struggle with other members of his family following his brothers' death to establish himself, and it was not until 1948 that he was able to gain a seat on the board. See, C. Bainbridge and R. Stockdill, *The News of the World Story* London, 1993, pp. 165–66.
10. Engel, *Tickle the Public*, p. 234.
11. House of Commons Debate 29 October 1946, vol. 428 columns 452–577.
12. House of Commons Debate 28 November 1952, vol. 508 columns 962–1062; 8 May 1953 vol. 515 columns 748–806.
13. Royal Commission on the Press Report (1949), pp. 131–34.
14. House of Commons Debate 8 May 1953, vol. 515 columns 748–806.
15. Ibid.
16. Ibid.
17. S. Chibnall (1977) *Law and Order News: An Analysis of Crime Reporting in the British Press* London, Tavistock, 1977, p. 65.
18. A. Bingham, *Family Newspapers? Sex, Private Life, and the British Popular Press 1918–1978.* Oxford, 2009, p. 144.
19. Bingham, *Family Newspapers*, p. 146.
20. House of Commons Debate 17 May 1957 vol. 570 columns 725–819.
21. H. Proctor, *The Street of Disillusion*, 2nd edition, Brighton, Revel Barker, 2010, p. 61.
22. N. Root, Frenzy! *Heath, Haigh & Christie: The First Great Tabloid Murderers*, London, 2011. When Rae died (1962) he had worked for the *NOTW* for 27 years.

23. Bainbridge and Stockdill, *The News of the World Story*, pp. 148–50.
24. Procter, *The Street of Disillusion*, back cover.
25. House of Commons Debate 08 May 1953, volume 515, columns 748–806.
26. ibid.
27. See A. Bingham, '"A stream of pollution through every part of the country": Morality, regulation and the modern popular press' in M. Bailey (ed.) *Narrating Media History*, Abingdon, Oxon, 2009, pp. 112–24.
28. Bainbridge and Stockdill, *The News of the World Story*, p. 176.
29. K. Bradley, '"All Human Life is There": The John Hilton Bureau of the *News of the World* and Advising the Public, 1942–1969,' *English Historical Review*, CXXIX (539), 2010, 888–910. This figure dwarfed the number of letters to advice columnists such as Marjorie Proops in the *Daily Mirror* in the 1970s, which received over 43,000 annually.
30. K. Bradley, 'All Human Life is There', p. 888.
31. Bradley, 'All Human Life is There', p. 896.
32. Engel, *Tickle the Public*, p. 239.
33. Somerfield, *Banner Headlines*, p. 119.
34. Bainbridge and Stockdill, The *News of the World Story*, p. 167.
35. Bingham, *Family Newspapers*.
36. Bingham, 'Morality, regulation and the modern popular press', p. 115.
37. Bainbridge and Stockdill, The *News of the World Story*, p. 234.
38. Bradley, 'All Human Life is There', p. 910.
39. http://www.bbc.co.uk/blogs/adamcurtis/posts/WHAT-THE-FLUCK; The 'mucky bits' included how Dors's husband used the two-way mirror to watch couples having sex, taped them and then played the tape back to the entire household the next day. She also described the violence in their marriage, and Hamilton's financial scams.
40. Greenslade, *Press Gang*, p. 172.
41. M. Engel, *Tickle the Public*, p. 236.
42. B. Levin, 'It's always Dors on Sunday', *Spectator*, 9 February, 1960, p. 6.
43. Greenslade, *Press Gang*, p. 128.
44. Greenslade, *Press Gang*, p. 127.
45. Press Council, Annual Report 1960, 31; 'Standards of Three Sunday Newspapers "A Disgrace",' *The Times* 31 March 1960.
46. G. Murray, *The Press and the Public: The Story of the British Press Council*. Carbondale, IL, 1972, p. 77.
47. Greenslade, *Press Gang*, p. 172.
48. Somerfield, *Banner Headlines*, p. 112.
49. G. Robertson, *People Against the Press*, London, 1983, p. 11.
50. R. Cohen-Almagor, 'Press Self-Regulation in Britain: A Critique', *Science and Engineering Ethics*, March 2014, DOI 10.1007/s11948-014-9538-8.
51. The Second Royal Commission in 1961 considered how the council could better represent the public. It recommended the introduction of lay members onto the council including the position of chairing the body, which was implemented and successive enquiries have seen further developments in public representation. The major reports since the 1960s are: *Royal Commission on the Press 1961–2 Report*, HMSO, 1962; *Royal Commission on the Press 1974–7 Final Report*, HMSO, 1977; *Report of the Committee on Privacy and Related Matters*, 1990; *Review of Press Self-Regulation*, 1993.
52. Greenslade, *Press Gang*, p. 174.
53. Bainbridge and Stockdill, *The News of the World Story*, p. 192.

54. General Press Council, Annual Report, 1963, p. 19.
55. Vassall was convicted of spying for the Soviet Union in 1962.
56. N. Wilkinson, *Secrecy and the Media: The Official History of the United Kingdom's D-Notice System*, London, 2009, p. 207.
57. Greenslade, *Press Gang*, p. 176.
58. Somerfield, *Banner Headlines*, Chapter 20.
59. Burden, *News of the world?, Fake Sheikhs & Royal Trappings* London, 2008, p. 53.
60. See Bainbridge and Stockdill, *The News of the World Story*, Chapter 21; Engel, *Tickle the Public*, pp. 240–42.
61. S. Clayton, 'Television and the Decline of Deference', *History Review*, 68, December 2010. http://www.historytoday.com/stuart-clayton/television-and-decline-deference (accessed 7 July 2013).
62. The paper did not actually make a payment to those who arranged the filming; they had taken their story to the *Sunday People* who handed over the cash.
63. G. Rhodes, 'The Younger Committee and Research, *Public Administration* 51 (4), 449–60, December, 1973.
64. Editors such as Bernard Shrimsley, Derek Jameson, David Montgomery, Patsy Chapman and Wendy Henry had run the newspaper in a more or less traditional manner. These editors continued to pay attention to investigations such as the exposé in July 1970 of an abortion racket, and in September 1972 revelations about property speculators buying up derelict houses with the help of improvements grants and selling them on at large profits, which led to legislation increasing the powers of local councils to make profiteers pay back grants.
65. Bainbridge and Stockdill, *The News of the World Story*, p. 238.
66. R. Greenslade, 'Hacking book: how Murdoch's papers twisted the news to his advantage' Greenslade Blog *The Guardian,* 12 September 2012. http://theguardian.com/media/greenslade
67. Ibid.
68. Ibid.
69. Mediawise Trust, *Pity the poor citizen complainant*, formal statement of evidence to The Leveson Inquiry into the Culture, Practice and Ethics of the Press, Mediawise Trust, University of West of England, Bristol, 2012.
70. See A. Bingham, 'Drinking in the last chance saloon', *Media History*, 13 (1), 2007, pp. 79–92.
71. Jukes, *The Fall of the House of Murdoch*, https://fothom.wordpress.com/2014/07/30/other-dark-arts-at-the-news-of-the-world-fake-sheikh-investigated-by-police-just-before-phone-hacking-operation/
72. M. Moore, 'Did the PCC fail when it came to phone hacking?' *Media Standards Trust,* December 2011, http://mediastandardstrust.org/wp-content/uploads/downloads/2012/02/Did-the-PCC-fail-when-it-came-to-phone-hacking.pdf (accessed 9 June 2014).
73. *NOTW*, 8 June, 2003.
74 . Inforrms Blog, Journalism, Entrapment and the Public Interest 30 August 2010, http://inforrm.wordpress.com/2010/08/30/journalism-entrapment-and-the-public-interest, (accessed 9 June 2012)
75. See for example Sly Bailey's evidence to the Leveson enquiry. Evidence to the Leveson Inquiry, 16 January 2012. http://www.levesoninquiry.org.uk/evidence/?witness=sly-bailey
76. This was not the first time the paper had used private investigators but by the 2000s their use had become systematic.

77. See Leveson, An inquiry into the culture, practices and ethics of the press, Report chapter 4, Vol. 2, November 2012. http://www.levesoninquiry.org.uk

78. http://www.theguardian.com/media/2011/jul/24/phone-hacking-scandal-bullying-intimidation (accessed 26 June 2012).

79. S. Jukes, 'The Perfect Storm', in Karen Fowler-Watt and Stuart Allan (eds), *Journalism: New Challenges,* Bournemouth, 2013.

80. The Culture, Media and Sport (CMS) Select Committee published a report into press standards, privacy and libel in 2010 that accused the *NOTW* of ignoring illegal phone hacking and 'blagging' (the practice of obtaining information through deception) by its reporters. See House of Commons, Culture, Media and Sport Committee, *Press Standards, Privacy and Libel*, Second Report of Session 2009–10, London: HMSO.

81. See Greenslade, 'Hacking Book'.

13
'Gross Interference with the Course of Justice': The *News of the World* and the Moors Murder Trial

Adrian Bingham

Introduction

It was, declared the *News of the World*'s (*NOTW*) front page on 17 April 1966, 'The Murder Trial of the Century', and, for once, the hyperbolic language was justified. The prosecution of Ian Brady and Myra Hindley for the murder of three children – 12-year-old John Kilbride, 10-year-old Lesley Ann Downey and 17-year-old Edward Evans – generated huge interest both in Britain and around the world. Over 150 journalists, and 5 authors, attended the trial, all aiming to satisfy the intense public curiosity in the so-called 'Moors Murders', and 300 hundred extra policemen were drafted in to ensure the participants in the case safe passage in and out of the courtroom amidst the noisy crowds gathered outside.[1] The attention elicited by the case was not hard to explain. The sheer brutality of the murders, the unusual presence of a glamorous young woman in the dock, the widespread suspicion that the accused were a product of the 'permissive' mores of modern society and the knowledge that, if guilty, they would narrowly avoid the death penalty, following the suspension of capital punishment the previous year – all of these ingredients heightened the controversy and the outrage surrounding the trial. No one at the time could have predicted, however, the extent to which the case would continue to haunt the public imagination, and be played out in the pages of the popular newspapers, in subsequent decades as two more victims – Pauline Reade and Keith Bennett – were confirmed and the grim search for bodies on the moors continued. A study of the press in 1985 found that the 'Moors Murderers' featured more prominently than all other 'sex criminals' in custody put together; Ian Brady still had sufficient news value in 2013 to earn several front-page lead stories.[2]

Having introduced the trial in such sensational terms, and fully primed to provide characteristically detailed coverage, the *NOTW* team found itself in the unusual position of being wrong-footed by events in the court room.

During his cross-examination, David Smith, the 17-year-old chief prosecution witness who went to the police after watching the grisly killing of Edward Evans, revealed that he had been promised £1,000 by the *NOTW* for his story, and thus had a financial incentive in the conviction of Brady and Hindley. There was understandable uproar. The judge, Mr Justice Fenton Atkinson, was dismayed that there seemed 'to be a gross interference with the course of justice', and the Attorney-General, Sir Elwyn Jones promised an investigation.[3] Mr Justice Atkinson observed in his summing-up that the 'extraordinary arrangement' with the paper had 'handed the defence a stick with which to beat Smith and his wife Maureen', but, fortunately for the *NOTW*, he eventually decided that the substance of Smith's testimony had not been altered by his agreement with the paper.[4] Nevertheless, the *NOTW*'s actions had jeopardised the prosecution of the most notorious murderers in recent British history. Questions were subsequently raised in both Houses of Parliament, and the Press Council was prompted to produce its first Declaration of Principle, banning the payment of witnesses in advance of trials. Given the gravity of the offence, though, the *NOTW* escaped lightly, and the paper's editor expressed little remorse for the actions of his journalists.

This controversy has featured in studies of press regulation, accounts of the *NOTW*'s history and the many popular narratives of the 'Moors Murders', but it has not yet received the detailed examination it deserves.[5] It has become all the more pertinent since the closure of the paper in 2011 following allegations of phone hacking, most notably of the phone of the murdered schoolgirl Milly Dowler. In both cases, the single-minded pursuit of a story about a murdered child led journalists to disregard ethical considerations and bring opprobrium on the paper; one might go further and suggest that the weakness of the regulatory response in 1966 contributed to the entrenchment and further development of an ultra-competitive, scoop-based culture in the *NOTW* and across the press more broadly. Nearly derailing 'the trial of the century' brought few serious consequences, and it proved possible to ignore the Press Council's strictures about crime reporting. This was the great missed opportunity for the regulatory regime to develop a robust response to press misbehaviour.

This chapter is divided into three parts. The first provides the necessary context to the Moors Murders controversy by examining the changing culture of the *NOTW* in the 1960s as it shifted from its traditional reliance on court reporting towards a more intrusive, scoop-based formula that prized 'the story behind the story'. The new policies inevitably involved greater risk-taking by journalists and an increased use of the editorial chequebook. The second section discusses the *NOTW*'s coverage of Brady and Hindley's crimes, and, in particular, the paper's much-criticised relationship with David Smith. It suggests that in the race to secure an exclusive there was little concern for the integrity of the judicial process. The final part focuses on the political and professional debates once the *NOTW*'s actions had been revealed. It highlights the Labour government's desire for the press to put its own house in order without outside intervention.

The *News of the World* and the culture of crime reporting

A widespread and deep-rooted public fascination with transgressive behaviour has ensured that stories of crime and punishment have been a staple of British popular culture for hundreds of years in the form of ballads and broadsheets. In the mid-nineteenth century, the commercial exploitation of law, police and court news was taken to a new level with the emergence of new high-circulation Sunday newspapers such as *Lloyd's Weekly News* and the *NOTW*.[6] The authority of the judicial process gave legitimacy to the coverage of subjects that would have been considered inappropriate for discussion in other contexts. This was a cheap, convenient and reliable means of providing material that enthralled, entertained and shocked readers. By the First World War, the *NOTW* had become the most popular paper in Britain through its mastery of the court reporting genre. The paper expertly squeezed every last drop of human interest from legal proceedings around the country: its coverage was more professional, more extensive and more explicit than any of its rivals. Particularly serious or sensational cases, or those involving prominent figures, were described as fully as possible, but considerable amounts of space were also devoted to recording relatively mundane cases of assault, deception or indecency. The paper was aptly described by one Fleet Street veteran as the 'Hansard of the Sleazy.'[7]

The price of commercial success obtained in this way was sustained moral criticism from political, religious and cultural elites. The *NOTW* was the least respectable of the mainstream national papers, and was widely agreed to exist in a class of its own. The Conservative MP Major Birchall did not need to identify the publication to which he was referring when he complained to the House of Commons in 1926 that 'one Sunday newspaper' devoted half of its news space to 'matters of crime of every kind, very largely connected with sexual offences'. This was, he argued, material that 'degrades and pollutes the reader's mind'. One of his colleagues agreed that it was possible to single out 'one newspaper that has been wrong in this matter'.[8] There were similar exchanges before the Royal Commission on the Press in 1947–48.[9] The *NOTW* was a special case, both in the circulations it achieved and the censure it attracted.

In this period, the editors of the *NOTW* were well aware that the paper's editorial formula would never win over educated critics. Their task was rather to ensure that the paper contained enough to interest and titillate a mass working-class readership without becoming so unrespectable that too many potential buyers or advertisers were put off. It was essential for circulation and advertising success that the *NOTW* should be able to present itself as a 'family newspaper', suitable for all. Two strategies were essential to this balancing act. The first was self-censorship. Court reports were compiled very carefully, with the most sensitive evidence either omitted completely or described euphemistically. Accounts of sexual misdemeanours were particularly evasive and oblique, relying on traditional circumlocutions rather than modern sexual terminology. Editors could therefore protest that the newspaper contained only what was 'fit to print' and that it excluded unnecessary information about criminal and indecent activities. The key to this form of popular journalism, of course, was suggestion: tantalising headlines introduced stories that gave just enough detail to set readers' imaginations racing. A vocal support for the law, the police and conventional morality was the second key strategy. There must be no suspicion at all that the *NOTW* condoned the behaviour it recorded. Reporters scrupulously described the mechanics of the judicial process, giving prominence to the comments of the judge and the sentence that was handed down. The paper's standard defence to accusations that it dwelt on the worst aspects of human behaviour was that it reported not crime but punishment, and thereby helped to teach readers what they should not do.[10] Post-war the paper's leading crime reporters, such as Norman Rae (1896–1962), worked hard to forge a close relationship with the police and the judiciary, trading favourable publicity for tip-offs and sympathetic treatment. Leading detectives and members of the bench were often able to secure lucrative deals for the serialisation of their memoirs.[11]

The success of the *NOTWs* editorial formula enabled the paper to reach the spectacular peak circulation of 8.44 million copies per issue in June 1950, the highest in British newspaper history. At this time, it was read by more than half of all adults in Britain, and was thus deeply woven into British popular culture.[12] The circulation growth of the first half of the century abruptly came to a halt in the 1950s, however, and by 1959 sales had fallen sharply to 6.4 million copies a week. The *NOTW* still led the Sunday market, but the gap to its main rivals, the *People* and the *Sunday Pictorial*, was much reduced. In its evidence to the Royal Commission on the Press 1961–62, the paper blamed wider social changes for its difficulties, notably 'the increased competition in the past decade for the leisure time of the people' in the form of motoring, gardening and DIY, altered patterns of housing and sociability, and the rise of television:

> This especially applies to the Sunday newspapers which are bought by a non-working public who are increasingly tending to spend the week-end away from home or out of doors. This tendency over the years could have a serious effect on the Sunday newspaper habit. There has been some evidence, mainly from the New Towns and the recently built Council Estates, that the high wages paid to teenagers and young people and the tendency for such persons to marry earlier [mean they] are not inculcating

the newspaper habit; it is possible that as they grow older they will prefer to take their news and entertainment from television rather than from newspapers.[13]

This was a perceptive analysis, as the evidence of subsequent decades would demonstrate: the decline of Sunday newspaper circulations occurred at a significantly faster rate than that of dailies. However, this was far from the whole explanation of the *NOTW*'s decline in the 1950s. After all, both its main competitors had gained readers during the decade, almost certainly from the faltering market leader. The deeper problem was that the *NOTW*'s traditional formula was designed for a society in which censorship was strict, moral judgements were severe and class positions were stable. The more sexualised, affluent, secular and youth-orientated society that was emerging from the late 1950s produced different expectations of newspapers. There was a greater demand for stories about celebrities, consumer information and advice about personal relationships. In particular, there was an expectation of a different approach to sex. As the American journalist Thomas Matthews observed in 1957, the *NOTW*, while still 'extremely sex-conscious, still clings to the outmoded, moralistic view of sex as something delightfully furtive and shocking'.[14] The *Daily Mirror* and its sister paper the *Sunday Pictorial*, by contrast, shared the attitude of the 'rising generation' that 'takes sex at its declined but up-to-date value, as just a bit of good healthy fun'.[15] The *Mirror* and the *Pictorial*, both enjoying circulation success in the 1950s, had adapted to the social and cultural shifts of the period far more adroitly than the *NOTW*.

Stafford Somerfield, a brash and vivacious journalist who had joined the *NOTW* in 1945, replaced Reginald Cudlipp as editor in 1960 and was charged with halting the decline in circulation. He recognised immediately that fundamental editorial changes were necessary to compete with the paper's more nimble rivals. He was adamant that '[i]t was not enough to print straightforward court reports': this was 'the day of investigative journalism, the story behind the story.' He urged his journalists to be 'bolder', and to ensure that the paper was 'talked about'. He insisted that the paper's make-up be brightened with 'bigger pictures and bigger type' and 'more up-to-date language'.[16] He also spotted the public's growing appetite for celebrity journalism, and increased the resources devoted to securing features involving major stars: he signalled his intent with a high-profile serialisation of the life story of the actress Diana Dors, which cost the paper £36,000.[17]

Somerfield's more aggressive and intrusive style of journalism brought some circulation gains, but it also brought the paper into conflict with the Press Council, the self-regulatory body that since 1953 had been charged with overseeing the standards and conduct of the press. The Council declared that the Dors serialisation and a rival set of articles run by the

Sunday Pictorial in a bid to compete contained 'material that was grossly lewd and salacious' and were 'a disgrace to British journalism'.[18] Somerfield, appearing on the television show *The Editors*, was entirely unrepentant, and accused the Press Council of being 'quite out of step' and having 'lost sight' of its proper job.[19] The disquiet about the *NOTW's* new approach intensified three years later when Somerfield sanctioned the payment of £23,000 to secure the Christine Keeler's story as the Profumo scandal broke. This five-part serialisation of the 'Confessions of Christine' generated a flood of criticism from politicians and religious leaders. The Press Council responded with the most damning adjudication it had yet delivered. It condemned the 'publication of personal stories and feature articles of an unsavoury nature where the public interest does not require it'. The Council concluded that the *NOTW* had exploited 'vice and sex for commercial reward' and thereby 'done a disservice both to public welfare and to the Press'.[20] Once again, Somerfield was defiant, arguing that 'the public is entitled to know what is going on.' He claimed that only by speaking to Keeler could the facts of the affair be ascertained, and 'to provide the facts we had to pay'. Nothing the paper had published, he added, 'sought to disguise as virtue that which is vicious', and he concluded by appealing to the court of public opinion: 'A prodigious and mounting readership tacitly acknowledges the rightness of the course we have followed.'[21] If commercial success, rather than any form of ethical consideration, was to be the determining factor in the paper's activities, further controversies were inevitable. It was not surprising that they would be caused by the pursuit of a sensational murder story.

Reporting the Moors Murders, searching for a scoop

What became known as the 'Moors Murders' were on the *NOTW's* radar even before the arrests of Brady and Hindley in October 1965. Reporter Jack Nott and northern news editor George McIntosh had registered the disappearances of a number of children from the same area, and Nott ran a story including a plea for public help from Detective Inspector Joe Mounsey.[22] Once Edward Evans's body was discovered and suspects were taken into custody, the case quickly started attracting attention. The *Manchester Evening News*'s front-page exclusive headlined 'Police in Mystery Dig on Moors' propelled the story into the nationals, and the discovery in quick succession of the bodies of Lesley Ann Downey and John Kilbride generated frenzied interest. Hundreds of members of the public travelled to the Moors to watch the police search, and dozens of national and international journalists flocked to the area. Thousands of mourners watched the funeral processions for the young victims.[23] For Clive Entwistle, a young journalist from Rochdale, the case was beyond anything he had witnessed: 'The whole thing just exploded. We had the world's press coming to us. Not just Britain, but everywhere – New Zealand, America, Japan, France... It was a colossal story.'[24]

David Smith, the chief witness, and his pregnant wife Maureen, Myra Hindley's sister, quickly became the focus of intense press scrutiny. Reporters posted cards wrapped in five-pound notes through their letter box, inviting them for a 'drink and a chat', and photographers trained their cameras on the couple's balcony and door. Smith, traumatised by his experience and resentful of the attention, responded by shovelling dog excrement onto the cars of the waiting journalists.[25] He had an obvious weakness, however, that experienced journalists were able to exploit. Even before the murder of Edward Evans, he had been struggling for money. Now unable to work, and tainted by his association with Brady and Hindley, he was in severe financial difficulty. Others in his family recognised the opportunity to make money and were prepared to set it up. Smith's father and uncle fielded two substantial offers from Sunday papers: £1,000 from the *NOTW*, and £6,000 from its rival, the *People*. The *NOTW*'s lower bid was accepted because of the prospect of additional syndication rights. As Smith later recalled, the paper 'convinced Dad and Uncle Bert to think long-term gain rather than short-term solution', enticing them with the 'thousands we might earn through syndication, serial rights and all that malarkey'.[26] When David and Maureen met Jack Nott and George McIntosh, they were given £20 apiece and persuaded to sign a contract. The agreement stipulated that the couple would be paid £15 a week until the trial, with a lump sum of £1,000 paid for a series of articles if Brady and Hindley were convicted. There were further promises of fees from syndication rights.[27]

Using the editorial chequebook to secure scoops in high-profile murder cases was nothing new. In 1949, the *NOTW* spent over £10,000 paying for the defence of the 'acid bath murderer' John Haigh in return for his life story.[28] Paying a witness in advance of a major trial was very risky, however, and it should not have been difficult to predict exposure and the resulting furore. This was clearly the sort of journalistic 'boldness' that Somerfield believed was necessary to halt the *NOTW*'s declining circulation. It was no surprise that the *People* was the other bidder. The Sundays were under increasing pressure in the field of crime journalism because dailies, since the early 1950s, had become less euphemistic and were increasingly prepared to print explicit details of cases revealed in court transcripts.[29] This greater frankness, combined with the natural advantage that dailies had in being able to cover every twist and turn of sensational cases, left Sundays struggling to produce distinctive and appealing copy. There was, as Somerfield recognised, a pressing need for Sundays to lure readers with 'the story behind the story'. The *People*, seeking both to narrow the circulation gap to the *NOTW*, and to fend off the commercial challenge of the *Sunday Pictorial*, was equally willing to go the extra mile for such a big exclusive. There was little that could not be justified in the race for a scoop.

Having secured their prize, the *NOTW* protected it carefully. When the Smiths were attacked by hostile local people suspicious of their involvement in the murders, the paper paid for a ten-day holiday in France, with little thought of how the trip would be perceived by the court or the wider public. During the court proceedings, held at Chester Castle, the couple were kept closeted in their room and forbidden to talk about the case. In between, David was interviewed so extensively about his interactions with Brady and Hindley that he absorbed the words and phrasing of the *NOTW* reporters. Some of his courtroom responses that so struck observers – such as his comment about Brady dealing with Evans's body that 'I have seen butchers working in the shops show as much emotion as he did when they are cutting up a sheep's ribs' – had their origins in these earlier conversations.[30] As he later admitted, 'I ended up talking like a hack, picking up their way of speech, and it wasn't good.'[31] Even if the *NOTW*'s reporters had no intention of altering the factual basis of Smith's testimony, they inevitably shaped the style in which it was delivered. At the same time, the paper was ensuring that its readers understood the full magnitude of the case. The Sunday before the trial opened, the *NOTW*'s front page led on 'the murder trial that is gripping the world more than any other in our time', and familiarised readers with the protagonists by printing pictures of David and Maureen Smith, the three victims and the judge, Mr Fenton Atkinson (who had heard, the paper noted, the appeal of the Great Train Robbers, another case that had been turned into a media event). Further details of the case were provided in a further article inside the paper.[32]

Despite the sensational build-up – the *People* joined the *NOTW* in labelling it the 'trial of the century' – and the almost obsessive press interest in the murders afterwards, the media coverage of the case was, in most cases, relatively restrained and muted.[33] The details of the case were so gruesome, and some of the evidence so upsetting, that many editors and journalists felt uncomfortable sensationalising it; indeed, some veteran crime reporters were haunted for years afterwards by what they had heard.[34] This restraint was most evident in the *People*'s coverage, despite – or perhaps because of – the paper's failed attempt to secure David's Smith's testimony. The *People* found that 'the horrifying nature of the allegations produces a kind of vocal numbness when anybody tries to raise the subject', and described local people avoiding newspapers with coverage of the court proceedings. It went on to halt its coverage of the case completely.[35] Jeremy Tunstall, at that stage a young media sociologist, spent a day at the *Daily Mirror*'s offices during the trial, and was struck by the editorial team placing the story sixth in its line-up: he recorded that 'there was clearly a strong directive from on high not to sensationalize the Moors murders.'[36] The *Mirror* gave very few details of the tape recording of Lesley Ann Downey's murder, and printed an editorial explaining that 'certain evidence in the case is of a nature that few people would wish to print in a paper read by millions of people of all ages.'[37] Before 1969, when Rupert Murdoch's *Sun* intensified the competition in the popular daily market, the *Mirror* was not under much pressure to push back boundaries in search of new readers. The BBC and ITV also demonstrated considerable caution in what they broadcast about the case.[38] Even so, the coverage was still sufficiently extensive – with the *Daily Express* leading the way in space devoted to the case – to draw criticism from certain quarters.[39] The *Lancet* argued that the detailed reporting of violent crime was a 'public nuisance', while the Conservative MP John Tilney called for restrictions on the coverage of murder cases, in a manner similar to that achieved for the divorce courts by the Judicial Proceedings (Regulation of Reports) Act of 1926.[40] Support for such legislation was limited, but such public criticism testified to a fairly widespread unease about the media's court reporting practices. Papers that were perceived to be stepping over the mark – as the *NOTW* would be in this case – could not be surprised by the strong condemnation that followed.

The *NOTW* did not, however, have the opportunity to provide its readers with its particular brand of sensational coverage because its big scoop was undermined in the first week of the trial. On the third day, Brady and Hindley's barristers both probed Maureen Smith, the first prosecution witness, about the arrangement with an (unnamed) newspaper, and she admitted that her husband received 'between £10 and £20 a week'.[41] The following day, when David Smith took the stand, the exchanges became more confrontational. Having admitted to Brady's counsel, Mr Emlyn Hoosen, QC, that the newspaper deal meant that he had 'a vested financial interest' in Brady and Hindley's conviction, David Smith would not name the paper involved, despite several direct questions from both the barrister and the judge. Risking contempt of court – perhaps because of a fear of losing out on the promised money – Smith defiantly stated that he would not answer without 'the sanction of the newspaper'. Only after several further exchanges, and an opportunity to discuss the matter with his own legal team during a recess, did Smith relent and identify the *NOTW*. Expressing his grave concern at the arrangement, the judge asked Sir Elwyn Jones, the Attorney-General who was also leading the prosecution, 'Isn't this a matter for investigation?' Jones agreed, promising to do so 'immediately and most thoroughly'.[42] Leading figures in the *NOTW* feared the worst. The paper's counsel told Somerfield, 'My God, you've done it this time.' Somerfield joked to Rosalie Shann, one of the reporters on the case, that they would soon be sharing a cell.[43]

These courtroom exchanges were fully reported across the press, although there was a widespread reluctance in Fleet Street to criticise the *NOTW* directly. Despite the fierce competition between rivals, proprietors, editors and journalists had very little appetite for closer legal or regulatory scrutiny. The *NOTW*, for its part, did not shy away from reporting the controversy, but its enthusiasm for the case clearly dwindled in the aftermath of

Smith's evidence. In subsequent weeks, the case was restricted to a single inside page – indeed, the guilty verdicts were covered in less than half a page, without photographs.[44] None of the material gathered from David and Maureen Smith was used, although they were paid the remainder of the £1,000 fee. Even in the restricted space available, though, there were flashes of the lurid reporting style that attracted many and appalled others. 'In all murder trials there are peaks and sloughs', the paper reported on 1 May:

> As for the peaks – who will say which was the more electric moment: when Ian Brady left the D-shaped dock with its screen of bulletproof glass and walked over to the witness box with its built-in mike – or when, in the most breathless hush you can imagine a tape recorder was switched on? There were 16 minutes of tape with a child – her mother has said it is Lesley-Ann's voice – screaming and whimpering and crying: "Please God help me".[45]

The language of 'peaks and sloughs' betrayed the paper's view that court-room drama was entertainment for the masses.

Paying witnesses: the public debates

The *NOTW* was saved, in this instance, by a comparison of David Smith's original statements to the police and his courtroom testimony showing that he had not altered or strengthened his evidence about Brady and Hindley – if anything, his original statement was even more damning for Hindley. Hindley's defence agreed not to persist with questions about the news-paper deal in order to ensure that the original statement was not brought to the courtroom. In his summing-up, Mr Fenton Atkinson condemned the arrangement with the *NOTW*, but he made clear that he did not 'think it is really suggested that the substance of his evidence has been substantially affected'.[46] There was plenty of other strong evidence against Brady and Hindley, and very little desire to see the case retried or for the accused to escape justice. Asked by the Conservative backbencher Gresham Cooke on 11 May 1966 whether he would instruct the Director of Public Prosecutions to bring legal proceedings against the *NOTW* for paying Smith – 'in view of the fact that such payments have the effect of suborning witnesses' – Sir Elwyn Jones fell back on the same reasoning. 'After careful consideration', he would not charge the paper because '[t]here is no evidence that the testi-mony of any witness in the murder trial referred to was affected by the payments in question.' He accepted, nevertheless, that the case had revealed 'serious problems in relation to the administration of justice', and declared that the government would 'examine these problems with a view to making such changes in the law as may prove necessary'.[47] Rather unconvinced, Cooke emphasised the extent of public disquiet: 'many people think that practices of this nature ... should be stamped on very hard.' Other members, from both sides of the House, were keen to voice their support for Cooke. Fred Blackburn, Labour MP for Stalybridge and Hyde, where the Smiths lived, highlighted that there was 'a great deal of resentment' about the *NOTW* deal in his constituency. Mark Carlisle, a Conservative backbencher, argued that it was 'wholly monstrous for a payment to be made to an important witness prior to his giving evidence'. Sir Elwyn assured the House that he was 'aware of the public feeling on this matter', but made clear that he wanted the industry to take the lead in responding to the concern about the case: 'I hope that, even before any Government action is taken, Fleet Street will now put its house in order.'[48]

The controversy over the trial provided the perfect opportunity for a reform-minded government, buoyed by an election victory only a couple of months earlier, to make an example of the *NOTW* and to explore ways of ensuring that the system of press regulation was more rigorous. Few could deny that the paper had risked interfering with the course of justice, and there was sufficient public and political disquiet to mobilise in support of robust action. The *NOTW* had, moreover, brazenly ignored the Press Council's critical adjudication of September 1963 in response to the Keeler articles, and had exposed the weakness of the regulator. Yet with economic difficulties mounting and Britain's seamen about to launch a bitter strike, there was very little appetite at the heart of government to take on Fleet Street. On 12 May, the day after the Commons debate on the matter, Prime Minister Harold Wilson and the Attorney-General met Lord Devlin, the chair of the Press Council, agreed to discuss the problem of 'chequebook journalism'. Sir Elwyn's note of the meeting makes clear that he and Wilson both expressed 'the wish that the Press would put its own house in order so as to make legislation ... unnecessary'.[49] Sir Elwyn believed that '[l]egislation to cover the position will be very difficult to draft and may not succeed in getting at the mischief.'[50] Given that government intervention would effectively signal the failure of the Press Council, Devlin was prompted into a rapid response, and suggested to Sir Elwyn five days later that rather than just issue another critical adjudication, the Council would ask newspapers to 'subscribe to a statement' of good practice. Devlin was, however, rather complacent about the scale of the problem, writing to Sir Elwyn that 'I think that the *NOTW* is the only newspaper which blatantly disregards what I believe is now the prevailing morality in Fleet Street,' and reassuring him that 'this is the first occasion on which the views of the Council ... have been openly flouted.'[51] By focusing on the contraventions of the main offender – and ignoring the evidence from Brady and Hindley's trial that other newspapers had been willing to entice the Smiths with money – Devlin avoided asking difficult questions about the broader culture and practices of Fleet Street.

By late October 1966, Devlin had drafted a three-part 'declaration of principle' on payments to witnesses. It declared that no payment should be made by a newspaper 'to any person known or reasonably expected to be a witness in criminal proceedings already begun'; nor should newspapers question witnesses about their evidence until after the trial. A third clause stated that 'no payment should be made for feature articles to persons engaged in crime or other notorious misbehaviour where the public interest does not warrant it.' Submitting the draft to Sir Elwyn for his comments, Devlin noted that such was the attachment to journalistic freedom, the declaration was 'regarded in Fleet Street as rather a revolutionary thing to have done'.[52] Devlin expected little dissent from the first two rules, although he expected that 'some will jib – certainly the *NOTW* will – about the wording of the third.' This third rule was, he admitted to Sir Elwyn in a phrase that betrayed the Council's lack of authority, 'a bit of a bonus anyway', a continuation of the efforts begun in 1963 to clamp down on what the Press Council regarded as the glamorisation of vice. The limitations of the Press Council's power were further evident in Devlin's admission that because they anticipated 'disagreement' with the wording, 'we have given up the idea of inviting editors to sign the Declaration. We have invited them instead, as you see, to state the policy of their newspaper.'[53] Despite these concessions, Sir Elwyn was broadly content, writing to the Prime Minister that the declaration went 'quite a way' to meeting the anxieties expressed about press conduct, and that he was prepared to 'see how the new code of conduct works in practice'.[54] Sir Elwyn's remark to Devlin that he had 'so far, been able to fend off pressure for action to prevent recurrence of the practices disclosed in the Moors Trial' demonstrated that there was still a significant current of opinion in favour of a firmer response, but he, and the Prime Minister, clearly wanted the matter to be dealt with by the Press Council.

The declaration of principle was eventually issued on 27 November 1966. There was, as predicted, open resistance from the *NOTW*. Somerfield was prepared to accept the ban on payments to witnesses while legal proceedings were ongoing, but regarded the third point as a 'blatant attempt to muzzle the Press'. He had also recognised the Council's lack of resolution, writing later that he 'felt the Council was piling it on and didn't really intend doing much about it'.[55] The paper printed a defiant leader describing the third rule as 'another step on the road to censorship':

> We do not believe that the public interest is served by the Council trying to impose a general restriction in advance … on the judgement of editors as to what they may or may not publish. The public interest demands that matters which are criminal, vicious and unsavoury should be exposed and not concealed. The greater the evil, the greater the need for exposure.[56]

For some commentators, the Council's declaration of principle was a 'landmark decision'; others have argued that under Devlin's leadership, the

Council was accorded a new respect.[57] Yet, with no powers to enforce its judgements or to punish newspapers, the Press Council could do nothing to prevent its work being treated with contempt. Somerfield remained unapologetic, and the *NOTW* was not prompted into any period of self-reflection. David and Maureen Smith were left to fend for themselves in a community bitter about the way they had exploited their circumstances for financial gain. Both were physically and verbally abused almost every time they left their house, and spent years struggling to deal with the vicious legacy of the case.[58] Fleet Street paid lip service to the 'declaration of principle', while bending or breaking it whenever there was a prospect of a major scoop. Witnesses were still approached and inducements offered for their information, for example during the 1979 trial of Jeremy Thorpe, the former Liberal Party leader, and in the journalistic frenzy after the arrest of Peter Sutcliffe, the so-called 'Yorkshire Ripper', in January 1981.[59] In these cases, papers other than the *NOTW* were the prime offenders. Devlin had attempted to isolate the *NOTW* as the moral outcast of 1960s Fleet Street, but rather than turning their backs, other papers learned that there were few dangers in imitating it. The opportunity to set out some proper limits to the aggressive, scoop-based culture of crime reporting was therefore missed, and the intrusive pursuit of intimate 'revelations' and 'confessions', featuring a liberal use of the editorial chequebook, became even further entrenched.

The longer history of press regulation suggests that while newspapers are adept at fending off criticisms about their treatment of celebrities and high-profile figures, they are far more vulnerable to accusations that they have wronged 'ordinary' members of the public or impeded the workings of the judicial system. Traducing the victims of the Hillsborough stadium disaster in 1989 put the *Sun* on the defensive and prompted a damaging boycott of the paper on Merseyside; the revelations about the hacking of Milly Dowler's phone led directly to the decision to close the *NOTW* in 2011. That the *NOTW*'s actions during the Moors murders trial had so few negative repercussions for the paper testifies not only to the weakness of the regulatory regime, but also to its lack of pragmatism. The government and the Press Council let a crisis go to waste, with serious consequences for the future.

Notes

1. *NOTW,* 17 April 1966, p. 1; David Smith and Carol Anne Lee, *Evil Relations* [Kindle version], London 2012, location 3723.
2. Keith Soothill and Sylvia Walby, *Sex Crime in the News,* London 1991, p. 87; *Sun* and *Daily Mirror,* 26 June 2013, p. 1.
3. *Daily Mail,* 23 April 1966, p. 7.
4. *NOTW,* 8 May 1966, p. 10.

5. For example, Tom O'Malley and Clive Soley, *Regulating the Press*, London, 2000; Cyril Bainbridge and Roy Stockdill, *The News of the World Story: 150 Years of the World's Bestselling Newspaper*, London, 1993; Smith and Lee, *Evil Relations*.

6. M. Conboy, *The Press and Popular Culture*, London, 2002, Chapters 4–5.

7. R. Greenslade, *Press Gang: How Newspapers make Profits from Propaganda*, London, 2003, p. 30.

8. 200 H.C. Debs 5s, Judicial Proceedings (Regulation of Reports) Bill, 10 December 1926, colums 2445, 2447.

9. Royal Commission on the Press 1947–49 [RCP], *Minutes of Evidence*, Day 13, London 1948, Cmd. 7351, p. 9.

10. For example, RCP, *Minutes of Evidence*, Day 22, Cmd. 7398, p. 27.

11. Bainbridge and Stockdill, *The News of the World*, pp. 141–50.

12. D. Butler and G. Butler, *Twentieth-Century British Political Facts 1900–2000*, 8th edn, Basingstoke, 2000, p. 538; Jeremy Tunstall, *Newspaper Power: The New National Press in Britain*, Oxford, 1996, p. 13; Hulton Press Survey 1952, as summarised in *World Press News*, 19 September 1952, p. 3.

13. National Archives, HO 252/12, *News of the World evidence to 1961–62 Royal Commission on the Press*, Replies to Questionnaires, 5 July 1961 – Questionnaire A, Q. 37.

14. T.S. Matthews, *The Sugar Pill: An Essay on Newspapers*, London, 1957, p. 153.

15. Ibid.

16. Stafford Somerfield, *Banner Headlines*, Shoreham-by-Sea, 1979, p. 111.

17. News of the World Archive, EDF/ 61, 61/1 Christopher Shaw, Director of London International Press Ltd, to Acting Editor of NOTW, 16 January, 1960; Somerfield, p. 111.

18. Press Council, *The Press and the People*, London, 1960, pp. 31–32.

19. Somerfield, *Banner Headlines*, pp. 112–13.

20. Press Council, *The Press and the People: Annual Report 1964*, London, 1964, p. 19.

21. Ibid., p. 18.

22. Bainbridge and Stockdill, *The News of the World*, p. 199.

23. Smith and Lee, *Evil Relations*, 2975, 3062, 3354.

24. Ibid., 3062.

25. Ibid., 3420.

26. Ibid. 3571.

27. Ibid.

28. Bainbridge and Stockdill, *The News of the World*, p. 145.

29. Adrian Bingham, *Family Newspapers? Sex, Private Life and the British Popular Press, 1918–1978*, Oxford, 2009, pp. 144–47.

30. Pamela Hansford Johnson, the novelist, thought this phrase captured the emergence of an 'affectless society': *On Iniquity: Some Personal Reflections Arising out of the Moors Murder Trial*, London 1967, p. 35.

31. Smith and Lee, *Evil Relations*, 3791.

32. *NOTW*, 17 April 1966, pp. 1 and 11.

33. *People*, 17 April 1966, p. 12.

34. Greenslade, *Press Gang*, p. 232.

35. *People*, 24 April 1966, p. 12.

36. Tunstall, *Newspaper Power*, p. 45.

37. *Daily Mirror*, 29 April 1966, pp. 1–2.

38. Smith and Lee, *Evil Relations*, 3723.

39. Tunstall, *Newspaper Power*, p. 45.

40. *Daily Mirror*, 29 April 1966, p. 24.
41. *Daily Mail*, 22 April 1966, p. 13.
42. *Daily Mail*, 23 April 1966, p. 4; *NOTW*, 24 April 1966, pp. 8–9; Smith and Lee, 3824–3897.
43. Bainbridge and Stockdill, *The News of the World*, p. 202.
44. *NOTW*, 1 May 1966, p. 10; 8 May 1966, p. 10.
45. *NOTW*, 1 May 1966, p. 10.
46. Smith and Lee, *Evil Relations*, 3897–3979.
47. H.C. Debs, 11 May 1966, 728, column 400.
48. Ibid., columns 401–03.
49. National Archives, PREM 13/1067, Sir Elwyn Jones, Attorney-General to Harold Wilson, Prime Minister, 13 May 1966.
50. Ibid., Sir Elwyn Jones to Harold Wilson, 20 May 1966.
51. Ibid., Lord Devlin to Sir Elwyn Jones, 17 May 1966.
52. Ibid., Lord Devlin to Sir Elwyn Jones, 27 October 1966.
53. Ibid.
54. Ibid., Sir Elwyn Jones to Harold Wilson, 22 November 1966.
55. Somerfield, *Banner Headlines*, p. 116.
56. *NOTW*, 27 November 1966, p. 10.
57. Greenslade, *Press Gang*, p. 233; O'Malley and Soley, *Regulating*, p. 66.
58. Smith and Lee, *Evil Relations*.
59. S. Freeman and B. Penrose, *Rinkagate: The Rise and Fall of Jeremy Thorpe*, London, 1997; Greenslade, *Press Gang*, pp. 435–41.

14

Harbingers of the Future: Rupert Murdoch's Takeover of the News of the World Organisation

Julian Petley

A very British company

In 1968, the chairman of the News of the World (*NOTW*) Organisation, Sir William Carr, had been in place for 16 years and owned 32 per cent of the voting shares. However, he also had serious health problems, which were not helped by heavy drinking. Like his predecessors, he ran the paper very much as a family concern, and, as Michael Leapman[1] put it,

> saw nothing wrong in using its resources for his personal comfort and amusement. The family enjoyed company boxes at Ascot races and the Covent Garden opera. There were company golf courses in Surrey and Spain where Sir William played. The paper owned racehorses and a stud farm and sponsored a race at Goodwood. Carr would regularly host black-tie stag dinners at the company flat at Cliveden Place – one floor below his own plush quarters. All this affected profitability and the share price, and that was compounded by an unadventurous record of expansion.[2]

What diversification had actually taken place was largely in print-related areas, and included subsidiaries such as the paper-making firm Townsend Hook and colour presses in Liverpool. By this time the *NOTW*'s readership had fallen to just over six million from well over eight million in 1950. It was still by a good margin the best-selling national newspaper in Britain, but profits had dropped by nearly £1 million in five years, standing at below £2 million in 1968. All of Britain's national newspapers had suffered a steady decline in readership in the post-war period, due partly to competition from broadcasting, but as a paper whose stock in trade was moral outrage (however hypocritical) at what it painted as sexual deviance of one kind or another, the *NOTW* also had the disadvantage of finding itself somewhat at odds with the spirit of the 'swinging sixties' or the 'permissive society' that the Christine Keeler episode explored later in this chapter dramatically illustrated. As Bruce Page puts it: 'During the 1960s, a behavioural Berlin Wall was crumbling, and when tolerance widens, moral and editorial sensibility is needed to prevent exposé journalism becoming, not just offensive, but tediously irrelevant'.[3]

The second largest block of voting shares, 25 per cent, was owned by Carr's cousin, Professor Derek Jackson. The two did not get on, and when Jackson announced that he was going to sell his shares, on account of worries about eventual death duties, Carr feared that these might fall into unfriendly hands and that he might lose control of the company. So he instructed his bank, Hambros, to offer Jackson 28s. (£1.40) per share, which was the current market price. Rothschild's Bank, who were handling the sale for Jackson, regarded the offer as too low, and found a willing buyer in Robert Maxwell, the high-profile Labour MP for Buckingham and owner of the scientific publisher Pergamon Press, who bid 37s. 6d. (£1.87) per voting share.

'A complete stranger'

On 16 October 1968, Sir Max Aitken, chairman of the Express Group, phoned Carr, who was ill in bed, and told him that the London *Evening Standard* was carrying a story to the effect that Maxwell had put in a bid of more than £26 million for the NOTW Organisation. This sent the share price soaring. Carr dismissed the bid as 'impudent'.[4] Neither he nor his editor, Stafford Somerfield, who was also a close friend and drinking companion, wanted Maxwell, who had already established a reputation for throwing his weight around. However, in the eyes of the extremely conservative Carr and Somerfield, he also had three other deeply unattractive characteristics: he was a foreigner (albeit a naturalised one), a Jew and a member of the Labour Party. Thus, four days after Maxwell's interest in the paper became known, Somerfield published an editorial on its front page, which began: 'We are having a little local difficulty at the *NOTW*. It concerns the ownership of the paper. Mr Robert Maxwell, a Socialist MP, is trying to take it over.'[5] It went on to argue that 'Mr Maxwell, formerly Jan Ludwig [actually Ludvik] Hoch' who was 'a complete stranger as far as Fleet Street and this newspaper are concerned', should not be allowed to gain control of a newspaper which is 'as British as roast beef and Yorkshire pudding'.[6] Noting that Maxwell had said that 'he would cease to be a Socialist MP if he gained control', Somerfield enquired: 'But is it possible for him to support the Socialists one day and become completely impartial the next? I do not think so.'[7] Deeply ironically, in the light of the paper's imminent take-over by the Australian Rupert Murdoch, the editorial concluded: 'This is a British newspaper, run by British people. Let's keep it that way.'[8] The editorial was widely condemned as xenophobic.

It should also be noted that the unions at the *NOTW* were as opposed to Maxwell taking the paper over as they would be when he tried to acquire the *Sun* from the International Publishing Corporation (IPC) in 1969. Thus the Imperial Father of the Federated House Chapel at Bouverie Street, the paper's headquarters, wrote to Carr assuring him of the unions' loyalty to the Carr family and the board and stating that:

> Your employees feel deeply the apparent threats that the Maxwell hierarchy are making to destroy this newspaper.... We reiterate our determination to stand fast and support the management in its stubborn fight to survive the onslaught from these destructive pressures.[9]

Deeply worried by Maxwell's offer to buy Jackson's stake in the NOTW Organisation, Carr instructed Hambros to place £750,000 at the disposal of its stockbrokers to enable them to buy every share in the company on the market. However, this could be regarded as a clear breach of at least the spirit of the code of practice recently introduced by the new City Takeover Panel, under which companies were forbidden to buy shares in their own business in order to fight off a takeover bid. Within days, Hambros owned 10 per cent of its client's shares. The brokers secured pledges of support from other shareholders for a payment of 10*s*. (50 p) each, and *NOTW* employees were given shares on a temporary basis. By these means, Carr was guaranteed 48 per cent of the votes. Six days after his initial bid, Maxwell upped his offer to £34 million, valuing the voting shares at 50*s*. (£2.50) each.

'Your saviour is here'

Whilst all this activity was taking place, Rupert Murdoch's company News Limited had been steadily buying up shares in IPC, which at that time published the *Daily Mirror,* the *Sunday People* and the *Sun.* However, realising that this could be a very long game, he turned his attention elsewhere, and specifically to the *NOTW.* Murdoch operated through Morgan Grenfell, merchant bankers to the Queen, whose director, Lord Catto, was a personal friend who also had considerable banking interests in Australia.

News Limited had been founded in 1923 and originally owned papers in Melbourne, Adelaide and Brisbane. In October 1952, Rupert's father, Sir Keith, died, and death duties reduced his estate to just two small papers in Adelaide. His son, only 23, set about rebuilding the family newspaper empire. As Roy Greenslade put it, 'he soon discovered that sleaze equals sales',[10] as is particularly clearly illustrated by the transformation of Sydney's *Daily Mirror* after his purchase of it in 1960. Four years later, he launched the country's first genuine national daily, the *Australian.* In 1959, he entered the television arena with the Adelaide-based station NWS-9. He then began to consider expanding his ever-growing empire beyond Australia's shores.

Nothing if not prescient, he pointed out to a conference of newspaper executives shortly after his takeover of the NOTW Organisation that:

> What most people don't realise is that publishing empires are going out beyond national boundaries. Whether it be in the transmission of news between countries or satellite programmes, you have got to think in terms of numbers much greater than you can achieve in Australia.[11]

Murdoch had already acquired 3.5 per cent of voting shares in the NOTW Organisation, and as soon as Catto informed him about Maxwell's bid for the company he dropped everything and flew straight to England. On 22 October, accompanied by Catto, he presented Carr with a plan whereby the NOTW Organisation would acquire part of Murdoch's publishing interests in Australia, including *Truth*, a Melbourne-based weekly based on sex and sport, the women's magazine *New Idea* and the racing guide *Best Bets*; in return, Murdoch, through an issue of new shares allotted to News Limited, would acquire the majority shareholding in the NOTW Organisation. He would become joint managing director with Clive Carr, a cousin of Sir William, who would himself remain as chairman and consultant. Murdoch also gave assurances that a member of the Carr family would remain as chairman of the company for the foreseeable future and that he would not seek to increase his shareholding above 40 per cent, which would give him control of the company. Carr agreed to this arrangement, as he was convinced that this was the only way in which he and his family could maintain a degree of control. Murdoch produced a written record of the agreement, in which he told Carr that he looked forward 'with keen anticipation to working with you and your colleagues for many years to add to the strength and prosperity of the *NOTW* and further the interests of the shareholders.'[12]

On 23 October News Limited began buying shares in the NOTW Organisation, and word of the operation broke. The following day, Murdoch gave a press conference at which he announced that he intended to acquire 40 per cent of the NOTW Organisation. Carr and Murdoch now owned just over half the shares between them. Somerfield, who was actually a director of the company, had known nothing about all this until a friend from the *Express* rang up on 23 October and said: 'Your saviour is here. It's young Rupert Murdoch from Australia'.[13]

Dubious practices and dirty tricks

Approval of the new share issue would have to be sought at an extraordinary general meeting of the NOTW shareholders. Dealings in the shares were thus suspended by the stock exchange for two months in order to give shareholders an opportunity to make up their minds about the offer.

Maxwell complained to the City Takeover Panel that the company had been effectively buying its own shares in order to frustrate his bid for it. Jackson made the same argument to the panel, but as Anthony Crosland, the President of the Board of Trade, pointed out: 'As there are very few sanctions at the Panel's disposal, it will have to rely mainly on the respect shown for its views.'[14] This, it would appear, was minimal on the part of the big beasts of the City jungle, although Maxwell was convinced, both at the time and later, that the panel failed to act not because it was feeble but because its members disliked him, and his political views in particular. Murdoch was later to observe that 'I could smell that the Establishment wouldn't let Maxwell in',[15] an observation that turned out to be entirely correct.

Murdoch then started a dirty tricks campaign against Maxwell, his Sydney *Daily Mirror* accusing encyclopaedia salesmen working for Pergamon of dubious selling practices. In turn, Maxwell and his City ally Sir Isaac Wolfson tried to persuade Carr that Murdoch was not to be trusted. Maxwell warned him that 'you will be out before your feet touch the ground'. This turned out to be entirely correct, but Carr would have none of it, retorting: 'Bob, Rupert is a gentleman.'[16] This turned out to be entirely incorrect as, already scenting victory, Murdoch began to change the terms of the deal with Carr. Now he would be the sole managing director, dispensing altogether with Clive Carr, although Sir William would remain as chairman. This assurance was to be broken the following year.

In December, Carr set out for shareholders the terms of the deal with Murdoch – the NOTW Organisation would issue 5.1 million voting ordinary shares, amounting to 35 per cent of the expanded voting stock, to News Limited, in exchange for Australian assets owned by News Limited, which would then own 40 per cent of the reconstructed NOTW Organisation. Murdoch would put six directors on a reconstituted board.

On 2 January 1969, the shareholders voted. Under pressure from Crosland, the City Takeover Panel had roused itself sufficiently to rule that the 15 per cent of shares acquired since the Maxwell bid should not count for voting purposes, which somewhat weakened the position of the Murdoch/Carr grouping, which now possessed 38 per cent of the voting shares, whilst Maxwell had 32 per cent. About 30 per cent were uncommitted. According to William Shawcross:

> Lady Carr and her family had spent days and days trying to persuade as many of the smaller shareholders as possible to attend and vote the Carr-Murdoch ticket. They suggested to those who could not attend the meeting that they sign over their shares temporarily to *News of the World* staff who would be present and could vote with them. Lady Carr gave her friends one share each so that they could attend and vote against an adjournment. Under the articles, an adjournment could be passed on a show of hands – so the turnout of shareholders might be crucial.[17]

Carr was greeted by a long ovation when he appeared on the dais. Murdoch made a very brief speech about the benefits that would flow from a liaison between the British and Australian newspaper groups; he also paid tribute to Carr, repeating the undertaking to keep him on as chairman. Maxwell, who was booed when he rose to speak, attacked the company's record and the tactics of their bankers, accusing both of rigging the meeting. After a number of angry exchanges, Carr told him to sit down, and members of the audience shouted 'Go home!' In the event, the deal was decisively carried, on a show of hands, by 299 votes to 20. Carr then announced that the matter was so important that a poll had to be taken. The result was closer, 4,526,822 votes to 3,246, 937, but still the same. Maxwell protested that 'we are back to the laws of the jungle. We played according to the rules while the other side treated them with cynical disregard,'[18] whilst Jackson pronounced: 'I regard the News of the World board as raving mad.'[19]

Friends in high places

This deal could have caused problems for Murdoch in Australia, since the Liberal government, and, in particular, the Treasurer, William McMahon, were unhappy about overseas corporations taking control of Australian assets. Furthermore, the operations in the London stock market required exchange control approval in Canberra. As Page points out: 'Involved here were the resources of a business built largely on public licenses granted for the development of Australian television.'[20] Furthermore, Murdoch had used his papers to campaign against McMahon when, during the previous year, it had looked as if he might stand for the leadership of the Liberal Party. Had McMahon launched a review of News Limited's manoeuvre, it would have torpedoed the whole scheme. However, Murdoch was extremely friendly with the Deputy Prime Minister, John 'Black Jack' McEwen, who, whilst McMahon was away for a weekend, asked the Prime Minister, John Gorton, for whom Murdoch had campaigned, to sign the necessary papers, which he did willingly.[21] Thus, not for the first time and by no means for the last, Murdoch's carefully nurtured political contacts played a key role in helping him to clinch a media deal.

'Only one executive boss'

On 21 January Murdoch wrote to Carr informing him that he was going to buy 'some of the Jackson shares, probably about a million'[22] which Rothschild was putting on the market, thus breaking his word about not attempting to acquire a majority of shares. But by now there was growing concern about Murdoch amongst the *ancien régime* at the *NOTW*, not least on the part of Somerfield, and the new arrival felt that he had to act fast in order to consolidate his position. Thus on 7 March he wrote to Carr, stating: 'The plain fact, which I am sure you are as aware of as I am, is that a company of this nature can have only one executive boss. As managing director (and in control of a virtual majority of the voting shares) that person has to be me' (Shawcross, p. 142). Although many of the executives were old friends of Carr, he was told that in future he could contact them only through Murdoch, who also asked him to resign from the subsidiary companies in the organisation. Three months later he asked him to resign as both chairman and a director, proposing to take over as chairman himself. On 19 June, Carr resigned, giving no hint then or subsequently that he had been forced out. At a subsequent meeting of the board, Murdoch was elected chairman. Not long after this, Carr became seriously ill once again, remaining an invalid for the last seven years of his life. When he died in 1977, Murdoch's offer to pay for a memorial service was rejected by Lady Carr.

After Murdoch's takeover of the NOTW Organisation, his relationship with Somerfield was never good. Early on, Murdoch ordered Somerfield to fire various reporters and columnists (the latter included Battle of Britain ace Douglas Bader), and it was the new boss who chose their successors. He started altering advertising material that Somerfield had already approved, and told him not to send correspondents abroad without his agreement. In May 1969, Somerfield broke off a holiday in Spain when he was told that Murdoch was making radical changes to the paper, including removing the leader page. On his return he arrived on the editorial floor and said loudly: 'Somebody's been messing about with my newspaper',[23] following which he reversed all Murdoch's changes. He then sent a letter to the directors about editorial responsibility. This stated:

> As Editor, I am responsible for the newspaper and its contents. The responsibility is both traditional and inveterate [sic]. Whether the editor is present or absent or whether he has actual knowledge of the particular contents of the paper, his responsibility remains. This is true in law or in ethics or morality or generally in accordance with long-established custom in Fleet Street. The editor is the servant of the board, and contractually answerable to the board and the managing director. But this does not mean that the chief executive, acting independently of the board, can take his chair, seek to discharge his functions or introduce fundamental changes in the paper without consultation.[24]

After Cardinal Heenan had refused to write for the paper because of the serialisation of Christine Keeler's memoirs, which were trailed in the paper on 28 September 1969 and began in earnest on 5 October, Somerfield was quoted in the *Daily Mail*, 2 October, as stating that:

> I think it's extraordinary that people who have the opportunity to use the columns of the *News of the World* in the way Cardinal Heenan does

do not seize the chance to preach. Is it better to talk to the converted in a cathedral or go into the market place and talk to sinners? *The News of the World* is a market place. The *News of the World* can offer to any cleric 16 million sinners to talk to, and if Cardinal Heenan doesn't want to talk to sinners...well, what an unfortunate situation. Didn't Jesus Christ go into the market place to preach to sinners?

Murdoch was furious, writing an apology to the Cardinal and castigating Somerfield's remark as 'tasteless and unnecessary'. He told Somerfield: 'We will win this debate, I am sure, but there can be only one spokesman and that's me. In future, please say nothing or clear it with me first. I must be firm about this – there is a lot more at stake than one newspaper.'[25] The 'lot more' referred to Murdoch's plans to acquire the *Sun*, a project by now well advanced. (The process was completed on 20 October when the Board of Trade formally approved his bid for the paper.) The inevitable finally arrived in February 1970 when Murdoch asked Somerfield to resign. He refused, and was sacked. According to Leapman[26] he was paid off with a lump sum of around £100,000, since his contract still had seven years to run, but Bainbridge and Stockdill[27] claim that he was given £50,000 and a consultancy agreement worth £6000 a year for the remaining six years of his contract.

An interventionist proprietor

Murdoch made it clear from the start that he was going to be an interventionist proprietor. In an early interview in the UK he revealed that 'I do get involved in the newspaper I am responsible for. I am not a backroom businessman or simply chairman of the company. I am the chief executive.'[28] And on the matter of editorial control, he stated in 1969:

> As proprietor I'm the one who in the end is responsible for the success, or failure, of my papers. Since a paper's success or failure depends on its editorial approach, why shouldn't I interfere when I see a way to strengthen its approach? What am I supposed to do, sit idly by and watch a paper go down the drain, simply because I'm not supposed to interfere? Rubbish! That's the reason the *News of the World* started to fade. There was no-one there to trim the fat and wrench it out of its editorial complacency.[29]

He also put it rather more bluntly to Somerfield: 'I didn't come all the way from Australia not to interfere. You accept it or quit!'[30] As Matthew Engel observed:

> He would not tolerate for a moment Somerfield's sacerdotal incantation of an editor's holy rights and responsibilities; he could do what he liked

when he liked with the newspapers he owned. Having made his point, he had little wish to interfere once they were being run smoothly, i.e. profitably, and by editors who did not presume they were acting as free agents.[31]

Another Profumo scandal

Before Somerfield was fired, however, he was to embroil Murdoch in an affair that was to have lasting repercussions for him in Britain. Five years before Murdoch's arrival, the paper had paid £26,000 for the serialisation rights to Christine Keeler's memoirs. Now Keeler had spiced up the story, and the papers were bidding again. Somerfield urged Murdoch to enter the fray, and Murdoch paid £21,000 and won. On 28 September 1968 the memoirs were trailed as the front page lead, under the headline 'Storm over Keeler Book', by-lined The Editor, and an article below promised 'Next Week: First Lessons on Love.' That week, on 5 October 1969, 150,000 extra copies of the paper were printed, and the first extracts were announced on the front page, again by The Editor, under the inevitable headline 'The Story They Don't Want You to Read.' In a fascinating BBC news item on 2 October fronted by David Dimbleby,[32] Somerfield and Murdoch are seen at an editorial meeting discussing the imminent serialisation. Somerfield states that 'the line I'm proposing to take on it is the storm of the book, and people who are trying to get it stopped.' Murdoch adds, to much head-nodding around the table, that the line to take in the controversy is 'to say forgive the individual by all means, but you can't forget it [the story]', and to ask: 'Are these people proposing that whenever anyone writes history in future they're never going to mention this incident?' He concludes: 'We should take the offensive ... and if it keeps it boiling for six weeks then so much the better.'

However, by now, the man at the heart of the affair, John Profumo, had redeemed himself by working tirelessly amongst the poor at Toynbee Hall in Aldgate in London's East End, and there was an angry reaction to the serialisation. Murdoch had anticipated that this might happen, but was taken aback by the sheer amount of criticism and, in particular, was concerned that this episode might jeopardise his plans to buy the *Sun*. The Independent Television Authority (ITA) banned all television advertisements for the paper until the serialisation ended, the Press Council condemned the serialisation as a 'disservice both to the public welfare and to the press',[33] and Cardinal Heenan, the Archbishop of Westminster and Britain's most senior Roman Catholic, withdrew from a commitment to write an article on the 'permissive society' for the paper. The Archbishop of Canterbury, Dr Michael Ramsay, also backed out of writing a piece.

During his interview with Murdoch (who seems decidedly ill at ease), Dimbleby asks him if he has any qualms about the story as 'muckraking and going back over an old scandal that should be dead and buried by now'. Murdoch responds: 'No, no, certainly not, and it shouldn't be dead and buried either...We can forgive Mr Profumo, we can do what we can to see that he is rehabilitated, because he has tried very hard. By all means forgive the individual, but you can't forget it.' Dimbleby also quotes back at him his reported remark that 'people can sneer as much as they like, but I'll take the 150,000 extra copies we're going to sell' and suggests 'you are lining your pocket with rather sleazy material.' Murdoch replies: 'I don't believe it's sleazy for a minute' and concludes: 'Certainly it will sell newspapers, and other stories we'll put in will sell newspapers, we're not ashamed of that.'

However, this interview was nothing compared to the ferocious grilling that he received at the hands of David Frost on the *Frost on Friday* programme on London Weekend Television (LWT) on 3 October 1969.[34] This was described by Michael Wolff as 'perhaps the only public enquiry into Murdoch's tabloid philosophy,'[35] although that was written before Murdoch appeared before the Department of Culture, Media and Sport select committee in July 2011 and at the Leveson Inquiry in April 2012.

Things got off on the wrong foot for Murdoch when Frost started the programme by asking the audience whether they approved of the publication of the Keeler memoirs: only 9 out of the 230 present did so. The second part of the programme contained a recorded interview with Cardinal Heenan, following which Murdoch complained bitterly that 'this easy glib talk that the *News of the World* is a dirty paper is a downright libel and it is not true and I resist it completely.'[36] When Murdoch sought to defend the serialisation as a 'cautionary tale', Frost enquired: 'A cautionary tale about the best way to make £21,000?', and in the face of Murdoch's repeated attempts to justify publication on the grounds of the public interest, he retorted: 'It's pathetic to say that that's a social document of our time.'[37]

Murdoch vs the Establishment: round one

Murdoch then launched one of his first attacks on what was soon to be a very familiar target indeed, namely the British establishment, which he accused of hypocrisy for whipping up a controversy over Profumo whilst at the same time not wanting to be associated with him in public. As Roy Greenslade put it:

> Having placed his faith firmly in the market place he wrote a script that was to become his mantra: hostility towards him was orchestrated by the 'establishment'; he was honest and straightforward, a regular bloke; circulation was king; ethics were the province of a narrow elite of bleeding-heart, wishy-washy liberals whom he viewed as hypocrites and parasites.[38]

Similarly Shawcross stated: 'The incident hurt and angered Murdoch. He felt that he was once more a victim of British hypocrisy, as he had been at Oxford. It coloured his whole attitude towards the British, and in particular towards that amorphous and uncertain entity, the British Establishment.'[39] However, as we have seen, Murdoch was already on very good terms with members of the Establishment, such as Lord Catto, and in future years would be on even better ones. Thus, as Leapman suggested, Murdoch's anti-establishment rhetoric should not be taken entirely at face value:

> He knew that if he was to become an accepted and respected newspaper proprietor he would have to come to terms with the British establishment that, rightly or wrongly, believed him to have behaved caddishly in raking over Profumo's anguish. In public he affected a swaggering disregard for such matters. What did acceptance into the inner circles of power matter to him? He would ask rhetorically. But to his friends it was clear that it did matter.[40]

It is also possible, particularly in the light of Murdoch's later activities, to regard his anti-establishment diatribes as something of a mask, concealing what Page calls his 'capacity to traffic with established power, legitimately or otherwise',[41] and also as 'necessary camouflage for a business specialising in privatised government propaganda'.[42]

'The "dirty" bits'

The interview also contained a classic demonstration of the kind of hypocrisy that would become such an unpleasant hallmark of papers such as the *NOTW* and the *Sun*. Leapman revealed that when Somerfield had first suggested serialising the new version of Keeler's memoirs 'Murdoch wrote to him enthusiastically, urging him to buy it, though the "dirty" bits in the early part should be held out.'[43] When asked by Frost if he had cut anything for the *NOTW* on the grounds of taste or morality, Murdoch appeared to try to ingratiate himself with his critics by readily admitting that 'I certainly sub-edited a tremendous amount' out of Keeler's memoirs, material from the first part of the book, which he considered was 'unpleasant' and not 'relevant or decent', and which he 'watered down or cut to pieces'. According to Murdoch, what was interesting about the Profumo affair was 'the search for a scapegoat. The way that scapegoat was treated', but Frost pointed out that the first episode of the serialisation was all 'from that early part you found so unpleasant. There was not a bit of scapegoat. You changed the phrases to having sex and so on from what is in the original text and so on, but there is none of that scapegoat social message and so on in the first episode, was there? It was pure sexual encounters.' He also pointed out that the paper had trailed the second episode of the serialisation as describing 'first lessons in love', 'the bathing party at…', and 'a night with the Russian Huggie Bear'.[44] In other words, titillating the readers with mild sexual details was permissible, indeed desirable, up to a point, but anything too sexually explicit was clearly out of bounds for a 'family newspaper' – because it might endanger the all-important sales figures. The give-away word here is, of course, 'decent'.

According to David Frost: 'As he strode from the studio he told a reporter, "London Weekend has made a powerful enemy tonight". One of his party said later that that was the bowdlerised version. What he had said privately was "I'm going to buy that blankety-blank company".'[45] And that is precisely what Murdoch set about doing. Thus, Murdoch's acquisition of the NOTW Organisation can be seen not only as his first foray into the British press but also as a prelude to his involvement in British television.

Fulfilling a promise

In 1967 LWT was licensed by the Independent Television Authority (ITA) to broadcast to the London area from Friday to Sunday evenings.[46] It was formed by a consortium of big-name television stars and businessmen. As Leapman explained:

> They won the contract on the strength of their names and of a programme prospectus that assumed an unsatisfied taste among British viewers for weekend fare of a more cerebral nature than they had hith-erto been offered, emphasising plays, documentaries, news and interview programmes.[47]

However, by 1970 it was in dire financial straits.

On 13 July 1970, Murdoch met Sir Robert Fraser, the director general of the ITA (another example of Murdoch fraternising with the hated establish-ment). Murdoch told him that he had contacted LWT's major shareholders, and that 63 per cent of the company's shares had been offered to him. He was thus interested in what the authority's attitude would be if he decided to purchase all or some of these. Fraser responded that the authority wanted ITV companies to retain the same ownership throughout the time that they held a franchise (a licence to broadcast) granted by the ITA, and stressed that any transfer of voting shares required its prior approval; he also made it clear that the authority would not allow a franchise to be controlled by a single shareholder. However, in November the ITA allowed Murdoch's NOTW Organisation to acquire 7.5 per cent of voting shares and 16 per cent of non-voting shares held by Sir Arnold Weinstock's General Electric Company (GEC). Murdoch then took Weinstock's place as a non-executive director on the LWT board.

As Murdoch forcefully pointed out soon after arriving, by the end of 1970 LWT had run through its authorised and fully-paid share capital of £1.5 million non-voting shares and £15,000 voting shares; that the loan stock of just over £3 million was rapidly being used up; and that the company had overdrafts of around £2.5 million. He argued that the company needed new programmes in order to improve its ratings, but that it lacked the necessary funds, and offered to inject £500,000 for programme making in return for new shares and a seat on LWT's executive committee. The LWT Board thus agreed to issuing a one-for-three rights issue, which Murdoch agreed to underwrite through his NOTW Organisation – an arrangement not dissimilar to the one that had helped him to gain control of that company in the first place. Of course, the arrangement had to be approved by the ITA, but the LWT chief executive, Tom Margerison, told Anthony Pragnell, the deputy director-general of the ITA, that without Murdoch's funds, LWT would have to merge with Thames Television (which broadcast to the London area on weekdays), an outcome that the ITA was very keen to avoid. The ITA board thus agreed to the proposal, somewhat unwillingly, and Murdoch underwrote the issue to the tune of £505,000, in so doing becoming the owner of 35 per cent of the non-voting shares. He announced that he would attend meetings of the executive directors and devote part of his time to the affairs of the company, although the ITA made it clear that under the Television Act 1964 he could not involve himself in programming. On 31 December 1970 the new share issue was formally approved by the ITA. As David Docherty pointed out: 'It had taken over a year, but Murdoch had fulfilled the promise which he made to himself when he stood outside Wembley studios in October 1969.'[48]

However, the company was still financially weak. On 18 February 1971, Murdoch became chairman of the executive committee formed to run the company, even though under the Television Act no one could hold executive authority in a television company whilst also controlling a major newspaper. However Murdoch, who was accustomed to a far lighter television regulatory regime in Australia, either did not understand or did not care how the ITA operated, and the members of the LWT Board were delighted that he was determined to put the company on a sound financial and organisational footing.

'Like the Mafia'

Murdoch's arrival at LWT sounds remarkably like his arrival at British Satellite Broadcasting (BSB) following its effective takeover by Sky in 1990. According to Docherty: 'Murdoch exploded into LWT', and he quotes one employee as stating that he and his entourage toured the building 'like the Mafia'.[49] He immediately drafted a new programme schedule and began to explore ways in which staffing could be streamlined and production costs lowered. In terms of programming, he announced that he would take charge of the selection of feature films for the next quarter; that *On the Buses*, LWT's most popular show, should be broadcast every week; that *Aquarius*, the station's only arts programme, should be pushed back to 11.15 pm, and that *Survival*, Anglia's documentary series about the natural world, should be replaced by quiz shows, one of which would be fronted by Hughie Green. Brian Young, who had taken over from Sir Robert Fraser as director general of the ITA, refused to accept Murdoch's changes, but by now staff departures had begun in earnest. Most left of their own accord, but chief executive Tom Margerison, who had actually supported Murdoch's involvement in the company but who soon found himself marginalised and outmanoeuvred by him, was asked by the Board on 17 February, at Murdoch's instigation, to tender his resignation, which he duly did.

As Docherty puts it: 'It very quickly became clear that although Murdoch was a non-executive director with no formal power or authority he had become, de facto, Managing Director and Controller of Programmes.'[50] Pragnell wrote to the ITA's solicitors on 19 February stating that 'I feel sure that the Authority would take the view that the changes announced yesterday, which seem to put Mr Murdoch in executive charge of the company, would have meant that LWT would not have got the contract had they been in operation before the contract was entered into.'[51] It is important in this context to understand that Section 11 of the Television Act stated that the appointment of the manager, editor or other chief executive of any ITV company should be approved by the ITA, and that Section 12 laid down that:

If at any time there are newspaper shareholdings in the programme contractor, and it appears to the Authority that the existence of those shareholdings has led or is leading to results which are contrary to the public interest, the Authority may, with the consent of the Postmaster General, by notice in writing to the programme contractor, taking effect forthwith or on a date specified in the notice, determine or suspend for such period as may be so specified or until further notice is given, the Authority's obligation to transmit the programmes supplied by the programme contractor.

In the Commons, there were demands for an enquiry, but the Minister for Posts and Telecommunications (Christopher Chataway) argued that the responsibility for the matter lay with the ITA. Murdoch was attacked in the press for threatening to dilute LWT's original mission. For example, Clive Irving, a former member of the board, wrote a letter to *The Times*, 25 February 1971, demanding a formal enquiry into the transfer of power at LWT, adding: 'The company's initial philosophy was too ambitious, but it is one thing to concede that. It is another to make undiluted commercial expediency the alternative.'[52] According to Docherty:

> Murdoch, believing that Irving was a front man for Frost, called the letter writer 'His Master's Voice.' A few days later Murdoch announced that LWT would not be able to afford to pay Frost's salary and that the latter would either have to accept a substantial reduction for the next series of Frost programmes or he could take his talents elsewhere.[53]

But before Murdoch could take his revenge on Frost, the ITA intervened.

Murdoch vs the Establishment: round two

In a letter to Brian Young, Murdoch had already argued that he subscribed to the programme philosophy of the original consortium and attributed LWT's problems not to 'unrealism or unattainable ideals' but to 'very bad management and a company structure which led to nobody being really accountable'.[54] On 23 February, Young set out for the ITA the arguments for and against action. As summarised by Potter these were as follows:

> On the one hand, the company was indisputably a different one; Murdoch indisputably held the main executive power; and 'the fact that Murdoch's newspapers are what admirers call popular and detractors call vulgar increases the discrepancy between Peacock's promise [Michael Peacock was LWT's original managing director] and Murdoch's method.' On the other hand, the company was likely to become more effective under Murdoch's leadership; sixteen employees had left, but a thousand remained, and did not deserve a second total upheaval in three years; the shareholders would get a raw deal; and the only practical alternative was a merger with another ITV company.[55]

The ITA met on 25 February, and agreed that the sacking of Margerison and the Establishment of an executive committee headed by Murdoch contravened the Television Act and thus entitled it to cancel LWT's contract. However, rather than taking immediate action it invited the chairman and the LWT board to put a submission before the authority at a meeting to discuss the company's future plans for its management and programme provision. It also made clear that LWT should, in consultation with the ITA, choose a new managing director and programme controller. The decision was not welcomed by the press, which feared that Murdoch would take LWT down-market, and criticised the ITA for being feeble and in dereliction of its duty in failing to terminate LWT's franchise.

In early March, Murdoch returned from Australia and, ever suspicious of machinations against him within the British establishment, personally accused the ITA of besmirching his reputation. But as Jeremy Potter contended:

> While there can be little doubt that he was the buccaneering kind of entrepreneur not favoured by the Authority during the Young years, it had been scrupulous in not personalising the dispute and was able to reassure him in a mollifying letter deploring some of the newspaper comments and enclosing copies of its own press statements.[56]

Murdoch was suitably mollified, and denied that he had ever intended to play an executive role in LWT; he did, however, declare his intention of taking an active interest in running the company and supporting its newly appointed chairman and chief executive. The latter was John Freeman, famous for his interviews on the BBC series *Face to Face*, who had in fact been named as prospective deputy chairman of LWT in its original franchise application. However, at that time he could not take up the post, as he was High Commissioner to India. However, as he had just retired as British ambassador to Washington, he was open to the suggestion by David Frost, who had recruited him to the consortium in the first place, that he become LWT's new chief executive and chairman. The two roles were combined partly at Freeman's insistence and partly because Murdoch had demanded the resignation of the then current chairman, Aiden Crawley, for not supporting him in his battle with the ITA. Freeman also stipulated that the appointment would have to be approved by Murdoch, who would have to agree to give him a free hand. Murdoch approved and agreed, and Freeman was duly appointed.

Holding Murdoch in check

As Docherty pointed out: 'Despite the widespread relief which greeted Freeman's appointment, LWT still had to go through the mechanics of virtually reapplying for its franchise.'[57] It was invited to present its case for the continuation of its franchise on 22 April. The team included Murdoch but was headed by Freeman. Among other things, the meeting noted that the executive committee headed by Murdoch, of which the ITA had disapproved so strongly, had been disbanded. The ITA was clearly impressed by the way in which Freeman had evidently taken control of the company's affairs in such a short space of time, and announced that the franchise was secure.

Murdoch did more or less leave him to his own devices, but Freeman left him in no doubt that he would resign if Murdoch interfered, which would undoubtedly spell the end of the franchise. As he himself put it:

> It was my job to hold Murdoch in check, because to have allowed him to continue interfering in the company would have spelt simple and rapid

disaster. I had very strong views about how the company should be run, but frankly I didn't give a bugger whether I stayed or not – I merely had to do the best I could. I intended to run the company my way and to hell with anyone who wanted it done differently. I always treated Murdoch with the respect which he commands personally, because he is a very formidable and able man, but I simply did not concede that he had any right to interfere in the day-to-day running of the company...Our relationship was based on the fact that I had to prevent him doing what he wanted to do until eventually, and quite inevitably, he decided to focus his energies elsewhere.[58]

Murdoch quit the board when he began to involve himself in the media in the USA, and in 1979 sold nearly all his shares in LWT when he needed cash in order to acquire United Telecasters Sydney Limited, which owned the city's TEN-10 television station.

'I'll still get the bastard one day'

Frost thus survived Murdoch's arrival and carried on making programmes for LWT, although from 1969 to 1972 he also fronted the thrice-weekly *The David Frost Show* in the US. He sold his shares in LWT in 1976. Accounts vary of the Frost/Murdoch relationship at the company. According to Bainbridge and Stockdill, after the famous programme 'there was an angry exchange of correspondence in which both agreed to differ. "Let us not worry too much," Murdoch wrote. "It is in the past and I certainly won't fall for it again". Later, they bumped into each other at Les Ambassadeurs restaurant and agreed to re-establish social contact.'[59] However, tucked away in an endnote in Michael Wolff's book on Murdoch we find an extract from an interview in October 2007 in which Murdoch states:

I swore I would never, ever have anything to do with Frost on any level in any way and I made it my, for at least twenty years I never spoke to him [sic]. He'd be all over me at parties, 'Oh Rupert...' I've never had a one-on-one with him since and I've always been very cold to him, but I've been in situations where I've had to have social conversation. But I thought he was such an arrogant bastard, a bloody bugger...I feel like saying I'll still get the bastard one day, but he'll die before I get him.[60]

As, indeed, he did. Similarly, according to Shawcross, Murdoch's treatment by the ITA continued to rankle: 'Murdoch was angry that the Independent Television Authority should have the power to exclude him. He saw it as another example of the Establishment hatred of him. He was determined that one day he would break into British television.'[61]

Decidedly the boss

As far as the *NOTW* was concerned, Murdoch continued to make it very clear to Somerfield's successors that he was a highly activist proprietor and decidedly the boss. In this respect, it is surely significant that from 1891 to 1970 the paper had just six editors – in the years after Somerfield was fired, it had no fewer than sixteen. The paper lost Bernard Shrimsley (1975–80) because of rows with Murdoch about the paper becoming a tabloid, which Shrimsley wanted and Murdoch did not, although Murdoch finally relented in 1984. In spite of being a legendary tabloid editor, Derek Jameson (1981–84) did not last long. The reasons for his dismissal are unclear, but Jameson himself has suggested that it was on account of his publishing of a story implying that Harold Holt, the Australian Prime Minister who disappeared from a beach in 1967, had been a communist spy and had been whisked away by a Chinese submarine. Holt had been a friend of Murdoch's mother, Dame Elisabeth Murdoch, and the Murdoch family were outraged by the story's appearance.[62] Murdoch had also advised Jameson against suing the BBC over remarks in the Radio 4 satirical programme *Week Ending* which described him as an 'East End boy made bad' and said that he was 'so ignorant he thought erudite was a type of glue'. Jameson did sue, but lost the action when it came to court in February 1984. Murdoch, then as now, disapproved of anything that might serve to put his papers under the spotlight, and he disliked his employees becoming 'personalities' in their own right – and, for that matter, becoming too powerful within his companies. Wendy Henry (1987–88), with her insatiable appetite for stories about sex scandals, might have appeared to be the perfect *NOTW* editor, but Murdoch (who, it should be remembered, had cut out what he called the 'dirty bits' from the Keeler memoir) baulked at what she was prepared to publish, and fired her. The tipping point was apparently reached when the paper ran a story about Sir Ralph Halpern, the former Burton boss, and his girlfriend Fiona Wright; Henry turned Wright's allegation that Halpern had wanted to 'goose' Mrs Thatcher at No. 10 into an assertion that he had actually done so, causing him to complain personally to Murdoch, who was absolutely furious with his editor.[63]

Conclusion

There are very significant parallels between the way in which Murdoch took over the NOTW Organisation and the manner in which he attempted to take control of LWT. In particular, in both instances he operated with utter ruthlessness and a buccaneering contempt for the niceties of traditional business practice. In both cases, his arrival was marked by his new acquisition lurching, or rather, in the case of LWT, threatening to lurch, downmarket for primarily commercial reasons. Moreover, the two narratives are obviously intimately linked by the Keeler affair. However, important though this was, its significance should not be overstated, as it is clear that Murdoch was already determined to expand his television interests outside his native Australia. Yet, there is also a significant difference between the events at the *NOTW* and those at LWT. In the former case, 'self-regulation' in the form of the City Takeover Panel proved utterly incapable of stopping Murdoch (not to mention unwilling to do so), and his actions fell outside the remit of the Monopolies and Mergers Commission. However, even if they had engaged the Commission, it is highly unlikely that it would have acted to stop Murdoch since, not once in its history, did it ever act to stop a national newspaper changing hands. Nor did his actions remotely engage the Press Council, which was anyway a largely supine body. By contrast, in the case of LWT, Murdoch ran up against not only a law, namely the Broadcasting Act 1964, which stood in his way, but also a public body, the Independent Television Authority, which was determined to see that the law was not flouted, even if it failed to act as robustly as many would have liked. Clearly, Murdoch was furious that his broadcasting ambitions in Britain had been to a considerable extent thwarted, but there was little he could do about this. Yet, as Shawcross noted, it rankled.

It is thus entirely possible that the endless propaganda campaign against public service broadcasting and in favour of its 'deregulation' (for which read re-regulation in the interests of big business) that has for so long been such a prominent feature in Murdoch's newspapers had its genesis in the LWT episode. Similarly, the absolute ruthlessness of Murdoch's dealings with the Carr family and his trouncing of Robert Maxwell foreshadow his brutal treatment of all those who would stand in his way in future, such as the print unions at Wapping in 1986 and rival satellite broadcaster BSB in 1990. Furthermore, the help that he received from high-ranking Liberal politicians in Australia in his acquisition of the NOTW Organisation uncannily prefigures the support that he was granted by Margaret Thatcher in his purchase of Times Newspapers in 1981 and by Tony Blair in the addition of highly Murdoch-friendly clauses to the Communications Act 2003. Finally, the manner in which Murdoch, in the Dimbleby programme, is seen repeatedly attempting to justify the Keeler serialisation on what would now be called 'public interest' grounds, when, clearly, there isn't one iota of such content in it, looks forward to the *NOTW*'s increasingly desperate and threadbare attempts to invoke 'public interest' in defending itself in court against Max Mosley's libel action in 2008. Similarly, the way in which the paper ignited a scandal, by buying and serialising the new version of Keeler's memoirs, and then assiduously made the scandal a key part of the story itself, is an early example of a now highly familiar tabloid tactic.

With the benefits of 20/20 hindsight, it can be argued that the manner of Murdoch's acquisition of the NOTW Organisation should have rung loud warning bells, but this would be to ignore a number of inconvenient truths. First, the acquiescence of Sir William Carr in his own fate: driven as he was by xenophobia (not to say anti-Semitism) and hatred of socialism, he placed himself in the hands of a 'saviour' who turned out to be his nemesis. Second, the print unions were firmly behind the takeover of the paper by their future nemesis. Finally, the authorities were unable actually to stop Murdoch, as noted above. It is hard not to read the story of Murdoch's takeover of the NOTW Organisation as something of a parable of capitalist succession in modern Britain, with the scions of the Establishment firmly convinced that if this particular piece of profit-generating endeavour was not to remain with 'one of us' it was far safer in the capable hands of this Australian capitalist than in the clutches of a Czech-born Jew and socialist.

If certain ingredients of this narrative look forward to Murdoch's future acquisition of large parts of the British media, others recall a time when liberal values were rather more common in the British press than they are now. In particular, the negative reactions to Somerfield's editorial about Maxwell, the revulsion at the serialisation of the Keeler memoirs and the demands for the LWT franchise to be revoked following Murdoch's involvement in the company, although not universal, were to be found in a wide variety of papers. Today, given similar circumstances, it is very doubtful if such views would be expressed outside the pages of the *Guardian/Observer* and *Independent*. And their relative absence would be less the result of fear of a counter-strike by the Murdoch press (though such fears most certainly exist) than a consequence of the corrosive spread of a thoroughly illiberal, raucous populism throughout much of the press (and not simply the tabloids), which, for many, is Rupert Murdoch's main legacy to British journalism.

Notes

1. The best and fullest accounts of Murdoch's takeover of the News of the World Organisation are to be found in M. Leapman, *Barefaced Cheek: the Apotheosis of Rupert Murdoch*, London and Sydney, 1983; and C. Bainbridge and R. Stockdill, *The News of the World Story*, London, 1993, to which the main narrative of this chapter is inevitably indebted.
2. Leapman, *Barefaced Cheek*, pp. 42–43.
3. B. Page, *The Murdoch Archipelago*, London and New York, 2003, p. 124.
4. Quoted in Bainbridge and Stockdill, *The News of the World Story*, p. 217
5. Quoted in ibid., p. 217.
6. Quoted in Leapman, *Barefaced Cheek*, p. 44
7. Quoted in ibid., p.44.
8. Quoted in ibid., p. 44.
9. Quoted in Bainbridge and Stockdill, *The News of the World*, p. 218.
10. R. Greenslade, *Press Gang: How Newspapers Make Profits from Propaganda*, Basingstoke and Oxford, 2003, p. 212.
11. Quoted in Bainbridge and Stockdill, *The News of the World*, p. 225.
12. Quoted in ibid., p. 221.

13. Quoted in Leapman, *Barefaced Cheek*, p. 45.
14. Quoted in ibid., p. 46.
15. Quoted in W. Shawcross, *Rupert Murdoch: Ringmaster of the Information Circus*, London, p. 137.
16. Quoted in Leapman, *Barefaced Cheek*, p. 46.
17. Shawcross, *Rupert Murdoch*, p. 138.
18. P. Thompson and A. Delano, *Maxwell: a Portrait of Power*, London, 1991.
19. Quoted in Leapman, p. 48.
20. Page, p. 122.
21. Ibid., pp. 122–23.
22. Quoted in Shawcross, *Rupert Murdoch*, p. 142.
23. Quoted in Matthew Engel, *Tickle the Public: One Hundred Years of the Popular Press*, London, 1996, p. 241.
24. Quoted in Bainbridge and Stockdill, *The News of the World*, p. 227.
25. Quoted in ibid., p. 229.
26. Leapman, *Barefaced Cheek*, pp. 54–55.
27. Bainbridge and Stockdill, *The News of the World*, p. 227.
28. Quoted in ibid., p. 226.
29. Quoted in Shawcross, *Rupert Murdoch*, p. 144.
30. Quoted in ibid., p. 144.
31. Engel, *Tickle the Public*, p. 252.
32. http://www.bbc.co.uk/programmes/p00dr94w. 'Talk at the BBC', episode 3.
33. Quoted in Greenslade, *Press Gang*, p. 214.
34. For a full account of this encounter see D. Frost, *David Frost: an Autobiography. Part One – From Congregations to Audiences*, London, 1993, pp. 493–501.
35. M. Wolff, *The Man Who Owns the News: Inside the Secret World of Rupert Murdoch*, London, 2010, p. 128.
36. Quoted in Leapman, *Barefaced Cheek*, p. 52.
37. Quoted in ibid., p. 52.
38. Greenslade, *Press Gang*, p. 214.
39. Shawcross, *Rupert Murdoch*, p. 147.
40. Leapman, *Barefaced Cheek*, p. 53.
41. Page, p. 405.
42. Ibid., p. 452.
43. Ibid., p. 49.
44. The quotes are drawn from Frost, *David Frost*, pp. 495–500.
45. Quoted in ibid., p. 500.
46. The most detailed accounts of Murdoch's involvement in LWT are to be found in J. Potter, *Independent Television in Britain: Vol. 3: Politics and Control, 1968–80*, Basingstoke and London, 1989; and D. Docherty, *Running the Show: 21 Years of London Weekend Television*, London, 1990, and the narrative of the final part of this chapter acknowledges its debt to these sources.
47. Leapman, *Barefaced Cheek*, p. 59.
48. Docherty, *Running the Show*, p. 70
49. Ibid., p. 72.
50. Ibid., p. 73.
51. Quoted in Potter, *Independent Television*, p. 51.
52. Quoted in ibid., p. 51.
53. Docherty, *Running the Show*, p. 74.
54. Quoted in Potter, *Independent Television*, p. 51.

55. Ibid., pp. 51–52.
56. Ibid., p. 53.
57. Docherty, *Running the Show*, p. 81.
58. Quoted in ibid., p. 82.
59. Bainbridge and Stockdill, *The News of the World*, p. 230.
60. Quoted in Wolff, *The Man*, p. 423.
61. Shawcross, *Rupert Murdoch*, p. 158.
62. D. Jameson, *Last of the Hot Metal Men: From Fleet Street to Showbiz*, London: Penguin, pp. 92–94.
63. Bainbridge and Stockdill, *The News of the World*, p. 279.

15
The Downfall of the *News of the World*: The Decline of the English Newspaper and the Double-edged Sword of Technology

James Rodgers

The effect was the same as the Saturday phone call before the splash hit the news stands on Sunday: a shock. This time, though, it was the scandal-seeking scribes who were on the receiving end of the stunning blow. Like a wayward politician, bribe-taking official or a footballer 'playing away', the *News of the World* (NOTW) only learned too late the extent of the trouble in which it found itself. By then, there was no way back. The court of public opinion, on this occasion, offered only the briefest of rights of reply. In any case, nothing was going to change the sentence imposed by an under-pressure Rupert Murdoch: a lifetime ban. Just as the *News of the World* had made ending careers its stock-in-trade, so finally it found itself exposed, with no way back. Unlike a rock star shamed for a 'drink and drugs hell', though, there was no option of going through rehabilitation in the hope of relaunching a career some years later. This was closure in the sense of shutting down for good. Mr Murdoch's expression of humility at a parlia-mentary hearing[1] had not, of itself, proved repentance enough. The *NOTW* had to go.

Its departure pleased its critics; dismayed its admirers. The back page of the final edition, on 10 July 2011, used George Orwell's picture of pre-war Sunday afternoon peace (how, or why, should they have resisted it?) as if to remind those happy to see them done down of the place the paper had once occupied in public life, and, indeed, in letters. The effect of the whole was an attempt to create a feeling of nostalgia for a time when the *NOTW* was able to do what it was best at. Yet perhaps there was another nostalgia: deeper than that for pre-war snoozes on the sofa, or for Sundays that would never be the same again. It was nostalgia for a time when the printed news-paper had only its counterparts for commercial rivals, a time when the Internet, giving away for free scandals that had previously been saleable, did not exist. 'Lots of mistakes were made 20 years ago, at the dawn of the web,' Sly Bailey, then Chief Executive of Trinity Mirror, told the Media Society in 2010. 'We can't make the same mistakes we made 20 years ago – poorly thought-through assumptions based on what we thought was good for us as publishers, with virtually no consumer insight in to who would pay and for what.'[2] Bailey was talking about ways in which the mistakes could now be, if not corrected, then at least compensated for. Her suggested solution involved, '"The Three Ps" of portability, personalisation and payment mechanisms,'[3] various permutations of which have been tried, and are still being tried today, in an attempt to offset revenue lost from print sales, which continue to fall. The challenge also lies in facing up to a world in which, as Bailey put it, 'The multiplicity of news products online and the very nature of the online environment has seen the willingness of consumers to pay for content dissipate almost completely.'[4] It is, in other words, a world as far distant from the era of reliable print sales as we now find ourselves from George Orwell's pre-war Sunday afternoon.

'Lots of mistakes': the phrase could apply to many eras of press and broadcasting history. To survive in a business that, in Britain at least, has often been highly competitive has long required an ability to gaze into the future, and then make the right decisions based on what you see there. That is not to say that even those who proved to be successful survivors always got their predictions right. For example, Ralph D. Blumenfeld, later to become a legendary editor of the *Daily Express*, pronounced in 1887, 'I doubt if type-setting by machinery will ever be as efficient or indispensable as hand-setting.'[5] Over at the *Daily Mail*, the great rival of the *Express*, Lord Northcliffe had sounder instincts about which forces might dominate the future. He would later come to appreciate correctly the significance of the advent of broadcasting for news media. As Briggs and Burke put it, 'Northcliffe had been keenly interested in exploiting the power of the press not only in politics, but in the advancement of new technology too.'[6] They even wondered, 'If Northcliffe had not become mentally disturbed and died in 1922, the year of the foundation of the BBC, he might have played as important a part in the history of broadcasting as he had done in the history of the press.'[7]

On one level, the story of the downfall of the *NOTW* is the story of the end of a newspaper whose conduct, once exposed, proved to be so unacceptable, in the eyes of so many, that the owner decided to close it. Doing so – closing that rarest of British newspapers in the twenty-first century, a profitable one – seemed a sensible decision for the longer term. With the wayward member of the Murdoch newspaper stable out of the way, the rest could be allowed to continue. Mr Murdoch would be seen to have taken a difficult decision, and, in doing so, have experienced the 'most humble day of my life'. Yet, there is another way of seeing the end of the *NOTW*, too: as the downfall of a newspaper that was a victim of changes that it, like other newspapers – as Sly Bailey noted in the speech referred to above – did not fully understand. In the case of the *NOTW*, technological change – in the shape of relatively insecure mobile telephony – gave the newspaper and its hired agents the opportunity to hack into messages. It did so at a time when the pressure, always huge, on red-top tabloids to land exclusives was increasing to unprecedented levels precisely because of another aspect of technological change: online competition. Technological change gave the *NOTW* the chance to stay ahead of the game by hacking phones. The ultimate price was too high. The newspaper's decision to abuse new technology, in the way it did, led eventually to its downfall. Evidence given to the Leveson Inquiry in 2012 offers some clues as to the effects that bewilderingly rapid technological change had on journalism. Aside from the closure of the *NOTW*, the setting-up of the Inquiry was the most visible consequence of the phone hacking scandal. The Inquiry's brief was to consider the 'Culture, Practice, and Ethics of the Press.'[8] Yet, the Inquiry could not approach its task in anything like the required detail without also considering companies and organisations that were outside the press and that, in the age of the Internet, were encroaching on what had once been indisputably press territory. For example, towards the end of January 2012, the Inquiry was hearing evidence from three media firms that, if not always supplying material that would once have come only from newspapers, were at least making claims on time that might otherwise have been spent reading them. 'Leveson inquiry: Facebook, Google, Popbitch executives appear. Full coverage as executives from the social network, search giant and gossip website appear at the media standards inquiry'[9]. *Facebook, Google, Popbitch*: the names would have been meaningless for most of the *NOTW*'s existence. In the years before its closure, they had become names without which the media world could not be understood.

The *Guardian*'s piece is instructive as to one part in particular of the challenges that print and other media faced as they sought to confront the competition emerging online. Presented in the form of a live blog (itself something that a conventional newspaper would have been technically incapable of producing), the page reports an exchange between Lord Leveson and Camilla Wright of *Popbitch* (which describes itself on its website as 'a free weekly celebrity gossip email').[10] 'I'm not sure that there is a great difference between what you do and what newspapers do,' Lord Leveson said to Camilla Wright at one point.[11] There was, however, a key difference between the way that *Popbitch* – and other websites – and newspapers were regulated. While newspapers published in the UK were subject not only to the Press Complaints Commission (the perceived inefficacy of which had led campaigners such as the group Hacked Off to demand something different, something stronger), but also to the law in a way that many websites could never be. This, in a way, was one of the challenges that the *NOTW* faced. Not only did it have to contend with new competitors working in new media, it had to do so while bearing in mind laws of libel and contempt of court.

Blogs, social media and even some gossip sites (if, unlike Popbitch, they were not UK-based) were not operating under the same constraints. This was a point made by those who did not agree with the purpose of the Leveson Inquiry. Senior Conservative politicians were among them, as presumably, the *NOTW* itself would have been had it lived to see the day the inquiry opened. Referring to the then recent publication in France of topless photographs of the Duchess of Cambridge, Angie Bray, a Conservative member of the British Parliament's Culture, Media and Sport Committee, advanced the following argument:

> Why should the mainstream press have its hands tied behind its back when everyone can say what they like on Twitter and the Internet? It is illogical, unreasonable, and makes the whole thing pointless.
>
> I look at France which has a regulated press and the pictures of the Duchess of Cambridge still came out. It is not the solution.[12]

The issue of the Internet was also referred to in the exchange between Lord Leveson and Camilla Wright. Ms Wright had said in her statement:

> Some newspapers have tried to use Popbitch to post stories that they wouldn't do themselves so that they can quote them as being on the Internet and therefore they can publish as in the public domain. I have tried to avoid Popbitch being used for this purpose.[13]

In the months before the closure of the *NOTW*, there had been a number of instances of court injunctions, designed to prevent the publication of details of prominent people's alleged extra-marital affairs, being rendered largely ineffective because the parties had been named on social media. The case of the Manchester United football player, Ryan Giggs, was one example.[14] There was a suspicion that Fleet Street journalists had employed the same 'post it on the Internet' technique of getting scandalous stories in the public domain, only with more success than Camilla Wright suggested they had apparently enjoyed with Popbitch. This was the time when Twitter, in particular, was rapidly growing in importance as a means of gathering and distributing news. As the *Mail* Online said in a June 2011 headline, 'Twitter's British audience jumps by a third as millions log on to discover details about celebrity scandals.'[15] Despite concerns about the Internet such as those raised by Angie Bray, the Leveson Iinquiry's remit remained clearly the 'Culture Practice and Ethics of the *Press*' (emphasis added). In July 2011, adding detail to his earlier announcement that the inquiry was to be set up, the British Prime Minister, David Cameron, did tell parliament, 'We have also made it clear that the inquiry should look not just at the press, but at other media organisations, including broadcasters and social media if there is any evidence that they have been involved in criminal activities.'[16] The crucial phrase was 'if there is any evidence that they have been involved in criminal activities.' It was not necessarily Lord Leveson's remit to uncover such evidence; the inquiry was only intended to respond to it should it come to light.

So, while posting material on the Internet might have afforded some journalists some opportunities, conventional newspapers found themselves generally put at a great disadvantage. Social media had given their audience opportunities to disclose and to discover scandals for themselves: scandals that might not have met the editorial standards of the newspapers, never mind the legal requirements of the courts. One consequence, perhaps the most alarming for newspapers trying to make enough money to remain in business, was endlessly tumbling circulations. This was such a serious problem that the closure of the *NOTW* became a cloud with only the most short-lived of silver linings. Those of the *NOTW*'s rivals who were looking to take a share of its readers after its demise did not get all they probably hoped for. As the *Guardian* website reported on 13 January 2012, 'Nearly half of the News of the World's s buyers give up on Sunday papers. Tabloid rivals of News International's now-defunct Sunday red-top have collectively lost 542,247 copy sales since July.'[17] In other words, while the five titles – *Daily Star Sunday,* the *Sunday Express,* the *People,* the *Sunday Mirror* and the *Mail on Sunday* – which might have seen themselves as alternative choices for *NOTW* readers did inherit some readers, their circulation figures, nevertheless, began to fall again: suggesting that the *NOTW*'s readers, like Jeanne Hobson who wrote to the paper's last edition, really could not imagine Sundays without it. Instead, it seemed, they were getting used to Sundays without a newspaper at all – as were many of the once-devoted readers of their rivals. The gossip and scandal that had once been the exclusive reserve of the Sunday tabloids was now also available on the Internet. So was a lot of other material such as music videos, games and chat on social networks: all of them taking up the leisure time of the descendants of the newspaper reader whom George Orwell imagined nodding off on the sofa on 'Sunday afternoon, preferably before the war.'[18]

It is important to stress that that world did not end because news values changed. George Orwell may have regretted the 'decline' of the kind of murder that was as much meat and drink to the press as the Sunday roast was to his imaginary reader. He did not suggest that murders in general had lost their appeal. Around the same time – 'preferably before the war' – that Orwell's sated Sunday newspaper reader was settling on the sofa, a fictional journalist was outlining the secret of a great story. 'Look at it this way. News is what a chap who doesn't care much about anything wants to read. And it's only news until he's read it. After that it's dead.'[19] The explanation is offered by Coker, a news agency reporter trying to explain to William Boot, the naive main character of Evelyn Waugh's novel, *Scoop,* what he needs 'to learn about journalism'.[20] Coker's definition of news has survived pretty well into the present century. A class of journalism students today might be able to guess the era in which it was written only because of the word 'chap' – a little old-fashioned now, and sexist in its assumption that the putative reader is inevitably male. That aside, it serves pretty well today: news is still something that will shake the casual observer out of his or her indifference, even if only for the time it takes to satisfy that mild curiosity. What has changed beyond all recognition is the way in which news can now be gathered and distributed. There are countless examples that might be given here: the emergence of user-generated content (UGC) as a vital source of material during the suicide bomb attacks on the London public transport system on 7 July 2005; the amount of footage sent and received via smart phone during the Japanese earthquake in February 2011; the videos distributed via the Internet around the world during the war in Syria from 2011 onwards. Charlie Beckett, though, summarises the effect especially well when he recalls in his book *Supermedia* (2008) the realisation he had when working as an editor at Channel 4 News in 2005. The story in question was the controversy, and eventually rioting, that followed the publication by the Danish newspaper *Politiken* of cartoons depicting the Prophet Mohammed. Beckett described the Channel 4 News team thinking long and hard about whether they should show the drawings on air. Most interpretations of Islam forbid the depiction of Mohammed; some of these cartoons were considered especially offensive because they portrayed Mohammed as a terrorist. In the end, Beckett realised that the lengthy discussion of editorial ethics had, to some extent, missed the point.

> The lesson of the Cartoons … is that journalism cannot pretend to operate in a vacuum. If news journalists are not conscious of their audiences then other people will be. If we do not find a way of connecting people then other people will.[21]

Beckett was writing some years before the closure of the *NOTW*, but he described very well the dilemma that all news media, not just newspapers, were facing as a result of technological change. As the falling sales mentioned above suggest, their long-established economic model, based on revenue from both sales and advertising, was under threat. That was especially true for newspapers – although more recent data, discussed at the end of this chapter, suggest that there might be the possibility of improvement in the future. It was not, however, only the existing economic models that were under threat. Editorial ones were, too. This is what I take Beckett to mean when he wrote, 'If news journalists are not conscious of their audiences, then other people will be.' In other words, if an established news organisation decides not to publish something on the grounds of impartiality, taste, fairness to those involved or decency, such a decision is no longer enough to keep the content in question out of the public domain.

No amount of lengthy discussion of editorial ethics can alter that. The only exception would be if the news organisation in question had the material exclusively. Even then, there is no guarantee that the situation would stay that way. Journalists themselves, just like non-journalists, now have unprecedented opportunities to publish – perhaps 'leak' might be a better word here – material that would not otherwise see the light of day. Where once, for Fleet Street reporters at least, that might have meant finding a sympathetic colleague at the satirical magazine *Private Eye*, the possibilities have now greatly multiplied. There is a good example of this in action in a story related to Rupert Murdoch and, indirectly, to the *NOTW*. In December 2010, the British Government's Business Secretary, Vince Cable, was secretly recorded by undercover reporters saying that he had 'declared war' on Mr Murdoch, specifically in relation to the latter's ambition to take a controlling share in BSkyB, the satellite broadcaster in which he held a substantial minority stake. As Business Secretary, Mr Cable was due to oversee the process that would decide whether or not a successful bid by Mr Murdoch would be in the public interest. Once the remarks came to light Mr Cable's role was passed to another cabinet minister on the grounds that he could no longer be considered impartial. The story was broken by the BBC's Business Editor, Robert Peston. Yet, he was not the person who had got the scoop. The undercover reporters were from the *Daily Telegraph*. In order to get their story, they had posed as constituents of Mr Cable. Having got the story, though, they did not run it – not immediately, at least. As the BBC News website put it, 'The BBC's Robert Peston said the *Telegraph* chose not to publish the "most explosive" part of its investigation. But a transcript was passed to him by a whistleblower.'[22] Speculation followed about the identity of the 'whistleblower' (itself an interesting choice of word – one more usually associated with someone passing information to a news organisation, rather than a source within a news organisation), with the *Guardian*'s Media Section,[23] following up a Reuters story suggesting that a former *Telegraph* senior executive, by then working for Mr Murdoch, had been Robert Peston's source.[24] The conclusion which might be drawn here is that a source sympathetic to Mr Murdoch, perhaps one of his employees, as the Reuters report suggested, leaked the story in order to discredit Mr Cable as an disinterested party. It might also be concluded that the *Telegraph* had originally decided to keep quiet about what the BBC called the 'most explosive' part of the story because it was content for Mr Cable's 'war' on Mr Murdoch to be prosecuted successfully. In any case, some seven months later, and just days after the closure of the *NOTW*, Mr Cable told the *London Evening Standard* that he was, 'delighted to discover that everyone in Britain and the House of Commons now agrees with me.'[25] Mr Murdoch's fortunes had suffered a major reverse in the intervening period. The seriousness with which the *Telegraph* took the leak is reflected in the fact that, as the Reuters story cited above reports, they hired 'a leading private investigations firm', Kroll, to try to identify its source. From the point of view of understanding this as a moment in media history, perhaps the most interesting element (aside from the many issues raised about how ownership, and business interests, shape content) is this:

> Because so many people, including people outside the Telegraph group, had access to the section of the Cable audio that discussed Murdoch, Kroll advised the *Telegraph* that while it could eliminate several categories of potential leakers as suspects, the circle of people with possible access was too large to enable them to pinpoint the leakers for certain.[26]

For this is a defining characteristic of the media environment in which the *NOTW* met its end: the world in which, as Beckett notes above, 'other people will' find a way of connecting people. Whatever the *Telegraph*'s reason for not initially publishing Mr Cable's 'declaration of war', because 'so many people ... had access', it was to prove impossible to keep the recording out of the public domain. Details of the discussions and the decision-making process at the *Telegraph* might not have become public, but the content that was the subject of those discussions could not be kept secret. Writing some years before the phone hacking scandal came to light, and in a work published only after his death in 2006, Roger Silverstone neatly summarised the way this lack of privacy, even the lack of the possibility of privacy, was affecting so many aspects of human activity:

> The pursuit of political life, the management (or mismanagement) of markets, the conduct of diplomacy and the fighting of wars, as well as the construction of lifestyles and the capacity to get through the day, signifi-cant each in their own terms and perfectly capable in principle (once upon a time) of being conducted in exclusively unmediated or private contexts, are no longer free to be so.[27]

It was perhaps not Mr Cable's kind of 'war' which Professor Silverstone had in mind when he mentioned the 'fighting of wars', but certainly the expo-sure of Mr Cable's remarks in the news media fall under the 'pursuit of political life' category. It is important to note that undercover reporting, and secret recordings, are journalistic techniques that are almost as old as journalism itself (even if electronic recordings came only later, once the technology was available). What places this incident so firmly in the early twenty-first century is the subject – Mr Murdoch's bid to take control of BSkyB – and the technological and financial factors that prevent even crack private investigators from identifying the leakers. Computer systems, and business models that rely on contracting out services – with the conse-quence that many people, including people outside the Telegraph Media Group, had access – ensured that. In its own way, the decline of the *NOTW* also represented a new departure from the older, established, techniques of stings and secret recordings. These are legitimate strategies of the press as the 'Fourth Estate', an idea, as Francis Williams noted in *A Dangerous Estate*, first published in 1957, that has its roots as far back as the eighteenth and nineteenth centuries:

> The press has been seen as a weapon of freedom, a sword in the hands of those fighting old or new tyrannies, the one indispensable piece of ordnance in the armoury of democracy. It has been called by Macaulay in honour and by Burke in despair, 'The Fourth Estate of the Realm,' ranking only just, if at all, behind the Lords Temporal, the Lords Spiritual, and the Commons.[28]

Perhaps the most striking example of the *NOTW*'s investigative journalism serving the public interest in the paper's later years was its exposure in July and August 2010 of a match-fixing scandal in Test cricket.[29] The match-fixing scandal, headlined simply 'Caught!' led to a police investigation and, eventually, jail sentences. It was a strong piece of investigative reporting that told readers, and those in authority, of wrongdoing that might other-wise have continued. It was included in the collection of front-page scoops that were reprinted in the farewell edition of 10 July 2011. There were also various tales of adulterous footballers and cocaine-sniffing stars – some of them stories that might fall into the category of worthwhile activity for the Fourth Estate, others that might struggle to do so. As time went on, there a more sinister side to this kind of journalism emerged. Journalists have always been of interest to security services of governments of all political persuasions. They often have access to information that is beyond the reach of diplomats or secret policemen. As Curran notes,[30] the political connec-tions of newspapers in the eighteenth century often meant revenue in the form of political subsidies – a system which continued well into the next century 'the last English newspaper to receive a clandestine government grant was the *Observer* in 1840.'[31] In the late twentieth- and early twenty-first centuries, relations have been less cosy. A BBC journalist working in the North Caucasus in 1999 found himself, in a very overcrowded café, sharing a table with a man whom the press corps suspected of being a Russian secret policeman. 'I am X', said the BBC journalist, giving his first name as he introduced himself to his co-diner. 'I know,' came the reply. In the early 2000s, a tale circulated in the foreign press corps in Jerusalem of one of their number who told an allegedly anti-Israeli joke at a private dinner party. The reporter later received a voicemail message that contained only a recording of his telling the joke. In other words, the security forces of whichever country keep a close eye on journalists, especially those who might know things that they would like to find out, or whose reporting might not please them. Journalists falling into those categories find them-selves the object of close surveillance, or worse. In the case of the later years of the *NOTW*, the newspaper seemed on occasion to abandon the role of the press 'as a weapon of freedom, a sword in the hands of those fighting old or new tyrannies', defined by Francis Williams, above, as central to any idea of the press as a Fourth Estate. Instead, the *NOTW* seemed occasionally to adapt the techniques of oppressive regimes to use in their newsgathering. Consider this description, taken from written evidence given to the Leveson Inquiry by the actress Sienna Miller:

> journalists and photographers would often turn up in meeting places that I had arranged on the phone and that no one else knew about. I also had men in cars sitting outside my house and I was convinced that they could somehow listen to my conversations. My paranoia and suspicion naturally spread to those around me.[32]

The detail of 'men in cars sitting outside my house' is especially chilling. While the stakeout, as it would be known in journalistic (and perhaps police?) slang can be seen as a legitimate technique – especially for tracking down suspected criminals who have refused all opportunity to give their side of the story – no responsible news organisation would use it just as a matter of course, as seems to have happened here. In the case of phone hacking, the 'weapon of freedom' was not used against tyrannies, but used to behave almost like one. This transformation took place against the background of bigger ones. As noted above, technological change in the shape of the Internet, and the news sites to which it gave a home, provided new competition for the Sundays and other printed media. When the *NOTW*'s methods were being exposed and discussed at the Leveson Inquiry, journalists, and anyone involved in political communication, were becoming increasingly aware of the way that this change was not only a 'weapon of freedom', but also a double-edged sword. 'There is no longer "off the record",' Jamie Shea, NATO's Deputy Assistant Secretary General for Emerging Security Challenges, told a conference at Royal Holloway, University of London on 11 April 2013.[33] From one point of view, this might seem a positive development: the end was perhaps in sight for poisonous briefings from faceless spin doctors. From another, it means that journalists' sources were less likely to be frank. 'Off the record', whatever its shortcomings, can be an important channel of communication for reporting any sensitive issue. It is hard to imagine British political reporting, especially in print, without reference to 'senior Labour figures' or 'Cabinet sources'. New technologies, especially smart phones and social media, have given journalists countless possibilities for both the gathering and distribution of news material. The actions of Wikileaks and Edward Snowden would have been impossible, in scale at least, in an earlier age. As with many ages of transformation, though, there are negatives side, too. One of those is that, with material so easy to share, it is also difficult to keep secrets, which presents particular problems for journalists trying to protect information given to them by their contacts. Writing on the subject for the BBC Academy's Journalism blog, in February 2012, the BBC World Affairs producer, Stuart Hughes, asked, 'with so much potentially sensitive information sitting on laptops and smartphones, and being shared through phone calls, emails and text messages, how can a journalist ensure the safety of their sources without acting like an amateur James Bond?'[34] Hughes' article, headlined, 'Be paranoid – protecting sources in the digital age', went on to outline a series of measures which journalists should take in order to prevent their material falling into the wrong hands. As he noted, 'For journalists covering stories involving repressive regimes, however, the main concern isn't that our sources could end up in court – it's that they could be exposed or even killed for sharing information the authorities would rather keep secret.'[35] Suggested techniques included encrypting especially sensitive information or concealing documents in misleadingly titled folders. In the matter of a couple of decades, the world of journalism had moved from one in which some reporters listened in to voice messages on insecure mobile phone networks to one where the 'Fourth Estate' itself might struggle to keep its secrets safe.

George Orwell ends his essay 'Decline of the English Murder' with an account of the 'Cleft Chin murder', killings committed 'by an eighteen-year-old ex waitress named Elizabeth Jones, and an American army deserter, posing as an officer, named Karl Hulten'.[36] He points to what he sees as the 'lack of feeling'[37] in the murders for which they are eventually tried and convicted. He concludes:

> Perhaps it is significant that the most talked-of English murder of recent years should have been committed by an American and an English girl who had become partly americanized. But it is difficult to believe that this case will be so long remembered as the old domestic poisoning dramas, product of a stable society where the all-prevailing hypocrisy did at least ensure that crimes as serious as murder should have strong emotions behind them.[38]

Orwell's concern over the decline in the quality of the English murder – from those provoked by 'strong emotions' to those committed with a 'lack of feeling' – was a product in part, perhaps, of the time in which he was writing. His essay was published in 1946, and the 'Cleft Chin' case was from the years of the Second World War. The weariness with war had perhaps led to a callousness, a disregard for human life, that might have been less prevalent in peacetime. Orwell might have been cheered had he lived to read of cases such as the 'Lady in the Lake', in the 1970s, when Peter Hogg, a 'personable Air Europe holiday pilot flying Boeing 757s'[39] dropped 'the weighted body of his strangled wife from an inflatable rowing boat into the watery grave of England's deepest lake' and 'was sure he had got away with it'.[40] There might be a similar lesson here for those who are convinced that phone hacking at the *NOTW* and the huge disruption to journalism as a job and as a business as a result of the technological changes of the last two decades mean that journalism itself is in decline.

For all the damage done to journalism's reputation by the scandal, it is worth remembering that it was journalists, principally, in the first place, from the *Guardian* and the *New York Times*, who exposed that scandal. While some *NOTW* reporters might have used criminal methods to pursue celebrity stories, it did not mean that journalism itself had become rotten. As Orwell regretted the passing of, 'Our great period in murder, our Elizabethan period, so to speak...between roughly 1850 and 1925',[41] so others have expressed concern over the consequences of the 'collapse in newspaper readership and the spread of social media', where 'everyone gets little snippets of information, and never fully understands the implications', as the respected author and journalist Misha Glenny put it in a 2013 interview with Alison Smale of the *New York Times*.[42] Mr Glenny and others are right to worry at the prospect of a world where no one reads in depth. The consequences for journalism, and for society, would be dire.

Yet at a time when the *NOTW* exists only in the memories of readers such as Jeanne Hobson and in the pages of histories of journalism, there might be hints of a way through this age of uncertainty for the news media. Despite introducing a paywall for their websites in 2010, *The Times* and the *Sunday Times* reported in October 2013 an increase in subscriptions for both their print and digital editions.[43] In other words, they seemed to have found a business model that might spell future profits for the newspaper industry – the traditional economics no longer reliably making money. Writing in 2011 on what was seen by some as the decline of newspapers' news agendas, Conboy persuasively placed it in a broader historical context when he suggested that, 'A longer view of lifestyle features and the popularization of mainstream journalism, for instance, culminating in the contemporary concentration on celebrity, confirms that these are threads emanating from the nineteenth century.'[44]

While the closure of the *NOTW* was a result of pragmatic decisions taken as a response to its criminal activity, it occurred at a time when newspapers were facing challenges that they had never before encountered: challenges to which they were unsure how to respond. In order for us to understand fully the reasons for the *NOTW*'s downfall, we need to consider too the point in the history of journalism at which it happened.

Notes

1. BBC, 2011. *Phone Hacking Hearing: Key Quotes*. [Online] Available at: http://www.bbc.co.uk/news/uk-14202349 [Accessed 1 October 2013].

2. R. Andrews, *Sly Bailey: 'The Three Ps' Could Show News Business Out Of The Mire*, 2010 [Online] Available at: http://paidcontent.org/2010/11/16/419-sly-bailey-the-three-ps-could-show-news-biz-out-of-the-mire/ [Accessed 1 October 2013].

3. Ibid.
4. Ibid.
5. Cited in M. Engel, *Tickle the Public: One Hundred Years of the Popular Press*, London, 1997, p. 91.
6. A. Briggs and P. Burke, *A Social History of the Media*, Cambridge, 2009, p. 191.
7. Ibid.
8. The Leveson Inquiry, 13 July 2011. *The Leveson Inquiry*. [Online] Available at: http://www.levesoninquiry.org.uk/. [Accessed 7 October 2013].
9. *The Guardian* website, *Leveson inquiry: Facebook, Google, Popbitch executives appear*, 2012. [Online] Available at: http://www.theguardian.com/media/2012/jan/26/leveson-inquiry-facebook-google-popbitch-live [Accessed 7 October 2013].
10. *Popbitch*, 2013. [Online] Available at: http://www.popbitch.com/board.html [Accessed 7 October 2013].
11. The Leveson Inquiry, *Transcript of afternoon hearing 26 January 2012*. [Online] Available at: http://www.levesoninquiry.org.uk/wp-content/uploads/2012/01/Transcript-of-Afternoon-Hearing-26-January-2012.pdf [Accessed 7 October 2013].
12. S. Swinford, *State regulation of press "absolutely pointless" because of internet*, 2012. [Online] Available at: http://www.telegraph.co.uk/news/uknews/leveson-inquiry/9691688/State-regulation-of-press-absolutely-pointless-because-of-internet.html [Accessed 7 October 2013].
13. The Leveson Inquiry, 2012. *Transcript of afternoon hearing 26 January 2012*. [Online] Available at: http://www.levesoninquiry.org.uk/wp-content/uploads/2012/01/Transcript-of-Afternoon-Hearing-26-January-2012.pdf [Accessed 7 October 2013].
14. BBC, 2012. *Ryan Giggs can be legally named as 'affair' footballer*. [Online] Available at: http://www.bbc.co.uk/news/uk-17114875 [Accessed 17 October 2013].
15. *Twitter's British audience jumps by a third as millions log on to discover details about celebrity scandals*, Mail Online [Online] Available at: http://www.dailymail.co.uk/sciencetech/article-2008748/Twitters-audience-jumps-millions-log-tweet-celebrity-scandals.html [Accessed 7 October 2013].
16. D. Cameron, 2011, www.parliament.co.uk. [Online] Available at: http://www.publications.parliament.uk/pa/cm201011/cmhansrd/cm110720/debtext/110720-0001.htm#110720110001091 [Accessed 7 October 2013].
17. The *Guardian* Website, *Nearly half of News of the World's buyers give up on Sunday papers*, 2012. [Online] Available at: http://www.theguardian.com/media/2012/jan/13/news-of-the-world-abcs[Accessed 17 October 2013].
18. G. Orwell, 'Decline of the English Murder,' in *Essays*, London, 2000, p. 345
19. E. Waugh, *Scoop*, London, 1938, p. 66.
20. Ibid.
21. C. Beckett, *Supermedia*, Oxford, 2008, p. 142.
22. BBC, *Cable: 'I have declared war on Murdoch,'* 2010 [Online] Available at: http://www.bbc.co.uk/news/business-12053175 [Accessed 21 October 2013].
23. J. Halliday, *News Corp boss 'linked' to leak of Vince Cable's Rupert Murdoch comments*, 2011 [Online] Available at: http://www.theguardian.com/media/2011/jul/22/willlewis-telegraphmediagroup [Accessed 21 October 2013].
24. M. Hosenball, *EXCLUSIVE-News Corp executive suspected of "orchestrating" leak*, 2011. [Online] Available at: http://uk.reuters.com/article/2011/07/22/idUKL6E7-IM0PX20110722 [Accessed 21 October 2013].

25. Cited in J. Murphy, *Vince Cable: I declared war on Murdoch ... now everyone agrees with me*, 2011. [Online] Available at: http://www.standard.co.uk/news/politics/vince-cable-i-declared-war-on-murdoch-now-everyone-agrees-with-me-6422452.html [Accessed 19 November 2014].

26. M. Hosenball. *EXCLUSIVE-News Corp executive suspected of "orchestrating" leak,'*. 2011. [Online] Available at: http://uk.reuters.com/article/2011/07/22/idUKL6E7-IM0PX20110722 [Accessed 21 October 2013].

27. R. Silverstone, *Media and Morality: On the Rise of the Mediapolis*, Cambridge, 2007, p. 162.

28. F. Williams, *Dangerous Estate: The Anatomy of Newspapers*, Cambridge, 1957, pp. 5–6.

29. M. Mahmood, 'Caught!', *News of the World*, 29 July 2010, pp. 1–9.

30. J. Curran and J. Seaton, *Power without Responsibility*, 7th ed. Abingdon, UK, 2010, p. 6.

31. Ibid.

32. S. Miller, *Leveson Inquiry*, 2011. [Online] Available at: http://www.levesoninquiry. org.uk/wp-content/uploads/2011/11/Witness-Statement-of-Sienna-Miller.pdf [Accessed 24 October 24].

33. Mr Shea made this remark as part of his speech to the Media, War and Conflict 5th Anniversary Conference, Royal Holloway, University of London, 11 April 2013. The author tweeted it. J. Rodgers, 2013. *Twitter*. [Online] Available at: https://twitter.com/jmacrodgers/status/322304735103307776 [Accessed 24 October 2013].

34. S. Hughes, *Be paranoid – protecting sources in the digital age*, 2012. [Online] Available at: http://www.bbc.co.uk/blogs/blogcollegeofjournalism/posts/be_paranoid_-_protecting_sourc [Accessed 25 October 2013].

35. Ibid.

36. Orwell, 'Decline', p. 347.

37. Ibid.

38. Ibid, p. 348.

39. A. Irving, *The lady in the lake*, 2009. [Online] Available at: http://www.whitehavennews.co.uk/news/the_lady_in_the_lake_1_528275?referrerPath=   [Accessed 25 October 2013].

40. Ibid.

41. Orwell, 'Decline', p. 345.

42. Cited in A. Smale, *At Davos, Crisis Is the New Normal*, 2013. [Online] Available at: http://dealbook.nytimes.com/2013/01/22/at-davos-crisis-is-new-normal/?_r=0 [Accessed 25 October 2013].

43. J. Halliday, *Digital subscriptions to the Times and Sunday Times top 150,000*, 2013. [Online] Available at: http://www.theguardian.com/media/2013/oct/17/digital-subscriptions-times-sunday-news-uk#start-of-comments [Accessed 19 November 2014].

44. M. Conboy, *Journalism in Britain: A historical introduction*, London, 2011, p. 194.

16
Afterword:
Lessons of the Leveson Inquiry into the British Press

Neil Berry

Britain's Prime Minister, David Cameron, set up the Leveson Inquiry in July 2011 in response to widespread horror that the *News of the World* had hacked the mobile phone of the murdered Surrey school girl, Milly Dowler. The inquiry's purpose was to review the conduct of the British press, although it would be hard to peruse the report delivered by Lord Justice Brian Leveson in November 2012 without being struck by how much it also concerns the conduct of the Metropolitan Police Service. Throughout its history, the Sunday tabloid that the budding Australian media magnate, Rupert Murdoch, acquired in 1969 thrived on crime stories; without close ties with the police it could scarcely have become what it long was: a byword for lurid sensationalism. Yet the relationship between the *News of the World* and Scotland Yard can never have been more collusive than during the paper's latter years under Murdoch's ownership, the period that was to culminate, in July 2011, with Murdoch's ruthless closure of the 168-year-old British scandal sheet, which had become a toxic scandal in its own right.

The Leveson Inquiry left little doubt that the original Metropolitan Police investigation into phone hacking at the *News of the World* in 2005/2006 was less than meticulous, with two senior officers, Andy Hayman and John Yates, seeming to have been remarkably ready to accept that hacking had been confined to a single rogue reporter, Clive Goodman, acting in concert with the private investigator, Glenn Mulcaire, to eavesdrop on the Royal Household. It left little doubt either about the depth of the rapport that certain officers enjoyed with the *News of the World* and its parent company, News International, whose chief executive as the hacking scandal deepened was Rupert Murdoch's son, James, and whose other titles included the *Times*, *Sunday Times* and daily tabloid the *Sun*. By the time that, in July 2009, the *Guardian* reporter Nick Davies told the UK Parliament's Culture, Media and Sport Select Committee that the police had not pursued their inquiries diligently enough, Hayman had resigned from the police and found lucrative fresh employment as a columnist for *The Times* and the

News of the World – in which capacity he worked for the very organisation whose suspected malfeasance he had only recently been investigating. In Murdoch's papers, Hayman insisted that 'no stone was left unturned' in the original hacking inquiry. It was a claim that appeared risible following the revelations by Nick Davies in 2011 concerning the hacking of Milly Dowler's phone and the belated acknowledgement by the Metropolitan Police of the extensive nature of phone hacking involving the *News of the World*. The paper had evidently breached the privacy of celebrities and public figures galore, as well as that of ordinary individuals like Milly Dowler and her family.

Unlike the *News of the World*, the Leveson report was not meant to entertain. But it would be a solemn reader of Leveson's observations about the original role of the police in the hacking imbroglio who did not smile at the circumlocutory language with which the judge affirmed his faith in the integrity of police witnesses while also pointing out that the public could be pardoned for wondering if their investigations had been exactly zealous. But then, it seems unlikely that the report – which can be downloaded from the Leveson Inquiry website and otherwise exists in a cumbersome four volume hard copy version comprising 2,000 pages – will ever have many readers. Leveson himself worried that his efforts (which cost at least £5 million) would end up, like earlier inquiries into the British press, as mere archive material. However, where the Leveson Inquiry differed from previous such undertakings was in its extraordinary immediate impact as a media event. Televised and streamed online, it was followed keenly by a vast audience. If designed to project the impression that the British state took very seriously the concern of hacking victims and the wider public that the British newspaper industry was out of control, the inquiry succeeded admirably. With endless witnesses from every walk of British life being quizzed at length by the pertinacious QC Robert Jay and intermittently by Leveson himself, the inquiry not only made absorbing theatre but also gave every appearance of being a conscientious forensic effort to lay bare the abuses of News International and other newspaper organisations.

Yet many in the newspaper industry believed that its hidden agenda was to end the self-regulation the British press had long enjoyed and subject it to political control. Leveson would indeed propose stricter control – in the form of a new regulatory body set up by the press itself but beholden to a watchdog panel with legal powers. Others considered that the inquiry's paramount objective was to spare David Cameron and Rupert Murdoch even more acute embarrassment than they were already experiencing. The Prime Minster had, to be sure, good cause to be disturbed by the public perception that he was on unhealthily familiar terms with News International's key personnel. Before and after Cameron entered 10 Downing Street in May 2010, he repeatedly met Murdoch himself and counted as a personal friend Rebekah Brooks, who edited the *News of the World* from 2000 to 2003, and who later, in 2009, became Chief Executive of News International. Moreover, he had controversially recruited Brooks' colleague, Andy Coulson, as the Conservative Party's spin doctor, even though Coulson, who had resigned as editor of the *News of the World* in 2007 following the jailing of the paper's royal correspondent, Clive Goodman, was a compromised figure. Still more controversially, in 2010 he had made Coulson his Government's Director of Communications. Bloggers sneered that the Leveson Inquiry was a pantomime, a fresh instance of the British establishment closing ranks, with obfuscation masquerading as transparency. In view of how far short Leveson fell of seriously discomfiting the powerful figures who came before him, such cynicism might not have been wholly unwarranted. Consider, too, that, according to the *Independent on Sunday* (19 January 2014) the Leveson Inquiry turned a blind eye to vital evidence, ignoring a police intelligence report documenting how a senior ex-officer had leaked information damaging to the former Metropolitan Police Commissioner, Sir Ian Blair, to the *News of the World*.

Less probing perhaps than it appeared, the Leveson Inquiry was certainly completed with singular dispatch, its eight-month duration a fraction of the duration of other public inquiries. It is true that Leveson meditated a second part to his Inquiry, on unlawful press conduct, but felt that the trial that began in 2013 of Brooks, Coulson and others on charges in connection with phone hacking might render that superfluous. The especially cynical might suspect that David Cameron was anxious to defuse as speedily as possible a scandal with incendiary ramifications for his government and Rupert Murdoch alike, and that he also saw an opportunity to capitalise on public outrage at press malpractice with an official review that presented the case for regulation. They might further surmise that Cameron was banking on Lord Justice Leveson to extricate not only himself and Murdoch but also the Metropolitan Police from a public relations debacle. In the event, Leveson was to prescribe a press code that outlawed the immemorial informal contact between journalists and police that had been a force for good as well as ill. The *Observer*'s columnist Nick Cohen excoriated Leveson's report on the grounds that the judge made the transgressions of the *News of the World* a pretext for the wholesale curtailment of press freedom, while making no effort to address the issue of the unaccountability of the British police (*Observer*, 22 February 14).

None of this means that Leveson's recommendations are unworthy of being taken seriously. Plenty of respected commentators have indeed endorsed them, not least the former campaigning journalist, Brian Cathcart, now Professor of Journalism at Kingston University London. In his book *Everybody's Hacked Off: Why we don't have the press we deserve and what to do about it* (2012), Cathcart welcomed Leveson's proposal that the press set up a regulatory body answerable to independent adjudicators with legal powers. Noting how signally the newspapers had failed to honour their word and set their own houses in order after earlier official reports critical of their conduct, Cathcart argued that the press had forfeited the right to self-regulation. What had hitherto enabled the newspapers to evade statutory control, he remarked, was that they could rely on the desperation of politicians to win their support as general elections loomed. Time was always on their side and Cathcart feared that public amnesia might yet save them anew from being made properly accountable. Still, it was cause for satisfaction that the Internet and proliferating new media were already obliging newspapers to recognise that they could be challenged as never before. No longer helpless in the face of the 'press megaphone', victims of press abuse had gained the capacity to answer back. It was testimony to the increasing democratisation of communications that, hard though it tried, the Murdoch organisation was not able to shut down the hacking scandal, and now there was a public consensus that the press could not go on being its own umpire.

It was to counter public amnesia and keep the issue of press accountability high on the political agenda that Cathcart founded the Hacked Off campaign. In his book, Cathcart underlined how imperative it was never to forget the magnitude of News International's delinquencies or the rampant criminality in which the company had engaged. By the same token, he was at pains to record the lengths to which it went to deny that phone hacking ever extended beyond a single rogue reporter, protesting that it had conducted investigation after internal investigation and found nothing. It also needed to be remembered, he wrote, that most of the rest of the British press followed the example of News International in seeking to smother the hacking scandal. Rival newspaper groups were scarcely less determined to present it as the hobby-horse of the *Guardian*, an issue for left-wing cranks and of scant public interest.

How, Cathcart inquired, could such corporate evasiveness be understood other than as evidence that Murdoch's competitors knew that their own journalistic practices did not bear much scrutiny either? All the signs were of a *de facto* collective cover-up, a concerted abuse of power by newspapers that vaunted their role as public consciences whose mission was to hold the powerful to account. Cathcart piquantly recounted that 40 years earlier when he first arrived on the British newspaper scene, Murdoch himself had declared that just as a newspaper can stir up fruitful controversy and expose wrong-doing, it can also 'hide things and be a great power for evil'. In the light of the hacking scandal, it would require no little charity to believe that Murdoch's newspapers had done more of the former than the latter.

Although public opinion is on his side, it has increasingly appeared that Cathcart was right to worry that the Leveson Inquiry might prove no more effectual than earlier inquiries into the conduct of the British press. Leveson's proposal that the Press Complaints Commission be axed has admittedly borne fruit, but – except in that it is presided over by a judge – the body that replaced it in September 2014, the Independent Press Standards Organisation (IPSO), is – like its discredited predecessor – the creation of the very newspapers that it is meant to regulate. Moreover, not all newspapers have signed up to IPSO, and those that have remain fiercely resistant to Leveson's key recommendation of an ultimate monitor, a watchdog body to regulate the regulator backed by statutory royal charter. It is because, they insist, of its glaring flaws that, disingenuously or not, the *Guardian*, the *Independent* and the *Financial Times* have spurned IPSO altogether. In fairness, it is not hard to see the force of newspaper concerns that statutory control might spell the end of British press freedom – or to accept that there might be something in industry suspicions that what celebrities who have lobbied hard for a royal charter really want is a tame press afraid to cause offence. Not that any of this could be easily gathered from the sketchy media coverage of the upshot of the Leveson Inquiry. Many are bound to feel that the hacking scandal has been met with an all too British official fudge. Yet, it has also to be acknowledged that print journalism is in any event facing a hugely imponderable future and that it is not clear how far Leveson's proposals are relevant to a digital age of multiplying modes of communication as rapid as they are global.

Should British journalism end up increasingly constrained, it will be in no small measure because Rupert Murdoch spawned a newspaper culture whose scurrility and venality injured the whole British press. Yet for years his unabashed populism worked commercial magic in Britain. Murdoch's acquisition of the *News of the World* paved the way for his purchase of the daily tabloid, the *Sun* – a key event in the progress of his career. It was the profits of these British papers that bankrolled his expansion into the US media market and pan-continental broadcasting, and his ultimate apotheosis as a global communications baron based in New York. In 1970s Britain, he was seen as gambling on a moribund industry in a post-imperial country itself felt to be moribund. It could be said that Murdoch built a media empire on the ruins of the British Empire, and that the crude titillation purveyed by his tabloid titles held a peculiar escapist appeal for a nation in decline that had failed to furnish many of its citizens with an adequate education. Pro-Murdoch opinion has it that, however unsavoury his tabloid wares, Murdoch rescued the British press from disaster by facing down the recalcitrant London print unions who were obstructing its over-due embrace of new technology. It has been argued, too, that with his purchase of *The Times* and *Sunday Times* in 1981 he showed his commitment to journalism of quality and that in the case of *The Times* he chivalrously kept alive a famous but chronically insolvent broadsheet. However, it is equally arguable that Britain paid dearly for the semi-monopolistic position that Murdoch attained as a UK newspaper magnate. All the titles of this free market ideologue have sought to subvert social democratic values, missing no opportunity to smear the BBC, denigrate British membership of the European Union as a form of enslavement,

champion American foreign policy and advocate a privatised Britain dedicated to acquisitive individualism. It is hard to see how British democracy
has been served by any of this.

The journalist Bruce Page has maintained that Murdoch offered governments a private propaganda service. Britain's Conservative Prime Minister
Margaret Thatcher was glad to avail herself of this service during the 1980s,
as, in the late 1990s and the first decade of the twenty-first century, was the
leader of the New Labour government, Prime Minister Tony Blair. Indeed,
a point was reached where few British politicians or journalists dreamed of
criticising Murdoch, many among the latter group being mindful that even
if they were not currently dependent on him for a livelihood, circumstances
could easily arise in which they might be. Gradually it grew apparent that
London's old patrician establishment had given way to a diversified new
establishment dominated by Murdoch's print and broadcasting media and
the Murdoch family itself. If Britain's inveterate top people, ministers, diplomats and editors, attended his lavish parties as though paying court to a
Mafia don, so too did a fresh British breed of movers and shakers: plutocratic
entrepreneurs, show business impresarios and the likes of the ubiquitous
publicist Max Clifford. A visitor from another planet might have received the
impression that everybody in the United Kingdom who was anybody was in
a deferential relationship with Rupert Murdoch. It was a turn of events that
must have been highly gratifying to a media mogul who despised British
snobbery and retained bitter memories of how, despite being the privileged
son of an Australian newspaper tycoon, he was patronised as an ill-bred
colonial when he studied history at Oxford University in the early 1950s.

In many ways, the Leveson Inquiry marked the close of the era during
which Murdoch's power and influence in Britain seemed to be endlessly
burgeoning – if not the close of the old-style newspaper era itself. He was
after all 80 years old when the Inquiry took place and, against all expectation, his bid to achieve outright control of the broadcaster BSkyB – and thus
consolidate his dominance of the British media landscape had miscarried.
At the same time, there was a palpable backlash in Britain against his brand
of scabrous, furiously down-market tabloid journalism, a prevailing sense
that – whether or not from the other side of the Atlantic Ocean he himself
knew precisely what went on at the *News of the World* in east London – he
had nurtured a tabloid ethos that had debased the British body politic. Yet,
if Murdoch's newspapers had damaged the cultural fabric of Britain, that
damage was not going to be quickly undone. Besides, his most successful
British newspaper, the *Sun*, albeit with a contracted circulation, is still in
business, while the *News of the World* has after a fashion been reincarnated
in the shape of the *Sun on Sunday*.

In 1968, Sir William Carr, whose family had owned the *News of the
World* since 1891, had been anxious to stop Robert Maxwell from taking
over the paper. Declaring it to be as 'English as roast beef and Yorkshire

pudding', Carr recoiled at the prospect of the paper falling into the hands of a 'foreigner' – in this case, a Czechoslovakian-born Jew. Yet, the paper was to pass out of English hands anyway when Murdoch successfully prosecuted a rival take-over bid. In a literal sense, the antipodean Murdoch was a foreign body in Britain – though a foreign body in a country that was rapidly becoming a stranger to itself. If truth be told, the coarse, truculently right-wing, celebrity-fetishising popular newspapers of this hard-bitten outsider did much to define British society during an epoch of national transformation of dizzying pace and scale. In the 1980s, it was common to talk of 'Thatcher's Britain', but the same country could with equal justice have been dubbed 'Murdoch's Britain'. All that flowed from Rupert Murdoch's takeover of the Carr family's venerable Sunday scandal sheet is a big subject for the historians.

Appendix:
Circulation of the *News of the World*

Sharp-eyed readers of the entirety of our text will have seen the variety of figures that contributors have identified to support circulation estimates at specific periods in the paper's history, particularly between the repeal in 1855 of the newspaper stamp duty that had yielded official stamp returns and the advent of audited figures of the Audit Bureau of Circulations Ltd (ABC) which the *NOTW* joined only in 1946. As we note in the Introduction, A.P. Wadsworth called the period between the 1850s and 1930s, 'the period of secrecy',[1] and our variation of figures reflects the dearth of a single set of reliable accounts for this span of time. However, two volumes for 1906 and 1907 of Mitchell's *Newspaper Press Directory* include adverts for the *NOTW*, by the *NOTW*, that reproduce official letters from auditors; these attest to audited figures of 'over 1,100,000 copies weekly' for 30 September 1905 and 'over 1,300,000 copies weekly' for 27 April 1906. The latter figure is corroborated in the following list, but the former figure suggests that the *NOTW* reached a circulation of over a million earlier, by September 1905.[2]

The list of circulation figures below has been compiled by the archivists at the *News of the World* Archive, from various secondary sources in their archives between 1843 and 1945, and from the ABC 1946–2011. It is reproduced with the generous permission of News UK, which reflects its archivists' generosity towards the many queries we posed in the course of producing this book.

News of the World Circulation Figures

Compiled by the archivists at the *News of the World* Archive, News UK

1843–1945

- These figures are unaudited by the Audit Bureau of Circulations Limited which did not anyway come into existence until 1931. The News of the World did not join ABC until the beginning of 1946.
- The figures for this period are compiled from various secondary sources in the News of the World archive.
- The leap in circulation in 1854 can be attributed to the public's interest in the Crimea War.
- The 1855 figure represents the largest circulation attained by any newspaper up to that time.

1843	13,000	1915	2,277,495
1844	18,000	1916	2.327,806
1845	24,061	1917	2,434,590
1846	36,125	1918	2,663,755

1847	38,113	1919	2,843,010
1848	47,672	1920	3,060,829
1849	53,976	1921	3,105,208
1850	56,274	1922	3,134,185
1851	58,512	1923	3,184,829
1852	58,857	1924	3,173,458
1853	66,631	1925	3,426,654
1854	100,000	1926	3,360,645
1855	200,000	1927	3,352,110
1888	80,000	1928	3,388,278
1891	51,380	1929	3,440,481
1892	61,773	1930	3,376,390
1893	65,251	1931	3,463,304
1894	71,622	1932	3,461,459
1895	81,650	1933	3,529,277
1896	99,539	1934	3,645,451
1897	119,594	1935	3,818,900
1898	173,570	1936	3,827,677
1899	217,248	1937	3,850,072
1900	222,648	1938	4,035,711
1901	271,838	1939	4,121,604
1902	362,045	1940	4,077,938
1903	556,890	1941	4,069,114
1904	731,440	1942	4,454,062
1905	975,224	1943	4,708,640
1906	1,173,309	1944	5,228,352
1907	1,358,238	1945	5,752,667
1908	1,466,267		
1909	1,521,127		
1910	1,663,258		
1911	1,771,231		
1912	1,890,520		
1913	1,941,568		
1914	2,033,317		

1946–date

- The *News of the World* joined the Audit Bureau of Circulations Limited at the beginning of 1946. The figures below are taken from the six-monthly figures provided by ABC. [ABC only began additionally to breakdown the circulation into monthly figures in 1962.]
- On 18 June 1950 the News of the World achieved its largest print run when 8,659,090 copies were printed at Bouverie Street and at the plant in Manchester. This represents the highest print run in history of any English language newspaper. The total issued for sale was 8,501,219. [Source: Publishers Statement Book, 1949–1951. *News of the World* Archive, PUB/1/10.]

Year	Jan.-June	July-Dec.	Annual Av.	Year	Jan.-June	July-Dec.	Annual Av.
1946	7,412,383	7,505,192	7,458,788	1980	4,472,283	4,197,652	4,334,968
1947	7,725,425	7,891,275	7,808,350	1981	4,003,067	4,236,715	4,119,891
1948	7,887,488	7,844,166	7,865,827	1982	4,314,008	4,180,894	4,247,451
1949	8,382,356	8,428,113	8,405,235	1983	4,074,424	4,037,873	4,056,149
1950	8,443,917	8,440,014	8,441,966	1984	4,280,713	4,698,341	4,489,527
1951	8,406,844	8,209,061	8,307,953	1985	4,787,233	5,103,164	4,945,199
1952	8,230,158	8,162,865	8,196,512	1986	4,849,507	4,954,416	4,901,962
1953	8,168,820	8,138,569	8,153,695	1987	4,941,966	5,096,155	5,019,061
1954	8,134,826	8,073,622	8,104,224	1988	5,213,901	5,360,479	5,287,190
1955	7,971,020	7,769,981	7,870,501	1989	5,294,317	5,185,742	5,240,030
1956	7,493,463	7,297,274	7,395,369	1990	5,036,019	5,056,315	5,046,167
1957	7,241,396	7,030,499	7,135,948	1991	4,807,646	4,815,894	4,811,770
1958	6,767,348	6,665,169	6,716,259	1992	4,725,427	4,695,553	4,710,490
1959	6,555,485	6,432,896	6,494,191	1993	4,619,596	4,660,094	4,639,845
1960	6,455,531	6,664,035	6,559,783	1994	4,773,857	4,807,308	4,790,583
1961	6,733,596	6,643,287	6,688,442	1995	4,743,621	4,690,563	4,717,092
1962	6,644,501	6,484,445	6,564,473	1996	4,607,799	4,505,632	4,556,716
1963	6,289,271	6,334,385	6,311,828	1997	4,469,884	4,425,708	4,447,796
1964	6,224,174	6,251,316	6,237,745	1998	4,334,115	4,225,599	4,279,857
1965	6,174,640	6,176,317	6,175,478	1999	4,209,173	4,074,474	4,141,824
1966	6,183,584	6,120,768	6,152,176	2000	4,041,987	4,028,441	4,035,214
1967	6,149,019	6,274,169	6,211,594	2001	3,980,339	4,030,283	4,005,311
1968	6,191,142	6,131,134	6,161,138	2002	3,953,700	3,962,383	3,958,042
1969	6,227,684	6,421,089	6,324,387	2003	3,876,018	3,913,154	3,894,586
1970	6,215,079	6,242,270	6,228,675	2004	3,840,684	3,745,113	3,792,899
1971	6,170,890	6,085,680	6,128,285	2005	3,666,044	3,718,682	3,692,363
1972	6,014,010	5,976,657	5,995,334	2006	3,552,119	3,468,216	3,510,168
1973	5,950,645	5,937,170	5,943,908	2007	3,315,976	3,320,850	3,318,413
1974	5,872,028	5,775,900	5,823,964	2008	3,207,103	3,162,430	3,184,767
1975	5,645,671	5,312,845	5,479,258	2009	2,993,776	3,039,130	3,016,753
1976	5,162,136	5,113,517	5,137,827	2010	2,909,302	2,826,854	2,868,078
1977	4,934,284	4,978,403	4,956,344	2011	2,683,917		
1978	4,934,532	4,905,279	4,919,906				
1979	4,708,575	4,666,811	4,687,693				

The *News of the World* was closed as a result of the phone hacking scandal. Its last issue was published on 10 July 2011.

Notes

1. W.A.P. Wadsworth, 'Circulations, 1800–1954', *Transactions of the Manchester Statistical Society 1954–5*, Manchester, 1955, p. 1.
2. Mitchell's *Newspaper Press Directory,* London, 1906, p. 493 and 1907, p. 471.

Bibliography

[Anon.] (1856) 'The Sunday Papers', *Saturday Review*, 19 April, p. 493.

Bainbridge, C. and Stockdill, R. (1993) *The News of the World Story: 150 Years of the World's Bestselling Newspaper*, New York: HarperCollins.

Berrey, R. Power [1922] *'The Romance of a Great Newspaper'*, London: News of the World.

Berridge, V. (1972) 'Popular Journalism and Working-Class Attitudes, 1854–1886: A Study of *Reynolds's Newspaper*, *Lloyd's Newspaper* and the *Weekly Times*', unpublished doctoral thesis, University of London.

—— (1978), 'Popular Sunday papers and mid-Victorian Society' in G. Boyce, J. Curran and P. Wingate (eds) *Newspaper History: from the Seventeenth Century to the Present Day*, London: Constable, pp. 247–64.

Bingham, A. (2004) *Gender, Modernity and the Popular Press in Inter-War Britain*, Oxford: Clarendon Press.

—— (2007) 'Drinking in the last chance saloon', *Media History*, 13 (1), 79–92

—— (2009) *Family Newspapers? Sex, Private Life, and the British Popular Press 1918–1978*, Oxford: Oxford University Press.

—— (2009) "A Stream of Pollution through every part of the country?" Morality, regulation and the modern popular press' in M. Bailey (ed.) *Narrating Media History*, Abingdon and New York: Routledge, pp. 112–24.

Bradley, K. (2010) '"All Human Life is There": The John Hilton Bureau of the *News of the World* and Advising the Public, 1942–1969' *English Historical Review*, CXXIX (539), 888–910.

Brake, L. (1988) 'The Old Journalism and the New: Forms of Cultural Production in London in the 1880s' in J. Wiener (ed.) *Papers for the Millions: The New Journalism in Britain, 1850s to 1914*, New York: Greenwood, pp. 1–24.

Brake, L. and Demoor, M. (eds) (2009) *DNCJ: Dictionary of Nineteenth-Century Journalism*, Print: Gent and London: Academia Press and British Library; Online ProQuest.

Brake, L., King, E., Luckhurst R. and Mussell, J. (eds) (2012) *W.T. Stead, Newspaper Revolutionary*, London: British Library.

Brake, L. (2015) 'Journalism' in D. Felluga, P. Gilbert, L. Hughes (eds) *The Encyclopedia of Victorian Literature*, Maldon, MA, Oxford and Chichester: John Wiley & Sons, pp. 845–54.

—— (2016) 'Markets, Genres, Iterations' in A. Easley and A. King (eds) *Ashgate Research Companion to Victorian Periodicals*, Farnham and Burlington: Ashgate.

Bryant, M. (2000) *Dictionary of Twentieth-Century British Cartoonists and Caricaturists*, Aldershot: Ashgate.

Burden, P. (2008) *News of the World? Fake Sheikhs & Royal Trappings*, London: Eye Books.

Carr, E. (1931) 'The Sunday Press', *Newspaper World*, 14 March 1931, pp. 1, 10.

Chibnall, S. (1977) *Law and Order News: An Analysis of Crime Reporting in the British Press*, London, Tavistock.

Chippendale, P. and Horrie, C. (1992) *Stick It Up Your Punter: The Rise and Fall of the Sun*, London: Mandarin.

Conboy, M. (2002) *The Press and Popular Culture*, London: Sage.

——— (2004) *Journalism: A Critical History*, London: Sage.
——— (2006) *Tabloid Britain Constructing a Community Through Language*, Abingdon: Routledge.
Crone, R. (2102) *Violent Victorians: Popular Entertainment in Nineteenth-Century London*, Manchester: Manchester University Press.
Curran, J. (1978) 'The Press as an Agency of Social Control: An Historical Perspective' in G. Boyce, J. Curran and P. Wingate (eds) *Newspaper History from the Seventeenth Century to the Present Day*, London: Constable, pp. 51–75.
Davies, Nick. (2014) *Hack Attack*, London: Chatto and Windus.
Easley, A. and King, A. (eds) (2016), *Ashgate Research Companion to Victorian Periodicals*, Farnham and Burlington: Ashgate.
Ellegård, A. (1957) *The Readership of the Periodical Press in Mid-Victorian Britain*, Göteborg: Göteborgs Universitets Årsskrift.
Engel, M. (1996) *Tickle the Public: One Hundred Years of the Popular Press*, London: Gollancz.
Finkelstein, D. (ed.) (2006) *Print Culture and the Blackwood Tradition, 1805–1930*, Toronto: University of Toronto Press.
First Edition Club (1931) *A Catalog of Books and Newspapers Printed by John Bell and by John Browne Bell*, London: First Edition Club.
Fox Bourne H.R. (1887) *English Newspapers: Chapters in the History of Journalism*, 2 vols., London: Chatto and Windus.
Grant, J. (1871–2) *History of the Newspaper Press*, 3 vols., London: Routledge.
Greenslade, R. (2003) *Press Gang: How Newspapers Make Profits From Propaganda*, London: Macmillan.
Griffiths, D. (1992) *The Encyclopedia of the British Press: 1422–1992*, London: Macmillan.
Hampton, M. (2004) *Visions of the Press in Britain, 1850–1950*, Champaign, IL: University of Illinois Press.
Hanning, J. and Mulcaire, G. (2014) *The News Machine. Hacking. The Untold Story*, London: Gibson Square.
Harvey, D. (2004) *The Beginnings of a Commercial Sporting Culture in Britain, 1793–1850*, Aldershot: Ashgate.
Hoggart, P.R. (1984) 'Edward Lloyd, the Father of the Cheap Press', *The Dickensian*, 80, 33–38.
Houfe, S. (2002) *Phil May: His Life and Work, 1864–1903*, Aldershot: Ashgate.
Humpherys, A. (1990) 'Popular Narrative and Political Discourse in *Reynolds's Weekly Newspaper*' in L. Brake, A. Jones and L. Madden (eds) *Investigating Victorian Journalism*, New York: St. Martin's, pp. 33–45.
Humpherys A. and James, L. (eds) (2008) *G.W.M. Reynolds, Nineteenth Century Fiction, Politics and the Press*, Aldershot: Ashgate.
——— (2000) 'Coming Apart: The British Newspaper Press and the Divorce Court' in L. Brake, B. Bell and D. Finkelstein (eds) *Nineteenth-Century Media and the Construction of Identities*, London: Palgrave, pp. 220–31.
James, L. (2009) 'Sporting Journalism' in L. Brake and M. Demoor (eds), *Dictionary of Nineteenth-Century Journalism in Great Britain and Ireland*, Print: Gent and London: Academia Press and British Library; Online ProQuest, pp. 593–94.
Jones, A. (1996) *Powers of the Press: Newspapers, Power and the Public in Nineteenth Century England*, Aldershot: Ashgate.
Jukes, S. (2013) 'A Perfect Storm' in K. Fowler-Watt and S. Allan (eds) *Journalism: New Challenges*, Bournemouth: Centre for Journalism & Communication Research Bournemouth University, pp. 1–18. https://microsites.bournemouth.ac.uk/cjcr/files/2013/10/JNC-2013-Chapter-1-Jukes.pdf

Kamper, D.S. (2004) 'Popular Sunday Newspapers: Respectability and Working-Class Culture in Late Victorian Britain' in M. Huggins and J. Mangan (eds) *Disreputable Pleasures: Less Virtuous Victorians at Play,* London and New York: Frank Cass, pp. 83–102.

Kaul, C. (2003) *Reporting the Raj, The British Press and India,* Manchester: Manchester University Press.

——— (2006) 'Monarchical Display & the Politics of Empire: Princes of Wales and India, 1870s–1920s' *Twentieth Century British History,* 17 (4), 464–88.

——— (2013) 'You cannot govern by force alone': W.H. Russell, *The Times* and the Great Rebellion' in M. Carter & C. Bates (eds), *Global Perspectives, Mutiny at the Margins: New Perspectives on the Indian Uprising of 1857,* Sage: New Delhi & London, Vol. 3, Chapter 2, pp. 18–35.

Kofron, J. (2009) '*News of the World*' in L. Brake and M. Demoor (eds) *Dictionary of Nineteenth-Century Journalism,* Gent and London: Academia Press and the British Library, p. 451.

Knelman, J. (1992) 'Subtly Sensational: A Study of Early Victorian Crime Reporting', *Journal of Newspaper and Periodical History,* 8 (1), 34–41.

Koss, S. (1981) *The Rise and Fall of the Political Press in Britain. Volume 1: The Nineteenth Century,* 2 vols., London: Hamish Hamilton.

Langer, J. (1998) *Tabloid Television: Popular Journalism and the 'Other News',* London: Routledge.

Law, G. (2000) *Serialising Fiction in the Victorian Press,* Basingstoke: Palgrave Macmillan.

Lee, A. J. (1976) *The Origins of the Popular Press in England, 1855–1914,* London: Croom Helm.

Mackenzie, H. and Winyard, B. (eds) (2013) *Charles Dickens and the Mid-Victorian Press 1850–1870,* Buckingham: DJO and University of Buckingham Press.

Morison, S. (1930, reprinted 2009) *John Bell, 1745–1831: A Memoir,* Cambridge: Cambridge University Press.

Mussell, J. (2012) *The Nineteenth Century Press in the Digital Age,* Basingstoke: Palgrave Macmillan.

North, J. (2003) *Waterloo Directory of British Newspapers and Periodicals, 1800–1900,* Waterloo: Waterloo Academic Press.

O'Donoghue, D. (2011) 'End of the "World"', *Irish Times,* 9 July, p. 15.

O'Malley T. and Soley, C. (2000) *Regulating the Press,* London: Pluto Press.

Onslow, B. (2000) *Women of the Press in Nineteenth-Century Britain,* New York: Palgrave Macmillan.

Oram, A. (2007) *Her Husband was a Woman! Women's Gender-crossing in Modern British Popular Culture,* London: Routledge.

——— (2012), '"Love Off The Rails" or "Over the Teacups"?: Lesbian Desire and Female Sexualities in the 1950s British Popular Press' in H. Bauer and M. Cook (eds) *Queer 1950s: Rethinking Sexuality in the Postwar Years,* London: Palgrave, pp. 41–57.

Page, B. (2003) *The Murdoch Archipelago,* London and New York: Simon and Schuster.

Phegley, J. (2004) *Educating the Proper Woman Reader: Victorian Family Literary Magazines and the Cultural Health of the Nation,* Columbus: Ohio State University Press.

Proctor, H. *The Street of Disillusion.* 2nd new edition Brighton: Revel Barker, 2010.

Rafter, K. (2013) 'Evil Literature: The Banning of the *News of the World* in Ireland', *Media History,* 19 (4), 408–20.

Raymond, E.T. [Ernest Raymond Thompson] (1921) 'Old and New Journalists', *Portraits of the Nineties,* London: Fisher Unwin.

Robertson, G. (1983) *People Against the Press,* London: Quartet Books.

Seymour-Ure, C. (1996) *The Press and Broadcasting Since 1945,* 2nd edn. Oxford: Blackwell.

Simanowitz, S. (2011) 'The Phone-hacking Scandal: British Politics Transformed?' *Contemporary Review,* 293, 409–17.

Soothill, K. and Walby, S. (1991) *Sex Crime in the News,* London: Routledge.

Snoddy, R. (1993) *The Good, The Bad and the Unacceptable,* London: Faber and Faber.

Somerfield, S. (1979) *Banner Headlines,* Shoreham-by-Sea: Scan Books.

Stephen, J. F. (1856) 'The Sunday Papers', *Saturday Review,* 18 April, pp. 493–4.

Taylor, S.J. (1992) *Shock! Horror! The Tabloids in Action,* London: Black Swan.

Tunstall, J. (1996) *Newspaper Power: The New National Press in Britain,* London: Constable.

Turner, M.W. (1996) 'Towards a Cultural Critique of Victorian Periodicals', *Studies in Newspaper and Periodical History 1995,* 111–26.

Watson, T. and Hickman, M. (2012) *Dial M for Murdoch: News Corporation and the Corruption of Britain,* London: Penguin.

Underhill, W. et al. (2011) 'Rupert's Red Menace' *Newsweek,* 158 (4), 40–44.

Wadsworth, A.P. (1955) 'Newspaper Circulations, 1800–1954', in *Transactions of the Manchester Statistical Society 1954–5,* Manchester: Lockwood & Co. Ltd., pp. 1–41.

Wiener, J. (1988) 'How New Was the New Journalism?' in J. Wiener (ed.) *Papers for the Millions: The New Journalism in Britain, 1850s to 1914,* New York: Greenwood, pp. 46–71.

—— (2011) *The Americanization of the British Press, 1830s–1914: Speed in the Age of Transatlantic Journalism,* Basingstoke: Palgrave Macmillan.

Wilkinson, N. (2009) *Secrecy and the Media: The Official History of the United Kingdom's D-Notice System,* London: Routledge.

Williams, C. (2010) 'Contesting Radical Cultures: the Cartoons of J. M. Staniforth of the *Western Mail*' in K. Cowman and I. Packer (eds) *Radical Cultures and Local Identities,* Newcastle upon Tyne: Cambridge Scholars, pp. 149–76.

—— (2011) 'Staniforth, Joseph Morewood (1863–1921)', *Oxford Dictionary of National Biography,* Oxford: Oxford University Press.

Williams, K. (2009) *Read All About It! A History of the British Newspaper,* London: Routledge.

—— (2010) *Get Me a Murder a Day. A History of Media and communication in Britain.* 2nd edn. London: Bloomsbury Academic.

Williams, R. (1970) 'Radical/respectable' in R. Boston (ed.) *The Press We Deserve,* London: Routledge & Kegan Paul, pp. 14–26.

—— (1978) 'The Press and Popular Culture: An Historical Perspective' in G. Boyce, J. Curran and P. Wingate (eds) *Newspaper History from the Seventeenth Century to the Present Day,* London: Constable, pp. 41–50.

—— (1984) *The Long Revolution,* reprinted edn., Harmondsworth: Penguin.

Wolff, M. (2010) *The Man Who Owns the News: Inside the Secret World of Rupert Murdoch,* London: Vintage Books.

Online

The Leveson Inquiry: Culture, Practice and Ethics of the Press http://www.leveson-inquiry.org.uk.

Royal Commission on the Press, Minutes of Evidence, 19 February, 1948, 7406, House of Commons Parliamentary Papers online http://parlipapers.chadwyck.co.uk/marketing/index.jsp.

James, L. (2004) 'Reynolds, George William MacArthur (1814–1879)', *Oxford Dictionary of National Biography*, Oxford: OUP. Online edn, May 2008 http://www.oxforddnb.com/view/article/23414 [accessed 25 Feb 2015].

Moore, M. (December 2011) 'Did the PCC fail when it came to phone hacking?' *Media Standards Trust* http://mediastandardstrust.org/wp-content/uploads/downloads/2012/02/Did-the-PCC-fail-when-it-came-to-phone-hacking.pdf [accessed 9 June 2014].

Morris, A.J.A. (2004) 'Riddell, George Allardice, Baron Riddell (1865–1934)', *Oxford Dictionary of National Biography*, Oxford: OUP; Online edn. <http://www.oxforddnb.com/view/article/35749> [accessed 20 January 2015].

Smith, A. (2004) 'Carr, Sir (William) Emsley (1867–1941)', *Oxford Dictionary of National Biography*, Oxford: OUP; Online edn <http://www.oxforddnb.com/view/article/48272> [accessed 20 January 2015].

Archives

News of the World Archive: CRP/4/1; News Group Newspapers Ltd Archive, News UK and Ireland Ltd., 1 London Bridge Street, London SE1 9GF.

A note on the Archive, by Nick Mays

News UK holds the archive of the *News of the World*. This comprises a document and artefact collection in addition to the full back file of newspapers and the paper's picture collection, the document and artefact archive being the only one of a popular Sunday newspaper in the UK. It includes corporate records, 1891–1979; property records, 1920–69; staff and pension fund records, 1937–80; production and publishing records, 1893–97, 1931–86; editorial correspondence relating to features, 1930–72; advertising and promotion material, 1908–95 and circulation records, 1931–84.

There are also the surviving records of the John Hilton Bureau, which include series of administrative files (relating to the organisation and administration of the bureau and its relationship with the *News of the World*) and external and public papers (concerning the relations of the bureau with other organisations and with readers) covering the period 1942–74. The archive is open to researchers but operates an access policy that requires all readers to register prior to their initial visit.

National Archives, HO 252/12, *News of the World evidence to 1961–62 Royal Commission on the Press,* Replies to Questionnaires, 5 July 1961 – Questionnaire A, Q. 37.

Index

Page numbers in *italics* refer to illustrations; page numbers in **bold** indicate the most important instances.

Printed and bound by CPI Group (UK) Ltd, Croydon, CR0 4YY